A History of Early
Christian Literature

A History of Early Christian Literature

Justo L. González

WESTMINSTER
JOHN KNOX PRESS
LOUISVILLE · KENTUCKY

First edition
Published by Westminster John Knox Press
Louisville, Kentucky

19 20 21 22 23 24 25 26 27 28—10 9 8 7 6 5 4 3 2 1

Book design by Sharon Adams
Cover design by Buckley Design

Library of Congress Cataloging-in-Publication Data

Names: González, Justo L., author.
Title: A history of early Christian literature / Justo L. González.
Description: Louisville, Kentucky : Westminster John Knox Press, 2019. |
    Includes bibliographical references.
Identifiers: LCCN 2019001533 (print) | LCCN 2019005743 (ebook) |
    ISBN 9781611649543 (ebk.) | ISBN 9780664264444 (pbk. : alk. paper)
Subjects: LCSH: Christian literature, Early—History and criticism. |
    Apostolic Fathers.
Classification: LCC BR60.A65 (ebook) | LCC BR60.A65 G66 2019 (print) |
    DDC 270.1—dc23
LC record available at https://lccn.loc.gov/2019001533

Most Westminster John Knox Press books are available at special quantity discounts when purchased in bulk by corporations, organizations, and special-interest groups. For more information, please e-mail SpecialSales@wjkbooks.com.

Contents

Part 6. Transition into a New Age

Bibliographical Note

Throughout this work I have given bibliographical references only for direct quotations of ancient authors. When citing these references, I begin with the author's name, the title of the work, and then the standard division of the work into books, chapters, and/or sections, followed by the English translation I've used (so, for example: Augustine, *Confessions* 6.3.3; *NPNF¹* 1:91). If no English translation is available (or I prefer not to use one that is), I provide my own, citing instead information about the critical edition that contains the work in its original language (thus Cyril of Alexandria, *Against the Blasphemies of Nestorius* 1.1; PG 76:17, 21) To refer to these standard translations and critical editions, throughout the book I have employed the following abbreviations:

Translations

ACW Ancient Christian Writers. Westminster, MD: Newman Press; Mahwah, NJ: Paulist Press, 1946–.

ANF *Ante-Nicene Fathers*. Edited by Alexander Roberts and James Donaldson. 10 vols. American Edition. Buffalo: Christian Literature Publishing Co., 1885–96.

LCC Library of Christian Classics. 26 vols. Philadelphia: The Westminster Press, 1953–66.

NPNF¹ *Nicene and Post-Nicene Fathers*. Series 1. Edited by Philip Schaff. 14 vols. American Edition. Buffalo: Christian Literature Publishing Co., 1886–90.

NPNF² *Nicene and Post-Nicene Fathers*. Series 2. Edited by Henry Wace. 14 vols. American Edition. Buffalo: Christian Literature Publishing Co., 1890–1900.

Original Languages

BAC Biblioteca de autores cristianos. Madrid: Editorial Católica, 1943–.

PG Patrologia graeca. Edited by J.-P. Migne. 162 vols. Paris, 1857–86.

PL Patrologia latina. Edited by J.-P. Migne. 217 vols. Paris, 1844–64.

Introduction

It was a clear sign of genius when some remote ancestor of ours decided that by breaking a branch or placing one stone atop another, others could follow along the same path. For the first time, it was now possible for human beings to leave a message for others following later. Out of that first insight, writing was born—for that is precisely the purpose of writing: a way to be present where we are not, whether because we are in another place or because we are in another time.

When, many centuries later, Christian literature emerged, the art of writing had developed widely. All the main languages around the basin of the Mediterranean had some sort of alphabet, most of them derived from the ancient Phoenician alphabet. As a result, we now know about the origins of Christianity and its first centuries not only through archaeological remains, but even more so thanks to the literature that the early church produced and left behind—much like that early ancestor had done ages before. Since Greek was the lingua franca of the eastern Mediterranean, most of the earliest Christian documents that have survived, including the New Testament, are written in that language. Shortly thereafter, as Christianity made headway westward, Latin came to occupy a place parallel to Greek. It is in these two languages that most of the surviving ancient Christian writings have come to our day, although there are also some in other languages such as Syriac, Armenian, Coptic, and others.

In this book we shall not be dealing with the writings of the New Testament, about which much has been written and much is available. Rather, our starting point will be the earliest Christian documents we have that are not part of the New Testament.

The documents we shall be studying represent several different literary genres. During the first years, the most common genre will be the epistle.

1

Just as much of the New Testament consists of letters, so also much of early Christian literature takes the epistolary form. Apart from those that are now part of the New Testament, very few such epistles remain from the early years of Christianity, but these are of great value since they give us a glimpse of the inner life of the church as well as the challenges it was facing. Later, many more Christian epistles would be produced and preserved, to the point that as we advance in our study, we shall find authors of whom more than a hundred epistles exist.

Another literary genre, appearing quite early and persisting throughout antiquity, presents manuals of instruction for the worship of the church and life in it. Jointly with this genre, and frequently mixed with it, are exhortations and advice for Christian life, particularly for the practice of asceticism.

Third, there is the apologetic genre. Constantly threatened by persecution and often finding itself the object of evil rumors, the church was in need of defending and expounding its faith in ways others could understand, or at least respect. The early flourishing of the apologetic genre took place in the second century, but such works were continuously produced throughout the period we are studying.

Although very few early Christian sermons have survived, there are frequent homiletic elements in documents that present themselves as epistles. As with other genres, while our study advances, we shall find ever more numerous sermons; by the time we come to the end of this book, we will have extensive collections of sermons by some of the most important leaders of the church. Since the early use of the word "prophecy" did not necessarily refer to an announcement of the future, but was rather what today we call preaching, we shall find that many of the surviving ancient homiletic writings include visions, dreams, and other similar elements. The most ancient Christian example we have of this is the book of Revelation, in the New Testament, which calls itself a "prophecy" but is also an extensive sermon to be read aloud in the churches to which it is addressed.

The persecutions that inspired the apologetic genre also resulted in numerous "acts" telling of martyrdoms. Some of these accounts present themselves as a letter from one church to another. Others claim to be, or at least to include, the official acts of the judicial process and punishment of some martyrs.

Frequently pseudepigraphic literature presents itself as a gospel or a book of acts attributed to an apostle or to some other important figure in the very early church. Most of these books are pious legends about Jesus or the apostles, which were then collected and written in their present form. Similarly, there are also some Christian books that claim to record the words or actions of some of the characters of the Hebrew Scriptures. And there are also Jewish books into which Christians interpolated their own views. The result of all this is that the task of studying, dating, and determining the origin and purpose of some of these writings is quite difficult, so much so that in many cases scholars do not agree on these matters. Besides all this pious literature, there are also apocryphal writings, whose purpose was to promote views that other Christians rejected, most commonly Gnosticism.

The biographic genre, whose antecedents may be found in some of the writings just mentioned and in the acts of martyrs, does not frequently appear in the early church. Later in the period we are studying, biographies will become more common, consisting particularly of "lives" of saints. Then, when we come to Augustine's *Confessions*, we find a genre that goes beyond a mere biography and is the earliest existing spiritual autobiography.

Doctrinal essays, some dealing with a particular doctrine and others with a wider understanding of Christian faith, began appearing in the second century and continued developing until they become vast treatises, such as Augustine's work *The Trinity*. The origins of such treatises are to be found in the antiheretical literature that began appearing in the second century. At that time Christianity was not only suffering or threatened by persecution from both the government and the people, but also by the diversity of doctrines that existed within the church and the need to decide which among them should be considered legitimate. Thus antiheretical literature has a polemical character similar to that of apologetics, although its purpose is not to defend the faith against its detractors, but rather to show why a particular doctrine has no place within the church.

As was to be expected, much of ancient Christian literature is biblical commentary. Like other literary genres, such commentaries become more abundant with the passing of time. Toward the end of the time we are studying, some of these commentaries are quite extensive. In some cases, they are actually a series of sermons on a particular book of the Bible, and therefore they are also examples of the homiletical genre.

In the pages that follow, we shall deal with all of these literary genres. Although some early chapters will center attention on a particular genre, as in the chapter devoted to the second-century apologists, in general we shall follow a chronological order that shows how Christian literature developed through the centuries. As our narrative progresses, we shall encounter many authors whose writings include several different literary genres. To understand such authors, we must look at their entire production. For instance, if we centered our attention on the epistolary genre, we would have to discuss the seven letters that Ignatius of Antioch wrote early in the second century jointly with the hundreds of letters by Augustine and Jerome late in the fourth century and early in the fifth. Likewise, we would need to discuss authors such as Augustine under the heading of different literary genres: epistolary, homiletical, Bible commentary, dialogue, apologetics, antiheretical literature, autobiography, and doctrinal treatises.

All these genres are present in the literature that we are about to study. But as we do so, it is important to remember the genius of that ancient ancestor of ours who many centuries earlier placed one stone atop another and thus left a sign of the path just trodden. Likewise, in this ancient Christian literature our ancestors in the faith have left a witness not only of their path through this world, but also of their faith, of what their Lord did for them, of their doubts, struggles, and hopes. As we read their writings, we do not do this out of mere antiquarian interest, but also and above all because these authors are our brothers and sisters in the faith. Their witness is still valid in our days and will be throughout the ages. Just as that ancient ancestor was made present to any who saw those two stones, so do these ancestors in the faith make themselves present to us by means of their written words.

Finally, we must also remember that we do not have the original autograph of any of these documents. What we have are copies of copies, all of them resulting from the work of the generations linking those ancient authors with our time. Thus, in studying them these documents put us in contact not only with their original authors, but also with the many generations through whose efforts and faithfulness the documents themselves have come to us.

Let us then enter this vast field of ancient Christian literature both with the inquisitive spirit of the researcher and with the gratitude and respect that this great cloud of witnesses deserves.

PART 1

The Earliest Christian Literature outside the New Testament

Introduction to Part 1

It is interesting to note that, while Christians in general are fairly well acquainted with the books of the New Testament, other early Christian literature, some of it dating from the same time as the last books of the New Testament, is generally unknown. Yet that frequently ignored literature helps us understand the environment in which the New Testament was formed. It was a time when the church itself was taking shape, when it was not clear what was acceptable Christian teaching and what was not. A persecution whose legal and official parameters were not yet established was a constant threat. There were divisions and differences of opinion, at least as widespread as we find in the New Testament itself. There was no clear church organization, and many would-be leaders profited from such circumstances. Some were seeking to discover words and teachings of Jesus that had not been included in what became the four canonical Gospels. Among those four, the difference within the three of them and the fourth led some to doubt the authority of the latter. Those who did not agree with the teachings of those Gospels simply wrote their own. Some wrote about the supposed acts of a particular apostle in order to put forth their own ideas, which frequently differed from those of the rest of the church. Martyrs were highly esteemed, and the acts of their trials and sufferings circulated widely. In response to persecution, several books defending the faith, commonly known as "apologies," began to appear. These sought to show, on the one hand, that persecution itself was unjust; and on the other hand, that the teachings of Christianity were true. In brief, the result was a vast and multiform body of literature of which significant portions have come to our day.

Still, even though this is a vast body of literature with abundant information about the life and faith of that nascent church, there is not a single writing among all of these books that seeks to systematize or to expound the totality of Christian faith. Even joining all the information that can be gleaned from this literature, it does not give us a total vision of Christian faith and practice in those early times. What we do have, rather than systematic treatises, are letters, practical and administrative advice, homiletic materials, defenses of the faith in the face of criticism and persecution, stories of martyrs, and a motley collection of apocryphal or pseudonymous literature.

1

The Apostolic Fathers

A vast body of early Christian literature is jointly known as the "Apostolic Fathers." This name, employed for the first time in the seventeenth century and in general usage today, may be confusing. Although the "Apostolic Fathers" are eight, some among them are individuals whose writings have come to us, while others are anonymous or pseudonymous documents. This is also a varied body of literature, for it includes, besides a number of letters, a manual of discipline, a pseudonymous homily presented as a letter, a series of visions and allegories, a collection of purported words of the Lord, and an apology. (Since the latter, the *Address to Diognetus*, should actually be counted among the Greek apologists, it will be discussed in a chapter devoted to the early apologists.)

THE *DIDACHE*

Quite likely the most ancient of these documents is the one that bears the title of *Teaching of the Twelve Apostles*, commonly known as the *Didache* (a Greek word meaning "teaching").

This document was amply circulated in the ancient church, for it seems that even some of the other Apostolic Fathers knew and made use of it. Likewise, other ancient Christian writers quoted it. Through these other writers, it influenced some medieval literature. But eventually the book itself was forgotten, and modernity did not know it until the end of the nineteenth century. Later, following various clues, scholars have found versions or portions of this work in Coptic, Syriac, Georgian, Latin, and Arabic, which witnesses to the widespread use of this book in ancient times.

As to the date and place of its composition, there is no absolute certainty. The fact that it is quoted quite early is proof of its antiquity. Also, on the basis of the text itself and the environment it reflects, it would seem that the *Didache* originated in Syria or nearby. Quite likely it was already in existence by the year 70 or 80, although some scholars date it much later. Its style is clear and simple, rapidly getting to the point without ornament or circumlocution.

The book is divided into two parts. The first six chapters, frequently called the "Document of Two Ways," employs the very ancient metaphor of two ways: one the way of the good, or life; the other the way of evil, or death—a metaphor that appears not only in ancient Greek literature, but also in Scripture, both in the Gospels (Matt. 7:13–15) and in the Old Testament (Jer. 21:8). The second and most interesting part, chapters 7 to 16, includes valuable data and instructions regarding the worship and government of the church.

The Document of the Two Ways opens with the first and great commandment of loving God, joined with love for neighbor. From there it moves to a series of prohibitions in which one perceives echoes of the Decalogue. But in any case, the central emphasis of this first part of the book is on the obligation to share with the needy. Thus we read:

> Give to everyone that asketh thee, and ask it not back; for the Father willeth that to all should be given of our own blessings. Happy is he that giveth according to the commandment; for he is guiltless. Woe to him that receiveth; for if one having need receiveth, he is guiltless; but he that receiveth not having need, shall pay the penalty, why he received and for what, and, coming into straits, he shall be examined concerning the things which he hath done, and he shall not escape thence until he pay back the last farthing. But also now concerning this, it hath been said, let thine alms sweat in thy hands, until thou know to whom thou shouldst give. . . . Thou shalt not turn away from him that is in want, but thou shalt share all things with thy brother, and shalt not say that they are thine own; for if ye are partakers in that which is immortal, how much more in things which are mortal? (*Didache* 1.5–6; 4.8; *ANF* 7:377, 378)

The second part of the *Didache* begins in chapter 7 with interesting instructions about baptism:

> And concerning baptism, thus baptize ye: having first said all these things, baptize into the name of the Father, and of the Son, and of the Holy Spirit, in living water. But if thou have not living water, baptize in other water; and if thou canst not in cold, in warm. But if thou have not either, pour out water thrice upon the head in the name of Father and Son and Holy Spirit. (*Didache* 7.1–3; *ANF* 7:379)

Also regarding communion, the *Didache* offers a glimpse into some of the earliest Christian practices. A meal is to take place each week on the "day of the Lord," and participants will eat until they are satisfied—which is an indication of the early date of the *Didache*. Here we find also the oldest eucharistic prayer that we have:

> Now concerning the Thanksgiving, thus give thanks. First, concerning the cup: We thank thee, our Father, for the holy vine of David Thy servant, which Thou madest known to us through Jesus Thy Servant; to Thee be the glory for ever. And concerning the broken bread: We thank Thee, our Father, for the life and knowledge which Thou madest known to us through Jesus Thy servant; to Thee be the glory for ever. Even as this broken bread was scattered over the hills, and was gathered together and became one, so let Thy Church be gathered together from the ends of the earth into Thy Kingdom; for Thine is the glory and the power through Jesus Christ for ever. (*Didache* 9.1–4; *ANF* 7:379–80)

After other prayers to be raised following partaking in communion, the *Didache* moves on to a series of expectations and recommendations, most of which refer to the need to discern between the true and the false "apostles and prophets" (two titles that seem to be synonymous in the *Didache*). The principal means the *Didache* offers for such a discernment has to do with what such preachers do and ask for:

> Let every apostle that cometh to you be received as the Lord. But he shall not remain except one day; but if there be need, also the next; but if he remain three days, he is a false prophet. And when the apostle goeth away, let him take nothing but bread until he lodgeth; but if he asks for money, he is a false prophet. . . . Whoever saith in the Spirit, Give me money, or something else, ye shall not listen to him; but if he saith to you to give for others' sake who are in need, let no one judge him. (*Didache* 11.4–6; 12; *ANF* 7:380–81)

In summary, the *Didache* is a most valuable book, not because of the novelty of its ideas nor because of its elegant style, but rather because it reflects the practices, beliefs, and challenges of the first years in the life of the church.

CLEMENT OF ROME

While the *Didache* offers a glimpse into the life of the church in a remote area of Syria, the *Epistle to the Corinthians*, traditionally attributed to Clement of Rome, shows how quickly the Christian faith was being clothed in Hellenistic vestments.

Very little is known of the life of Clement, although there are abundant legends and traditions. According to some ancient writers, Clement accompanied Paul on some of his pastoral duties. Others attribute to him the Epistle to the Hebrews, which appears in the New Testament. There were stories about his conflicts with Simon Magus. All of this is extremely doubtful. What is certain is that Clement was bishop of Rome toward the end of the first century. Some ancient lists declare him to be the immediate successor of Peter, while others make him the third bishop of Rome. If he wrote this *Epistle to the Corinthians*, this is the only one of his writings that is extant.

From the letter itself, as well as from what little else is known with certainty about Clement, it seems that this letter was written about the year 95 or 96, that is, at about the same time when John was writing his visions on Patmos. Like John in his Revelation, Clement constantly refers to the Old Testament, as well as to other Jewish literature of the time. But, unlike John, Clement employs the same Greek translation of the Old Testament that most of the authors of the New Testament use, the Septuagint. Also, in contrast to John, Clement makes ample use of the resources of Greek rhetoric, with which he seems to be familiar. But even so, certain elements in the manner in which he uses the Greek language seem to indicate that, though he had studied the language, he had been shaped in a Jewish background. Therefore, it seems that Clement was a Jew who had either been converted to Christianity and then moved to Rome or who had lived in Rome and was one of the early converts in that city. In any case, there is no doubt that he was a cultured man, not only in his own Hebrew tradition, but also in terms of Hellenistic culture.

Although the Letter to the Corinthians is traditionally attributed to Clement alone, the epistle itself has the church in Rome addressing its counterpart in Corinth: "The Church of God which sojourns at Rome, to the Church of God sojourning at Corinth" (*1 Clem.* 1; *ANF* 1:5). Apparently the church in Corinth had not solved the conflicts and the divisions that are so prominent in Paul's correspondence with it, and therefore Clement writes about "that shameful and detestable sedition, utterly abhorrent to the elect of God, which a few rash and self-confident persons have kindled to such a pitch of frenzy, that your venerable and illustrious name, worthy to be universally loved, has suffered grievous injury" (*1 Clem.* 1; *ANF* 1:5).

The first nineteen chapters of the letter affirm that the church in Corinth was known for its faith and virtues, but then pride and envy have led to its present conflicts. By way of foundation, the epistle includes a fairly long review of the history of Israel, first of all showing how jealousy and envy lead to all sorts of evil, and then offering the alternative of an obedience that leads to unity. After referring to Cain and Abel, Clement comments:

Ye see, brethren, how envy and jealousy led to the murder of a brother. Through envy, also, our father Jacob fled from the face of Esau his brother. Envy made Joseph be persecuted unto death, and to come into bondage. Envy compelled Moses to flee from the face of Pharaoh king of Egypt. . . . On account of envy, Aaron and Miriam had to make their abode without the camp. Envy brought down Dathan and Abiram alive to Hades, through the sedition which they excited against God's servant Moses. Through envy, David underwent the hatred not only of foreigners, but was also persecuted by Saul king of Israel. (*1 Clem.* 4; *ANF* 1:6)

Then, after several examples and a call to repentance, Clement includes words that remind us of the Epistle to the Hebrews, chapter 11, although in this case what he proposes is not faith, as Hebrews does, but rather obedience and hospitality:

Let us take Enoch, who, being found righteous in obedience, was translated, and death was never known to happen to him. Noah, being found faithful, preached regeneration to the world through his ministry; and the Lord saved by him the animals which, with one accord, entered into the ark. Abraham, styled "the friend," was found faithful, inasmuch as he rendered obedience to the words of God. He, in the exercise of obedience, went out from his own country, and from his kindred, and from his father's house, in order that . . . he might inherit the promises of God. . . . On account of his hospitality and godliness, Lot was saved out of Sodom. . . . On account of her faith and hospitality, Rahab the harlot was saved. (*1 Clem.* 9–12; *ANF* 1:7–8)

All of this leads to an exhortation to meekness and humility, following not only the example of Jesus Christ, but also all the great figures of the Old Testament. And Clement concludes this first section of his letter with other words that again remind us of Hebrews:

Thus the humility and godly submission of so great and illustrious men have rendered not only us, but also all the generations before us, better; even as many as have received His oracles in fear and truth. Wherefore, having so many great and glorious examples set before us, let us turn again to the practice of that peace which from the beginning was the mark set before us; and let us look steadfastly to the Father and Creator of the universe. (*1 Clem.* 19; *ANF* 1:10)

These words then lead Clement to pen a lyrical passage about the harmony of God's creation, and hence the harmony that is found at the very center of the Christian faith. The high point of such faith is the resurrection of Jesus Christ, which is also the foundation of a call for a holy life. This life, including both faith and good works, is set forth in an order that one must obey. Such obedience is necessary for the working of the whole. In an army, for instance, "All are not prefects, nor commanders of a thousand, nor of a hundred, nor of fifty, nor the like, but each one in his own rank performs the things commanded by the king and the generals. The great cannot subsist without the small, nor the small without the great" (*1 Clem.* 37; *ANF* 1:15).

The same is true of the church, whose leaders are the successors of the apostles. All of this is based on a hierarchical order of faith, because just as Jesus was sent by the Father, so were the apostles sent by Jesus. These apostles "preaching through countries and cities, they appointed the first-fruits, having first proved them by the Spirit, to be bishops and deacons of those who should afterwards believe" (*1 Clem.* 42; *ANF* 1:16). The order that should prevail in armies as well as in the church is similar to the order that exists throughout the universe, where each thing has its place, and all is under the sovereign rule of God. Furthermore, all of this is grounded on the fact that there is only one God and one faith: "Have we not one God and one Christ? Is there not one Spirit of grace poured out upon us?" (*1 Clem.* 46; *ANF* 1:17). As he approaches the end of his letter, Clement reminds the Corinthians of their ancient dissensions and how Paul confronted them, calling them once again to mutual love. This leads to a description of that love which also reminds us of what Paul wrote to the Corinthians on the same subject. According to Clement:

> Love unites us to God. Love covers a multitude of sins. Love beareth all things, is long-suffering in all things. There is nothing base, nothing arrogant in love. Love admits of no schisms: love gives rise to no sedition: love does all things in harmony. By love have all the elect of God been made perfect; without love nothing is well-pleasing to God. In love has the Lord taken us to Himself. On account of the Love he bore us, Jesus Christ our Lord gave His blood for us by the will of God; his flesh for our flesh, and His soul for our souls. (*1 Clem.* 49; *ANF* 1:18)

Finally, without explaining why he does so, Clement closes his epistle with an extensive prayer, which does not appear in all manuscripts and seems to be the earliest extant example of what came to be called "the prayer of the faithful": the intercessory prayer of the entire church for the rest of the world. In the early church it was customary to begin the service of the table or communion by raising such an intercessory prayer. The church is called to be a priestly people, and therefore part of its task is to pray not only for itself and for its members, but also for the entire world. After a prayer of praise to God, who undoes the happiness of the proud, destroys the thoughts of nations, raises the humble, and humiliates those who exalt themselves, Clement closes with what is clearly an intercessory prayer:

We beseech Thee, O Lord, to be our help and protection. Save the troubled, have mercy on the humble, raise the fallen, show Yourself to those in need, heal the sick, bring back those among the people who have strayed, feed the hungry, redeem our captives, give strength to the weak, consolation to the worried. Let all nations know that only You are God, and Jesus Christ is Your Servant, and we are Your people and sheep of your flock. . . . Give peace and single-mindedness to us and to all who inhabit the earth, as You gave it to our ancestors who called upon You in holiness and truth.

Make us obedient to Your most holy and omnipotent name, and also to the rulers and authorities on earth. By Your magnificent and ineffable strength You placed them in royal authority so that we, knowing the glory that You gave them, would be subject to them without opposing their will. Lord, give them health, peace, harmony and firmness so that they may exercise the power You gave them without stumbling. Because it is You, Lord and royal celestial ruler of the centuries, that give the sons of men glory and honor and power over things on earth. Lead their minds so that, employing the power that You gave them in meekness, peace and piety, they may attain your mercy.

It is You, the only one who can do these and even greater things among us whom we confess by means of the High Priest and defender of our souls, Jesus Christ, through whom be glory and magnificence now and from generation to generation, and forevermore. Amen. (*1 Clem.* 59.4–61.4; Greek text in BAC 65:233–35)

Because of Clement's fame, soon other writings were attributed to him. The most ancient among these seem to be the so-called *Second Epistle of Clement to the Corinthians* and the two *Epistles to the Virgins*. The latter seem to have been written in the third century, which produced abundant material on the subject of virginity and therefore do not properly belong in the present chapter. The document commonly known as the *Second Epistle of Clement to the Corinthians* is neither by Clement nor an epistle. It is rather a homily or sermon whose origin seems to date a few decades after Clement. Therefore, it vies with the *Pascal Sermon* of Melito of Sardis for the distinction of being the earliest surviving Christian homily. A number of reasons lead scholars to affirm that it came originally from Rome, where it was written and preached around the middle of the second century. In any case, contrasting with Clement himself, this preacher does not seem to have roots in the Hebrew tradition, but comes mostly from the Gentile world. As he himself declares, he had a pagan background: "We were deficient in understanding, worshipping stones and wood, and gold, and silver and brass, the works of men's hands; and our whole life was nothing else than death" (*2 Clem.* 1; *ANF* 7:517).

The main purpose of this homily is to call believers away from idolatry and immorality. But there are at least two other elements in its theology that merit special attention. The first of these is its call not to despise the flesh or the body. During the second century, due partly to gnostic influences, some Christians thought that only the spiritual was important. Over against such attitudes, this preacher declares:

> Let no one of you say that this very flesh shall not be judged, nor rise again. Consider ye in what state ye were saved, in what ye received sight, if not while ye were in this flesh. We must therefore preserve the flesh as the temple of God. For as ye were called in the flesh, ye shall also come to be judged in the flesh. As Christ the Lord who saved us, though He was first a Spirit, became flesh, and thus called us so shall we also receive the reward in this flesh. (*2 Clem.* 9; *ANF* 7:519)

The second element in the theology of this homily that is particularly interesting is its ecclesiology. According to this preacher, the church was founded before the sun and the moon. What has happened in more recent times is that this spiritual church has been made manifest in the flesh of Christ. And that manifestation of the church is also a foundation for respecting the flesh:

> Now the Church, being spiritual, was manifested in the flesh of Christ, thus signifying to us that, if any of us keep her in the flesh and do not corrupt her, he shall receive her again in the Holy Spirit: for this flesh is the copy of the spirit. No one then who corrupts the copy, shall partake of the original. . . . But if we say that the flesh is the Church and the spirit is Christ, then he that hath shamefully used the flesh hath shamefully used the Church. (*2 Clem.* 14; *ANF* 7:521)

IGNATIUS OF ANTIOCH

In the entire body of literature that those ancient times have bequeathed to us, possibly none is as valuable, and certainly none is as inspiring, as the seven letters that Ignatius of Antioch wrote while on his way to martyrdom. In probably the year 107, Ignatius, to whom several ancient writers refer as bishop of Antioch, had been condemned to death because of his faith. Since a great celebration was about to take place in Rome, Ignatius was sent to the capital so that he would be part of the projected spectacles. On his way to Rome, he wrote seven letters that have survived. Six of them were motivated by visits that he had received from Christians as he moved toward his martyrdom. The seventh was addressed to the church in Rome, where he expected to offer his life as a witness to his Savior. While he was in Smyrna, he was able to write letters to the churches in Ephesus, Magnesia, Tralles, and Rome. Shortly thereafter, from Troas, he wrote to the churches in Philadelphia and Smyrna as well as to Polycarp, who was then bishop of Smyrna. As was to be expected, these letters follow the canons of epistles written at that time, saying first who sends them and then to whom they are addressed. This is followed by a few words of encouragement and congratulations before the author moves into the body of the epistle. And it all ends with a few words of farewell.

The *Epistle to the Ephesians* expresses Ignatius's gratitude for the visit of the delegation from that church, presided over by Bishop Onesimus (the same that appears in Paul's Epistle to Philemon?). In reading this letter we find several themes that are also in the others. One of them is martyrdom and Ignatius's understanding of it, as he declares that he is merely beginning to be a disciple of the Lord, and that the chains that hold him are like precious strings of pearls.

Another central theme in this epistle and in several of the others is the need to obey and follow properly established ecclesiastical authorities. Ignatius exhorts Christians in Ephesus to be "subject to the bishop and the presbytery" (Ign. *Eph.* 2; *ANF* 1:50) so that they may be fully sanctified. And he also affirms that "it is fitting that ye should run together in accordance with the will of your bishop, which thing also ye do," and that "your justly renowned presbytery, worthy of God, is fitted as exactly to the bishop as the strings are to the harp" (Ign. *Eph.* 4; *ANF* 1:50).

An outstanding feature of this letter is its profoundly eucharistic spirituality, for Ignatius calls his readers never to withdraw from communion. This is a subject that he expands in his other letters.

But probably the most astounding feature of this letter is the high concept that Ignatius has of Jesus Christ as God incarnate. For him, the blood of Jesus is "the blood of God." Referring to Jesus, he says, "There is one Physician who is possessed both of flesh and spirit; both made and not made; God existing in flesh; true life in death; both of Mary and of God; first passible and then impassible,—even Jesus Christ our Lord" (Ign. *Eph.* 7; *ANF* 1:52). The power and dignity of this incarnate God are such that Ignatius declares that Jesus allowed his head to be anointed because this granted incorruption to the church. In other words, since the oil touched the head of Jesus, now the entire church rejoices in this ointment of incorruptibility. And a similar theology is seen later in the same epistle when Ignatius declares that Jesus was baptized "that by His passion He might purify the water" (Ign. *Eph.* 18; *ANF* 1:57).

And, referring to the incarnation of God in Jesus at the time of the nativity, he affirms that "Every kind of magic was destroyed, and every bond of wickedness disappeared; ignorance was removed, and the old kingdom abolished, God Himself being manifested in human form for the renewal of eternal life. And now that took a beginning which had been prepared by God. Henceforth all things were in a state of tumult, because He mediated the abolition of death" (Ign. *Eph.* 19; *ANF* 1:57).

The *Epistle to the Magnesians* is much shorter. It emphasizes the authority of the bishop. The bishop of Magnesia, named Damas, had led a commission that visited Ignatius and seems to have been quite young, for Ignatius insists that he must be obeyed in spite of his youth. According to Ignatius, anyone who seeks to receive the visible bishop is in fact obeying the invisible one, Jesus Christ. The concord that is necessary for the good of the church takes place "while your bishop presides in the place of God, and your presbyters in the place of the assembly of the apostles, along with your deacons, who are most dear to me, and are entrusted with the ministry of Jesus Christ" (Ign. *Magn.* 6; *ANF* 1:61) Furthermore, apparently Ignatius feared the possible presence of Judaizing elements in Magnesia, although he does not say much about their actual teachings. According to him, "It is absurd to profess Christ Jesus, and to Judaize. For Christianity did not embrace Judaism, but Judaism Christianity, that so every tongue which believeth might be gathered together to God" (Ign. *Magn.* 10; *ANF* 1:63).

The *Epistle to the Trallians* is a word of greeting that Ignatius sends to that church, apparently through its bishop Polybius, who had come to visit him. As in his other letters, Ignatius insists on the authority of the bishop and his representatives, coming to the point of declaring that "apart from these there is no Church" (Ign. *Trall.* 3; *ANF* 1:67). But in this case what seems to be his main concern is not divisions, but rather incorrect teachings. There were new movements that sought to incorporate the names of Jesus and of Christ in their speculations, sometimes counting him as one of the spiritual aeons, and denying his true incarnation. Such an opinion, commonly called "Docetism," turned the humanity of Jesus into a mere appearance. It is against these teachings that Ignatius writes lines that underscore the reality of the incarnation and the falsehood of Docetism:

> Stop your ears, therefore, when any one speaks to you at variance with Jesus Christ, who was descended from David, and was also of Mary; who was truly born, and did eat and drink. He was truly persecuted under Pontius Pilate; He was truly crucified, and died, in the sight of beings in heaven, and on earth, and under the earth. He was also truly raised from the dead. His Father quickening Him, even as after the same manner His Father will so raise up us who believe in Him by Christ Jesus, apart from whom we do not possess the true life.
>
> But if, as some that are without God, that is, the unbelieving, say that He only seemed to suffer (they themselves only seeming to exist), then why am I in bonds? Why do I long to be exposed to the wild beasts? Do I therefore die in vain? Am I not then guilty of falsehood against the Lord? (Ign. *Trall.* 9–10; *ANF* 1:69–70)

The last of Ignatius's four letters written from Smyrna is very different from the rest. His *Epistle to the Romans* is not, as the others, a word of gratitude and guidance for churches that had sent representatives to him, but rather a petition to the Christian community in Rome. Apparently Ignatius had heard that the church in Rome would seek to save him from martyrdom—although it is not clear whether they planned to employ whatever influence they had among the authorities or somehow to arrange for his flight. But the elderly bishop of Antioch did not want to be free from martyrdom. In his letter he begs them:

> For I am afraid of your love, lest it should do me an injury. For it is easy for you to accomplish what you please; but it is difficult for me to attain to God, if ye spare me. . . . For if ye are silent concerning me, I shall become God's; but if you show your love to my flesh, I shall again have to run my race. (Ign. *Rom.* 1–2; *ANF* 1:74)
>
> I write to the Churches, and impress on them all, that I shall will-ingly die for God, unless ye hinder me. I beseech of you not to show an unseasonable good-will towards me. Suffer me to become food for the wild beasts, through whose instrumentality it will be granted me to attain to God. I am the wheat of God, and let me be ground by the teeth of the wild beasts, that I may be found the pure bread of Christ. . . . Then shall I truly be a disciple of Christ, when the world shall not see so much as my body. (Ign. *Rom.* 4; *ANF* 1:75)
>
> Permit me to be an imitator of the passion of my God. (Ign. *Rom.* 6; *ANF* 1:76)

The first of his three letters from Troas is addressed to the church in Phila-delphia. Here we find a hint as to why Ignatius was so insistent on the unity of the church under the authority of the bishop. He tells of an incident that took place in Antioch: without having any knowledge of the dissension that was brewing, moved by the Holy Spirit, he had warned: "Give heed to the bishop, and to the presbytery and the deacons" (Ign. *Phld.* 7; *ANF* 1:83). On the basis of this experience, Ignatius insists on the need to obey proper ecclesiastical authorities and to show the unity of the church in its worship:

> For as many as are of God and of Jesus Christ are also with the bishop. . . . If any man follows him that makes a schism in the Church, he shall not inherit the kingdom of God. If any one walks according to a strange opinion, he agrees not with the passion [of Christ].
>
> Take ye heed, then, to have but one Eucharist. For there is one flesh of our Lord Jesus Christ, and one cup to [show forth] the unity of His blood; one altar; as there is one bishop, along with the pres-bytery and deacons, my fellow-servants: that so, whatsoever ye do ye may do it according to God. (Ign. *Phld.* 3–4; *ANF* 1:80–81)

The last two letters of Ignatius, also written from Troas, are addressed to Smyrna, one to the church in that city, and the other to its bishop, Polycarp.

There he again underscores the authority of the bishop and the need to be subject to him, while he also warns about Docetist doctrines that apparently were already circulating among Christians in the area. As in his letter to the Trallians, Ignatius insists on the reality of the incarnation and of the physical sufferings of Jesus. After summarizing those sufferings, he writes:

> Now He suffered all these things for our sakes, that we might be saved. And He suffered truly, even as also He truly raised up Himself, not, as certain unbelievers maintain, that He only seemed to suffer, as they themselves only seem to be. And as they believe, so shall it happen unto them, when they shall be divested of their bodies, and be mere evil spirits. For I know that after His resurrection also He was still possessed of flesh. (Ign. *Smyrn.* 2–3; *ANF* 1:87)

This emphasis on the reality of the physical body of Christ also has practical consequences. Those who do not believe in the value of the flesh or in the incarnation of God in Christ will also neglect the physical needs of others: "They have no regard for love; no care for the widow, or the orphan, or the oppressed; of the bond, or of the free; of the hungry, or of the thirsty" (Ign. *Smyrn.* 6; *ANF* 1:89).

The last of the seven letters of Ignatius is addressed to the young bishop of Smyrna, Polycarp. Once again, Ignatius insists on the importance of unity among believers. That unity is grounded in obedience to the bishop, who in turn must be obedient to God and to Christ, and to do nothing without God. The bishop is then to attend to his entire flock, no matter their virtue or lack of it: "If thou lovest the good disciples, no thanks are due to thee on that account; but rather seek by meekness to subdue the more troublesome" (Ign. *Pol.* 2; *ANF* 1:93).

As in the case of Clement, the fame of Ignatius was such that soon other literature arose falsely bearing his name. Besides extensive interpolations added to his genuine letters, we have supposed letters from Ignatius to Antioch, Tarsus, and others. There is also a supposed correspondence between Mary of Cassobola and Ignatius, in which she asks him to send certain specific leaders to her church, and he agrees.

POLYCARP OF SMYRNA

In his letter to Polycarp, Ignatius tells Polycarp that since he must leave Troas for Neapolis, he has not been able to write to other churches in the area, so he asks Polycarp to contact them in his name. Apparently Polycarp followed his instructions and wrote to the Philippians, through whose city Ignatius and those who accompanied him had gone on the way to Rome, asking them for news. The main interest in this document is what it shows about how churches communicated among themselves:

> Both you and Ignatius wrote to me, that if any one went into Syria, he should carry your letter with him; which request I will attend to if I find a fitting opportunity, either personally or through some other acting for me, that your desire may be fulfilled. The Epistles of Ignatius written by him to us, and all the rest which we have by us, we have sent to you, as you requested. They are subjoined to this Epistle, and by them ye may be greatly profited; for they treat of faith and patience, and all things that tend to edification in our Lord. Any more certain information you may have obtained respecting both Ignatius himself and those that were with him, have the goodness to make known to us. (Pol. *Phil.* 13; *ANF* 1:36)

Although the letter itself doesn't tell us much about Polycarp, shortly thereafter his disciple Irenaeus would tell us that Polycarp had been a disciple of John in Ephesus and that therefore he guarded the apostolic tradition. Regarding his death, there is a very valuable document to which we shall return in chapter 3, when discussing the acts of the martyrs: the *Martyrdom of Polycarp*.

THE *EPISTLE OF BARNABAS*

Among the Apostolic Fathers is a document known as the *Epistle of Barnabas*. However, this document is not really a letter, but rather an extensive sermon or exhortation, and there seems to be no real reason to relate it to the Barnabas who appears in the book of Acts. It enjoyed great prestige and authority, particularly in Alexandria, where still in the third century Origen quoted it as Scripture.

The document may be divided into two parts. The first, which is also the most extensive, deals with the interpretation of the Scriptures of Israel and their relationship with Christian faith and moral life. The second deals with the subject of the "two ways," which we have already found in the *Didache*.

The first part of the document is clearly anti-Jewish. "The Son of God therefore came in the flesh with this view, that He might bring to a head the sum of their sins who had persecuted His prophets to the death (*Barn.* 5; *ANF* 1:140). And "He declared that circumcision was not of the flesh, but they transgressed because an evil angel deluded them (*Barn.* 9; *ANF* 1:142). By way of conclusion, this preacher tells his audience: "Take heed now to yourselves, and not to be like some, adding largely to your sins, and saying, 'The covenant is both theirs and ours.' But they thus finally lost it, after Moses had already received it" (*Barn.* 4; *ANF* 1:138).

At any rate, the mode in which this preacher understands and interprets the Hebrew Scriptures is what is commonly known as "typology." According to this method, the events, practices, and commandments of the Old Testament are "figures" or "types" of Jesus and his gospel. Isaac being offered upon the altar is a type of the sacrifice of Jesus on the cross, and the same can be said about the despised goat that was sent into the desert. The 318 men whom Abraham circumcised represent Jesus and his cross, for in Greek the number 318 is written as IHT: the first two of these letters are also the first two letters of the name of Jesus, while the T stands for the cross. The rest that God commanded for the seventh day of the week was a sign of the culmination of all time, when there will be true rest.

In referring to the "two ways," this document does not call them the ways of life and death, as does the *Didache*, but rather the ways of light and darkness. And, even more than the *Didache*, this document relates the way of life with service to the neighbor:

> Thou shalt communicate [share] in all things with thy neighbor; thou shalt not call things thine own; for if ye are partakers in common of things which are incorruptible, how much more of those things which are corruptible. . . . Do not be ready to stretch forth thy hands to take, whilst thou contractest them to give. . . . Thou shalt not hesitate to give, nor murmur when thou givest. "Give to every one that asketh thee," and thou shalt know who is the good Recompenser of the reward. (*Barn.* 19; *ANF* 1:148)

In contrast to this, those who follow the path of darkness

> pity not the needy, labour not in aid of him who is overcome with toil; who are prone to evil-speaking, who know not of Him, that made them, who are murderers of children, destroyers of the workmanship of God; who turn away him that is in want, who oppress the afflicted, who are advocates of the rich, who are unjust judges of the poor, and who are in every respect transgressors. (*Barn.* 20; *ANF* 1:149)

THE SHEPHERD OF HERMAS

The most extensive of all the books and documents counted among the Apostolic Fathers is the Shepherd of Hermas. Beyond what can be gathered from his own writings, we know about the life of Hermas thanks to a note in the Muratorian Fragment, a document that may well date from the second century or the third and was published in the eighteenth century. There we are told that Hermas wrote this book in Rome, when his brother Pius was bishop of that city. Since Pius was bishop of Rome approximately from 140 to 150, this seems to indicate the time when Hermas composed his book. In it, he tells us that as a child he had been a slave and that his master sold him to a woman named Rhoda. When helping her out of a bath in the river, Hermas lusted after her. Sometime later, as he slept, he had a vision in which Rhoda told him that in lusting after her, he had gravely sinned. As he was still trembling after that vision, an elderly woman in shining vestments appeared to him and told him that his sin had not been only in lusting after Rhoda, but also in not correcting his own children and thereby allowing for their waywardness. For this reason, Hermas had been punished in his secular business, about which we know no more. Then the elderly woman read to him words that he could not completely understand, but which however indicated that the end was near and that God would punish some and reward others. When Hermas tells her that he does not like her first words, having to do with destruction and punishment, but that he cherishes her words of love and forgiveness, she answers: "The last are for the righteous; the first are for the heathens and apostates" (Herm. *Vis.* 1.4; *ANF* 2:11).

This is the beginning of a long series of experiences, visions, and revelations that Hermas reports in his book. Apparently it is in fact a combination of various teachings and homilies of Hermas, who seems to have been a "prophet" or preacher in the church of Rome. In its final triplex form, the work includes five *Visions*; twelve commandments, or *Mandates*; and ten parables, or *Similitudes*.

The second vision takes place a year after the first, and at the same place. Here the same woman gives Hermas a book that he does not understand. After a period of fasting and prayer, Hermas finally understands what is written. The woman chastises him for not having been sufficiently concerned over his wife and his children, telling him, "You, Hermas, have endured great personal tribulations on account of the transgressions of your house, because you did not attend to them, but were careless, and engaged in your wicked transactions" (Herm. *Vis.* 2.3; *ANF* 2:12). For this reason, his children as well as his wife have committed serious sins. But now they're being offered a new opportunity for repentance at a fixed time. Hermas is to announce to them this message of God's grace and at the same time cleanse himself of his resentment against them, so that they may accept this opportunity for repentance. But "if any one of them sin after a certain day which has been fixed, he shall not be saved" (Herm. *Vis.* 2.2; *ANF* 2:11).

The third vision is the most extensive one as well as most often quoted. Once again the guiding woman appears to Hermas, who now sees, among other things, a great tower that is being built. A multitude of angels (as he is later told) brings stones for the construction, while another six lay them in the building. While some of these stones are perfectly fitted for the tower that is being built, others are different. Some break into pieces, some roll afar, and some remain at the foot of the tower, apparently waiting for a time when they will be ready to be added to the building. The woman now explains to Hermas that each of these kinds of stones represents a different kind of Christian. Among those who are rejected, some are those people who, having sinned, have not yet repented, and therefore they are placed aside until they are ready. Those who cannot fit in the tower because they are round "are those who have faith indeed but they also have the riches of this world" (Herm. *Vis.* 3.6; *ANF* 2:15), which leads them to deny their Lord. Such people cannot be added to the tower until they leave their riches aside, just as a round stone cannot be added to the building until it is pared down.

The fourth vision is a brief announcement of the coming tribulations, thus reminiscent of some chapters in the Revelation of John. In the fifth, which is even shorter, the Shepherd finally appears, telling Hermas to write down his mandates and similitudes. Thus this fifth vision is both a conclusion of the series of visions and an introduction to the rest of the book.

The first commandment, which is also rather brief, tells Hermas that he must believe in the God who is creator of all that exists and obey that God. The second, while warning him about various sins, calls him to practice almsgiving, without any concern about whether the one receiving his alms is worthy or not, for in the end this will be determined by God. The third commandment is a call to reject falsehood and speak the truth, while the fourth commends chastity. In this fourth mandate the Shepherd responds to the concern of Hermas about those who have sinned after their baptism. The Shepherd tells him that if anyone "sins after that great and holy calling in which the Lord has called His people to everlasting life, he has opportunity to repent but once. But if he should sin frequently after this, and then repent, to such a man repentance will be of no avail; for with difficulty will he live" (Herm. *Mand.* 4.3; *ANF* 2:22). The fifth mandate commends patience. The sixth says that in every person there is an angel of goodness and justice and another of evil and injustice, and that it is necessary to believe and follow the guidance of the first and reject that which comes from the second. The seventh calls for fear of God and obedience to God, while the eighth points out that in some things moderation is necessary, and the exact opposite is true of other things. One must practice continence in the face of evil, but there should be no limit when it comes to "helping the widows, looking after orphans and the needy, rescuing the servants of God from necessities" (Herm. *Mand.* 8; *ANF* 2:25) and other similar things. The very brief ninth mandate insists that one should continue coming to God in spite of one's own sin, since God has no rancor toward humans. The tenth includes an interesting discussion of sadness. While, on the one hand, sadness is usually connected with a lack of faith, being sad over an evil that one has committed opens the way for the action of the Holy Spirit, which brings joy. The eleventh mandate is actually a call to discern between the true and false prophets. The main means for such discernment is examining their actions: "First, he who has the Divine Spirit proceeding from above is meek, and peaceable, and humble, and refrains from all iniquity and the vain desire of this world, and contents himself with fewer wants than those of other men" (Herm. *Mand.* 11; *ANF* 2:27).

The last of this series of mandates is a brief exhortation to amend the evil desires and practice justice, truth, and meekness. This is followed by a brief epilogue on the possibility of keeping these various mandates. As to the doubts of Hermas, the Shepherd tells him that those who do not keep the commandments of God cannot possibly be saved, and that their damnation will also extend to their family and children. The devil is constantly seeking to persuade believers that they cannot obey the commandments of God. But in truth the devil has no power over the children of God and therefore should not be heard.

The ten similitudes vary greatly in their length and significance. The first, which is relatively short, deals with the citizenship of believers, which is not in the present world, but in the heavenly city. As aliens, believers must be ready "when the master of this city shall come to cast thee out for disobeying his law" (Herm. *Sim.* 1; *ANF* 2:31). Furthermore, being an alien, a believer should lead a different life, with different purposes: "Instead of lands, therefore, buy afflicted souls, according as each one is able, and visit widows and orphans, and do not overlook them; and spend your wealth and all your preparations which ye received from the Lord, upon such lands and houses. For to this end did the Master make you rich, that you might perform these services unto Him" (Herm. *Sim.* 1; *ANF* 2:31).

The second similitude refers to how in some vineyards the grapevines are tied to elm saplings. Just as an elm bears no fruit, neither do the rich. But if the rich support the poor, the fruit of the poor will be also counted for them, as the fruit of the grapevines is also the fruit of the elms. The third similitude once again employs examples taken from the countryside and agriculture. Just as during the winter all trees seem to be dead, but only some are actually dead, while others have a hidden life, so will the coming age reveal who are just and who are not. The same imagery is then carried into the fourth similitude, now dealing with summer.

In the fifth similitude, after a brief discussion of fasting—which is not simply abstaining from food, but rather doing good—Hermas presents a parable about a vineyard, a story reminiscent of the Gospels. In this case, the slave who was left in charge of the vineyard did more than the master had commanded him, and that was why the master rewarded him. Therefore, "if you do any good beyond what is commanded by God, you will gain for yourself more abundant glory, and will be more honoured by God than you would otherwise be" (Herm. *Sim.* 5.3; *ANF* 2:34).

The sixth and seventh similitudes speak of two shepherds, one being "the angel of luxury and deception," and the other "the angel of punishment." Although the guidance of the latter is not pleasant, it is a call to repentance and new life. This explains the situation of Hermas himself, whose sins are not so grave, but whose family has indeed committed serious sins, and the tribulation that he now suffers is also an invitation to their repentance and purification. The eighth similitude is rather confusing, speaking of a willow tree from which a number of twigs were taken and distributed. These twigs were in various conditions, some completely dry and others green, showing different levels of obedience to God. The ninth similitude, the most extensive of all, is a repetition and amplification of the third vision, once again employing the imagery of a tower under construction, although now with greater detail. Finally, the tenth similitude summarizes the main thrust of the entire book:

> Enjoin all who are able to act rightly not to cease well-doing; for to practice good works is useful to them. And I say that every man ought to be saved from inconveniences. For both he who is in want, and he who suffers inconveniences in his daily life, is in great torture and necessity. Whoever, therefore, rescues a soul of this kind from necessity, will gain for himself great joy. For he who is harassed by inconveniences of this kind suffers equal torture with him who is in chains. Moreover many, on account of calamities of this sort, when they could not endure them, hasten their own deaths. Whoever, then, knows a calamity of this kind afflicting a man, and does not save him, commits a great sin, and becomes guilty of his blood. Do good works, therefore, ye who have received good from the Lord; lest, while ye delay to do them, the building of the tower be finished, and you be rejected from the edifice. (Herm. *Sim.* 10.4; *ANF* 2:55)

THE FRAGMENTS OF PAPIAS

Among the documents usually included in the Apostolic Fathers are the remains of a vast work in five books that is commonly called *Expositions of the Oracles of the Lord*. Its author was the bishop of Hierapolis, Papias. According to Irenaeus, he was a disciple of John jointly with Polycarp. All that remains of this vast work are a few fragments quoted by later authors, particularly by Eusebius of Caesarea. These fragments are interesting for two main reasons: the first is what they say about the origins of the Gospels, which is now not generally accepted by scholars. According to Papias, Mark was Peter's interpreter, and Matthew wrote his Gospel originally in Hebrew. The second reason why the fragments of Papias are interesting is a quotation preserved by Irenaeus in which Papias says that Jesus spoke about the abundance of the promised future: "The days will come, in which vines shall grow, each having ten thousand branches, and in each branch ten thousand twigs, and in each true twig ten thousand shoots, and in each one of the shoots ten thousand clusters, and on every one of the clusters ten thousand grapes, and every grape when pressed will give five and twenty metretes of wine" (*Fragments* 4; *ANF* 1:153).

2

The Greek Apologists

As has been the case through the centuries, the ancient church had on the one hand to deal with internal matters of its own life, organization, worship, and theological debates; and on the other with external matters involving its relationship with the society in which it lived. This was a time when the church was at best despised, and at times persecuted. The documents that we discussed in the previous chapter refer primarily to the inner life of the church. They are letters from some Christians to others, a manual on church order and worship, and at least one homily. In this second chapter we turn our attention to the manner in which the church addressed its own defense to the society around it. It was around the middle of the second century that such literature appeared and, since it was all written in Greek, its authors are commonly called the "Greek apologists of the second century"—a title in which the word "apology" is not to be understood as an expression of regret, but rather as a defense.

The writings of these apologists served a dual purpose. On the one hand, they tried to show their readers that Christianity is not an uncouth, absurd, and even immoral religion, as many thought. On the other hand, they sought to convince authorities that the persecution of Christians was unjust and therefore should cease. Among the apologists, some addressed mainly the first of these purposes, and some the second. Thus, among these writings we find appeals to established authority as well as arguments trying to show the reasonableness of Christianity and describing various aspects of the inner life of the church in order to convince readers that Christians are not the dross of society, but rather a shining light within it.

THE *ADDRESS TO DIOGNETUS*

There is an ancient and intriguing document, usually included among the Apostolic Fathers, but in truth an apology, commonly known as the *Address to Diognetus*. It is intriguing in part because there is no certainty about its author or about its addressee, Diognetus. Yet even more intriguing, it is possibly the most ancient of extant Christian apologies. In his *Church History*, Eusebius of Caesarea says that a certain Quadratus produced a speech in favor of Christianity, which he presented to Emperor Hadrian. Eusebius's description of that apology seems to fit the text addressed to Diognetus. But even more, the word "Diognetus" was employed not only as a name, but also as title of honor. Before he became emperor, Hadrian had been given that title in the city of Athens. Therefore, it is possible that the *Address to Diognetus* is that lost apology of Quadratus to which Eusebius refers. Since Hadrian reigned from 117 to 138, if *To Diognetus* was actually addressed to him, this would make it the earliest Christian apology.

This document is valuable not only for its antiquity, but also for its style, which makes it a jewel within early Christian literature. There is no doubt that its author was well acquainted with the rhetorical canons of his time. His use of classical rhetoric and his refined language make it extraordinarily elegant. Furthermore, this document reflects a new development that was taking place within Christianity. It was becoming increasingly Gentile and therefore harbored many erroneous or inexact views of Judaism, which had been the religion of the earliest Christians. Within the document itself are but faint echoes of the Hebrew Scriptures, which has led some to suggest that the author was not very familiar with them.

After an introductory paragraph, the author undertakes first to refute idolatry, and then Judaism. It is in the refutation of idolatry that we find the clearest echoes of the ancient Jewish Scriptures, for his arguments are reminiscent of the prophets of Israel:

> Come and contemplate, not with your eyes only, but with your understanding, the substance and the form of those whom ye declare and deem to be gods. Is not one of them a stone similar to that on which we tread? Is not a second brass, in no way superior to those vessels which are constructed for our ordinary use? Is not a third wood, and that already rotten? Is not a fourth silver, which needs a man to watch it, lest it be stolen? (*Diogn.* 2; *ANF* 1:25)

Then the document turns to Judaism, which is praised for forsaking idolatry, but errs in offering sacrifices to God, who does not need such things, and in its observance of ridiculous rules. "But as to their scrupulosity concerning meats, and their superstition as respects the Sabbaths, and their boasting about circumcision, and their fancies about fasting and the new moons, which are utterly ridiculous and unworthy of notice,—I do not think that you require to learn anything from me" (*Diogn.* 4; *ANF* 1:26).

However, the most memorable parts of the document are those in which he describes Christians and their life by pointing out a series of paradoxes, a commonly used rhetorical device of the time.

> For the Christians are distinguished from other men neither by country, nor language, nor the customs which they observe. For they neither inhabit cities of their own, nor employ a peculiar form of speech, nor lead a life which is marked out by any singularity. The course of conduct which they follow has not been devised by any speculation or deliberation of inquisitive men; nor do they, like some, proclaim themselves the advocates of any merely human doctrines. But, inhabiting Greek as well as barbarian cities, according as the lot of each of them has determined, and following the customs of the natives in respect to clothing, food, and the rest of their ordinary conduct, they display to us their wonderful and confessedly striking method of life. They dwell in their own countries, but simply as sojourners. As citizens, they share in all things with others, and yet endure all things as if foreigners. Every foreign land is to them as their native country, and every land of their birth as a land of strangers. They marry, as do all [others]; they beget children; but they do not destroy their offspring. They have a common table, but not a common bed. They are in the flesh, but they do not live after the flesh. They pass their days on earth, but they are citizens of heaven. They obey the prescribed laws, and at the same time surpass the laws by their lives. They love all men, and are persecuted by all. They are unknown and condemned; they are put to death, and restored to life. They are poor, yet make many rich; they are in lack of all things, and yet abound in all; they are dishonoured, and yet in their very dishonour are glorified. They are evil spoken of, and yet are justified; they are reviled, and bless; they are insulted, and repay the insult with honour; they do good, yet are punished as evil-doers. When punished, they rejoice as if quickened into life; they are assailed by the Jews as foreigners, and are persecuted by the Greeks; yet those who hate them are unable to assign any reason for their hatred. (*Diogn.* 5; *ANF* 1:26–27)

As to its theology, the *Address to Diognetus* centers attention on the incarnation of God in Jesus Christ. After exalting the name and power of God, the author asks to what end such a powerful God would send a representative to earth.

Was it then, as one might conceive, for the purpose of exercising tyranny, or of inspiring fear and terror? By no means, but under the influence of clemency and meekness. As a king sends his son, who is also a king, so sent He Him; as God He sent Him; as to men He sent Him; as a Saviour He sent Him, and so seeking to persuade, not to compel us; for violence has no place in the character of God. As calling us He sent Him, not as vengefully pursuing us; as loving us He sent Him, not as judging us. For He will yet send Him to judge us, and who shall endure His appearing? (*Diogn.* 7; *ANF* 1:27)

Part of the reason why God has done such a thing is to invite humans to imitate the divine. Strange as it may seem, human beings, made after the image of God, are capable of imitating God.

And if you love Him, you will be an imitator of His kindness. And do not wonder that a man may become an imitator of God. He can, if he is willing. For it is not by ruling over his neighbours, or by seeking to hold the supremacy over those that are weaker, or by being rich, and showing violence towards those that are inferior, that happiness is found; nor can any one by these things become an imitator of God. But these things do not at all constitute His majesty. On the contrary he who takes upon himself the burden of his neighbor; he who, in whatsoever respect he may be superior, is ready to benefit another who is deficient; he who, whatsoever things he has received from God, by distributing these to the needy, becomes a god to those who receive [his benefits]: he is an imitator of God. (*Diogn.* 10; *ANF* 1:29)

THE *APOLOGY OF ARISTIDES*

Eusebius of Caesarea says that, almost at the same time as Quadratus, the Athenian Aristides delivered to Emperor Hadrian a defense of Christianity and that as a result Hadrian instructed the proconsul of Asia that he should refrain from condemning Christians unless they were proved to have committed a crime. This latter statement, although not necessarily false, is not corroborated by any ancient Christian writer. At any rate, the *Apology of Aristides* was lost until late in the nineteenth century, when an Armenian text that claimed to be the lost apology was published in a Latin translation. Shortly thereafter an American scholar pointed out the very similar text in the fictional writing known as *Barlaam and Josaphat*, where Barlaam takes episodes from the life of Buddha and uses them as part of his argument to convince Josaphat, an Indian prince, to remain firm in the Christian faith. There is no doubt that the author of this legend took this part of his work from an ancient manuscript of the *Apology of Aristides*. From that point onward, other texts and fragments have surfaced. This includes a Syriac version which seems to be older than the extant Greek text, even though at some points it appears to be summarizing the original text. Therefore, it is impossible to reconstruct the text of the *Apology* in any detail. But it is possible to reconstruct the essence of its argument, and in some cases there is sufficient agreement among the various versions that one may quote the text with some confidence.

This apology is characterized by its philosophical tone, for Aristides seeks to prove that the Christian faith is more reasonable than any other. So it divides humankind into three groups (three groups in the Greek text, four in the Syriac version). The first includes most of the intended audience of Aristides, whom he calls "worshipers of what you call gods." The other two are Jews and Christians. The first group includes not only Greeks, but also others such as the Chaldeans and the Egyptians. They all err, declares Aristides, although in different ways. Some claim that the sky is a god; others, that the earth is a god; and others that the wind, the sun, the moon, or human beings are divine. Since this group includes the Greeks, and they are the true audience of this writing, Aristides describes in greater detail some of their religious myths, to show that the Greek gods are in truth the invention of humans who sought to give divine sanction to their immorality by attributing it to the gods.

> This shows, O king, that the Greeks introduced stupid and ridiculous words in calling such things gods. They are not. They did this following their evil desires so that those gods would justify their evil, leaving them free to practice adultery, plunder, murder, and all sorts of evil. Because they say that, since the gods did all these things, why would not those who worship them? Thus the result of all these works of error was that people suffered continuous wars and slaughters as well as bitter captivity. (*Apol.* 9.4–6; BAC 116:122)

As to the Jews, although they have the revelation of God, who first was manifested to the patriarchs and later in leading them out of slavery in Egypt, besides giving them laws and doing wonders among them, they also failed, for they disobeyed God and killed the prophets, and also because

> when the Son of God decided to come to earth, first they insulted him, and then they turned him over to Pontius Pilate, the Roman governor, and he condemned him to die on the cross, forgetting all the good he had done them and the many marvels he had performed. And they perished for their own iniquity. . . . Thus they worship the only Omnipotent God, but without true understanding, for they reject Christ, who is the Son of God. No matter how much they seem to approach truth, in fact they have strayed from it. (*Apol.* 14.1–2; BAC 116:129)

All of this leads Aristides to close his treatise with an affirmation of Christian faith and a description of the life that flows from it:

> These are the ones who better than anyone else in the world have found truth, for they know God the creator and shaper of all things in the Only Begotten and the Holy Spirit and worship no other God. The commandments of this Lord Jesus Christ are written on their hearts, and they keep them, while they await the resurrection of the dead and life in the age to come. They do not commit adultery or fornication. They do not bear false witness. They do not covet what is not theirs. They honor their father and mother, love their neighbor, and judge justly. They do not do unto others what they do not wish done unto them. They call on those who do them evil to be their friends. They seek to do good to their enemies. They are meek and gentle. They abstain from every impurity or illicit union. They do not scorn the widow nor sadden the orphan. Those who have share abundantly with those who do not. If they see a stranger, they welcome him under their roof and rejoice with him as with a brother. (*Apol.* 15.3–7; BAC 116:130–31)

JUSTIN MARTYR

Up to this point we have dealt with authors of whom we only have short treatises or letters. When we come to Justin Martyr, the situation is different. The ancient historian Eusebius of Caesarea gives a list of many of his works. Only three of them have come to our time. But even these three by themselves are as extensive as the total work of the other apologists in the present chapter.

The three works of Justin that have survived are his *First Apology*, his *Second Apology*, and his *Dialogue with Trypho*. According to the witness of Eusebius, the first of these was addressed to Emperor Antoninus Pius, and the second to his successor Marcus Aurelius. Since Antoninus Pius ruled from 138 to 161, and Marcus Aurelius from that time until 180, these apologies are to be placed at the middle of the second century. (Yet some scholars suggest that the second is simply an appendix to the first, leaving the two as a single work.) The *Dialogue with Trypho* is a conversation or debate between Justin and a rabbi by that name, a conversation that sometimes is quite respectful and not so much so at other times.

Justin was raised in the city of Flavia Neopolis in the region of Syria, which had been founded by Emperor Vespasian on the site of the ancient city of Shechem. Since his name as well as his father's are of Roman origin, it seems that his roots were Roman, or at least Latin. Even so, like all cultured Romans of the time, he knew Greek quite well, and it was in that language that he wrote. He himself tells us that what caused him to consider the faith of Christians was their witness when they were killed:

> For I myself, too, when I was delighting in the doctrines of Plato, and heard the Christians slandered, and saw them fearless of death, and of all other things which are counted fearful, perceived that it was impossible that they could be living in wickedness and pleasure. For what sensual or intemperate man, or who that counts it good to feast on human flesh, could welcome death that he might be deprived of his enjoyments, and would not rather continue always the present life, and attempt to escape the observation of the rulers; and much less would he denounce himself when the consequence would be death? (2 Apol. 12; ANF 1:192)

Even though what attracted him to Christianity was the witness of martyrs, Justin was above all a philosopher, and therefore he sought to establish bridges between his faith and the reigning philosophy. Having settled in Rome, he founded a school attended by both those who were Christian and those who were not, and he gained wide respect. This eventually led to a debate with the pagan philosopher Crescentius. According to various reports, which probably reflect Christian prejudices, Justin was a clear winner in that debate. Shortly thereafter, perhaps as a result of accusations and maneuvers by Crescentius, Justin was arrested and condemned to die, just as the martyrs whom he had earlier admired—although, being a Roman citizen, he was beheaded.

Since Justin's two apologies deal with the relationship between Christian faith and philosophy, and his *Dialogue with Trypho* refers to the relationship between Christianity and Judaism, we shall begin by considering the first matter and then the latter.

In contrast with some of the apologists whom we shall study in the rest of this chapter, Justin shows great respect and even admiration for Greek philosophers, particularly Plato. His purpose is not to prove that philosophy is wrong, but rather to show that Christianity is the "true philosophy," the culmination of all the earlier great philosophical systems.

Although Justin's apologies are not as well organized as the one written by Aristides, their scope is much wider. The explicit purpose is to convince the emperor and those around him that they should cease persecuting Christians unjustly:

> For we have come, not to flatter you by this writing, nor please you by our address, but to beg that you pass judgment, after an accurate and searching investigation, not flattered by prejudice or by a desire of pleasing superstitious men, nor induced by irrational impulse or evil rumours which have long been prevalent. . . . We demand that the charges against the Christians be investigated, and that, if these

be substantiated, they be punished as they deserve. But if no one can convict us of anything, true reason forbids you, for the sake of a wicked rumour, to wrong blameless men. (*1 Apol.* 2–3; *ANF* 1:163)

But in fact these two apologies also have another purpose. Justin wishes to show not only that the persecution against Christians is unjust, but also that Christian truth is above every other truth, and whatever may be found to be true in any other philosophy comes from the same Word of God whom Christians worship in Jesus Christ. Thus he proposes to prove that "whatever we assert in conformity with what has been taught us by Christ, and by the prophets who preceded Him, are alone true, and are older than all the writers who have existed; that we claim to be acknowledged, not because we say the same things as these writers said, but because we say true things" (*1 Apol.* 23; *ANF* 1:170).

Jointly with the long sections seeking to show the moral superiority of Christians, and that what was said by the ancient prophets of Israel has been fulfilled in Jesus Christ, Justin tries to show that the wisdom of the philosophers coincides with that of Christians, although the latter is higher. While he employs the rather unconvincing argument that Moses lived before Plato, and therefore anything to be found in the latter was taken from the Hebrew Scriptures, Justin goes beyond that. Those ancient philosophers had repeatedly spoken of the Logos, Word, or reason that is the origin and foundation and of all true knowledge. Arguing then that this eternal Word is the one who was incarnate in Jesus Christ, Justin can accept and claim any good that may be found in the wisdom of the ancients:

> We have been taught that Christ is the first-born of God, and we have declared above that He is the Word of whom every race of men were partakers; and those who lived reasonably are Christians, even though they have been thought atheists; as, among the Greeks, Socrates and Heraclitus, and men like them; and among the barbarians, Abraham, and Ananias, and Azarias, and Misael, and Elias, and many others whose actions and names we now decline to recount because we know it would be tedious. (*1 Apol.* 46; *ANF* 1:178)

On the other hand, this does not mean that everything the philosophers have said is to be believed. The philosophers only had a partial knowledge of the Word, and this is why they committed errors and contradictions. Therefore,

> our doctrines, then, appear to be greater than all human teaching; because Christ, who appeared for our sakes, became the whole rational being, both body, and reason and soul. For whatever either lawgivers or philosophers uttered well, they elaborated by finding and contemplating some part of the Word. But since they did not know

the whole of the Word, which is Christ, they often contradicted
themselves. (*2 Apol.* 10; *ANF* 1:191)

This had enormous significance, for it was the means whereby Christians
were able to take possession of philosophy and turn it into an ally rather
than an opponent. Many other authors after Justin would use what he had
said in order to build bridges between Christian faith and the surrounding
culture.

The two apologies of Justin—especially the first—are also important
because in them may be found valuable descriptions of Christian life and worship in the middle of the second century. Thanks to Justin, we know that,
from a very early date, when pagans decided to join the church, they were to
undergo a period of instruction, prayer, and fasting before being baptized:

> As many as are persuaded and believe that what we teach and say
> is true, and undertake to be able to live accordingly, are instructed
> to pray and to entreat God with fasting, for the remission of their
> sins that are past, we praying and fasting with them. Then they are
> brought by us where there is water, and are regenerated in the same
> manner in which we were ourselves regenerated. For, in the name of
> God, the Father and Lord of the universe, and of our Saviour Jesus
> Christ, and of the Holy Spirit, they then receive the washing with
> water. (*1 Apol.* 41; *ANF* 1:183)

This is followed by two parallel descriptions of Christian worship. The
first of these, mostly describing what happens with those who have just been
baptized, then moves to the eucharistic celebration:

> But we, after we have thus washed him who has been convinced and
> has assented to our teaching, bring him to the place where those who
> are called brethren are assembled, in order that we may offer hearty
> prayers in common for ourselves and for the baptized person, and
> for all others in every place, that we may be counted worthy, now
> that we have learned the truth, by our works also to be found good
> citizens and keepers of the commandments, so that we may be saved
> with an everlasting salvation. Having ended the prayers, we salute
> one another with a kiss. There is then brought to the president of the
> brethren bread and a cup of wine mixed with water; and he taking
> them, gives praise and glory to the Father of the universe, through
> the name of the Son and of the Holy Ghost, and offers thanks at con-
> siderable length for our being counted worthy to receive these things
> at His hands. And when he has concluded the prayers and thanksgiv-
> ings, all the people present express their assent by saying Amen. This
> word Amen answers in the Hebrew language to [the Greek] γένοιτο
> [*genoito*, so be it]. And when the president has given thanks, and all the
> people have expressed their assent, those who are called by us deacons

give to each of those present to partake of the bread and wine mixed with water over which the thanksgiving was pronounced, and to those who are absent they carry away a portion.

And this food is called among us Εὐχαριστία [*Eucharistia*, the Eucharist], of which no one is allowed to partake but the man who believes that the things which we teach are true, and who has been washed with the washing that is for the remission of sins, and unto regeneration, and who is so living as Christ has enjoined. For not as common bread and common drink do we receive these; but in like manner as Jesus Christ our Saviour, having been made flesh by the Word of God, had both flesh and blood for our salvation, so likewise have we been taught that the food which is blessed by the prayer of His word, and from which our blood and flesh by transmutation are nourished, is the flesh and blood of that Jesus who was made flesh. (*1 Apol.* 65–66; *ANF* 1:185)

Also within this context, Justin offers a brief description of Christian worship, providing information that would otherwise be unknown today:

And on the day called Sunday, all who live in cities or in the country gather together to one place, and the memoirs of the apostles or the writings of the prophets are read, as long as time permits; then, when the reader has ceased, the president verbally instructs, and exhorts to the imitation of these good things. Then we all rise together and pray, and, as we before said, when our prayer is ended, bread and wine and water are brought, and the president in like manner offers prayers and thanksgivings, according to his ability, and the people assent, saying Amen; and there is a distribution to each, and a participation of that over which thanks have been given, and to those who are absent a portion is sent by the deacons. And they who are well to do, and willing, give what each thinks fit; and what is collected is deposited with the president, who succours the orphans and widows. (*1 Apol.* 67; *ANF* 1:186)

In reading these passages, it is important to remember that they are addressed to people outside the church, and that therefore they seek to employ the language that will be understood in those circles. Thus, for instance, the person who in other writings is called "presbyter" or "bishop" here is simply called "the president." Likewise, Justin speaks of "the day called Sunday," which was the name that pagans gave to that day, while in his *Dialogue with Trypho* he refers to it as "the first day of the week." This is because Romans commonly understood the week to begin on the day of Saturn, which for Jews and Christians was not the first day of the week, but the seventh, and therefore Justin has to give it the pagan name, "the day of the sun."

The context and the tone are very different when we come to the *Dialogue with Trypho*. All that is known about this Trypho is what we learn from this dialogue. Much later, Eusebius of Caesarea says that this was the famous Rabbi Tarpho, whose name appears in the Talmud. Scholars are not in agreement as to whether this is correct. If Trypho is in fact that famous rabbi, we know that he died around the year 155, and therefore the dialogue that provided the foundation for Justin's writing must have been composed toward the middle of the century. At any rate, there is no doubt that the Trypho who appears in this dialogue is an educated Jew who at the same time does not seem to have great sympathy for the hellenized forms of Judaism that were then circulating.

As Justin tells the story, the dialogue began as Justin was strolling by the gymnasium: Trypho approached him and began the conversation. When Trypho asks him about his philosophy, Justin tells him that "philosophy is, in fact, the greatest possession, and most honorable before God" (*Dial.* 2.1; *ANF* 1:194). But he then goes on to tell Trypho that, after first having followed the philosophy of the Stoics, then those of the Aristotelians, the Pythagoreans, and finally the Platonists, an old man approached him and asked him about the true philosophy. Justin then tells Trypho the conversation that he held with that man, which led him to become a Christian.

> When he had spoken these and many other things, which there is no time for mentioning at present, he went away, bidding me attend to them; and I have not seen him since. But straightway a flame was kindled in my soul; and a love of the prophets, and of those men who are friends of Christ, possessed me; and whilst revolving his words in my mind, I found this philosophy alone to be safe and profitable. Thus, and for this reason, I am a philosopher. Moreover, I would wish that all, making a resolution similar to my own, do not keep themselves away from the words of the Saviour. (*Dial.* 8; *ANF* 1:198)

Upon hearing this, Trypho advises Justin: "First be circumcised, then observe what ordinances have been enacted with respect to the Sabbath, and the feasts, and the new moons of God; and, in a word, do all things which have been written in the law; and then perhaps you shall obtain mercy from God" (*Dial.* 8; *ANF* 1:198–99).

This opens a dialogue that generally shows mutual respect, although occasionally Trypho accuses Justin of blasphemy, and on his part, Justin, while affirming that he worships the same God as the Jews, is free with criticisms that show the degree to which anti-Semitism was making headway in the church. For instance, Justin says that circumcision was given to the Jews in order to remind them of their unfaithfulness. And now that their land has been conquered, "these things have happened to you in fairness and justice, for you have slain the Just One, and His prophets before him" (*Dial.* 16; *ANF*

1:202). Furthermore, according to Justin, whenever they have been able to do so, Jews have persecuted and oppressed Christians, and the only reason why they do not do so now is that the authorities will not allow it.

In any case, the error of the Jews, besides not acknowledging Jesus as the Christ, is taking literally the biblical commandments and not understanding their spiritual sense. This is particularly true of circumcision, which pointed to the true circumcision of the heart. In an interesting passage, Justin argues that the fact that only males are circumcised shows that it has no saving significance, for when it comes to justification, there is equality between the sexes:

> And furthermore, the inability of the female sex to receive fleshly circumcision, proves that this circumcision has been given for a sign, and not for a work of righteousness. For God has given likewise to women the ability to observe all things which are righteous and virtuous; but we see that the bodily form of the male has been made different from the bodily form of the female; yet we know that neither of them is righteous or unrighteous merely for this cause, but by reason of piety and righteousness. (*Dial.* 23; *ANF* 1:206)

Almost all the rest of the dialogue is devoted to discussing the meaning of various biblical passages, particularly from the Pentateuch, the Prophets, and Psalms. Without reviewing each of these passages, it is important to notice that in his biblical interpretation Justin makes use of both prophecy and of typology. The first is simply taking the words of the prophets and other authors in the Hebrew Bible and showing how they are fulfilled in Jesus. Typology sees in the actions, ceremonies, and events of Jewish history signs or "types" of Jesus Christ. Justin affirms both: "For the Holy Spirit sometimes brought about that something, which was the type of the future, should be done clearly; sometimes he uttered words about what was to take place, as if it was then taking place, or had taken place" (*Dial.* 114; *ANF* 1:256). There are many examples of this. The blood with which the children of Israel marked their houses so that the angel of death would pass over them was a figure or type of Christ, who saves those who are sealed with his blood. Furthermore, the paschal lamb is roasted in the shape of a cross, which is also an announcement of the cross of Jesus. The offering of flour that was required pointed to the bread in Christian communion, and circumcision was a prefiguring of the "true circumcision" that Christ has brought to the world.

According to Justin, this means that it is no longer necessary to keep the Mosaic law, since once the reality has come, the type or sign that announced it is no longer necessary. On the other hand, Justin acknowledges that some Christians still insist in keeping the ancient Jewish laws. And, although there are Christians who will have no communion with them, Justin himself would tolerate them, as long as they do not insist that others must follow the same laws.

The *Dialogue with Trypho* ends in a stalemate, for neither side is able to convince the other. But at the end both Justin and Trypho show mutual respect. When Justin is about to take a ship to sail away, Trypho asks that he remember him and his fellows as friends, and Justin invites them to follow the path of joy that he has been describing.

TATIAN

Tatian is the best known of Justin's disciples, with whom he studied in Rome and whom he succeeded as a teacher in that city. But, as several ancient writers tell us, he abandoned Christian orthodoxy, declaring that every sexual act was a sign of corruption and therefore marriage is to be avoided. Later, those who held this position were called "Encratites," and Tatian was said to have been the founder of this "sect"; yet Encratism does not really appear to have been a sect, but rather a practice and an opinion fairly prevalent in some circles within the church. Finally, Tatian returned to the East (Syria? Armenia?), where he is said to have founded a school around the year 172. At that point he disappears in the shadows of time, although it seems that he had died by 185.

Tatian was the author of a harmony of the Gospels, the *Diatessaron*, which enjoyed wide distribution in the region of Syria, where it was frequently employed instead of the four Gospels, at least until the fourth century.

Tatian wrote an *Address to the Greeks* and is therefore one of the Greek apologists of the second century. While he praises his teacher Justin, the tone as well as the content of his apology stands in strong contrast to his teacher. Although Justin affirmed the value of Greek philosophy and sought to show the continuity or connection between it and the Christian message, Tatian's views are diametrically opposed. His work is a stark rejection of all that could be called Greek and provides a defense of the Jewish "barbarians" among whom Christian faith arose. The very tone of this writing seems to indicate that he was not addressing a Greek audience, as the title suggests, but rather other believers whom he sought to strengthen for facing the opposition of the culture and society.

According to Tatian, any good that may be found in Greek culture has been taken from the "barbarians." Since Moses lived long before Homer, both the latter and all Greek philosophers have drawn from his teachings, although without understanding them properly. This is why philosophers contradict one another and each Greek city has different laws. Furthermore, precisely because they did not know the commandments of God, the Greeks have abandoned themselves to all sorts of immorality.

In summary, Tatian is an example of an apologetic attitude that takes the opposite tack from Justin's, trying to show that all that is not Christian is inferior and even despicable.

ATHENAGORAS

Very little is known about this Christian apologist. Athenagoras certainly was interested in philosophy and was probably an Athenian. Two of his works have been preserved: the *Plea for the Christians* and *On the Resurrection of the Dead*. The first, addressed jointly to Emperors Marcus Aurelius and Commodus, must have been written between 176 and 180, during which time these two shared the imperial throne. The second seems to have been written shortly thereafter, for at the end of the *Plea* Athenagoras says: "Let us defer the discourse concerning the resurrection" (*Plea* 36; *ANF* 2:148).

Like Justin, Athenagoras shows sincere appreciation for Greek philosophy, particularly Platonism. But his main purpose is not to show the relationship between that philosophy and his own faith, but rather to expound Christian faith in such a way that the emperors will realize how unjust and unnecessary persecution is: "We venture, therefore, to lay a statement of our case before you—and you will learn from this discourse that we suffer unjustly, and contrary to all law and reason—and we beseech you to bestow some consideration upon us also, that we may cease at length to be slaughtered at the instigation of false accusers" (*Plea* 1; *ANF* 2:129).

Then Athenagoras says that he proposes to refute the three main accusations made against Christians. The first of these is atheism, of which Christians were accused because they had no visible gods. The other two are rumors claiming that Christians practiced cannibalism and incest. Although in an introduction Athenagoras says that he will deal with these three accusations, in fact thirty of the thirty-six chapters of his work deal with the first. About the last two, Athenagoras simply says that, in view of the high moral principles of Christians and their belief in the final judgment and resurrection, it is inconceivable that they should do such things. As to atheism, Athenagoras's main argument is that, if Christians are atheists because of what they say about their God, so also were several of the greatest figures in Greek history:

> If, therefore, Plato is not an atheist for conceiving of one uncreated God, the Framer of the universe, neither are we atheists who

acknowledge and firmly hold that He is God who has framed all things by the Logos, and holds them in being by His Spirit. . . . That we are not atheists, therefore, seeing that we acknowledge one God, uncreated, eternal, invisible, impassible, incomprehensible, illimitable, who is apprehended by the understanding only and the reason, who is encompassed by light, and beauty, and spirit, and power ineffable, by whom the universe has been created through His Logos, and set in order, and is kept in being—I have sufficiently demonstrated. (*Plea* 6,10; *ANF* 2:132–33)

In his other work, *On the Resurrection of the Dead*, Athenagoras responds to the various objections that could be raised against such a doctrine. For instance, what will happen to those whose bodies have fallen into the sea and whose particles are now dispersed among the many fish that ate them? Or, to whom will the various particles that have been shared through the centuries by different people belong? Athenagoras responds to such objections by appealing to divine omnipotence. The God who created bodies out of nothing is also able to overcome such difficulties. At any rate, this doctrine is of great importance for Athenagoras: "Nor again is it the happiness of soul separated from body: for we are not inquiring about the life or final cause of either of the parts of which man consists, but of the being who is composed of both" (*Res.* 25; *ANF* 2:162).

THEOPHILUS OF ANTIOCH

The most important fact that is known about Theophilus of Antioch is that he was a bishop of that city and therefore a successor, though not an immediate successor, of Ignatius. We have the titles of several other works that he wrote and have been lost. Probably the most important among these was *Against Marcion*. The work that remains, his *Three Books to Autolycus*, is an extensive apology in which the author tends to condemn and reject anything that is of Greek origin. When he mentions something with approval, he goes on to claim that any such things the Greeks said, they learned from the Hebrew Scripture. At any rate, this work is a long disquisition, rather poorly organized, with abundant quotations from ancient writers, not all of them accurate. Who this Autolycus was to whom Theophilus writes this book is not known. Theophilus depicts him as a pagan, which he remained after his discussions with Theophilus.

Probably the best lines in the entire work appear quite near the beginning, where Theophilus tells Autolycus:

But if you say, "Show me thy God," I would reply, "Show me yourself, and I will show you my God." Show, then, that the eyes of your soul are capable of seeing, and the ears of your heart able to hear. . . . For God is seen by those who are enabled to see Him when they have the eyes of their soul opened: for all have eyes; but in some they are overspread [diseased], and do not see the light of the sun. Yet it does not follow, because the blind do not see, that the light of the sun does not shine. (*Autol.* 1.2; *ANF* 2:89)

For the rest, if Theophilus is accused of not worshiping the emperor, he responds by affirming that he serves the emperor better by praying for him than by worshiping him, for the emperor is not a god, but his power and rule do come from God.

The second book generally repeats what was said in the first. It does include a long commentary on the history of creation and the fall, and then about Adam and Eve and their descendants, the flood, the patriarchs, and so on. Although Theophilus does not develop the subject, in the second book he makes a distinction between the Word of God as it existed within God eternally and the uttered Word. Later this led to long controversies and would eventually be rejected by most theologians.

The most interesting section in the third book is a long calculation of the time between the creation and the time when Theophilus himself was writing his book. He concludes:

From the creation of the world to the deluge were 2242 years. And from the deluge to the time when Abraham our forefather begat a son, 1036 years. And from Isaac, Abraham's son, to the time when the people dwelt with Moses in the desert, 660 years. And from the death of Moses and the rule of Joshua the son of Nun, to the death of the patriarch David, 498 years. And from the death of David and the reign of Solomon to the sojourning of the people in the land of Babylon, 518 years 6 months 10 days. And from the government of Cyrus to the death of the Emperor Aurelius Verus, 744 years. All the years from the creation of the world amount to a total of 5698 years, and the odd months and days. (*Autol.* 3.28; *ANF* 2:120)

HERMIAS

Some collections of the apologists of the second century include a short writing by a certain Hermias, *Mockery of the Pagan Philosophers*. So little is known about this writing and its author that some scholars place it in the second century, while others date it as late as the sixth. In any case, the book is simply a repetition of arguments already found in Tatian, based on the mutual contradictions among philosophers. It is marked by mordant sarcasm, making it appear that the philosophers themselves were irrational and capricious.

Apparently content with this, the author says nothing about Christian faith beyond a few brief biblical references.

MELITO OF SARDIS

Eusebius of Caesarea quotes a few short sections from a lost apology that Melito of Sardis addressed to Emperor Antoninus Pius. Eusebius also mentions other works by Melito, all of which have been lost. But Eusebius refers to two books on the paschal feast, and it appears likely that an Easter homily discovered in relatively recent times may have been part of that work. It appears to be a sermon by Melito, who was bishop of Sardis around the year 160 or slightly later. In this rather poetical homily, Melito builds a bridge between the ancient history of Israel and the gospel, showing how the former announced the latter, and the history of Israel prefigures the history of Jesus: "He is the Pascha of our salvation. It is he who in many endured many things: it is he that was in Abel murdered, and in Isaac bound, and in Jacob exiled, and in Joseph sold, and in Moses exposed, and in the Lamb slain, and in David persecuted, and in the prophets dishonored" (*On Pascha* 69; S. G. Hall, ed. and trans., *Melito of Sardis: "On Pascha" and Fragments* [Oxford: Clarendon Press, 1979], 37).

Most of the homily is a beautiful exaltation of Jesus, contrasting his power with his sufferings, and ending with a song in his praise:

> He is the Alpha and the Omega; he is beginning and end, beginning inexpressible and end incomprehensible; he is the Christ; he is the King; he is Jesus; he is the captain; he is the Lord; he is the one who rose from the dead; he is the one who sits at the Father's right hand; he carries the Father and is carried by the Father. To him be glory and power for ever. Amen. (*On Pascha*, 105; Hall, *Melito*, 61)

3

The Acts of the Martyrs

The same conditions that led the apologists to write their defenses of the faith also gave rise to another literary genre generally known as the "acts of the martyrs." In some ways, these have their antecedents in the Hebrew tradition and also in the New Testament, with the well-known story of Stephen's stoning and death. As persecution became increasingly general, some believers sought to preserve the memory of the suffering and valor of the martyrs. Since there often was a formal trial, official acts were recorded by the authorities. Some of them made their way into Christian hands and were then employed in a more elaborate story about the martyrs to which they referred. Others seem to have been written from the memory of what had taken place, and perhaps even simply as a product of the imagination of the faithful. As persecution advanced, and even after it ceased, the number of these "acts" increased. For these reasons, there is still much debate about how much of these documents is actually taken from official documents, how much is based on memory, and how much is just the result of pious imagination.

THE *MARTYRDOM OF POLYCARP*

Probably the most ancient of these documents that has been preserved is the *Martyrdom of Polycarp*, which takes the form of a letter that the church of Smyrna addressed to the church in Philomelium, but is in fact intended to be read also by other churches. According to this letter, Polycarp "waited to be delivered up even as the Lord had done" (*Mart. Pol.* 1; *ANF* 1:39).

What led to Polycarp's death was that a martyr by the name of Germanicus, when brought before the beasts, taunted them so that they would attack him. Angered by such valor, the mob began shouting that the leader of all Christians in the city, Polycarp, was to be punished. At the same time, however, a certain Quintus, moved by what he was witnessing, offered himself as a martyr; but at the last minute he denied the faith. In its letter, the church in Smyrna uses this example as proof that martyrdom is not to be sought, but that when it comes, it is to be received willingly: "Wherefore, brethren, do not commend those who give themselves up [to suffering], seeing the Gospel does not teach so to do" (*Mart. Pol.* 4; *ANF* 1:40).

This serves as an introduction to the story of Polycarp, who repeatedly hid until he was finally convinced that it was the Lord himself who had set him apart for martyrdom. At that point he would no longer flee from those who were seeking him, and when they finally found him, he ordered that they be fed while he took some time to pray.

It is in chapter 9 of the *Martyrdom of Polycarp*, when Polycarp finally meets the proconsul, that we come to the part of the document that was possibly taken from the acts of his trial. Several decades earlier Pliny the Younger, governor of Bithynia, had written to Emperor Trajan regarding Christians. Pliny reported to the emperor that he had given Christians brought before him three opportunities to recant, and if they refused to do so, he would condemn them to death. Trajan responded commending him for his policy, and from that point on this became the general policy followed throughout the empire. The *Martyrdom of Polycarp*, while not referring explicitly to this policy, tells us that Polycarp is given the three required opportunities. The proconsul invites him to take his old age into account and declare, "Away with the Atheists"—by which the proconsul means the Christians. Polycarp, pointing to the mob who wishes him dead, employs the words suggested by the proconsul, yet making it clear that to his mind they actually refer not to Christians, but rather to the pagan multitude. As to his age, Polycarp says: "Eighty and six years have I served Him, and He never did me any injury: how then can I blaspheme my King and Saviour?" (*Mart. Pol.* 9; *ANF* 1:41).

The proconsul then threatens him with beasts and with fire, and Polycarp answers: "Thou threatenest me with fire which burneth for an hour, and after a little is extinguished, but art ignorant of the fire of the coming judgment and of eternal punishment, reserved for the ungodly" (*Mart. Pol.* 11; *ANF* 1:41).

At this point the narrative moves beyond the acts of the trial and tells of a series of miracles, whose purpose seems to be to show that God was truly with Polycarp. We are also told that together with Polycarp twelve other Christians from Philadelphia were also killed—although there is no explanation as to why they were in Smyrna.

THE MARTYRDOM OF PTOLEMY

In Justin's *Second Apology*, discussed in the preceding chapter, there is a story of three martyrs, Ptolemy, Lucius, and an unnamed third. Since Justin is addressing the emperor and speaking of his previous imperial acts, there is no doubt that what he says here is true. What is not known is whether Justin takes his materials from the official acts of the trial of Ptolemy and his companions, or from some other source. At any rate, the legal process followed against Ptolemy is described in such a way that the entire story is usually counted among the early acts of the martyrs. Justin wrote this apology around the year 160, some five years after Polycarp's martyrdom. Therefore the events that he narrates must have taken place near the time of Polycarp's martyrdom.

According to Justin, what happened was that a woman who jointly with her husband had been leading a dissolute life became a Christian. Her husband employed all possible means to have her return to her previous life. Eventually the tension was such that she decided to divorce him. In retaliation, the husband accused her of being a Christian. She then petitioned the emperor that she be allowed to respond to these charges after she had made proper plans for the disposition of her possessions. When the emperor agreed to this, the husband—who apparently was more interested in his wife's possessions than in her—turned his wrath against Ptolemy, who had brought the woman to Christianity. He also made certain that the centurion who arrested his wife and the prefect of the city of Rome, Urbicus, would hasten the trial of Ptolemy, who declared that he was indeed a Christian. Lucius, who witnessed the haste with which the trial was conducted, protested and then declared himself also to be a Christian. The third martyr, whose name is not given, also protested against what seemed to be a miscarriage of justice and joined the other two in their death. (As to what happened to the woman who had been converted, Justin does not say.)

THE *MARTYRDOM OF JUSTIN*

Shortly after writing about these events, it was Justin's turn to follow the path of Ptolemy and his companions. Historian Eusebius of Caesarea leads us to believe that Justin was accused by the cynic philosopher Crescentius, whom Justin had defeated in a public debate. The document relating Justin's martyrdom does not mention this matter. The text itself seems to have been taken from the official acts of the trial, although obviously it has been edited by Christians, for at the very beginning we are told that "in the time of the lawless partisans of idolatry, wicked decrees were passed against the godly Christians in town and country, to force them to offer libations to vain idols" (*Mart. Justin* 1; *ANF* 1:305). The very fact that the document offers this explanation seems to indicate that, since conditions have changed and persecution has ended, its author has had access to the official acts of the trial. This is one of many reasons that lead most scholars to declare that the acts of Justin's martyrdom are authentic. The Christian author seems to have added only the already-quoted introduction and a brief conclusion in which he declares that the martyrs glorified God as they marched to the place where they would be beheaded, and that some other believers took their bodies and buried them. The rest seems to have been taken literally from the official acts.

The judge at the trial is the prefect of Rome, Junius Rusticus, a distinguished and learned man to whom Emperor Marcus Aurelius attributed much of his own wisdom. In the trial, the prefect begins by addressing Justin, apparently without having given him an opportunity to speak, and ordering him to believe in the gods and obey the emperors. Justin responds that it is Jesus whom he must obey. When Rusticus gives him leave to express his beliefs, Justin tells him that although he has tried to learn as much as possible from all philosophers, he is a firm believer in Christian doctrines, "even though they do not please those who hold false opinions" (*Mart. Justin* 1; *ANF* 1:305). After a dialogue in which Rusticus declares him to be miserable, Justin expounds the essence of his faith declaring that his doctrine is

> that according to which we worship the God of the Christians, whom we reckon to be one from the beginning, the maker and fashioner of the whole creation, visible and invisible; and the Lord Jesus Christ, the Son of God, who had also been preached beforehand by the prophets as about to be present with the race of men, the herald of salvation and teacher of good disciples. And I, being a man, think that what I can say is insignificant in comparison with His boundless divinity. (*Mart. Justin* 1; *ANF* 1:305)

The prefect tries to force Justin to tell him where Christians meet, but he refuses to do so and instead simply declares where he himself can be found. Finally, Rusticus asks him if he is a Christian, and Justin tells him that indeed he is.

Then Rusticus addresses the others who have been accused, five men and a woman. When the first three are asked if they are Christians, they all respond that they are. One of them, Evelpistus, is a servant of the emperor, but declares that as a Christian he has been "freed by Christ."

Rusticus is still interested in finding out more about other Christians and repeatedly asks who has taught them such doctrines. They all declare that it was not Justin, although one of them says that he has willingly listened to

Justin's teachings. When Rusticus turns again to Justin and asks him if he truly believes, in spite of all his knowledge, that if he is beheaded, he will rise to heaven, Justin answers: "I do not suppose it, but I know and am fully persuaded of it" (*Mart. Justin* 4; *ANF* 1:306).

And then the other six join Justin, declaring, "Do what you will, for we are Christians, and do not sacrifice to idols" (*Mart. Justin* 4; *ANF* 1:306). In response to this, Rusticus pronounces his verdict: "Let those who have refused to sacrifice to the gods and to yield to the command of the emperor be scourged, and led away to suffer the punishment of decapitation, according to the laws" (*Mart. Justin* 5; *ANF* 1:306).

THE MARTYRS OF LYONS AND VIENNE

In book 5 of his *Church History*, Eusebius of Caesarea includes a letter from the churches of Lyons and Vienne, in Gaul, to the churches in the provinces of Asia and Phrygia. It is quite likely that the reason why they write to the churches in those areas is that it was from there that many of the Christians who were now living in Gaul had come. The letter is a report of what took place in Gaul when a mob mentality unleashed its fury against Christians. It all began in 177, when there were riots against Christians, and the authorities imprisoned a large number of Christians while waiting for the arrival of the governor, who would be their judge. The letter gives many details about several of the martyrs, their witness, and their sufferings. As the trial opened, a man by the name of Epagathus showed such sympathy for the accused that he was asked if he was a Christian; upon declaring that he was, he was added to those on trial. Apparently the number of those imprisoned was enormous, for the document says that many of them died of asphyxiation due to the pressure of the number of prisoners. Several among those who had been put in prison denied their faith in order to avoid the torture that threatened them. The slaves of some believers, threatened with torture, declared that it was true that Christians ate children, practiced incest, and other similar things.

As the process went on, some among those who had denied the faith were arrested anew, and on this occasion many of them reaffirmed their faith and remained firm to the end. The means of torture were many and varied. An outstanding member of the group of martyrs was the young slave Blandina, an apparently frail woman whose steadfastness was such that she was an inspiration to the rest. In order to convince her and another young slave to abandon their faith, they were made to witness the sufferings of some of the rest. When she was hung from a cross so she could see the suffering of others, some of these others declared that looking at her hanging there evoked for them the image of Jesus hanging from the cross. Bishop Pothinus, who was more than ninety years old, suffered an exemplary death. Christians were not allowed to bury the bodies of the martyrs, which were guarded so that they would be left to be eaten by dogs.

THE SCILLITAN MARTYRS

There is also a very brief document that recounts the martyrdom of a number of believers in the small village of Scillium, in North Africa. Persecution does not seem to have reached North Africa until then, or shortly before. But in 180 persecution broke out in that small village in the province of Numidia. The brevity of the document, as well as its style, attest to its authenticity as the act of a trial in which a group of Christians was brought before proconsul Saturninus, in Carthage. The document, just over two pages long, is made even more stark by its brevity.

The most interesting words in this document are spoken by a Christian by the name of Speratus when he is commanded to swear by the emperor. His words point to a certain subversive dimension in the faith of many Christians, even though they obeyed the laws: "I know of no empire of this world, but rather serve a God whom no one can see with these eyes of the flesh. I have never stolen, and in any business I perform I pay my taxes promptly, because I know my Lord, ruler and King of all nations" (*Martyrs of Scillium* 6; BAC 75:353). In total, twelve Christians were executed.

OTHER MARTYRS OF THE SECOND CENTURY

The martyrs of the second century were many. Most of the acts referring to their martyrdom are much later and almost certainly spurious. However, there are a few documents that can be classified among the acts of the martyrs and that may indeed date from the second century, although some scholars question their authenticity.

One of these acts tells the story of a widow Felicity and her seven sons. According to this document, their martyrdom took place under the reign of Antoninus Pius and was presided by the prefect of Rome Publius Salvius Julianus. From other sources, it is known that in that position he was a successor of Urbicus, who had presided over the trial of Justin. On the basis of the dates of the reign of Antoninus, the events narrated in this document took place slightly before 161. The document recounts the trial and witness of Felicity and her sons. When, in a private audience, Publius encourages

Felicity to abandon her faith and threatens her with death, we are told that she says: "Your blandishments will not convince me, nor will your threats break me, for I have with me the Holy Spirit, who will not allow me to be overcome by the devil. Therefore I am certain that while I live I shall triumph over you. And if you kill me, being dead I shall vanquish you even more" (*Martyrdom of Felicitas and Her Sons* 1; BAC 75:294). As Felicity remains firm in her faith and urges her sons to do likewise, Publius condemns them to death, appointing various judges so that each of the seven martyrs will face different sufferings.

There are mainly two reasons for doubting the authenticity of this document. First, the story of Felicity and her sons is very similar to another found in Second Maccabees and seems to be a Christian version of that ancient Jewish tradition. Second, the first Christian writer to mention it is Gregory the Great, who late in the sixth century preached a sermon about Felicity and her sons.

Another doubtful document is the martyrdom of Roman senator Apollonius. Eusebius of Caesarea briefly tells the story of Apollonius, tried and condemned by Roman prefect Perennius, who held that position from 183 to 185. The present *Martyrdom of Apollonius* seems to be an expansion of what Eusebius says. Its high point is the radical confession of faith of the prospective martyr: "Perennius, you need to know that the God who is high above emperors and senators and every other authority, no matter how great, high above rich and poor, free and slave, great and small, wise and ignorant, has established a common death for all and, after that death, a judgment that will encompass all humankind" (*Mart. Apollonius* 24; BAC 75:368).

There are several versions of this document, and the differences among them are such that it is impossible to reconstruct the original text. While the Greek text—from which the passage just quoted has been translated—seems to be the most ancient, its author confuses Senator Apollonius with the early Christian preacher Apollo. This is an indication that the author is not well informed.

Finally, a word must be said about the *Martyrdom of Carpus, Papylus, and Agathonica*, which claims to tell the story of the trial and the punishment of three martyrs in the city of Pergamum at an uncertain date. Since the proconsul refers to an imperial decree ordering that all must sacrifice, it seems that the document refers to events in the latter half of the third century, after Emperor Decius issued such a degree. Carpus is tried first, and as he is being tortured, Papylus is brought before the court. His answer to the judge is reminiscent of similar words in the *Martyrdom of Polycarp*. Both are nailed to a post and burned to death. When Carpus is about to die, he laughs, and when asked why, he answers that this is because "I have seen the glory of the Lord and I have rejoiced, and also because I will be free from you and will no longer have to deal with your evil" (*Mart. Carpus* 39; BAC 75:381). At that point Agathonica, a woman who has been watching the events, has a similar vision and therefore jumps into the arena and nails herself to the post. This last detail leads some scholars to suggest that the document originated in Montanist circles, for Montanists praised "spontaneous" martyrs, those who voluntarily offered themselves for martyrdom, while the rest of the church rejected such a practice.

THE *MARTYRDOM OF PERPETUA AND FELICITAS*

Although the events to which it refers took place in 203, and therefore take us beyond the strict limits of the second century, the *Martyrdom of Saints Perpetua and Felicity* may well be seen as the culmination of this literary genre, and therefore deserves an important place at the end of this chapter. This document is unique in that whoever wrote it, rather than only telling what was taking place, also included extensive sections of Perpetua's diary. For this reason, she is the only ancient Greek or Roman woman from whose hand we have an inner or intimate diary. As we shall see, this not only shows the faith, but also the soul and the angst of its author.

There are many signs that the document is Montanist in origin. Among other things, it praises catechist Saturus for having offered himself willingly in order to accompany his disciples in their martyrdom. But above all, the document stresses the significance of revelations and visions given by the Holy Spirit, declaring that "new things are to be highly esteemed as being part of the last days," that "we acknowledge the new visions and the new prophecies," and that the very purpose of telling this story is so that it will be made clear that "the grace of God was not limited to the ancients, neither in the confession of martyrdom nor in revelations" (*Mart. Perpet. and Felic.* 1; BAC 35:419–20).

Emperor Septimus Severus had decreed that conversions to Judaism or Christianity would not be allowed, for both religions were rapidly spreading among the population. What the emperor found most galling was that both Jews and Christians insisted on the existence of a sole God who would admit no other, and this was clearly opposed to the syncretistic policies that the emperor followed. It is significant that all those arrested are catechumens, people preparing to receive baptism and thereby violating the imperial edict forbidding conversions.

Events begin unfolding in the outskirts of the city of Carthage, where a group of catechumens is arrested. One of these is Perpetua, a young aristocratic woman who is nursing a child. She is accompanied by servants Felicity and Revocatus, as well as by two others, Saturninus and Secundulus. Apparently because of the high standing of the family, those who have been arrested are allowed to remain at home as they await their trial.

It is at this point that Perpetua's diary begins. She says that her father, the only member of the family who is not a Christian, tries to convince her not to be baptized, but rather to deny her faith and thus save her life. Perpetua records the ensuing dialogue:

> "Father," said I, "do you see, let us say, this vessel lying here to be a little pitcher, or something else?"
> And he said, "I see it to be so."
> And I replied to him, "Can it be called by any other name than what it is?"
> And he said, "No."
> "Neither can I call myself anything else than what I am, a Christian." (*Mart. Perpet. and Felic.* 1; *ANF* 3:699–700)

Frustrated by such words, her father becomes violent yet eventually simply gives up. A few days later, Perpetua and her friends are baptized, in open disobedience to the imperial decree. Shortly thereafter they are imprisoned, and Perpetua writes about her distress: "O terrible day! O the fierce heat of the shock of the soldiery, because of the crowds! I was very unusually distressed by my anxiety for my infant" (*Mart. Perpet. and Felic.* 1; *ANF* 7:700).

Two deacons from the church pay the jailers so that for a few hours each day the prisoners are allowed a bit more room. There Perpetua's family is able to visit her and bring her child so that she can nurse him. Eventually she is able to keep the child with her in prison. So then she writes: "The dungeon became to me as it were a palace" (*Mart. Perpet. and Felic.* 1; *ANF* 3:699–700).

It is at this point that Perpetua begins writing about her visions. Her brother tells her that her devotion is such that now she can demand a vision from God, and she tells him that in fact she does speak quite familiarly with God. She also promises that the next day she will tell her brother about the vision that she expects to have that night. What she then tells him is a vision of a high and narrow bronze stairway, surrounded by weapons and instruments of torture; it was necessary to climb the steps one at a time. At the foot of the stairway was a dragon, and the catechist Saturus, who was also part of Perpetua's vision, told her that she must beware of the dragon. She marched forward, stepped on the dragon's head, climbed the stairs, and reached a place where she had a vision of the Lord surrounded by thousands dressed in white. The next day, Perpetua and her brother agree that the vision is a promise of martyrdom.

Perpetua's father is still urging her to abandon her faith. This continues to such a point that when Perpetua is being questioned, her father comes with his small grandson and insists so much in trying to get Perpetua to change her mind that the judge loses patience and orders that he be expelled from the court and beaten. He then refuses to return her child to Perpetua, who comments, "Even as God willed it, the child no longer desired my breast, nor did my breast cause me uneasiness, lest I should be tormented by care for my babe and by the pain of my breasts at once" (*Mart. Perpet. and Felic.* 2; *ANF* 3:701).

This is followed by two visions in which Perpetua says, first, that she sees her very young brother, who has died of cancer of the face, now suffering in a dark place; and second, that after praying for her brother, she has a vision that he is now in heaven.

The day before her martyrdom, Perpetua has a new vision in which she is in the arena, facing a terrible Egyptian gladiator backed by others, while she is surrounded by her own supporters. She declares that "I was stripped, and became a man"—apparently as a way of covering her shame. Then she sees a huge man dressed in purple and carrying "a green branch upon which were apples of gold" (*Mart. Perpet. and Felic.* 3; *ANF* 3:702). This brings to mind the gladiatorial games in Carthage that were dedicated to Apollo, where victors received golden apples. In her vision, after a strenuous combat, Perpetua is the victor and is given the apples. Upon awakening, she understands the vision as meaning that her great enemy will not be the beasts, but the devil himself, and that in spite of that, she will win the struggle.

At this point the document turns to a vision of Saturus, the catechist who has offered himself to accompany his disciples in martyrdom. In that vision he and his companions are gathered with other martyrs in the presence of the Lord. As they leave that place, they meet a bishop and a presbyter who apparently are having difficulties and ask the martyrs to help them be reconciled.

Meanwhile Felicity, eight months pregnant, fears that this will impede her martyrdom, for the judges might have mercy on her child. In answer to the prayers of her companions, Felicity gives birth to a girl three days before her martyrdom. One of the officers present comments that if she moans so much during childbirth, she will not be able to withstand the tortures awaiting her. To this she answers: "Now it is I that suffer what I suffer; but then there will be another in me, who will suffer for me, because I also am about to suffer for Him" (*Mart. Perpet. and Felic.* 5; *ANF* 3:704).

Three days later the martyrdom takes place, and the narrator writes:

> The day of their victory shone forth, and they proceeded from the prison into the amphitheatre, as if to an assembly, joyous and of brilliant countenances; if perchance shrinking, it was with joy, and not

with fear. Perpetua followed with placid look, and with step and gait as a matron of Christ, beloved of God; casting down the luster of her eyes from the gaze of all. Moreover, Felicitas, rejoicing that she had safely brought forth, so that she might fight with the wild beasts; from the blood and from the midwife to the gladiator, to wash after child-birth with a second baptism. (*Mart. Perpet. and Felic.* 6; *ANF* 3:704)

The narrative continues with a series of tortures that the martyrs suffer. We are told that in each of them it is Jesus who suffers in their stead, and that because of this at least some do not feel the pain. Perpetua herself, who has been told that she will be attacked by a savage cow, after the attack takes place and she is tossed about by the cow, asks when will the cow be coming.

Finally the document ends with words that may well serve as a summary of much that we have read in the present chapter:

O most brave and blessed martyrs! O truly called and chosen unto the glory of our Lord Jesus Christ! Whom whoever magnifies, and honors, and adores, assuredly ought to read these examples for the edification of the Church, not less than the ancient ones, so that new virtues also may testify that one and the same Holy Spirit is always operating even until now, and God the Father Omnipotent, and His Son Jesus Christ our Lord, whose is the glory and infinite power for ever and ever. Amen. (*Mart. Perpet. and Felic.* 6; *ANF* 3:705–6)

4

The Beginnings of Apocryphal, Popular, and Heretical Literature

The vitality of early Christianity was also shown in an abundant number of popular writings, many of them in imitation of the authors of the New Testament, and often claiming to be written by one of those authors. Much of this literature is called "apocryphal." This is a word that requires explanation, for although today it generally means false, and perhaps—particularly in some recent fiction—even forbidden, originally the word simply referred to something unknown or hidden. As the canon of the New Testament was being formed, the discussion was not primarily about which books were orthodox and which were not, but rather about which should be read in worship as sacred writings. Naturally, this involved excluding any heterodox book. But also many doctrinally orthodox books were excluded. Thus, among the "apocryphal" books are many that are not heterodox in any way and have never been forbidden. This is particularly true of the Old Testament, whose "apocryphal" books are simply those that are not included in the Hebrew Bible, but they are part of several ancient Christian Bibles and still part of the Catholic Bible. Such is the case, for instance, of the books of Judith and of Maccabees.

In the case of the New Testament, the books called "apocryphal" are an entire series of writings that claim to tell stories about Jesus or the apostles, yet with no canonical authority. Although certain people criticized what some of them said, none of them was "forbidden" in the literal sense—among other reasons, because in those early centuries the church had no means to forbid books. They were simply excluded from among those that were to be read in worship. Some of them, such as the *Revelation of Peter* and the *Third Epistle of Paul to the Corinthians*, were read in some churches for a time, until general consensus developed around the books that now compose the New Testament. Many of the apocryphal books of the New Testament continued circulating without hindrance through the ages, and there are numerous reminders of them, as in medieval cathedrals, where one finds art depicting stories found only in those books. Some others written to defend the position of a group that the church considered heretical disappeared, not because the church had forbidden them, but simply because as the group that held to such teachings disappeared, no more copies were produced. Some of these have been recently rediscovered. Thus it is true that there are many apocryphal books conveying doctrines that the church rejected. But in fact most of the apocryphal books are simply pious writings by someone with a creative imagination. Since such writers do not represent the entirety of the church, in these books one may find some doctrines or ideas that are not entirely orthodox. The most common of these is Encratism, which some ancient Christian writers call a "sect," but which does not seem to have ever been a real sect or rival church, but simply an extremely ascetical movement that for a time was quite popular among some believers. But there are also books that are clearly gnostic, written with the obvious purpose of providing apostolic authority to a particular gnostic school.

The Apocrypha of the New Testament include all the literary genres that appear also in the New Testament: gospels, acts, epistles, and apocalypses. In this chapter we shall also mention some similar books that, instead of claiming the authorship of one of the great figures of the New Testament, claim to be connected with someone in the Old Testament or in the early church.

This literature is so numerous that all we can do here is deal with a part of it, which can serve as a sufficient example of their tone and contents. Beyond that, many other documents are mentioned by ancient writers, many of which have been lost or remain only in brief fragments quoted by those ancient writers themselves. For instance, in the fourth century Epiphanius wrote that the Ebionites employed an altered text of the Gospel of Matthew, which they called the "Hebrew Gospel." And apparently the most ancient gnostic gospel was the now lost *Gospel of the Egyptians*, of which all that remains are a few very brief references by orthodox writers. To further complicate the matter, besides the fragmentary nature of these remains, many of these ancient books have been preserved in different versions and languages that do not entirely agree among themselves. In many cases, the reconstruction of the original text is quite difficult, and scholars do not agree as to that text. Given the nature of the present study, here we shall simply employ the texts most commonly accepted among scholars.

THE APOCRYPHAL GOSPELS

The *Protevangelium of James*

Possibly the most influential, and certainly one of the most ancient among these documents, is the one commonly called the *Protevangelium of James*. It should probably be dated in the second century and deals only with stories of the birth of Jesus, although adding much to what the canonical Gospels say. It is here that we find the well-known tradition that Mary's parents were named Joaquim and Anna. This is then followed by the birth of Mary and her early years. Joseph is a widower selected by high priest Zechariah as a husband for Mary, following a process in which all the widowers of Israel participate, and Joseph is miraculously chosen. From then on, the author weaves together the nativity stories of Matthew and Luke, to which he adds dramatic episodes relating particularly to Mary's pregnancy and Joseph's response. The document ends with the coming of the magi from the east and the slaughter of the innocents. Herod believes that the new king who has been born is John the Baptist, and for that reason orders that he be killed. But Elizabeth flees with him to a mountain that opens in order to hide them. In his anger, Herod orders that Zechariah be killed. Finally, the priests name the elderly Simeon (the same person who appears in the Gospel of Luke) in order to fill the vacancy left by the death of Zechariah.

This document, which was never taken to be part of the New Testament, circulated widely during the Middle Ages, particularly in the Eastern church. It also circulated in the Western church with some slight variations. Although never read in church as Scripture, it has left its mark in much medieval art and on popular piety.

The *Gospel of Thomas*

This document, probably dating from late in the second century, should not be confused with another *Gospel of Thomas* that is part of a gnostic library discovered in the twentieth century, to which we shall refer later. The one now being discussed is a gospel about the childhood of Jesus and the miracles that he did, some of them rather incompatible with the Jesus who appears in the canonical Gospels. For instance, when another child disturbs him, he simply tells him to die, and he does. Some other miracles in this gospel have become part of popular legend. Jesus shapes birds out of clay and makes them fly. When a rabbi tries to teach Jesus his first letters, Jesus shames the rabbi, who is shown to be relatively ignorant, so that the teacher ends up saying, "I cannot follow the flight of his intelligence. Woe is me. I have deceived myself.

I wished to have a disciple and I have found a teacher" (*Gospel of Thomas* 7.2; BAC 148:309). When Jesus drops a clay vessel and it breaks, he simply covers it with his coat, and the pieces come back together. In brief, this document is an indication of the manner in which popular piety was amplifying the stories and legends about Jesus.

GNOSTIC GOSPELS

Among the apocryphal literature of the New Testament are several gospels that seek to read the story of Jesus from a gnostic perspective. Among these is the *Gospel of Judas*; its existence was always known, but it drew public attention in the late twentieth century when a partial text of it was discovered. The Gnosticism of this document, with its dislike for all that is physical or bodily, may be seen in the manner in which it interprets the role of Judas in the passion of Jesus. According to the document, Judas is the only one who knows that Jesus wishes to leave the prison of the body, and therefore Judas serves that purpose by turning him over to those who are seeking to kill him.

Another document generally included among the apocryphal gospels is the (gnostic) *Gospel of Thomas*, which is not a narrative, as are the other gospels, but rather a collection of sayings of Jesus. It can probably be dated to the middle of the second century. It is generally included among the gnostic gospels because it was found in the twentieth century as part of a library that is clearly gnostic (the library of Nag Hammadi, sometimes called of Chenoboskion). Approximately half of the sayings of Jesus in this document are also part of the canonical Gospels. It is in the other sayings that there may be a rather moderate gnostic influence. For instance, Jesus tells Thomas three secret words that he will not share even with the other disciples. And, referring to the soul and the body, he speaks of the first as dwelling in the poverty of the latter.

More clearly gnostic is the *Gospel of Truth*, which is part of the same gnostic library. Even before its discovery, we knew of the existence of this document because Irenaeus declares it to have been the work of the gnostic teacher Valentinus. But there is a vast difference between what this document says and what Irenaeus tells us about the teachings of the Valentinians. One does not find here the endless speculations about aeons or the origins of the world that Irenaeus attributes to the followers of that sect. But at the same time there is much in this book that reflects what Irenaeus says. For this and several other reasons, most scholars believe that the *Gospel of Truth* dates from the middle of the second century, and that what Irenaeus seems to have known was not the original teachings of Valentinus, but the manner in which these had evolved some thirty or forty years later, when Irenaeus encountered them.

At any rate, this document is not a gospel in the normal sense of the word, for it is not a story about Jesus, but rather a meditation on the author's understanding of the gospel. The book begins by affirming the joy of those who are able to know the truth through the Word that has come from "the plenitude." Since the word "plenitude," *plērōma*, was the name that gnostics gave to the beginning and end of all things, from its very opening this document shows that it comes from gnostic circles. Furthermore, it repeatedly praises the gnostics, who are the ones who have been illumined and awakened from their dream of materiality. One also notes that this gospel includes no reference to any historical events—not even stories or sayings of Jesus.

Something similar may be said about the *Pistis Sophia*. This document, which is preserved in a Coptic manuscript from the end of the fourth century or early in the fifth, had been forgotten until it was rediscovered late in the eighteenth century. It was probably written late in the third century or early in the fourth. It is not a gospel in the strict sense, for it does not deal with Jesus and his teachings before his death and resurrection, but rather with what Jesus taught his disciples as well as Mary, Martha, and Mary Magdalene, during the eleven years that he supposedly remained on earth after his resurrection. Although the name of "Sophia," meaning "Wisdom," is often given to Jesus in Christian tradition, here Sophia is the feminine aeon that serves as a counterpart to the masculine Jesus.

APOCRYPHAL ACTS OF THE APOSTLES

Just as some believers sought to amplify what the canonical Gospels said about Jesus, others set out to expand what was known of the apostles through the book of Acts. In spite of its title, that book in the New Testament says little about the work of the Twelve. After the first few paragraphs, Acts speaks only of John and Peter, and eventually seems to abandon them in order to center its attention on Paul. But popular imagination wished to know more about the apostles themselves, and this gave birth to several apocryphal acts of various apostles.

Five of the most ancient of these apocryphal acts stand in close relationship, those of Andrew, John, Peter, Paul, and Thomas. Although the stories they tell are different, their theological perspective is so similar that at a time it was thought that they were the work of a single author. Today scholars are in general agreement not only that their authors are different, but also that some of them have more than one author. But even so, there is no doubt that there is a close connection among them. There is certainly a relationship of dependence, for some of the authors of these books show that they have read others. But the typical note that links them most closely is their Encratist tendency. Encratism, which some ancient Christian writers call a "sect," seems to have been a rather strong movement of highly ascetic tendencies that involved a large part of the ancient Christian community; the rest of the church did not favor the Encratist excesses. Besides the well-known fact that they denounced matrimony and all sexual activity, many of them abstained from wine and flesh. As we shall see in studying the already-mentioned five apocryphal acts, they all speak negatively about marriage, and they observe frequent eucharistic celebrations with only bread and no wine.

In some cases, the Encratism of the movement seems to have a liberating note for women in a society in which they are not respected and are taken as mere sexual objects. Repeatedly, while it is men who oppose the preaching of the apostles in these books, it is women who defend them. This has led some modern scholars to suggest that these apocryphal acts are in fact the product of a circle of Encratite women for whom this doctrine, besides giving them a hope of salvation, served as a means of protest against the sexual abuse of women.

The *Acts of Andrew*

Probably the oldest of these apocryphal books is the *Acts of Andrew*. Andrew's claim to be the first of the apostles whom Jesus called plays an important role in this document as a means for asserting his authority. Although an extensive part of the book still exists, most of the pages we have deal with the martyrdom of Andrew. In the sixth century Gregory of Tours wrote a summary of the book, and from that summary we know that the story of the martyrdom of Andrew is only the end of a much more extensive original text. To complicate matters further, the section that has survived also includes several later additions, making it difficult to determine the exact original text.

Nevertheless, there is no doubt that the *Acts of Andrew* come from Encratite circles. The emphasis on total sexual abstinence, even within marriage, is a dominant theme in the martyrdom of Andrew. The author seems to have been a fairly well-educated person with a Hellenistic background, making frequent use of the main resources of Greek rhetoric. In its style, it is wordy and sometimes takes on the characteristics of a novel.

The action takes place in the Greek city of Patras, in the house and among the family of Aegatus, the prefect of the city. His wife, Maximilla, is a Christian and jointly with Andrew is the protagonist of the story. This begins when the brother of Aegatus, Estratocles, comes to the city, and one of his most esteemed servants seems to be possessed by a demon. Maximilla tells him that there is in the city a man of God who can heal such an illness; she has

Andrew come to the house. He heals the servant, and Estratocles becomes a believer. This is a cause of great rejoicing in the Christian community of the town, which meets frequently in Aegatus's praetorium. But Aegatus, a firm believer in traditional religion, has no idea that this is taking place, for Christians are using his home without his knowledge. On a certain occasion, when Aegatus arrives unexpectedly and is about to discover the Christian meeting, Andrew prays, with the result that Aegatus suffers an urgent need to go to the bathroom, and the Christians escape while the prefect attends to his physical needs.

But in general the story revolves around the theme of the relationship between Maximilla and her husband, Aegatus. She decides that, since she is a Christian, she will have no sexual relations with her husband. When he insists, she responds with the ruse of sending a servant to the matrimonial bed and making her husband believe that it is Maximilla. When the deception is discovered, the servant pays with her life. Furthermore, since he does not want the world to know what he considers his shame, he orders that the servants who had made him aware of the matter also be executed. As a result of this entire episode, Aegatus throws Andrew in jail and forbids Maximilla to visit him. But through a series of miracles, she and a companion can visit him repeatedly. After several such meetings, marked with speeches and exhortations by Andrew, he is crucified. Aegatus kills himself, and thereafter Maximilla leads a tranquil life of sexual abstinence.

The *Acts of John*

If the textual history of the *Acts of Andrew* is complex, that of the *Acts of John* is even more so. Besides several fragments from various sources, we have a fairly extensive text that scholars have been able to reconstruct in part, but still presents serious difficulties. One of these is a radical change in style, and also to a degree in theology, that takes place in the middle of the book. This seems to indicate that the book as it has now come to us had at least two authors. While the entire book shows gnostic and Encratite leanings, these become much more obvious and extreme in the second part of the book. As to its date, it is clear that the present book was known by the author of the next work to be discussed, the *Acts of Peter*. Since the latter seems to date from the third century, scholars suggest that the first part of the *Acts of John* was written in mid-second century, and the rest somewhat later. It is also possible that the text as we now have it includes later additions. For instance, the book refers to the destruction of the temple of Artemis in Ephesus, which did not take place until the year 262, when the Goths burned it. It is hard to imagine that while this temple was still in existence, a Christian author would speak of it as if it had been destroyed in the first century as the work of John. Therefore, either this is a later addition or the book was written quite some time after that date.

At any rate, throughout the book we find a Jesus who appears to be human, but in truth is purely spiritual. His sufferings are not real. When John flees to the Mount of Olives after seeing Jesus suffer on the cross, Jesus appears to him and tells him that he is not really suffering, and John returns from the mountain rejoicing. Some people see Jesus one way and some in another. When he calls John and James, the first sees Jesus as a youngster, while John sees him as a mature man. Shortly thereafter John sees Jesus almost bald-headed but with a thick beard, while James sees him as a beardless young man.

The Encratism of the book is shown in the story of Drusiana, to which we shall return, and also in John's conviction that it was the Lord himself who on three different occasions impeded his plans to marry, and then turned his heart in such a way that even the sight of a woman became odious to him.

Most of the narrative takes place in Ephesus, where John resurrects one of the rulers of the city and his wife who has also died. Shortly thereafter, seeing that most of the widows in the city are suffering some kind of illness, he calls them all to the theater, where he heals them wholesale. After a long speech with gnostic overtones, John confronts Artemis in her own temple, with the result that a good portion of it collapses and its priest dies when a falling beam strikes him. But John resurrects the priest, who is then converted. When he encounters a young parricide who is repentant for what he has done, John resurrects his father. When he is traveling with some companions and has to sleep in a bed full of bedbugs, he orders them to depart. His companions laugh, but in the morning they find that all the bedbugs are gathered in a corner. John then gives the insects leave to return to the bed and comments that even bedbugs obey the word of God, while humans will not.

The stories of John raising the dead reach their high point in the account of Drusiana, a devout and Encratite woman who "for religious motives had for some time abstained from contact with her husband" (*Acts of John* 63; BAC 646:405). A young man falls in love with her, and she does not accept his overtures. When she dies, the young man bribes the manager of the cemetery to be allowed to go to the sepulchre and violate the woman who in life rejected him. When they are in the sepulchre, a snake kills the manager and makes the young man fall on the ground. Later John and a group of Christians go to the sepulchre and discover the scene. John resurrects the manager, the young man is converted, and Drusiana also rises again. When the administrator continues practicing evil, John announces his death, which takes place soon thereafter.

After another speech, John partakes of a eucharistic meal—though only with bread and no wine—and prepares to die. He then goes to the outskirts of the city, where he tells two believers to dig a tomb; John says farewell to life, enters the tomb, and dies joyfully.

The *Acts of Peter*

The *Acts of Peter* does not exist as a complete document; instead, it is a compilation by modern scholars of a series of documents and fragments that may or may not have been part of a single original writing. They include some incidents attributed to the life of Peter that have become an integral part of popular Christian tradition, and also others that are not as well known. The author's Encratism appears repeatedly. When Peter's daughter is about to be raped by a rejected suitor, she becomes a paralytic, and Peter rejoices because in this manner God has made certain that his daughter will not tempt others. Toward the end of the book, when we come to Peter's martyrdom, we are told that the reason why he was killed is that he had led four of the emperor's concubines to abandon the royal bed, and that he had likewise persuaded the wife of a friend of the emperor to abstain from conjugal relations. It is these two men, as well as others who have similar experiences, who seek Peter's death.

But most of the book centers on the conflicts between Peter and Simon Magus. Having been forced to leave the Holy Land as a result of Peter's miraculous powers, Simon goes to Rome, were his wonders soon make him famous to such a point that most Christians abandon their faith in order to follow Simon. God then sends Peter to Rome, where there is an ongoing competition in which both Peter and Simon are trying to show his own miraculous powers as greater than the other's. As in other apocryphal acts of the apostles, but to an even greater degree, here we have repeated stories of resurrections and other wonders. Peter makes a dog and a baby speak and chastise Simon. Finally, one day when Simon is flying above the city, Peter prays to the Lord, and Simon falls, breaking a leg that eventually has to be amputated and leads to his death. The conflicts between Peter and Simon that are part of the apocryphal *Acts of Peter*, amplified even more by Christian imagination, came to be a frequent theme in later popular Christian literature.

It is also in this book that we first find the tradition that Peter was crucified upside down. And it is also there that we find the well-known episode of the *Quo vadis?* According to that legend, when Peter is fleeing from Rome, Jesus appears to him. Peter asks the Lord, "Where are you going? [*Quo vadis?*]," and Jesus answers that he is going to Rome to be crucified. It is this vision that compels Peter to return to Rome, where he is to die.

The *Acts of Paul*

As in some of the other apocryphal acts of the apostles, these also exist only in a series of long fragments that scholars seek to rebuild into a single text. One of these fragments is the so-called *Third Epistle of Paul to the Corinthians*, to which we shall return. It too is an Encratite document in which sexual abstinence is exalted and communion is celebrated without wine. But these Encratite tendencies are less marked in the *Acts of Paul* than in the other apocryphal acts of the apostles. According to the story, Paul dwells in the house of a married man and does not seem to think less of him because he is married. But near the beginning of the document there is a series of beatitudes that include this one: "Blessed are those who have a wife as if they did not" (*Acts of Paul* 5.1; BAC 656:737).

A large portion of the reconstructed *Acts of Paul* is the *Acts of Paul and Thecla*. Thecla is a young woman in Iconium who was promised in marriage. Hearing Paul, she decides that she will live in virginity and refuses to see her intended husband. He joins other men with similar grievances, and they have Paul arrested. Thecla flees from her home, bribes the jailer, and hides in Paul's prison, where she listens to him avidly. She is finally captured and condemned to death, while Paul is whipped and expelled from the city. When she is preparing for martyrdom, the story says: "There was a riot. The beasts roared, the people screamed, and the women who were seated together were shouting. The mob shouted, 'Bring out the blasphemer.' And the women cried out: 'Let this evil perish with the city. Proconsul, kill all of us! What a sad spectacle, what an evil sentence!'" (*Acts of Paul* 32.1; BAC 656:763).

When they try to burn her, a great storm drenches the fire and saves Thecla, also killing several of those present. Later, in Antioch, another incident takes place, when a frustrated accoster of Thecla accuses her. Taken before the beasts to be killed, she is saved once again by a series of miracles. When she tells Paul that she plans to return to Iconium, he directs her: "Go and teach the Word of God" (*Acts of Paul* 41; BAC 656:771)—interesting instructions, given the common image of Paul as being opposed to women's ministry.

The rest of this document, like the others we have been studying, is full of ever more surprising prodigies. Among others, a lion comes to Paul and asks to be baptized. Paul baptizes him and, in a clear reference to Encratite views, the lion is no longer interested in lionesses. Later, when Paul is condemned to be killed by the beasts, the lion that is supposed to kill him is the same one that he has baptized, and now this lion defends him from the other beasts.

The *Acts of Thomas*

There is a close connection between the *Acts of Thomas* and the *Acts of Paul*, but there is a debate among scholars as to which of these preceded and influenced the other. If, as most seem to think, those of Paul are earlier, this would mean that the *Acts of Thomas* should be dated in the middle of the third century. At any rate, unlike the other apocryphal acts that we have been studying, those of Thomas have come to us in a single book, and not as fragments or separate documents. Still a number of literary differences between the first sixty-one chapters and the rest of the book seem to indicate that it had at least two different authors. Also, there is no doubt that the writer or writers of the book included in it some elements that had earlier circulated independently, such as the "Hymn of the Bride" and the "Hymn of the Pearl."

As will become clear when we summarize part of the contents of the book, it is an Encratite text, although there are some portions that also reflect gnostic overtones, particularly the two hymns mentioned above. At any rate, the book shows its Encratism by insisting on the value of absolute sexual continence and in its repeated references to eucharistic celebrations without wine.

This document is particularly interesting because it includes the most ancient reference to the presence of Thomas in India. It begins with a scene in Jerusalem in which the apostles parcel out the world, determining what region each will evangelize, and India is assigned to Thomas. Thomas—who according to this book was a twin brother of Jesus—refuses to go, even when Jesus orders him to do so. Jesus then has Thomas sold as a slave and taken to India as such. It is interesting to note that Thomas, like his supposed twin brother, is a carpenter. On his way to India, at the wedding of a king's daughter, Thomas sings a strange hymn that is erotic in tone and that appears to be in honor of the bride, but in truth seems to refer to secret gnostic doctrines and hopes. Since he sings in Hebrew, only the flutist, a Jewish woman, understands the words. When the couple withdraws to their chamber, Jesus comes to them and calls them to leave aside "this filthy living together," so that they may become pure and holy temples. The two youths accept this calling and are converted. When the king knows what has happened, he orders Thomas to be arrested, but Thomas has already left for India.

After he has arrived there, the king orders Thomas to build him a palace. He repeatedly sends large sums to Thomas, who distributes them in alms to the poor. Thomas reports to the king that the construction is going well. When finally the king comes to see his palace and finds nothing at all, he is enraged and orders that both Thomas and the agent who brought him to India be imprisoned, then skinned alive and burned. But a brother of the king who has died returns from the dead in order to tell the king of the beautiful palace that Thomas has built for him in heaven. Next both the king and his brother are baptized in a strange rite with clear gnostic overtones, and they partake of a communion celebration of bread, with no mention of wine. Thomas then continues preaching a message that is markedly ascetic: "Men and women, boys and girls, young men and maidens, vigorous and aged, both bound and free, withhold yourselves from fornication, and covetousness, and the service of the belly; for under these three heads all wickedness comes" (*Acts of Thom.* 22.1; *ANF* 8:541).

As in the other apocryphal acts of the apostles, so in the *Acts of Thomas* there are prodigious narratives in which snakes and asses speak, and a demon rapes a woman until the apostle expels him. When, as a result of the preaching of Thomas, a woman refuses to share her husband's bed, the husband accuses Thomas before the king and has him arrested. It is there in prison that Thomas sings the already-mentioned "Hymn of the Pearl." Using cryptic language, the hymn tells of a heavenly messenger who has come to rescue the spiritual pearls trapped in this world. (In some manuscripts, apparently as an attempt to correct or lessen the heterodoxy of this hymn, there follows another that is more traditional in its content.) While Thomas is still in prison, the wife of the man who has accused him appears to Thomas; he baptizes her and shares communion with her: in this particular case, although the text is not completely clear, it seems that there is wine mixed with water. The story continues, and when the king sends his own wife to convince the wife of his friend to return to the matrimonial bread, the king's wife is also converted and refuses to have relations with the king. The son of the king tries to dissuade Thomas, but he too is converted. Finally the king decides to punish Thomas by forcing him to walk barefoot on sheets of red-hot metal. But there is a great flood that not only covers the metal but also nearly drowns the king. Thanks to the prayers of Thomas, the flood ceases, and the king orders that the apostle be returned to prison until he decides what to do with him. Still, Thomas and those who follow him are able to gather so that he baptizes all of them, and they share communion.

The document then includes a brief narrative of the martyrdom of Thomas: on the king's orders he is killed by four soldiers with lances. Sometime later, when his own son is gravely ill, the king takes dirt from the tomb of Thomas, uses it to heal his son, and is converted.

The *Acts of Thomas* is the earliest witness to a tradition, which eventually became widespread, that it was Thomas who took the gospel to India. Today most scholars doubt that it was so. The text exists both in Greek and in Syriac, and it is possible that it was originally written in Syriac, which was the language commonly used for trade and connections in the vast area between Syria and India. In the third century, Origen wrote that Thomas had visited the Persian

Empire. Thus there is a fairly ancient tradition that connects Thomas with the eastward expansion of Christianity. And, at least as early as the fourth century, there already was a church in India that called itself "St. Thomas Christians."

APOCRYPHAL EPISTLES

Just as some pious Christians wrote apocryphal gospels and acts of the apostles, there were also some who wrote epistles claiming to have been written by one of the apostles. Thus, toward the end of the second century someone wrote a so-called *Epistle of the Apostles*, whose obvious purpose is to reject gnostic doctrines and speculations. Since in Colossians 4.16 Paul speaks of a letter that he has written to the Christians in Laodicea, soon various versions of that purported epistle began to circulate. One of them to which ancient authors refer, but which has been lost, defended the teachings of Marcion. In response to it, someone wrote an *Epistle of Paul to the Alexandrians*, which has also been lost. A supposed epistle of James, commonly known as the *Apocryphon of James*, apparently written also in the second century, claims to be a report that James is sending to an unknown reader about the secret gnostic doctrines that Jesus taught James and Peter. The Nag Hammadi Library also includes an *Epistle of Peter and Philip*.

As stated above, some manuscripts of the *Acts of Paul* include a letter from the Corinthians to Paul and the latter's response, commonly known as the *Third Epistle of Paul to the Corinthians*. In this letter the Corinthians supposedly address Paul while he is in Philippi, giving a summary of what some are teaching in Corinth and making it clear that these are people of gnostic inclinations, holding that the body is evil, and that therefore Jesus cannot have come in human flesh:

The doctrines that they affirm and teach are as follows: "They deny that one should use the Prophets, that God is Almighty, that there will be a resurrection of the flesh, that Christ has come in human flesh and was born of Mary. They teach that the world does not come from God, but from the angels" (*Acts of Paul* 1.9–15, Heidelberg manuscript; BAC 656:805).

Much later, possibly in the fourth century, a supposed correspondence between Paul and Seneca began circulating. It includes eight letters from Seneca to Paul, and six from Paul to Seneca. At about the same time, or shortly thereafter, a supposed epistle from Titus in defense of monastic celibacy began circulating.

There were even letters supposedly written by Jesus himself. The most famous was the purported correspondence between Jesus and King Abgar of Edessa. According to this correspondence, the king writes to Jesus, asking him to come and heal him of a horrible disease, and Jesus answers by sending Thaddeus with a letter addressed to the king. Since it was around the year 200 that another King Abgar of Edessa became a Christian, and the earliest references to this correspondence date from the beginning of the fourth century, it seems likely that these supposed letters were written during the third century, as an attempt to prove the antiquity of the church in Edessa. In any case, the supposed letter of Jesus attained great popularity. It was translated into several languages, and some people would carry a copy of it in order to preserve them from evil spirits and from their enemies. In some cases, particularly in the area of Syria, it was read in worship jointly with canonical Scripture.

Finally, there is another supposed letter from the Lord, apparently composed late in the fifth century, which urges strict observance of Sunday. According to legend, it appeared as floating over the altar of a church in Rome, and it descended into the hands of the bishop after three days and nights of prayer. This letter too was widely distributed and translated into diverse languages, and even as late as the nineteenth century some people employed copies of it as a guard against evil.

APOCRYPHAL APOCALYPSES

Just as there were imitations of the canonical Gospels, Acts, and Epistles of the New Testament, there were also apocalyptic books following the pattern of Revelation, the Apocalypse of John. The most successful of these was the *Apocalypse of Peter*, most likely written during the second century and for a time considered by some to be part of Scripture. It is a brief text in which Jesus shows his disciples alternative visions, contrasting the beauty of heaven, where the faithful go, with the horrors of hell, to which sinners are destined. Later, in the third century, someone composed an *Apocalypse of Paul*, which, according to the fifth-century historian Sozomen, was still highly regarded by some monks, for there was a legend that it had been miraculously discovered in Paul's ancient house in Tarsus. Later, other similar works appeared and were attributed to figures such as Stephen, Thomas, and Mary.

OTHER PSEUDONYMOUS OR
INTERPOLATED LITERATURE

This may be the best place to mention the existence of ancient documents that are similar to the apocryphal writings that we have just discussed yet do not claim to have apostolic origins. Many of these are books of Jewish origin into which Christians introduced their own interpolations and interpretations. For instance, during the period between the two Testaments, there was a continuation of the history of Ezra. But now Christians added a *Fourth Book of Ezra*, which had a strong eschatological emphasis. Likewise, the *Book of Enoch*, a Jewish work that seems to have been written some 150 years before Jesus, had new sections added that turned it into a Christian book. The same was done with the *Testaments of the Twelve Patriarchs*. The *Ascension of Isaiah* is also an originally Jewish book telling the story of the martyrdom of the prophet, to which now Christians added several chapters describing how, after being taken to heaven, Isaiah saw the incarnation, death, resurrection, and ascension of Christ. This is a gnostic text in which Jesus descends from heaven without letting his passing be known by the angels that guard each celestial sphere, and then Jesus returns, manifesting his power so that now heaven is open to his followers.

An interesting case is that of the *Sibylline Oracles*. Sometime before the advent of Christianity an unknown Jew, apparently in order to support the proselytizing thrust of Judaism at the time, composed a series of poems claiming to be visions of the famous pagan seer known as the Sibyl, which corroborated Jewish teachings. Now Christians took those oracles and added to them a number of prophecies supposedly proving the truth of Christianity. Early in the twentieth century, the *Odes of Solomon* were discovered. This is a Christian collection of hymns with strong gnostic inclinations that seems to have circulated jointly with the so-called *Psalms of Solomon*, which were Jewish in origin. Both the *Oracles* and the *Odes* will be discussed further in chapter 8 (below).

Already as early as the middle of the second century, Justin mentioned some *Acts of Pilate*. But it is likely that the document now known by that title is a later production, perhaps inspired by the words of Justin, who seems to be referring to an official document. At any rate, the *Acts of Pilate* seems to have been written in order to blame Jews for the death of Jesus, thus exculpating Pilate and the Roman Empire itself.

Finally, the pseudo-Clementine literature must also be mentioned. This presents Clement of Rome at first as an aristocratic pagan seeking after truth, and later as Paul's companion. Here we find stories of the conflict between Peter and Simon Magus similar to those we have already encountered in the *Acts of Peter*. This literature seems to have a complex history, having been used at different times by various authors, and therefore it is impossible to determine a date for its composition.

In summary, the vitality and variety within the early Christian movement were such that an entire body of literature was produced that expressed feelings, opinions, and practices that do not always reflect the rest of the church. Many of these documents are gnostic in origin. Others reflect the extreme asceticism of the Encratites, who do not seem to have become a separate sect, but were simply a movement among very fervent Christians. Many are mere pious legends in which some believer has allowed imagination to run wild. As to their style, some of these books show a measure of literary and rhetorical refinement, while others reflect the style of less educated Christians.

Even though these books have long been considered apocryphal and have been excluded from canonical Scripture, some of them have left their mark on Christian tradition. It is from them that we draw traditions such as the names of Mary's parents, the manner in which Peter was crucified, the evangelization of India, and many other such matters that to this day are reflected in Christian art and devotion.

PART 2

Christian Literature in the Late Second Century

Introduction to Part 2

As the second century advanced, the great change that took place in the life and composition of the church was that the Christian movement, which had begun among Jews and whose first leaders were also Jewish, began making headway among Gentiles. Soon the majority of Christians no longer were of Jewish origins. This required an entire new system of formation for those who asked for baptism, who were now coming to the church without the religious and biblical background that the first Jewish converts brought, and who therefore could not be simply baptized as soon as they requested it.

As to the history of literature, which is our main concern here, the authors of most of the surviving Christian literature from this time and thereafter were Gentile in origin. While it is quite probable that among the writers we have been following up to this point many were Jews, with rare exceptions the ones to whom we shall now turn were Gentiles. Several of them were highly educated and therefore were able to employ the best rhetorical devices of classical antiquity. Now the matter of the relationship between Christianity and that ancient Greco-Roman culture became paramount for many of these authors. And, while most of them still wrote in Greek, the first Latin Christian writers emerged.

Beyond that momentous demographic and cultural change, the circumstances of the church did not change much during the second century. Persecution continued. It was still necessary to make clear the nature of the Christian faith in response to various different and even contradictory views. But now a new generation of Christian authors emerged who, while building on the foundations laid by the apologists of the first half of the century, produced works in which they dealt with the entirety of Christian doctrine; or at least, the total corpus of their writings is sufficiently extensive that we are able to reconstruct the essential points of their theology. Although there were many lesser authors, the three great figures of the late second century are Irenaeus, Clement of Alexandria, and Tertullian. As we read and study their works, we see that, while they were all orthodox and agreed that certain teachings must be rejected, they did not entirely agree on every point nor emphasize the same elements in Christian doctrine. Thus we see the beginning of various theological perspectives that would develop and interact over the course of the centuries. I have explored and developed this point in the book *Christian Thought Revisited: Three Types of Theology* (Maryknoll, NY: Orbis Books, 1989; rev. ed., 1999, 2002).

5

Irenaeus

HIS LIFE

The first among the theologians of the late second century that we will be studying—and the least commonly known—is Irenaeus of Lyons. Irenaeus seems to have been a native of Smyrna in Asia Minor, later living in Lyons. He was in Rome in the year 177, when a great persecution in Gaul led to the death of the bishop of Lyons. When Irenaeus returned to Lyons, the congregation elected him as their bishop. Although little is known about his life before those events, his writings seem to imply that he was a disciple of Polycarp in Smyrna, or at least that he was able to hear some of his teachings. On that basis, the date of his birth may be placed around the year 130. The reason for his moving to Lyons is unknown, although he was part of a Greek-speaking group that had settled in Lyons, apparently coming mostly from Asia Minor. It has been suggested that they were there as missionaries, but there is no reason to believe so. What is clear, as Irenaeus himself says, is that he then preached among the Celts. Toward the end of the century, around the year 190, he was involved in the Quartodeciman controversy because his church, following the traditions of Asia Minor, still celebrated Easter on the fourteenth day of the Jewish month of Nissan, while the rest of the church always celebrated it on a Sunday, following a long tradition to celebrate the resurrection of Jesus every first day of the week. During Irenaeus's lifetime, the controversy became sufficiently bitter to lead to mutual excommunications between the bishops of Rome and Ephesus. Irenaeus intervened, seeking to calm the waters. The details of the process are not known, but eventually all Christians agreed on celebrating the great day of the resurrection of Jesus on a Sunday. According to tradition, Irenaeus died as a martyr during the persecution of Septimus Severus in the year 202; but this is not absolutely certain, for it is only in the fourth century that this tradition arises.

HIS WORKS

Besides a number of fragments from other works, what we have are two main writings by Irenaeus. The most extensive of them, the *Destruction and Refutation of the False Knowledge [Gnosis]*, is usually known by a shortened title, *Against Heresies*, or simply by its Latin name, *Adversus Haereses*. The other work, which is much briefer, is the *Proof of the Apostolic Preaching*, also known as the *Epideixis*.

Of this latter work, only the title was known until early in the twentieth century, when an Armenian version was discovered. After careful study, scholars are now in agreement that this is indeed a translation of the lost work of Irenaeus. Famous historian Adolf von Harnack divided it into a hundred chapters, and that division is still employed. It is addressed to a brother by the name of Marcianus, of whom nothing else is known. Since its purpose is not to refute heresy, but rather to instruct the reader on matters of faith, this writing is not overburdened by numerous details about various gnostic systems that make the reading of *Against Heresies* difficult.

As its title says, *Against Heresies* is a polemical work. Although it deals with heresies in general, Irenaeus focuses his attention on the gnostic system of Valentinus, particularly as it had been developed by a disciple of Valentinus named Ptolemeus, and then also against the teachings of Marcion. The work is divided into five rather extensive books and was written in Greek. However, we do not have an entire Greek text, but only a Latin translation. Its style is such, and so different from classical writings in that language, that it has been suggested that it may have been the work of one of the Celtic disciples that Irenaeus says he had near Lyons. As to the original Greek, Irenaeus himself apologizes for his own style:

> Thou wilt not expect from me, who am resident among the Keltae, and am accustomed for the most part to use a barbarous dialect, any display of rhetoric, which I have never learned, or any excellence of composition, which I have never practiced, or any beauty and persuasiveness of style, to which I make no pretensions. But thou wilt accept in a kindly spirit what I in a like spirit write to thee simply, truthfully, and in my own homely way. (*Heresies* 1, Preface 3; *ANF* 1:316)

The first book, and much of the second, are devoted to a lengthy exposition of the gnostic system that Irenaeus seeks to refute. This includes a long and very detailed description of gnostic teachings, or at least of those gnostics against whom Irenaeus was writing. The reason why Irenaeus focuses his attention on this particular system is that he had learned that a friend had embraced it. At any rate, as already stated, what is said here about the Gnosticism of Valentinus and his disciples is different from what we find in the *Gospel of Truth* written by Valentinus or his disciple. Irenaeus presents Gnosticism as an endless series of speculations about the aeons that gave birth to the universe and about relations among the aeons. Although this first part of Irenaeus's work is of great interest to those who study Gnosticism, its style and its detailed discussion of gnostic speculations frequently lead readers to abandon the reading of the entire work, by which they miss much of the positive contribution of Irenaeus, which appears later in this work. One could wish that Irenaeus had limited himself to a principle that he proposes in his own work. In the middle of the second book, after numerous and lengthy pages about aeons and their relationships and about other similar matters, Irenaeus says:

> For it is not needful, to use a common proverb, that one should drink up the ocean who wishes to learn that its water is salty. But, just as in the case of a statue which is made of clay, but coloured on the outside that it may be thought to be of gold, while it really is of clay, any one who wishes to take out of it a small particle, and thus laying it open reveals the clay, will set free those who seek the truth from a false opinion; in the same way have I (by exposing not a small part only, but the several heads of their system which are of the greatest importance) shown to as many as who do not wish wittingly to be led astray, what is wicked, deceitful, seductive, and pernicious, connected with the school of the Valentinians, and all those other heretics. (*Heresies* 2.19.8; *ANF* 1:387)

At this point, a modern reader will probably think that a teaspoonful would have sufficed, instead of buckets and buckets of seawater! And most certainly, as he says, the outer gold covering that Irenaeus has removed in order to let the clay show is much more than a small piece.

Even so, this work of Irenaeus is of great importance: it offers significant insight into Christian thought during his time. Furthermore, the theology of Irenaeus—frequently hidden in the midst of his ample description of Gnosticism, and at other times clearly expressed, particularly in the last books of *Against Heresies* and on the *Proof of the Apostolic Preaching*—has made a significant impact in recent Christian theology. Although Irenaeus was not frequently read by a Latin public, Tertullian, to whom we shall turn in chapter 7, and who may well be called the father of Latin theological language, had read him, and therefore the influence of Irenaeus may be seen in Tertullian. Beginning in the twentieth century, students of Irenaeus—particularly in Sweden—have proposed a vast theological renewal inspired by insights drawn from Irenaeus.

Although a quick reading may give the impression that all that Irenaeus wishes to do is to ridicule Gnosticism, what he is trying to do is to separate from gnostic teachings that bit of truth that makes them credible. As he says at the beginning of his work, "Error, indeed, is never set forth in its naked deformity, lest, being thus exposed, it should at once be detected. But it is craftily decked out in an attractive dress, so as, by its outward form, to make it appear to the inexperienced . . . more true than the truth itself" (*Heresies* 1, Preface 2; *ANF* 1:315).

As the complete title of his great work makes clear, what Irenaeus proposes is both to describe and to refute gnostic heresy. The description appears mostly in the first book, and its detailed and lengthy exposition may be one of the reasons why the entire work is not more widely studied. For any who are not deeply interested in Gnosticism, there are so many details, and so much explanation, that it is difficult to maintain interest. In our evaluation of his work, we can apply his own principle: to prove that seawater is salty one does not need to drink all of it. We do so by simply quoting a few typical lines near of the beginning of his work:

> They maintain, then, that in the invisible and ineffable heights above there exists a certain perfect, preexistent Aeon, whom they call Pro-arche [First Principle], Propater [Pre-Father], and Bythos [Abyss], and describe as being invisible and incomprehensible. Eternal and unbegotten, he remained throughout innumerable cycles of ages in profound serenity and quiescence. There existed with him Ennoea [Thought], whom they call Charis [Grace] and Sige [Silence]. At last this Bythos determined to send forth from himself the beginning of all things, and deposited this production (which he had resolved to bring forth) in his contemporary Sige, even as seed is deposited in the womb. She then, having received this seed, and becoming pregnant, gave birth to Nous [Intellect], who was both similar and equal to him who had produced him, and was alone capable of comprehending his father's greatness. This Nous they also call Monogenes [Only-begotten], and Father, and the Beginning of all Things. (*Heresies* 1.1.1; *ANF* 1:316)

The rest of this first book—over a hundred pages in some editions—is similar to these few words. One also finds there a sort of genealogy of Gnosticism leading back to Simon Magus, and including teachers such as Menandrus, Saturninus, Basilides, Carpocrates, Cerinthus, Cerdo, and Marcion. This section includes interesting data about each of these and his teachings, thus serving as the main source for many later authors to describe Gnosticism and its main teachers. Unfortunately, it may well be that not all the information that Irenaeus gives here is trustworthy. And the matter has become even more complicated with the discovery of the *Gospel of Truth*, which presents a different picture of the teachings of Valentinus than the one Irenaeus offers.

At any rate, Irenaeus summarizes the contents of the first book in his preface to the second:

> In the first, which immediately precedes this, exposing "knowledge falsely so called," I showed thee, my very dear friend, that the whole system devised, in many and opposite ways, by those who are of the school of Valentinus, was false and baseless. I also set forth the tenets of their predecessors, proving that they not only differed among themselves, but had long previously swerved from the truth itself. (*Heresies* 2, preface 1; *ANF* 1:359)

Thus, after describing Gnosticism and its teachings in the first book, particularly the teachings of Valentinus and his disciple Ptolemeus, in the second book Irenaeus turns to their refutation. This first refutation is mostly based on logical and philosophical arguments, trying to show the contradictions in the teachings that Irenaeus wishes to refute. The arguments are varied. Some have to do with all gnostic doctrines, and some with a specific teaching of a particular leader. Most of it has to do with the nature of God and the relationship between God and the world. On this point, Irenaeus points to a great disagreement among the gnostics, for on the one hand they seem to claim that the world is the result of an error or a passion on the part of an inferior aeon, and on the other hand they seem to understand the world as an emanation of the divine, of whose nature it then participates. In the first case, Irenaeus claims that this would be an ignorant and powerless God, who does not even have control over the aeons emanating from him. In the second case, God would be an imperfect being, whose imperfection is manifest in the very creation that emanates from the divine. The classical doctrine of creation, which Irenaeus affirms, declares on the one hand that creation is the will of God, and on the other that it is a reality different from God. According to Irenaeus, the theories of Valentinus about creation come from pagan philosophers and poets, with the result that they "are thus convicted by their own views of blasphemy against that God who really exists, while they conjure into existence a god who has no existence, to their own condemnation" (*Heresies* 2.9.2; *ANF* 1:369).

Among other gnostic doctrines that Irenaeus refutes here is the notion that the human spirit is a spark or seed of the divine, so that humans share in divinity. Likewise he rejects the gnostics' numerologies, their denial of a physical resurrection of the dead, their belief in the transmigration of souls, and other similar matters.

The third book is the most interesting of the five, for here Irenaeus seeks to refute heresy on the basis of the teachings of the church, and therefore shows how he himself understands such teachings. This third book, jointly with the *Proof of the Apostolic Preaching*, is the main source that we have for the theology of Irenaeus himself. In the fourth book, Irenaeus refutes the doctrines of the gnostics on the basis of Scripture, which makes this fourth book an important source for our knowledge of the exegetical methods of the ancient church. Finally, the fifth book deals mostly with the end times, and therefore it is here that the impact of the Revelation of John on Irenaeus and the church of his time is most clearly seen.

HIS THEOLOGY

Since Irenaeus was probably a native of Asia Minor and a disciple of Polycarp, one can see in his theology a profound influence of the traditions of that area, and particularly of Johannine literature, both the Gospel and the Revelation of John. Reading the third book of *Against Heresies* in particular, as well as the entire corpus of the works of Irenaeus, we see that he understands the entire history of humankind and of creation as a great cosmic drama that begins with creation and leads to the consummation of all things.

Irenaeus summarizes this cosmic drama within a Trinitarian framework:

> And this is the drawing-up of our faith, the foundation of the building, and the consolidation of a way of life. God, the Father, uncreated, beyond grasp, invisible, one God the maker of all; this is the first and foremost article of our faith. But the second article is the Word of God, the Son of God, Christ Jesus our Lord, who was shown forth by the prophets according to the design of their prophecy and according to the manner in which the Father disposed; and through Him were made all things whatsoever. He is also, *in the end of times*, the recapitulation of all things, is become a man among men, visible and tangible, in order to abolish death and bring to light life, and bring about the communion of God and man. And the third article is the Holy Spirit, through whom the prophets prophesied and the patriarchs were taught about God and the just were led in the path of justice, on who *in the end of times* has been poured forth in a new manner upon humanity over all the earth renewing man to God. (*Proof* 6; trans. J. P. Smith, *Proof of the Apostolic Preaching* [New York: Newman Press, 1952], 51)

If we then turn to the doctrine of creation, we note that Irenaeus constantly refers to the early chapters of Genesis, on which he bases his understanding of creation. But when quoting the Genesis stories, he repeatedly calls them "the beginning of creation." This means that what God then made was not a completed work, but the beginning of an entire creative process through which God will take humanity to its final goal. Referring to Adam and Eve, he says that they were created "as children." Those first ancestors of all humankind were not already all that they were intended to be: they were created for a more intimate communion with God.

According to Irenaeus, the world was created and is ruled by God's "two hands," the Son and the Holy Spirit. The purpose of this image of hands is not to remove God from contact with creation, but the opposite: the relationship between God and creation is so close that the world is made by God's very hands, "by which Adam was fashioned, and we too have been formed" (*Heresies* 5.16.1; *ANF* 1:544). Human beings were created after the image of God, and Paul's Epistle to the Colossians (1:15) says that Jesus Christ is the image of God; thus the model that God employed in the creation of humankind was Jesus Christ, God incarnate. Although from the very beginning God employed this model in the shaping of humanity, the model itself was not known to us until the time of the incarnation:

> Then, again, this Word was manifested when the Word of God was made man, assimilating Himself to man, and man to Himself, so that by means of his resemblance to the Son, man might become precious to the Father. For in times long past, it was *said* that man was created after the image of God, but it was not [actually] *shown*; for the Word was as yet invisible, after whose image man was created. (*Heresies* 5.16.2; *ANF* 1:544)

Human beings, created as children, but destined to communion with God, were as princes who will someday become kings, but are now in need of tutors. This is a function of the angels, who are teachers of humanity, preparing us for the time when we shall reign jointly with God, for Paul declares that humans are to judge the angels. Irenaeus declares this explicitly: "So, having made the man lord of the earth and everything in it, He made him in secret lord also of the servants in it. They, however, were in their full development, while the lord, that is, the man, was a little one; for he was a child and had need to grow so as to come to his full perfection" (*Proof* 12; Smith, *Proof*, 55).

Irenaeus insists on the incomplete status of creation, and particularly of the human creature, who at the moment of humankind's creation is not yet all that it is called to be:

> If, however, anyone say, "What then? Could not God have exhibited man as perfect from the beginning?" . . . Created things must be inferior to Him who created them, from the very fact of their later origin; for it was not possible for things recently created to have been

uncreated. But inasmuch as they are not uncreated, for this very reason they come short of the perfect. . . . So also it was possible for God Himself to have made man perfect from the first, but man could not receive this [perfection], being as yet an infant. And for this cause our Lord, in these last times, when He had summed up all things into Himself, came to us, not as He might have come, but as we were capable of beholding Him. He might easily have come to us in His immortal glory, but in that case we could never have endured the greatness of the glory. (*Heresies* 4.38.1; *ANF* 1:521)

The sin of the first couple was in not trusting this God after whose image they had been made, but believing and following instead the advice of the Evil One, and thus becoming his subjects and slaves. Given the nature of that sin and its consequences, it was necessary to destroy the power that the Evil One now has over humankind. Christ did this in his incarnation, death, and resurrection. He who had been the image according to which God created humanity now was manifested as a human being, in order to conquer in the name of humankind.

As it has been clearly demonstrated that the Word, who existed in the beginning with God, by whom all things were made, who was also always present with mankind, was in these last days, according to the time appointed by the Father, united to His own workmanship, inasmuch as He became a man liable to suffering. . . .

For as it was not possible that the man who had once for all been conquered, and who had been destroyed through disobedience, could reform himself, and obtain the prize of victory; and as it was also impossible that he could attain to salvation who had fallen under the power of sin,—the Son effected both these things, being the Word of God, descending from the Father, becoming incarnate, stooping low, even to death, and consummating the arranged plan of our salvation. . . .

For He fought and conquered; for He was contending for the fathers, and through obedience doing away with disobedience completely: For He bound the strong man, and set free the weak, and endowed His own handiwork with salvation, by destroying sin. (*Heresies* 3.18.1, 2, 6; *ANF* 1:445–48)

So by the obedience, whereby He obeyed unto death, hanging on the tree, He undid the disobedience wrought in the tree. (*Proof* 34; Smith, *Proof,* 69)

This does not mean, however, that the Word who was incarnate in Jesus Christ was not present throughout human history long before the time of the incarnation. On the contrary, by means of God's two hands, the Word and the Holy Spirit, God continued shaping humanity and preparing it for the time of the incarnation. Irenaeus considers this to be of great importance, for many of the gnostic systems declared that the world was alien to the true God, who had nothing to do with it until a messenger was sent from on high who, taking the appearance of a human being, but without being truly human, came to bring a new message of salvation. Over against this, Irenaeus stresses the continuity of God's work throughout all of history, particularly the history of Israel. Concretely, it was this Word, later to be incarnate, who revealed himself repeatedly to Israel. He is the fulfillment of prophecy, the one awaited by the nations, the star of Jacob, the offshoot of Jesse, the promised king, the Suffering Servant. One can see this presence of the Word in Israel's history, as in the manner in which Irenaeus interprets the story of Moses:

> He [the Word] it was, who spoke with Moses in the bush, and said: *I have indeed seen the affliction of my people in Egypt, and I am come down to deliver them.* He it was, who was mounting and descending for the deliverance of the afflicted, taking us out of the domination of the Egyptians, that is, out of every idolatry and impiety, and freeing us from the Red Sea, that is, liberating us from the deadly turbulence of the Gentiles and from the bitter current of their blasphemy; for in these things our affairs were being rehearsed, the Word of God at that time prefiguring what was to be. (*Proof* 46; Smith, *Proof*, 77)

Irenaeus frequently refers to the work of Christ as a "recapitulation." This requires some explanation, for it does not mean, as in our current usage, a mere summary of what has gone on before. The word that Irenaeus employs here is the same word that appears in Ephesians 1:10, where we are told that the mystery of God's will was "to gather up all things in him." Literally, this word means joining all things under a single head, "re-heading." Thus, what Jesus Christ does is not simply to summarize earlier history, but rather he takes all of it to its culmination. He is creating a new humankind under a new head. Just as Adam was the head of the old humanity, now Christ is the head of this new humanity that is the church. He takes up all of history, from the time of creation to its culmination, creating a new humanity that, in contrast to the old humanity headed by Adam, is free from the slavery to sin and death. On this point, Irenaeus declares, "The Son of God did not come into being at that time, but rather existed always in the Father. But in being incarnate and becoming human he recapitulated [placed under a new head] the long line of humankind. . . . So that what we lost in Adam, the image and likeness of God, we may now receive in Christ Jesus" (*Heresies* 3.18.1, my translation).

Thus, the cosmic drama that begins with the creation and fall of humankind finds its culmination in the incarnation, death, and resurrection of Jesus Christ. Humanity, once subject to sin and to the Evil One because its head, Adam, had fallen, is now freed through the victory of a new head, a second Adam, Jesus Christ.

This drama, which leads to the victory of the risen Lord, comes to its denouement in the last times. Irenaeus devotes a large section of his fifth book to eschatology. Making certain that he rejects the negative attitude of gnostics toward material reality, Irenaeus affirms and argues that the just will literally receive the earth as their inheritance. "For it is just that in that very creation in which they toiled or were afflicted, being proved in every way by suffering, they should receive the reward of their suffering; and that in the creation in which they were slain because of their love to God, in that they should be revived again; and that in the creation in which they endured servitude, in that they should reign" (*Heresies* 5.32.1; *ANF* 1.561).

In these lines of Irenaeus, as well as in his entire eschatology, one can see the influence of the Revelation of John and of the millennialism we have already found in the fragments of Papias. There are echoes of Revelation in Irenaeus's discussion of the apocalyptic beast who is the head and summary of all evil. It is interesting to note that, just as Irenaeus sees the work of Christ as a recapitulation, so does the beast recapitulate evil and rebellion against God.

> There is therefore in this beast, when he comes, regulation made of all sorts of iniquity and of every deceit, in order that all apostate power, flowing into and being shut up in him, may be sent into the furnace of fire. Fittingly, therefore, shall his name possess the number six hundred and sixty-six, since he sums up in his own person all the commixture of wickedness which took place previous to the deluge. . . . For Noah was 600 years old when the deluge came upon the earth. . . . For that image which was set up by Nebuchadnezzar having indeed a height of sixty cubits, while the breath was six cubits. (*Heresies* 5.29.2; *ANF* 1:558)

Although passages such as the one just quoted remind us that Irenaeus was a man of the second century, and therefore was immersed—as were his contemporaries—in numerological speculation, this does not eclipse the importance of his thought both for his own time and for later centuries.

As to his own time, the arguments of Irenaeus against various forms of Gnosticism, but particularly that of Valentinus, became a source from which many other antiheretical writers drew. His insistence on the doctrine of creation, and therefore on the value of material reality, served as a caveat to those who would otherwise allow themselves to be led astray by the prevailing tendency to think that anything material was valueless and that only the spiritual was important. His vision of all of history leading from creation to consummation as a great cosmic drama gave unity to Christian doctrine, so that it would not be a mere list of disparate doctrines. As part of that drama, he insisted on the continuity between the history of Israel and the history of the church, for the protagonist of the entire drama is the same Word of God who spoke to Abraham, Moses, and the prophets, and who has now taken flesh in Jesus Christ.

As to the second, that is, the impact of Irenaeus on later Christian thought, one must begin by noticing that for centuries he was not given his due in the Western church. Since so much of his work was a refutation of gnostic teachings, once the church decided by consensus that such teachings would be rejected, and so the theories of Valentinus and other gnostics no longer seemed a threat to the church, the voluminous work *Against Heresies* no longer seemed important. And the *Proof of the Apostolic Preaching* was lost. Yet in more recent times, particularly after the mid-twentieth century, Irenaeus's theology has drawn much more attention, no longer as a mere refutation of ancient gnostic theories, but particularly as a sweeping vision of history in the light of redemption.

6

Clement of Alexandria

HIS LIFE

Clement of Alexandria was born near the middle of the second century, probably in Athens. His parents were pagans, and the manner in which he became a Christian is not known. Most likely when he was already a Christian, and seeking greater wisdom, he traveled widely through Italy, Syria, Palestine, and eventually to the city of Alexandria, at the mouth of the river Nile. He tells about those travels and the teachers whom he met in them:

> Of these the one, in Greece, an Ionic; the other in Magna Graecia; the first of these from Coele-Syria, the second from Egypt, and others in the East. The one was born in the land of Assyria, and the other a Hebrew in Palestine.
>
> When I came upon the last (he was the first in power), having tracked him out concealed in Egypt, I found rest. He, the true, the Sicilian bee, gathering the spoil of the flowers of the prophetic and apostolic meadow, engendered in the souls of his hearers a deathless element of knowledge. (*Miscellanies* 1.1; *ANF* 2:301)

This teacher whose constant search after truth led Clement to compare him with a Sicilian bee was most likely the famed scholar Pantenus, who had traveled as far as India and now in Alexandria led a Christian school. It was there in Alexandria that Clement spent the most productive years of his life until, probably in 202 or thereabouts, he was forced to flee because of the persecution of Septimus Severus. He then took refuge in Cappadocia, where he lived until his death, a decade later.

What Clement says about this teacher, whom he compares to a Sicilian bee that gathers nectar from every flower, also applies to him. In his writings, scholars have found almost four hundred references to other authors, mostly pagan ones. This is a sign of the nature and purpose of Clement's theology, in which he seeks on the one hand to prove to pagans that Christian faith is intellectually respectable, and on the other to lead Christians to a deeper understanding of their faith, based on a knowledge of classical wisdom.

A TRILOGY

As is the case with other ancient Christian writers, many of Clement's works have been lost. The most important of these would have been a series of biblical commentaries in eight books, of which only brief fragments remain as quotations within the work of others. His three major works that are still extant are a sort of trilogy: *Exhortation to the Greeks*, *The Instructor*, and the *Stromata*, or *Miscellanies*.

The *Exhortation to the Greeks* is an apologetic work. However, unlike other apologists whom we have already studied, Clement does not pay much attention to the false accusations that were made against Christians, for his real goal is not so much to defend his fellow believers as to invite his pagan readers to follow the path of Christianity. For this reason, this work is similar to others from classical antiquity whose purpose is to call the reader to a better life. The most widely read among these works that may have served as an example for Clement is the *Hortensius* (*On Philosophy*) of Cicero, a lost dialogue.

Since Clement's purpose is not to refute, but rather to convince and to invite, the *Exhortation to the Greeks* begins with a beautiful passage in which, after declaring that the ancient poets frequently sought to corrupt human life, Clement declares that his song is otherwise:

> But not so my song, which has come to loose, and that speedily, the bitter bondage of tyrannizing demons; and leading us back to the mild and loving yoke of piety, recalls to heaven those that had been cast prostrate to the earth. It alone has tamed men, the most intractable of animals. . . . But if one of those serpents even is willing to repent, and follows the Word, he becomes a man of God. . . . And so all such most savage beasts, and all such blocks of stone, the celestial song has transformed into tractable men. . . . Behold the might of the new song! It has made men out of stones, men of the beasts. Those, moreover, that were as dead, not being partakers of the true life, have come to life again, simply by becoming listeners to this song. . . . A beautiful breathing instrument of music the Lord made man, after His own image. (*Exhort.* 1; *ANF* 2:172)

Clement is most interested in showing that Christian truth, even though revealed recently, has deep roots that go back to the very origin of the universe. The song to which Clement refers is not new, as a house newly built, but is rather the song of all ages by which all things were made. As Clement boldly declares, long before such ancient people as the Phrygians and the Egyptians came into existence, this Song of God was being sung. "This is the New Song, the manifestation of the Word that was in the beginning, and before the beginning. The Saviour, who existed before, has in recent days appeared; He, who is in Him that truly is, has appeared; for the Word, who 'was with God,' and by whom all things were created, has appeared as our Teacher" (*Exhort.* 1; *ANF* 2:173).

Contrasting with the God of Christians, the ancient pagan gods were demons, for the stories that are told about them make them less than human beings. Anyone who in spite of that still follows them is truly dead, for these demonic gods are themselves idols of death. Pagans worship the sun, the moon, and the stars. But Clement considers this insufficient: "It is the Lord of the spirits, the Lord of the fire, the Maker of the universe, Him who lighted up the sun, that I long for. I seek after God, not the works of God. . . . For the sun never could show me the true God; but that healthful Word that is the Sun of the soul, by whom alone, when He arises in the depths of the soul, the eye of the soul itself is irradiated" (*Exhort.* 6; *ANF* 2:191).

Like other apologists, Clement claims that any good or truth that may be found in classical philosophy and literature is due to the illumination of the Word, even though the ancient philosophers and authors did not know it. He also responds to those who argue that there is no reason to forgo the ancient truth and religion that they have received from their ancestors in order to embrace this new teaching of Christians. "But you say it is not creditable to subvert the customs handed down to us from our fathers. And why, then, do we not still use our first nourishment, milk, to which our nurses accustomed us from the time of our birth? . . . Why do we not still vomit on our parents' breasts, or still do the things for which, when infants, and nursed by our mothers, we were laughed at?" (*Exhort.* 10; *ANF* 2:197).

Finally, Clement concludes this with an exhortation in which he employs the imagery of the chariot races that were so popular in his time:

> Let us haste, let us run, my fellow-men—us, who are God-loving and God-like images of the Word. Let us haste, let us run, let us take His yoke, let us receive, to conduct us to immortality, the good charioteer of men. Let us love Christ. He led the colt with its parent; and having yoked the team of humanity to God, directs His chariot to immortality, hastening clearly to fulfil, by driving now into heaven, what He shadowed forth before by riding into Jerusalem. (*Exhort.* 12; *ANF* 2:206)

The second element in Clement's trilogy is *The Instructor*. Clement's purpose here is not to teach or explain Christian doctrine, but rather to lead his readers to Christian life. As he says, "the Instructor being practical, not theoretical, His aim is thus to improve the soul, not to teach, and to train it up to a virtuous, not to an intellectual life" (*Instr.* 1.1; *ANF* 2:209). In the hands and under the care of this great Instructor, who is Jesus Christ, we are all children needing to be conducted. Furthermore, men and women are equal before God and are to receive the same instruction from the divine Instructor: "For if the God of both is one, the master of both is also one; one church, one temperance, one modesty; their food is common, marriage an equal yoke; respiration, sight, hearing, knowledge, hope, obedience, love all alike. And those whose life is common, have common graces and a common salvation; common to them are love and training" (*Instr.* 1.4; *ANF* 2:211).

The rest of this first book of *The Instructor* describes who this divine Instructor is and how he teaches. In the other two books, Clement turns to more concrete matters regarding the Christian life. Thus, for instance, he deals with what one is to eat and drink, and how to do it; with laughter and its proper measure; with footwear; with baths and other similar matters. Possibly the most interesting assertions regarding Christian life in these last two books of *The Instructor* are those having to do with wealth and its use. However, since this will be the main theme of another of Clement's books, *Who Is the Rich to Be Saved?*, we shall postpone that matter for our discussion of that other work.

At the end of *The Instructor*, Clement seems to promise a third work that would possibly be called *The Teacher*. There the Instructor says: "And now, in truth, it is time for me to cease from my instruction, and for you to listen to the Teacher" (*Instr.* 3.12; *ANF* 2:294). These words would lead us to expect that Clement would write a third and more systematic work devoted to expounding the doctrines of Christianity. But instead of that, what we have are the eight books of the *Stromata*, or *Miscellanies*. Here he follows a fairly common literary genre in antiquity, in which an author would comment on a number of subjects, without trying to give such comments any order or systematization. Of the eight books of *Miscellanies*, the most interesting are the first two, for five of the remaining are mostly a detailed refutation of Gnosticism, and the last is a list of disconnected notes that apparently Clement never intended to publish.

The main theme of the first two books of *Miscellanies* is the relationship between philosophy and Christianity. This is possibly the most important contribution of Clement to the development of Christian doctrine. Like Justin, he tries to build bridges between classical philosophy and the Christian faith, and he does this on the basis of the same doctrine of the Logos. But, while Justin's argument is addressed to pagans who consider Christianity an uncouth superstition that intellectuals should view with contempt, Clement's audience is mostly those Christians who need the principles whereby to relate their faith to the surrounding culture, particularly its philosophy. Comparing Christian life with the care of vineyards, Clement says: "Some, who think themselves naturally gifted, do not wish to touch either philosophy or logic; nay more, they do not wish to learn natural science. They demand bare faith alone, as if they wished, without bestowing any care on the vine, straightaway to gather clusters from the first. . . . We must lop, dig, bind, and perform the other operations" (*Misc.* 1.9; *ANF* 2:309).

Rejecting such notions, Clement insists on the value of philosophy as a path leading to God:

> Before the advent of the Lord, philosophy was necessary to the Greeks for righteousness. And now it becomes conducive to piety; being a kind of preparatory training for those who will attain to faith through demonstration. "For thy foot," it is said, "will not stumble, if thou refer what is good, whether belonging to the Greeks or to us, to Providence." For God is the cause of all good things; but of some primarily, as of the Old and the New Testament; and the others by consequence, as philosophy. Perchance, too, philosophy was given to the Greeks directly and primarily, till the Lord should call the Greeks. For this was a schoolmaster to bring "the Hellenic mind," as the law [brings] the Hebrews, "to Christ." Philosophy, therefore, was a preparation, paving the way for him who is perfected in Christ. (*Misc.* 1.5; *ANF* 2:305)
>
> As many men drawing down the ship cannot be called many causes, but one cause consisting of many, . . . so also philosophy, being the search for truth, contributes to the comprehension of truth; not as being the cause of comprehension, but a cause along with other things, and cooperator. . . . So, while truth is one, many things contribute to its investigation. But its discovery is by the Son. (*Misc.* 1.20; *ANF* 2:323)
>
> He made a new covenant with us; for what belonged to the Greeks and Jews is old. But we, who worship Him in a new way, in the third form, are Christians. For clearly, as I think, he showed that the one and only God was known by the Greeks in a Gentile way, and by the Jews Judaically, and in a new and spiritual way by us.
>
> And further, that the same God that furnished both the Covenants was the giver of Greek philosophy to the Greeks, by which the Almighty is glorified among the Greeks. (*Misc.* 6.5; *ANF* 2:489)

However, this does not mean that Clement is ready to accept without further investigation whatever philosophers say, nor that he would have philosophy and logic take the place of faith. Philosophical and logical knowledge is built on the foundation of a series of principles or axioms that are themselves incapable of demonstration. Such axioms are accepted by faith and not by proof. Thus, while faith ought to seek understanding, understanding is impossible without faith—at least that faith with which one accepts axioms or fundamental principles.

> Should one say that Knowledge is founded on demonstration by a process of reasoning, let him hear that first principles are incapable of demonstration. . . . Hence it is thought that the first cause of the universe can be apprehended by faith alone. For all knowledge is capable of being taught; and what is capable of being taught is founded on what is known before. . . . Accordingly, faith is something superior to knowledge, and is its criterion. Conjecture, which is only a feeble supposition, counterfeits faith; as the flatterer counterfeits a friend, and the wolf a dog. . . . Knowledge, accordingly, is characterized by faith; and faith, by a kind of divine mutual and reciprocal correspondence, becomes characterized by knowledge. (*Misc.* 2.5; *ANF* 2:350)

It is on the basis of this reciprocal relationship between faith and knowledge that Clement builds a bridge between the best of pagan culture and philosophy and Christian faith. If philosophy needed revelation in order to come to the true knowledge of the first principle of the universe, believers in Jesus Christ must also employ that very philosophy in order to know and understand their faith. Thus they will avoid the danger that their faith, instead of being truly such, may be merely a conjecture disguised as faith.

CAN THE RICH BE SAVED?

If we then turn to the other work of Clement that is still extant, *Who Is the Rich [Person] to Be Saved?*, we see that it is a more detailed discussion of a subject of Christian life discussed in a more general fashion in *The Instructor*, the use of goods and wealth. In that other work, Clement had already devoted a chapter to the need of being rid of luxury items, in which ostentation overcomes use:

> For though such of us as cultivate the soil need a mattock and plow, none of us will make a pickaxe of silver or a sickle of gold, but we employ the material which is serviceable for our culture, not what is costly. What prevents those who are capable of considering what is similar from entertaining the same sentiments with respect to household utensils, of which let use, not expense, be the measure? For tell me, does the table knife not cut unless it be studded with silver, and have its handle made of ivory? . . . Will the table that is fashioned with ivory feet be indignant at bearing a three-halfpenny loaf? Will

the lamp not dispense light because it is the work of the potter, not of the goldsmith? . . .

For in fine, in food, and clothes, and vessels, and everything else belonging to the house, I say comprehensively, that one must follow the institutions of the Christian man, as is serviceable and suitable to one's person, age, pursuits, time of life. For it becomes those that are servants of one God, that their possessions and furniture should exhibit tokens of one beautiful life. (*Instr.* 2.3; *ANF* 2:247)

This issue was so important for Clement that he devoted a separate work to it: *Who Is the Rich [Person] to Be Saved?* The city of Alexandria, where Clement lived, was an opulent center. There silk and spices from the East abounded, and much of the gold of Rome came to it in payment for the wheat produced in Egypt. But at the same time, as is so often the case with great cities, Alexandria was also noted for the poverty of many of its inhabitants. This was particularly the case for the Copts, the descendants of the ancient inhabitants of Egypt, against whom both Greeks and Romans discriminated. Given the onerous taxes that peasants had to pay and the growth of latifundia, many of the Copts, whose ancestors had grown wheat on the shores of the Nile, were now displaced and went to Alexandria, where they led a miserable life. Apparently there now began to be within the church some people from the higher echelons of society, and Clement was concerned over the inclination to mollify the requirements of Christian living, particularly in matters having to do with help for the needy. He therefore begins this treatise with a warning to those who praise the rich because of their wealth:

Those who bestow laudatory addresses on the rich appear to me to be rightly judged not only flatterers and base, in vehemently pretending that things which are disagreeable give them pleasure, but also godless and treacherous; godless, because neglecting to praise and glorify God, . . . they invest with divine honours men wallowing in an execrable and abominable life . . . and treacherous, because, although wealth is of itself sufficient to puff up and to corrupt the souls of its possessors, and to turn them from the path by which salvation is to be attained, they stupefy them still more, by inflicting the minds of the rich with the pleasures of extravagant praises, and by making them utterly despise all things except wealth, on account of which they are admired. (*Rich?* 1; *ANF* 2:591)

From that starting point, Clement declares that what moves him in his critique of luxury and ostentation is not hatred of the rich, but rather love, for his purpose is to lead them to salvation. At the same time, he has to make sure that the rich do not feel that they are already condemned and that the only way in which they can be saved is by tossing their wealth into the sea. What Clement wishes is for them to learn how to employ their wealth properly. This may be seen in the manner in which he interprets the story of the young man to whom Jesus says that if he wishes to be perfect, he is to sell all he has and give it to the poor. This is not to be taken literally, for those who have nothing cannot give, and an essential element in Christian life is sharing with the needy. What the young man must do is to "banish from his soul his notions about wealth, his excitement and morbid feeling about it, the anxieties" (*Rich?* 11; *ANF* 2:294). If he cannot do this, and wealth controls his life, Clement says that he must dispose of his riches, despise them, and flee from them. Those who truly possess things as believers do not possess them for their own benefit, but for their brothers and sisters, and would be just as happy in having them as in losing them.

This does not mean, however, that Clement is ready to tell the rich that they can set aside their obligations. On the contrary, he tells them that the love of riches is subversive and difficult to uproot, and that therefore they should find someone who is willing to advise them in the use of their wealth, who is ready to speak harsh words when they are not making good use of it. Wealth is like a viper that can be managed if held by the head; but if held by the tail it kills.

> The rich are to share with the needy even when they are not certain that the latter are worthy, for one's judgment may err, and it is better to help the unworthy in order to make certain of helping those who are truly needy than to forsake doing so in order not to help the unworthy.
>
> In any case, whoever makes good use of wealth, sharing it with the needy, is actually not making any sort of sacrifice, but actually doing good business:
>
> O excellent trading! O divine merchandise! One purchases immortality for money; and, by giving the perishing things of the world, receives in exchange for these an eternal mansion in the heavens! Sail to this mart, if you are wise, O rich man! If need be, sail round the whole world. Spare not perils and toils, that you may purchase here the heavenly kingdom. (*Rich?* 32; *ANF* 2:600)

Even though he devoted an entire treatise to the subject, as well as extensive paragraphs in *The Instructor*, the significance of Clement's work is not primarily in his teachings regarding wealth, which were soon disregarded. What did remain of his work was his effort to build a bridge between his faith and the surrounding culture. Through the doctrine of the logos, which Justin and several others had employed before, Clement could come to the conclusion that in Jesus Christ two great currents converge: Greek culture on the one side, and the faith of Israel on the other. In the next generation Origen and others followed Clement's lead and thus developed theological systems drawing both on Scripture and on philosophy. After that time, numerous Christian thinkers, no matter what their own cultural context, did similarly.

7

Tertullian

Tertullian is widely acknowledged as the creator of Latin Christian theological language. With a few minor exceptions, his writings are the earliest Christian witness to the growth of Christianity among the Latin-speaking population. Even the writers whom we have already studied from the western part of the Roman Empire, where Latin was generally spoken, wrote in Greek. Such was the case, for instance, of Clement, Hermas, and Irenaeus. In the next chapter we shall deal with the work of Minucius Felix, which may have been earlier than Tertullian's, but whose impact was much less. It was Tertullian who, in the very process of writing in Latin what others had discussed in Greek, developed the theological meaning of words that have become common in Western theology, words such as "person," "substance," and "catholic." Scholars have made lists of his neologisms, and these add up to almost a thousand.

HIS LIFE

Tertullian grew up in the north of Africa. This is important, for it was there, rather than in Rome or anywhere else in Europe, that Latin theology was centered throughout most of the time covered in this book. As we shall see later, among those who flourished in Africa were Cyprian, Augustine, and many others. Tertullian himself apparently was born around the year 160. He spent some time in Rome, where he studied law. Eusebius tells us that he was "a man well-versed in the laws of the Romans, and in other respects of high repute, and one of those especially distinguished in Rome" (*Church History* 2.2.4; NPNF[2] 1:106). Furthermore, it is even possible that this Christian

Tertullian is the same person by that name who is quoted in Roman jurisprudence. In any case, Tertullian would have been some forty or fifty years old when he was converted. He does not say much about his conversion, although he does indicate that his previous life left much to be desired. After his conversion he returned to Carthage, where he produced his vast writings. His great variety of works include apologies against the pagans, refutations of the teachings of Marcion and other heretics, and a vast number of moral and ascetic treatises on Christian life. Amid this period of vast literary production, Tertullian left the rest of the church and joined Montanism. This was a movement of rigorist tendencies, convinced that the rest of the church had abandoned the narrow path and that the Montanist leaders had received a special revelation from the Holy Spirit. Some ancient writers assert that at the end of his life, Tertullian left Montanism and created his own sect, which they call "Tertullianism." But such assertions are not completely trustworthy. Except in a few cases in which the influence of Montanism may be seen, it is difficult to be absolutely certain about the chronological order of his works. For that reason, rather than trying to discuss them chronologically, we shall organize them thematically, beginning with his apologetic works, then moving to his refutations of various heresies, and finally to the rest.

However, before discussing some of his works, some comments regarding Tertullian's manner of expression are important. His style is terse, combining classical rhetoric with cutting and memorable phrases. His arguments show his legal background. Often he employs irony against his opponents. As a writer, there is no doubt that his style is sharp and frequently mordant, abounding in unforgettable phrases, irreconcilable paradoxes, and mockery of his opponents. Thus, for instance, referring to the supposedly supreme God of Marcion, who was not the creator of the world, Tertullian wonders about the power of such a God, who is not even able to produce a cucumber. The result is that many of his phrases have become lapidary: "What indeed has Athens to do with Jerusalem? What concord is there between the Academy and the Church?" "The blood of Christians is seed." "It is by all means to be believed, because it is absurd." At a later point we shall return to such phrases, but here it is important to see them as a sign of Tertullian's character and style.

APOLOGETIC WORKS

Tertullian's apologetic works are several. The treatise in two books *To the Nations*, or *To the Gentiles*, seems to be a series of notes that Tertullian wrote in preparation for his great defense of Christianity, the *Apology against the Gentiles in Defense of Christians*, commonly known simply as the *Apology*. Along with these two, one must also mention two shorter writings that are also apologetic in nature: *The Testimony of the Soul* and *To Scapula*.

From the very first lines of the *Apology*, Tertullian shows his legal background, for he presents his work as a brief against a trial that is made impossible by persecution itself:

> Rulers of the Roman Empire, if, seated for the administration of justice on your lofty tribunal, under the gaze of every eye, and occupying there all but the highest position in the state, you may not openly inquire into and sift before the world the real truth in regard to the charges made against the Christians; if in this case alone you are afraid or ashamed to exercise your authority in making public inquiry with the carefulness which becomes justice; if, finally, the extreme severities inflicted on our people in recently private judgments stand in the way of our being permitted to defend ourselves before you, you cannot surely forbid the Truth to reach your ears by the secret pathway of a noiseless book. (*Apol.* 1; *ANF* 3:17)

The policy that the empire followed at that time with regard to Christians was that established several decades earlier by Emperor Trajan in his correspondence with Pliny, that Christians should not be sought after, but that those who were accused of being Christians and would not recant must be punished, if not for their crimes, at least for their obstinacy. As a good lawyer, Tertullian shows the contradiction implicit in such a policy:

> O miserable deliverance,—under the necessities of the case, a self-contradiction! It forbids them to be sought after as innocent, and it commands them to be punished as guilty. It is at once merciful and cruel; it passes by, and it punishes. Why dost thou play a game of evasion upon thyself, O Judgment? If thou condemnest, why dost thou not also inquire? If thou does not inquire, why dost thou not also absolve? Military stations are distributed through all the provinces for tracking robbers. Against traitors and public foes every man is a soldier; search is made even for their confederates and accessories. The Christian alone must not be sought, though he may be brought and accused before the judge; as if a search had any other end than that in view! And so you condemn the man for whom nobody wished a search to be made when he is presented to you, and who even now does not deserve punishment, I suppose, because of his guilt, but because, though forbidden to be sought, he was found. And then, too, you do not in that case deal with us in the ordinary way of judicial proceedings against offenders; for, in the case of others denying, you apply the torture to make them confess—Christians alone you torture, to make them deny; whereas, if we were guilty of any crime, we should be sure to deny it, and you with your tortures would force us to confession. (*Apol.* 2; *ANF* 3:19)

Tertullian then turns to the most common accusations made against Christians—accusations based on idle gossip, such as incest, infanticide, and cannibalism. He simply argues that it makes no sense to think that Christians, who hold to moral principles much higher than the rest of society, would do such things. Nor is it true that Christians worship the head of an ass, as is commonly said. And if any claim that Christians are committing a crime against the state in refusing to worship the emperor, Tertullian refutes this by saying, first, that the worship of the emperor is completely irrational; second, that it is not true that the gods protect the emperor, for in fact it is the emperor who protects the gods; and third, that in praying to the true and only God for the emperor, Christians offer him a greater service than all the idolatrous sacrifices of pagans.

> Let the emperor make war on heaven; let him lead heaven captive in his triumph; let him put guards on heaven; let him impose taxes on heaven! He cannot. Just because he is less than heaven, he is great. For he himself is His to whom heaven and every creature appertains. He gets his sceptre where he first got his humanity; his power where he got the breath of life. Thither we lift our eyes, with hands outstretched, because free from sin; with head uncovered, for we have nothing whereof to be ashamed; finally, without a monitor, because it is from the heart we supplicate. Without ceasing, for all our emperors we offer prayer. We pray for life prolonged; for security to the empire; for protection to the imperial house; for brave armies, a faithful senate, a virtuous people, the world at rest, whatever, as man or Cæsar, an emperor would wish. (*Apol.* 30; *ANF* 3:42)

Throughout the treatise, Tertullian expounds some of the basic teachings of Christianity, particularly regarding the one God who has created and ordered the world. At the end we find words that have become famous: "Nor does your cruelty, however exquisite, avail you; it is rather a temptation to us. The oftener we are mown down by you, the more in number we grow; *the blood of Christians is seed*" (*Apol.* 50; *ANF* 3:55, emphasis added). In the *Apology*, Tertullian had already declared that the human soul is by nature Christian. What he meant by this is that, no matter what it actually believes, the human soul is inclined toward the one true God. This is the main argument of *The Soul's Testimony*. There, as a lawyer would do, Tertullian questions the soul and forces it to become a witness for the one God. By showing that the soul yearns for that God and for eternal life, he comes to the conclusion that the soul, in refusing to accept Christianity, becomes not only a witness, but also the accused:

> There is not a soul of man that does not, from the light that is in itself, proclaim the very things we are not permitted to speak above our breath. Most justly, then, every soul is a culprit as well as a witness: in

the measure that it testifies for truth, the guilt of error lies on it; and on the day of judgment it will stand before the courts of God, without a word to say. Thou proclaimedst God, O soul, but thou didst not seek to know Him: evil spirits were detested by thee, and yet they were the objects of thy adoration. (*Test.* 6; *ANF* 3:179)

The treatise *To Scapula* is addressed to the man who served as proconsul of Africa around the year 212. Although it is impossible to date most of Tertullian's other works, we know that this one was written in 212 or slightly later, for it refers to a solar eclipse that took place on that date. This brief treatise begins by declaring that Christians do not make their defense on their own behalf, but rather out of love for those who persecute them, so that they may be spared the punishment due to them for having persecuted Christians. In a few words that may well have inspired the much more extensive treatise that Lactantius would later write on the subject, Tertullian refers to the punishments suffered by some of those who persecuted Christians and have been blinded or died after being riddled by worms. However, this is as nothing when compared with the eternal punishment that they will receive. Therefore, Tertullian ends with an exhortation to Scapula: "Spare thyself, if not us poor Christians! Spare Carthage, if not thyself!" (*Scap.* 5; *ANF* 3:108).

The writing by the title of *Against the Jews* is frequently included among Tertullian's apologetic works. Its argument is very similar to what is found in Justin's *Dialogue with Trypho*. But there is no certainty about the authorship of this writing, particularly its latter half, which clearly seems not to have been written by Tertullian.

POLEMICAL WRITINGS

Tertullian's polemical writings are numerous, partly because Tertullian himself was inclined to polemics. The most extensive of these is *Against Marcion*, in five books. But he also wrote *Against Hermogenes*, *Against the Valentinians*, and *Against Praxeas*. Also, seeking to refute those who undervalued the body, both the body of Christ himself and human bodies at large, he wrote *On the Flesh of Christ* and *On the Resurrection of the Flesh*. In order to refute those gnostics who denied the value of martyrdom, he wrote *Against the Scorpion*, or *Scorpiace*. To refute those who understood the nature of the soul in Platonic terms, he wrote *On the Soul*, where he rejects the notion of the reincarnation of souls and, following Stoic teachings, affirms that the soul is material, although its matter is much more subtle than that of the body. There he also affirms that God does not create individual souls, but rather that these are transmitted by parents in similar fashion to the transmission of bodies and their traits. All of these works are important expressions of Tertullian's thought and the multiple challenges facing the church at the time. But there is no doubt that his most important antiheretical work is *Prescription against the Heretics*.

To understand the title and the purpose of his work it is necessary to say a word about the term "prescription" in the legal usage of the time. This word was employed most commonly in two ways: First, a prescription in a trial was a previous argument seeking to determine if the trial itself was appropriate, if the judge had jurisdiction over the case, and other similar matters. Second, there was also the "prescription of antiquity," in which use of a property for an extended period of time without being questioned became a right of property. Such was the case, for instance, of a person occupying a piece of land and paying its taxes for an extended time, thereby becoming its rightful owner. Therefore, Tertullian's argument in this brief but very important writing does not seek to refute any particular error or heresy, but rather to deny the right of heretics to be part of the argument. According to Tertullian, heretics have no right to employ the Scriptures, for these belong to the church, in a possession that has never been questioned. "It ought to be clearly seen to whom belongs the possession of the Scriptures, that none may be admitted to the use thereof who has no title at all to the privilege" (*Prescr.* 15; *ANF* 3:250).

This leads Tertullian to the theme of apostolic succession. Some were claiming to be possessors of a secret teaching that Jesus had passed confidentially only to a favorite disciple. Tertullian's response is that there never was such a secret tradition. Jesus shared his teachings with all the apostles. These in turn passed these teachings to the same people to whom they entrusted the churches. Therefore, the churches able to show that their leaders are part of a succession connecting them to the apostles have the right to determine what is correct doctrine. It is only they, and other churches agreeing with them, that own Scripture and therefore are its legitimate interpreters.

It is also in this treatise that we find Tertullian's famous words: "What indeed has Athens to do with Jerusalem? What concord is there between the Academy and the Church? What between heretics and Christians?" (*Prescr.* 7; *ANF* 3:246). Tertullian is convinced that most of the blame for heresies is to be laid at the feet of philosophy. As he sees matters, what has happened is simply that some have allowed themselves to be carried away by vain philosophical speculation and thus have been led astray from correct doctrine. This is a subject that repeatedly appears in Tertullian's writings. But it is also necessary to point out that by "philosophy," Tertullian understood mostly the Platonic tradition, for he himself was profoundly influenced by Stoicism.

Tertullian has often been seen as an anti-intellectual, mostly because of his harsh criticism of philosophy, but also because he opened himself to such charges by his inclination to use striking paradoxes seeming to imply that he had little respect for reason itself. One such passage often quoted to support the view that Tertullian did not have much respect for reason appears in the work *On the Flesh of Christ*: "The Son of God was crucified; I am not ashamed because men must needs be ashamed *of it*. And the Son of God died; it is by all means to be believed, because it is absurd. He was buried, and rose again; the fact is certain, because it is impossible" (*Flesh of Christ* 3; *ANF* 3:525).

However, when we read Tertullian's work in its entirety, he clearly does not mean that the reason for believing something is that it is impossible or absurd, but rather that certain elements in Christian faith cannot be proved by reason and may even seem to be contrary to reason, but are still true.

This is shown in another of Tertullian's antiheretical writings that has left a profound footprint on Christian theology, *Against Praxeas*. It is impossible to determine exactly who Praxeas was. Some suggest that it may have been the bishop of Rome, whom Tertullian does not wish to mention by name. At any rate, it is clear that Praxeas so underscored the unity between the Father and the Son that there seemed to be no distinction between them. At the same time, he rejected Montanism and its emphasis on the activity of the Holy Spirit. For this reason, in one of his typical phrases, Tertullian declares that Praxeas "did a twofold service for the devil at Rome: he drove away prophecy, and he brought in heresy; he put to flight the Paraclete, and he crucified the Father" (*Prax.* 1; *ANF* 3:597). Apparently, the argument of Praxeas was that, since God is omnipotent, God could very well become Son and be crucified. Tertullian responds that to argue on the basis of divine omnipotence makes little sense. Certainly God is capable of doing anything; but what is important is not what God could do, but rather what God has indeed done:

> Of course nothing is "too hard for the Lord." But if we choose to apply this principle so extravagantly and harshly in our capricious imaginations, we may then make out God to have done anything we please, on the ground that it was not impossible for Him to do it. We must not, however, because He is able to do all things suppose that He has actually done what He has not done. But we must inquire *whether He has really done it*. God could, if He had liked, have furnished man with wings to fly with, just as He gave wings to kites. We must not, however, run to the conclusion that He did this because He was able to do it. He might also have extinguished Praxeas and all other heretics at once; it does not follow, however, that He did, simply because He was able. For it was necessary that there should be both kites and heretics. (*Prax.* 10; *ANF* 3:605)

However, the importance of *Against Praxeas* goes far beyond such matters. Among the many words to which Tertullian gave particular meaning within the context of Christian theology, none are more important than "substance" and "person," which he employs in this treatise to deal with both Trinitarian and christological doctrine. Making use of definitions taken from the field of law, Tertullian declares that God is a single substance existing in three persons. There has been much debate about the exact meaning in which Tertullian uses these words; but there is no doubt that it was he who proposed a terminology that has been repeatedly employed and debated in the course of Christian theology. Similarly, while discussing the incarnation of the Word in Jesus Christ, Tertullian says that in him there are two substances, the divine and the human, united in a single person. Later theologians, while following his lead, would prefer to speak of the humanity and the divinity of Christ as "natures" rather than as "substances."

Along with his apologetic and antiheretical works, Tertullian wrote about various aspects of Christian life. One of the most interesting among these works is *On Baptism*, written in response to the teachings of a woman in Carthage by the name of Quintilla, which seeks to refute the notion that baptism is unimportant or powerless. Referring to the ancient symbol of Christ as a fish, Tertullian says that, like fish, believers are born in water. The simplicity of the rite itself should not hide the great power of baptism. From the very beginning of creation, the Holy Spirit was moving over the face of the waters. Now that very Spirit comes to move over those who enter the water. In preparation for baptism, there must be a period of prayer, fasting, vigil, and confession of sins. Regarding infant baptism, Tertullian seems to take for granted that it is common practice and that it is valid, but at the same time he suggests that it is best to postpone baptism for two reasons: first, because children have not yet committed their worst sins, and the washing of baptism should be reserved for a time when it will be more necessary; and second, because those who commit to lead the child along the path of faith risk making promises that they will not be able to fulfill. Furthermore, those who are single should postpone baptism until such a time as marriage, age, or confirmed continence will keep them from falling into sin. Those who really understand the power and importance of baptism will be more afraid of receiving it than of postponing it. Although baptism should normally be administered by the authorities that the church has determined, in particular circumstances a layman may baptize. However, Tertullian makes it very clear that women should not baptize under any circumstance. Normally, baptism will take place on Easter or, if not, on Pentecost. As to the manner in which baptism is to be administered, Tertullian says that the person is to be introduced into the water (*demissus*), and then water is poured over the head (*tinctus*), while certain words are pronounced— apparently the Trinitarian formula, which Tertullian affirms throughout the entire writing. Upon coming out of the water, the neophyte is anointed as an indication that now the one baptized is part of God's holy priesthood, and the Holy Spirit is invoked with the imposition of hands. Although this treatise is very brief, it was the main source that scholars had to study ancient baptismal practices until the relatively recent discovery of the *Apostolic Tradition* of Hippolytus, which will be discussed in another chapter. Apart from his preference for the postponement of baptism, what Tertullian says agrees with the more detailed information we have from Hippolytus.

OTHER WORKS

Tertullian's works are so many and deal with such diverse issues that it is difficult to summarize them. *To the Martyrs*, apparently one of his earliest works, is addressed to a group of prisoners who had confessed their Christian faith and would soon face torture and death. Perhaps due in part to its brevity, it has been one of the most widely read writings of Tertullian. *On Prayer* is written for those preparing for baptism and includes a discussion and exposition of the Lord's Prayer. *On Spectacles* summarizes the origins and meaning of various public spectacles, such as those that took place in the circus or the arena. Tertullian rejects all of them as immoral, exciting passion, and leading the soul astray. At any rate, the greatest spectacle ever will be the coming of the Lord in glory, followed by the resurrection of the saints, the praise of the heavenly hosts, and the kingdom of God. This spectacle, which will be witnessed both by believers and by those who now persecute them, will outshine all the spectacles that now attract multitudes.

A similar rejection of the common practices of society is found in his work *On the Crown*, where Tertullian decries the pagan custom of crowning soldiers, and also declares that Christians must not be part of the army. In his treatise *On the Dress of Women* he follows the same direction, declaring that following the fashions of society and adorning oneself with gold and precious stones is not compatible with Christian faith. Although most of this writing refers to women, toward the end he says that the same is true of men. In any case, the strength of iron is more fitting to the life of faith than is the luster of gold. In his work *On Patience*, he exhorts his readers to cultivate that virtue, while he himself confesses that he is short of it. *On Penance* speaks of the repentance that is necessary before baptism, as well as of grave sins committed after baptism—about which Tertullian declares that there would be one more opportunity for repentance, but no more.

The treatises *On Chastity*, *On Monogamy*, and *To His Wife* deal specifically with the possibility of a second marriage after the death of a spouse. The first of these is addressed to a widower, whom he exhorts not to be married a second time, which would be almost as bad as fornication. The second likewise declares that such a second marriage is not legitimate. In the one addressed to his own wife, apparently written shortly before he became a Montanist, Tertullian gives his wife instructions about her life after his death. Among such instructions he tells her that, if she cannot continue living as a widow, at least she should marry a Christian. In his treatise *On the Veiling of Virgins*, he declares that modesty and chastity require that virgins cover their faces with a veil not only in church, but also in public life. *On Flight in Times of Persecution* shows Tertullian's Montanist inclinations in rejecting the teaching of the church at large, that martyrdom is not to be sought, and affirming that in times of persecution one must neither flee nor hide.

In the treatise *On Fasting*, he attacks Christians who do not practice fasting as rigorously as the Montanists do. In spite of its title, *On Modesty* is mostly about the established practice that it was bishops who could declare the forgiveness of sins. According to Tertullian, such authority must be reserved for men of a particular spiritual purity. (Later, this subject would become a matter of contention in North Africa, leading to the Donatist controversy.) Finally, in his very short *On the Pallium* Tertullian responds to those who have criticized him for having given up the Roman toga and wearing instead the more common vestment known as the pallium. According to Tertullian, the toga is a symbol of power and authority, while the pallium is a sign of humility and therefore a more proper dress for a Christian.

This long line of writings of various aspects of life, from marriage to clothing, shows Tertullian's interest in the moral life and in obedience to the strictest rules of behavior, an interest that eventually led him to break away from the rest of the church, which he considered too lax, and join the Montanists. But Tertullian's rigorism and even legalistic moralism should not obscure his enormous importance in the history of Christian literature and theology, for it was he who created much of the vocabulary that Western Christians still employ. Despite his exaggerated paradoxes and often unbecoming humor, Tertullian remains the founder of Western theological language.

8

Other Literature from the Same Period

Much of the literature discussed or mentioned in the foregoing chapters dates from the mid or late second century. Such is the case, for instance, of Clement's *Second Epistle to the Corinthians*, as well as several of the acts of the martyrs and much apocryphal literature. It is important to remember, however, that the works discussed and quoted in those earlier chapters are not the entirety of Christian literature in the second century. There is no doubt that much more has been lost than has been preserved. In the writings of Eusebius, Jerome, and others, we have abundant references to lost works of the authors already mentioned. We also find fragments of other prolific authors whose work has been mostly lost. Possibly the most important among them is Hegesippus.

Almost all we know about Hegesippus is what we find in allusions and quotes in the work of Eusebius of Caesarea. According to Eusebius, Hegesippus seems to have been a Jewish Christian who wrote about the various sects and heresies existing among the Jews as well as among Christians. However, since Eusebius is interested mostly in what Hegesippus says about the ancient church, the fragments that he quotes from Hegesippus say little about his style or the content of his writings.

Two other writings that may well date from the second century are the Odes of Solomon and the Sibylline Oracles. These stand at the very roots of Christian poetry. The Odes seem to have been originally written in Hebrew or Aramaic, but the text that was discovered early in the twentieth century is in Syriac and apparently translated from Greek. Some scholars suggest that they can see in this poetry dualistic tendencies indicative of gnostic origins. But the poetic nature of this material makes it difficult to determine whether or not such dualism really exists. The author of the Odes is unknown, and many scholars attribute them to an unknown Jewish Christian deeply imbued with the poetry and imagery of the psalms. In most of them, it appears that it is Christ who is speaking, although even that is subject to debate. As an example of the poetic style of these Odes, one may quote Ode 6, whose imagery is reminiscent of Ezekiel's vision of water flowing from the temple:

> A stream went forth
>   and became a long and broad river.
> It flooded and broke and carried away the Temple.
> Ordinary man could not stop it,
>   nor those whose art is to halt the waters.
> And it spread over the face of the whole earth,
>   filling everything,
> and the thirsty of the earth drank
>   and their thirst was quenched.
> The drink came from the highest one.
>   (Willis Barnstone, ed., *The Other Bible*
>   [San Francisco: Harper & Row, 1984], 271)

The Sibylline Oracles are a collection of fourteen books, of which two have been lost. Before the advent of Christianity, unknown Jewish writers produced a series of oracles that they attributed to a sibyl, apparently seeking to attract pagans to Judaism. In the second century a Christian author, also unknown, followed this lead, partly composing new oracles, and partly adding interpolations in the previous Jewish text. These oracles were very influential because many believed them to be proof that God had announced the gospel not only through the Hebrew prophets of old, but also through pagan seers.

A very different writing, also dating from the late second century, is the apologetic work of Minucius Felix known as the *Octavius*. There is still much disagreement among scholars as to whether this antedated Tertullian or not. There is no question that there is a connection between it and Tertullian's *Apology*. Yet it is not clear which of the two authors drew from the other. Since we know that Tertullian's *Apology* was written in 198, the *Octavius* must be dated late in the second century or early in the third.

At any rate, although there are great similarities in contents between the *Octavius* and Tertullian's writings, there is a marked difference in style. While Tertullian is harsh and cutting, and his Latin betrays abundant Hellenisms, the *Octavius* is a prime example of an elegant style worthy of Cicero and classical Rome. As to Minucius Felix himself, very little is known. Like Tertullian, he clearly was a lawyer in Rome before his conversion, and he may well have been a native of North Africa.

This apology takes the shape of a conversation among Minucius Felix himself, his Christian friend Octavius, and a pagan named Cecilian. Both Octavius and Cecilian hail from North Africa. The three are in Italy, making their way to Ostia, when Cecilian makes a gesture of adoration to Serapis, and Octavius criticizes him for it. The result is a friendly but firm debate in which Cecilian and Octavius discuss the nature and the truth of Christianity, while Minucius serves as a moderator or judge in the discussion. Cecilian's arguments are similar to those we have already encountered: Christians are ignorant, ready to speak of what they know not; they have no authors nor temples, and their god is invisible; the gods have made Rome great, and therefore Romans should not abandon them; it is said that Christians drink the blood of a child and practice incest; and so on. Octavius responds with arguments similar to what we have seen in other apologists. He simply sets aside the various accusations of immoral behavior, arguing that Christians, who abound in love and practice a superior style of life, would never be so degraded. Furthermore, the poverty for which Christians are criticized, and their low social status, help them to see eternal realities in the way that is impossible for the rich and powerful:

> Thus it is, that rich men, attached to their means, have been accustomed to gaze more upon their gold than upon heaven, while our sort of people, though poor, have both discovered wisdom, and have delivered their teaching to others; whence it appears that intelligence is not given to wealth, nor is gotten by study, but is begotten with the very formation of the mind. . . . What is wanted is not the authority of the arguer, but the truth of the argument itself: and even the more unskilled the discourse, the more evident the reasoning, since it is not coloured by the pomp of eloquence and grace; but as it is, it is sustained by the rule of right. (*Oct.* 16; *ANF* 4:181)

This response is particularly interesting since Minucius himself does not seem to belong to the lower classes, but to have been a highly educated person, as his style shows.

As to Cecilian's argument, that it was the gods who made Rome great, and that they therefore should not be abandoned, Octavius responds that Rome became great through theft and forcefully sacking its neighbors, and that therefore its power is not the result of its piety, but exactly the opposite. Cecilian seems to accept this understanding of the history of Rome, perhaps because he, like Octavius, is a native of one of the areas exploited by Rome. After Octavius finishes his argument, they take some time to mull over it:

> For some time we were struck into silence, and held our countenances fixed in attention and as for me, I was lost in the greatness of my admiration, that he had so adorned those things which it is easier to feel than to say, both by arguments and by examples, and by authorities derived from reading; and that he had repelled the malevolent

objectors with the very weapons of the philosophers with which they are armed, and had moreover shown the truth not only as easy, but also as agreeable. (*Oct.* 39; *ANF* 4:197)

After this pause, while Octavius remained silent, apparently waiting for Minucius to adjudge the result of the debate, Cecilian says:

I congratulate as well my Octavius as myself, as much as possible on that tranquillity in which we live, and I do not wait for the decision. Even thus we have conquered: not unjustly do I assume to myself the victory. For even as he is my conqueror, so I am triumphant over error. Therefore, in what belongs to the substance of the question, I both confess concerning providence, and I yield to God; and I agree concerning the sincerity of the way of life which is now mine. Yet even still some things remain in my mind, not as resisting the truth, but as necessary to a perfect training; of which on the morrow, as the sun is already sloping to his setting, we shall inquire at length in a more fitting and ready manner. (*Oct.* 40; *ANF* 4:197)

Finally, Minucius reports:

"But for myself," said I, "I rejoice more fully on behalf of all of us; because also Octavius has conquered for me, in that the very great invidiousness of judging is taken away from me. Nor can I acknowledge by my praises the merit of his words: the testimony both of man, and of one man only, is weak. He has an illustrious reward from God, inspired by whom he has pleaded, and aided by whom he has gained the victory."

After these things we departed, glad and cheerful: Cæcilius, to rejoice that he had believed; Octavius, that he had succeeded; and I, that the one had believed, and the other had conquered. (*Oct.* 41; *ANF* 4:197–98)

PART 3

Christian Literature
in the Third Century

Introduction to Part 3

During the third century, persecution became more systematic than before, for now for the first time the entire population was required to offer sacrifices before the gods and to carry proof that they had done so. Also, in order to stop the growth of Christianity, persecution now focused on the one hand on new converts and on the other on the leaders of the church, a policy that would lead to the great persecution of the early fourth century. In response to these conditions, several Christian authors continued the apologetic work that had begun earlier.

But there was also much other Christian literature moving in new directions and with more ambitious purposes. The most accomplished writer during this period was Origen, who is often credited with being the first author to seek to systematize all of Christian theology. At the same time, his work gave rise to discussions and clarifications that would lead to the great theological debates of the fourth century. But already in the latter half of the third century, disagreements and debates regarding the teachings of Origen took center stage in Christian theology.

There are also two important themes for which the literature of that period is of great importance. First, there was a matter of how to deal with those who abandoned the faith in times of persecution or committed some other grave sin. This became a central theme, for instance, in the writings of Cyprian and Novatian. Second, in the work of Hippolytus, the early third century also provides us with significant insights into early Christian worship, particularly regarding baptism and communion.

9

Hippolytus

HIS LIFE

Hippolytus was generally unknown and undervalued until some two centuries ago, when a series of discoveries and careful study of documents that were already known began bringing him to the foreground of theological and liturgical discussion. He seems to have been born around the year 175, and the place is not known. Details regarding his life and the list of his writings are so confused that some scholars have suggested that there were actually two persons with the same name. This is debatable, and is not a theory generally accepted. He spent much of his life in Rome, where Origen heard him preach in the year 212. At about that time he clashed with Bishop Zephyrinus (199–217), mostly on Trinitarian doctrine. Zephyrinus does not seem to have been very much interested in subtle theological matters, and during his episcopacy modalism made headway in Rome. (This was a way of understanding the Trinity that obscured the distinction among the three divine persons, claiming that each was a different mode, or face, of God.) Hippolytus opposed such views, and he felt that Zephyrinus not only tolerated but even favored them. When Zephyrinus died and his secretary Callixtus succeeded him, the controversy increased. Hippolytus accused Callixtus not only of heresy regarding the Trinity, but also of mishandling funds before becoming a secretary to Zephyrinus. Also, Callixtus was willing to readmit into the church, after requiring signs of repentance, those who were guilty of grave sins such as adultery or homicide. The result was a schism in which a party within the church in Rome elected Hippolytus as its bishop, so that now there were in the city two rival bishops. When persecution broke out under Emperor Maximinus Thrax, both Hippolytus and Callixtus's successor Pontianus were exiled, and we are told that in their exile they were reconciled. After the death of the two rivals, their remains were taken to Rome, where they were received with great honors. As a result, Hippolytus is the only antipope whom the Catholic Church lists among its saints. In the sixteenth century, in a Roman cemetery, an ancient statue of a man was discovered that bears the name of Hippolytus and also includes the titles of several of his works. This discovery was employed by scholars in order to restore to Hippolytus a number of writings that had been attributed to others.

THE *REFUTATION OF ALL HERESIES*

Hippolytus was a prolific writer. Although most of his writings have been lost, what remains is still significant. His most important extant works are the *Refutation of All Heresies*, also known as *Philosophoumena*, and the *Apostolic Tradition*. It is in the first of these two works that we find some of his strongest attacks on Callixtus. Like Tertullian before him, he was convinced that Greek philosophy had a negative influence on Christian thought and that this was the main source of heresy. The first book of the *Refutation of All Heresies* is a summary of the history of Greek philosophy, which Hippolytus seems to have known rather well. The second and third books, which have been lost, apparently continued along the same lines. The fourth describes and refutes the teachings and practices of astrologists and augurs. The remaining six books are mostly a catalog and refutation of a wide variety of heresies, mostly gnostic. Several of these are known to us only through the testimony of Hippolytus.

Finally, in the last three chapters of the last book, Hippolytus turns to an exposition of truth as he understands it. What he says here regarding the Word of God shows that, in his attempt to reject the modalism of Callixtus and others, he leans to subordinationism, so that the Word seems to be a lesser being and part of God's creation. In a strong rejection of gnostic teaching, he affirms that all that exists is God's creation. But this section also includes a strange discussion of masculine and feminine principles, in which the latter are claimed to be inferior. Thus he says, "I confess that angels are of fire, and I maintain that female spirits are not present with them" (*Refutation* 10.29; *ANF* 5:151). We also find here what we have already seen in Irenaeus and others, that the result of salvation is deification, although this is not to be interpreted in the sense that human beings become gods, but rather in the sense that they become immortal and therefore partake of that element of divinity:

And thou shalt be a companion of the Deity, and a co-heir with Christ, no longer enslaved by lusts or passions, and *never again* wasted by disease. For thou hast become God: for whatever sufferings thou didst undergo while being a man, these He gave to thee, because thou wast of mortal mould, but whatever it is consistent with God *to impart*, these God has promised to bestow upon thee, because thou hast been deified, and begotten unto immortality. (*Refutation* 10.13; *ANF* 5:153)

THE *APOSTOLIC TRADITION*

The other main work of Hippolytus, the *Apostolic Tradition*, has also had a confused history. The title of this work is among those listed on the statue found in Rome, but for a long time it was considered lost. Early in the twentieth century, several scholars came to the conclusion that a document generally known as *The Egyptian Church Order* was in fact the lost work by Hippolytus. This document had long been circulating in the Eastern churches in Coptic, Arabic, and Ethiopic translations. There is also a Latin translation dating from the fourth century. This is so literal that it can be used to reconstruct much of the original Greek text. Through these various translations, Hippolytus was instrumental in the shaping of the liturgies of the Eastern churches.

This discovery and reconstruction of the *Apostolic Tradition* has enormous importance for our knowledge of early Christian worship. At an earlier time, Justin and the *Didache* were our main sources in this respect, and both provide scant information. We also had Tertullian's *On Baptism*, of a slightly later date. Despite the numerous controversies in which Hippolytus was involved, there is no record of anyone within the church rejecting or criticizing what he says about worship practices and rites, which indicates that the practices that he describes were generally accepted and followed, at least in Rome. If one takes into account that Hippolytus was strictly conservative and was writing in order to reaffirm the worship of his youth and to make certain that the church preserved it, we may well suppose that he is describing practices that were common in the late second century. Furthermore, the *Apostolic Tradition* was one of the main sources for important later documents having to do with the worship and the organization of the church, as reflected in the Apostolic Constitutions of the fourth century. It even made a significant contribution to the liturgical renewal that took place late in the twentieth century and early in the twenty-first.

Hippolytus's conservative spirit is shown at the very beginning of the *Apostolic Tradition*, where he says that he has written it so that they who have been well trained, may, by our instruction, hold fast that tradition which has continued up to now and, knowing it well, may be strengthened. This is needful, because of that lapse or error which recently occurred through ignorance, and because of ignorant men. And [the] Holy Spirit will supply perfect grace to those who believe aright, that they may know how all things should be transmitted and kept by them who rule the church. (*Ap. Trad.* 1; trans. Burton S. Easton [Cambridge: Cambridge University Press, 1934], 33)

With this purpose in mind, the *Apostolic Tradition* begins with a discussion of the various offices in the church, and how those who occupy them are to be chosen and installed. Bishops are to be elected by the congregation and consecrated by means of the laying on of hands by other bishops. A bishop designated for that task will place his hand on the new bishop and pronounce a prayer that Hippolytus includes. After this, the bishop who has just been installed will be given the kiss of peace, and the deacons will bring to him the offertory of bread and wine for communion.

And he, laying his hand upon it, with all the presbytery, shall say as the thanksgiving:

The Lord be with you.
  And all shall say,
  And with thy spirit.
Lift up your hearts.
  We lift them up unto the Lord.
Let us give thanks to the Lord.
  It is meet and right.
    (*Ap. Trad.* 1.4; Easton, 35)

This is followed by a prayer summarizing the saving work of Jesus and the institution of communion. It is possible that some may bring wine, cheese, or olives, and in that case thanksgiving will also be pronounced over them.

The ordination of a presbyter is somewhat different, for in this case it is the bishop and the other presbyters who lay their hands on the ordinand. The deacons receive the laying on of hands from the bishop. Confessors—meaning those who have suffered and remained firm during times of persecution—who become presbyters or deacons will not receive the imposition of hands, for their confession itself has already consecrated them.

Hippolytus then turns to other offices within the church. Two of these are reserved for women, that of widow and that of virgin. A widow who decides to devote herself to the life of the church will not be acknowledged as such until she has been a widow for some time and it is clear that she will not marry again. Neither widows nor those who decide to live as virgins will have hands imposed on them, for they do not have "a sacred ministry." Likewise, those who claim to have the gift of healing will not be ordained for that purpose: "If anyone says, 'I have received the gift of healing,' hands shall not be laid upon him: the deed shall make manifest if he speaks the truth" (*Ap. Trad.* 1.15; Easton, 41).

We thus arrive at one of the most interesting sections in the *Apostolic Tradition*, dealing with new members and their admission to baptism. The text shows that the church devoted great care to the process of accepting new members. The first stage in the process was that of a "hearer." Hippolytus shows the seriousness with which this step was taken:

> New converts to the faith, who are to be admitted as hearers of the word, shall first be brought to the teachers before the people assemble. And they shall be examined as to their reason for embracing the faith, and they who bring them shall testify that they are competent to hear the word. Inquiry shall then be made as to the nature of their life; whether a man has a wife or is a slave. If he is the slave of a believer and he has his master's permission, then let him be received; but if his master does not give him a good character, let him be rejected. If his master is a heathen, let the slave be taught to please his master, that the word be not blasphemed. If a man has a wife or a woman a husband, let the man be instructed to content himself with his wife and the woman to content herself with her husband. But if a man is unmarried, let him be instructed to abstain from impurity, either by lawfully marrying a wife or else by remaining as he is. But if any man is possessed with demons, he shall not be admitted as a hearer until he is cleansed.
>
> Inquiry shall likewise be made about the professions and trades of those who are brought to be admitted to the faith. If a man is a panderer, he must desist or be rejected. If a man is a sculptor or painter, he must be charged not to make idols; if he does not desist, he must be rejected. If a man is an actor or pantomimist, he must desist or be rejected. A teacher of young children had best desist, but if he has no other occupation, he may be permitted to continue. A charioteer, likewise, who races or frequents races, must desist or be rejected. A gladiator or a trainer of gladiators, or a huntsman [in the wild beast shows], or anyone connected with these shows, or a public official in charge of gladiatorial exhibitions must desist or be rejected. A heathen priest or anyone who tends idols must desist or be rejected. A soldier of the civil authority must be taught not to kill men and to refuse to do so if he is commanded, and to refuse to take an oath; if he is unwilling to comply, he must be rejected. A military commander or civic magistrate that wears the purple must resign or be rejected. (*Ap. Trad.* 2.16; Easton, 41–42)

The list of impediments for becoming a hearer goes on. Hearers are to spend three years as catechumens, although in exceptional cases this time may be reduced. During those years, catechumens will pray in the church, the men on one side and the women on another. They will not take part in the kiss of peace, for they have not yet been purified. Women are to have the head covered by a heavy cloth, since a veil is insufficient. After this time of prayer with the rest of the church, the teachers or instructors of catechumens will lay their hands in blessing over each of their charges and dismiss them, while the church moves on to the service of the table.

Finally, after this long period of instruction and testing, the time comes to decide whether catechumens are ready to receive baptism. This decision will take place "after their lives have been examined: whether they have lived soberly, whether they have honoured the widows, whether they have visited the sick, whether they have been active in well-doing" (*Ap. Trad.* 2.20; Easton, 44). Those who have been thus approved will then prepare for their baptism with purifying ablutions on the Thursday of Holy Week, and with fasting on Good Friday. Early on Easter Sunday, those catechumens who are ready will be baptized. They will be baptized naked, first the children, then the men, and finally the women. This is the first explicit reference we have to the baptism of infants. There is no doubt that they are infants, for Hippolytus writes, "If they can speak for themselves, they shall do so; if not, their parents or other relatives shall speak for them" (*Ap. Trad.* 2.21; Easton, 45).

The rite of baptism that Hippolytus describes is not as simple as one might expect. In preparing for it, the bishop is to give thanks over a vessel of oil, called the "oil of thanksgiving," and then exorcise another vessel with "the oil of exorcism." Two deacons, each carrying one of the vessels, will stand on either side of the presbyter, who will then lead the candidate in an explicit renunciation of evil: "I renounce thee, Satan, and all thy servants and all thy work" (*Ap. Trad.* 2.21; Easton, 45). The presbyter will then anoint the candidate with the oil of exorcism and declare, "Let all spirits depart far from thee" (*Ap. Trad.* 2.21; Easton, 46). This will be followed by the act of baptism itself, in which a series of questions will be posed that reflect the evolution of the formula we now call the Apostles' Creed:

> And when he who is being baptized goes down into the water, he who baptizes him, putting his hand on him, shall say thus:
> Dost thou believe in God, the Father Almighty?
> And he who is being baptized shall say:
> I believe.
> Then, holding his hand placed on his head, he shall baptize him once. And then he shall say:
> Dost thou believe in Christ Jesus, the Son of God, who was born of the Holy Ghost of the Virgin Mary, and was crucified under Pontius Pilate, and was dead and buried, and rose again the third day, alive from the dead, and ascended into heaven, and sat at the right hand of

the Father, and will come to judge the quick and the dead? And when
he says:
    I believe,
he is baptized again. And again he shall say:
    Dost thou believe in [the] Holy Ghost, and the holy church, and
the resurrection of the flesh?
He who is being baptized shall say accordingly:
    I believe,
and so he is baptized a third time. (*Ap. Trad.* 2.21; Easton, 46–47)

Coming out of the water, the neophytes are anointed for a second time,
now with the oil of thanksgiving. After being dried and dressed, they join
the congregation, which has been gathered for some time. There they will
once again be anointed with the oil of thanksgiving, making the sign of the
cross on the neophyte's forehead. At this point they receive the kiss of peace
for the first time. Now finally considered part of the church, the neophytes
will partake for the first time in the prayer of the faithful, which they had not
been allowed to do before, for they were dismissed from services before this
point. Although Hippolytus does not explain it, other sources let us know that
this prayer of the faithful was a prayer for one another, for the entire church,
for the rest of the world, and even for the emperor who persecuted them.
The theological vision behind this practice was that the church is a priestly
people and that now, anointed as the priests of old were anointed in Israel, the
neophytes have come to be part of that people and to share in its ministry of
intercession for the rest of the world.

Then follows the celebration of communion, which is basically as has
already been described, except that on this particular occasion neophytes
will receive an additional chalice of milk and honey, indicating that they
have now entered the promised land, and another of water, indicating that
baptism is not only an outward matter but must reach into the very core of
one's being.

Communion is to be celebrated every Sunday, and all must practice fasting, particularly the widows and virgins. If some are ill and unable to attend
communion, the deacons will take it to their homes.

The rest of the *Apostolic Tradition* includes many more details and instructions regarding various ceremonies such as burials, stated times for prayer,
and offerings of firstfruits, yet deals particularly with the functions and obligations of each office, as well as instructions regarding daily meetings led by
deacons for the instruction of the faithful.

Finally, before leaving this document, one must acknowledge that the
import of some passages is still puzzling. One such case is the following
instruction:

Only certain fruits may be blessed, namely grapes, the fig, the pome-
granate, the olive, the pear, the apple, the mulberry, the peach, the
cherry, the almond, the plum. Not the pumpkin, nor the melon, nor
the cucumber, nor the onion nor garlic nor anything else having an
odour.

But sometimes flowers too are offered; here the rose and the lily
may be offered, but no other. (*Ap. Trad.* 3:28; Easton, 52)

OTHER WORKS

Hippolytus also wrote a treatise *On the Antichrist*, which is the oldest extant
discussion on the subject. He begins by warning the reader that he will be
dealing with important matters that are not to be scattered abroad or discussed
with unworthy people. Thus he recommends to a certain "Theophilus," to
whom the book is addressed: "Only see that you do not give these things over
to unbelieving and blasphemous tongues" (*Antichr.* 1; *ANF* 5:204). Also, while
insisting that such sacred things must not be given to unworthy people, Hippolytus points out that God's love is such that the divine revelation is adapted
so as to exclude no one:

> Do you wish then to know in what manner the Word of God, who
> was again the Son of God, as He was of old the Word, communicated
> His revelations to the blessed prophets in former times? Well, as the
> Word shows His compassion and His denial of all respect of persons
> by all the saints, He enlightens them and adapts them to that which is
> advantageous for us, like a skillful physician, understanding the weak-
> ness of men. And the ignorant He loves to teach, and the erring He
> turns again to His own true way. And by those who live by faith He
> is easily found; and to those of pure eye and holy heart, who desire to
> knock at the door, He opens immediately. For He casts away none of
> His servants as unworthy of the divine mysteries. He does not esteem
> the rich man more highly than the poor, nor does He despise the
> poor man for his poverty. He does not disdain the barbarian, nor
> does He set the eunuch aside as no man. He does not hate the female
> on account of the woman's act of disobedience in the beginning, nor
> does He reject the male on account of the man's transgression. But
> He seeks all, and desires to save all, wishing to make all the children
> of God, and calling all the saints unto one perfect man. (*Antichr.* 3;
> *ANF* 5:205)

The rest of the treatise is mostly a series of quotations from the prophets,
particularly from Daniel, Ezekiel, and Isaiah; and from the New Testament
book of Revelation. Apparently his purpose is to reject the notion that the

Roman Empire is the antichrist. Without defending the empire, which he believes to be the fourth beast in Daniel's vision (Dan. 7:7), Hippolytus tries to show that the antichrist is still to come.

This work set the pattern for discussions of the antichrist that many follow to this day. It is important to stress, however, that Hippolytus does not think that the antichrist is repulsive or an obvious destroyer. He is literally the anti-Christ, meaning that he tries to pass as Christ but is not Christ.

> For the deceiver seeks to liken himself in all things to the Son of God. Christ is a lion, so Antichrist is also a lion; Christ is a king, so Antichrist is also a king. The Saviour was manifested as a lamb; so he too, in like manner, will appear as a lamb, though within he is a wolf. The Saviour came into the world in the circumcision, and he will come in the same manner. The Lord sent apostles among all the nations, and he in like manner will send false apostles. The Saviour gathered together the sheep that were scattered abroad, and he in like manner will bring together a people that is scattered abroad. The Lord gave a seal to those who believed on Him, and he will give one in like manner. (*Antichr.* 6; *ANF* 5:206)

The brief writing *Against Noetus* seems to have been originally the ending of a larger work that has been lost. Very little is known about this Noetus. Apparently he was from Asia Minor, perhaps from Smyrna or Ephesus. What is clear is that he held to modalism or patripassionism, a doctrine that identifies the Father and the Son to such a point that one is led to conclude that the Father suffered the passion. According to Hippolytus, Noetus "alleged that Christ was the Father Himself, and that the Father Himself was born, and suffered, and died" (*Noet.* 10; *ANF* 5:223). Hippolytus responds that the affirmation that there is only one God does not mean that this is a lone God. The Father, without ceasing to be one, has begotten the Son and produced the Holy Spirit. God, "while existing alone, yet existed in plurality" (*Noet.* 10; *ANF* 5:226). The Son is to the Father "as a ray from the sun" (*Noet.* 11; *ANF* 5:226). However, in his zeal to refute and reject patripassionism, Hippolytus tends toward a view that subordinates the Son and the Holy Spirit to the Father, as if they were lesser beings. "It is the Father who commands, and the Son who obeys, and the Holy Spirit who gives understanding" (*Noet.* 14; *ANF* 5:228).

Only a few fragments remain of the treatise *Against Beron and Helix*. These deal mostly with the incarnation and show that on this matter Hippolytus agrees with what we have seen in Tertullian:

> And through the flesh He wrought divinely those things which are proper to divinity, showing Himself to have both those natures in

both of which He wrought, I mean the divine and the human, according to that veritable and real and natural subsistence, (showing Himself thus) as both being in reality and as being understood to be at one and the same time infinite God and finite man, having the nature of each in perfection, with the same activity, that is to say, the same natural properties; whence we know that their distinction abides always according to the nature of each, and without conversion. (*Beron and Helix* 1; *ANF* 5:231)

Hippolytus also wrote numerous Bible commentaries. Only fragments of most of them remain, and quite often in translations that are not necessarily exact. From his work on the *Song of Solomon*, for instance, all we have is commentary on the first three chapters of the biblical book, and this in a translation into Georgian of a previous translation of the original Greek into Armenian. Furthermore, the authenticity of several extant fragments is not certain. For this reason, it is difficult to say much about the biblical hermeneutics of Hippolytus.

Finally, Hippolytus composed two works on chronological matters, both inspired by practical considerations. The first is his *Chronicle*, whose purpose is to show that the end times are not as near as some claim. Adding numbers of years in the Bible, as many have done later, Hippolytus came to the conclusion that the world was created 5,738 years before the time he was writing. The six days of creation are a typology of future history: hence, before the second advent of the Lord, 6,000 years must pass, which will then be followed by the everlasting Sabbath of eternity. Therefore, writing in the year 5,768 after creation, Hippolytus concludes that the final consummation is still 262 years off. Since he was writing in 254, the end should come in 496. The *Chronicle* also includes data regarding the Mediterranean basin that Hippolytus seems to have taken from other authors.

Hippolytus's other chronological work deals with the date of Easter. It may be found in the already-mentioned inscription on his statue in Rome. Apparently he was trying to solve the debate regarding the celebration of Easter, and he was offering a way to calculate the dates when the moon would be full. Since by the middle of the fourth century these calculations did not match with observable reality, this has been used as proof that the statue in the Roman cemetery must be dated significantly earlier, probably around the year 250.

10

Origen

HIS LIFE

Origen is without question the most prolific Christian writer of the first three centuries. We have the titles of more than six thousand of his works. Although the vast majority of these have been lost, those that remain are still extensive and numerous.

Origen was born in Alexandria around the year 185, in a profoundly Christian family. During the persecution of Septimus Severus, when Origen was some seventeen years old, his father died as a martyr. Chroniclers report that young Origen wanted to accompany him in martyrdom and that in order to prevent him from doing so, his mother hid his clothes. At that time Origen wrote to his father, exhorting him to remain true to the faith, not being deterred by any consideration for the pain of his wife and children. By then young Origen was already known for his intellectual gifts, particularly for his knowledge of Holy Writ. His ascetic life gained him many admirers, Christians as well as pagans. He was some eighteen years old when Bishop Demetrius placed him at the head of the catechetical school where candidates for baptism were being prepared. Shortly thereafter, taking literally the words of Jesus about those who have made themselves eunuchs for the sake of the kingdom, he emasculated himself. Although at first Demetrius admired him for having done so, later he changed his mind.

While working at the catechetical school, Origen continued with a wide variety of studies. Among other things, he attended the lectures of the famous Platonist philosopher Ammonius Saccas, who at that time was beginning to develop what would later be called Neoplatonism. But Origen devoted himself mostly to writing. He was able to do so with the support of Ambrosius

(Ambrose), a rich believer who had been his disciple. Eusebius tells us how this contributed to Origen's vast production:

> For he dictated to more than seven amanuenses, who relieved each other at appointed times. And he employed no fewer copyists, besides girls who were skilled in elegant writing. For all these Ambrose furnished the necessary expense in abundance, manifesting himself an inexpressible earnestness in diligence and zeal for the divine oracles, by which he especially pressed him on to the preparation of his commentaries (Eusebius, *Church History* 6.23.2; *NPNF²* 1:271)

Origen was some forty-five years old when he clashed with the bishop and other leaders of the church in Alexandria because without their permission he had been ordained as a presbyter in Caesarea. The eventual result was that Origen left Alexandria and settled in Caesarea, where he spent the rest of his life. There he founded a school, and his fame became such that people came to hear him from distant places. When a debate was held in Arabia regarding the doctrine of the Trinity, he was invited there in order to resolve the issues. When, in mid-third century, the persecution of Decius was unleashed, Origen was imprisoned and tortured, although not killed. He finally died in Tyre in 253.

AGAINST CELSUS

Among the very numerous works of Origen, a good starting point is his work *Against Celsus*, an apology refuting what Celsus had said in his *True Word*. Not much is known about this Celsus, who apparently wrote late in the second century or early in the third. Origen did not know about Celsus more than what he could learn from the writing he was refuting. Reading Origen's work, we know that Celsus was a Platonist philosopher, or at least claimed to be one, for Origen declares that Celsus was not a very good philosopher. At any rate, Ambrose, Origen's financial sponsor, asked him to respond to what Celsus had written. As we begin reading *Against Celsus*, Origen says that, even though he himself is a student of classical philosophy in general, and accepts much of the teaching of the philosophers, he does not believe that mere philosophical argumentation can lead someone to faith. Although he has written this book at the request of Ambrose, he fears that someone might think that his arguments seek to lead the reader to faith. For this reason he makes it clear that he has written this book at his benefactor's request, not on his own initiative. According to Origen, since Jesus Christ himself was attacked, mocked, and killed without seeking to justify or defend himself, Christians must follow his example and not worry about defending themselves. Still, he is willing to accede to Ambrose's request:

> I know not, my pious Ambrosius, why you wished me to write a reply to the false charges brought by Celsus against the Christians, and to his accusations directed against the faith of the Churches in this treatise; as if the facts themselves did not furnish a manifest refutation, and the doctrine a better answer than any writing, seeing it both disposes of the false statements, and does not leave to the accusations any credibility or validity. (*Cels.*, Preface 1; *ANF* 4:395)

Origen continues expressing his doubts about the power of an intellectual apology to take someone to faith, and even declares, "I venture to say, then, that this 'apology' which you require me to compose will somewhat weaken that defense [of Christianity] which rests on facts" (*Cels.*, Preface 3; *ANF* 4:395). As he says, his work is not written "for those who are thorough believers, but for such as are either wholly unacquainted with the Christian faith, or . . . are weak in the faith" (*Cels.*, Preface 6; *ANF* 4:397).

It is important to underscore this, for Origen's constant use of philosophy might give the impression that he thought that faith can be reached by means of purely philosophical reasoning. This is far from the truth. While Origen did believe that God gave the Gentiles philosophy as a preparation for the gospel, he did not believe that philosophy or reasoning by themselves could lead to true faith.

This conviction is seen in the manner in which Origen responds to Celsus's argument that the sacred books of Christians are not as elegant as the writings of Plato and the philosophers, but seem rather simpleminded. Although, as we shall see later, he believed that some Christians are able to rise to higher levels of knowledge than others, Origen rejected the elitism implicit in Celsus's argument:

> Those . . . who turn away from the ignorant as being mere slaves, and unable to understand the flowing periods of a polished and logical discourse, and so devote their attention solely to such as have been brought up amongst literary pursuits, confine their views of the public good within very straight and narrow limits.
>
> I have made these remarks in reply to the charges which Celsus and others bring against the simplicity of the language of Scripture, which appears to be thrown into the shade by the splendour of polished discourse. For our prophets, and Jesus Himself, and His apostles, were careful to adopt a style of address which should not merely convey the truth, but which should be fitted to gain over the multitude, until each one, attracted and led onwards, should ascend as far as he could towards the comprehension of those mysteries which are contained in these apparently simple words. (*Cels.* 6.1–2; *ANF* 4:573)

This is the reason why, even though Celsus had claimed that he was a philosopher, and Origen himself was one of the wisest philosophers of his time,

Origen does not turn his book into a philosophical disquisition. The accusations of Celsus had to do mostly with issues such as the ignorance of Christians, the poor style of their sacred writings, their faith in miracles, and similar matters. Therefore Origen's response is not a philosophical nor a theological treatise, as Justin had written earlier, but simply a refutation of the claims of Celsus, many of them rather ridiculous and ill-informed.

ON FIRST PRINCIPLES

While Origen's apologetic work does not stand out among other writings of the same nature, the same is not true of his attempt to systematize Christian doctrine. If "systematic theology" is an organized discussion of Christian doctrine, beginning with the doctrine of God and creation and continuing to the final consummation of all things, one may well say that Origen wrote the first Christian systematic theology. His four books *On First Principles*, often known as *De principiis*, seek to expound the main doctrinal points of Christianity and should have sufficed for an adequate knowledge of his thought. Unfortunately, much of the Greek original has been lost, and what we have is a Latin translation by Rufinus dating from the late fourth century. Since in the preface to his translation Rufinus says that he has softened some of the more extreme or questionable views of Origen, in reading this work one must correlate it with the rest of Origen's corpus. Even so, in the translation by Rufinus there are still numerous speculations that most Christians would reject. This explains why Origen, who certainly was the most outstanding ancient Christian writer, has repeatedly been declared to have been a heretic.

Origen makes it quite clear that, while he is a firm believer in the teachings of the church, he also feels the need to inquire further about those matters that the apostles did not discuss.

> Now it ought to be known that the holy apostles, in preaching the faith of Christ, delivered themselves with the utmost clearness on certain points which they believed to be necessary to every one, even to those who seemed somewhat dull in the investigation of divine knowledge; leaving, however, the grounds of their statements to be examined into by those who should deserve the excellent gifts of the Spirit, and who, especially by means of the Holy Spirit Himself, should obtain the gift of language, of wisdom, and of knowledge: while on other subjects they merely stated the fact that things were so, keeping silence as to the manner or origin of their existence; clearly in order that the more zealous of their successors, who should be lovers of wisdom, might have a subject of exercise on which to display the fruit of their

> talents,—those persons, I mean, who should prepare themselves to be fit and worthy receivers of wisdom. (*Princ.*, Preface 3; *ANF* 4:239)

Later he adds:

> This also is a part of the Church's teaching, that the world was made and took its beginning at a certain time, and is to be destroyed on account of its wickedness. But what existed before this world, or what will exist after it, has not become certainly known to the many, for there is no clear statement regarding it in the teaching of the Church. (*Princ.*, Preface 7; *ANF* 4:240–41)

Origen is well aware of his superior intellect and is convinced that he is one of those to whom the Holy Spirit has granted the gift of being able to delve more deeply into apostolic teachings. This is the purpose of the entire treatise.

As was to be expected, Origen begins by discussing God and the divine nature. He affirms the Trinity, although interpreting divinity in the Platonic terms that by his time were becoming increasingly common among Christians. Thus, God is a pure intellectual nature, incomprehensible and incommensurable, and all that one can say about God is mere analogy, for God cannot be compared to anything else. This is why we must look to God's works as a sign of God's grandeur:

> Our eyes frequently cannot look upon the nature of the light itself— that is, upon the substance of the sun; but when we behold his splendour or his rays pouring in, perhaps, through windows or some small openings to admit the light, we can reflect how great is the supply and source of the light of the body. So, in like manner, the works of Divine Providence and the plan of this whole world are a sort of rays, as it were, of the nature of God, in comparison with His real substance and being. (*Princ.* 1.1.6; *ANF* 4:243)

Most of the first book of *On First Principles*, and a goodly part of the second, is devoted to this discussion of God's nature. What Origen says here is what many Christians have taught: God is immaterial, existing as Father, Son, and Holy Spirit. The manner in which Origen distinguishes among these three has to do with how they relate to creation, for creatures, "firstly, . . . derive their existence from God the Father; secondly, their rational nature from the Word; thirdly, their holiness from the Holy Spirit" (*Princ.* 1.3.8; *ANF* 4:255).

In chapter 8 of his second book, Origen begins laying out some of his particular views, many of which have been repeatedly rejected by most Christians. The subject of this chapter is the soul. For Origen, as for most thinkers in his time, the word "soul" refers to the principle of life in all living beings. All that has life, including the fish of the sea and the beasts of the field, has a soul. But, as Origen points out, most biblical references to the soul do not refer to its goodness or its eternity, but rather to its pain, anguish, and sin. Making use of a false etymology, Origen explains that the word "soul" (*psychē*) is related to a verb meaning "to cool," and that therefore a soul is an intellectual being that has cooled off and thereby lost its original nature. In other words, God originally created pure intellects or "understandings," and those among such intellects that have fallen are what we now call souls. He takes this to mean "that the understanding, falling away from its status and dignity, was made or named soul; and that, if repaired, and corrected, it returns to the condition of the understanding" (*Princ.* 2.8.3; *ANF* 4:288). This is a clear indication of Origen being influenced by the Platonic myth regarding the preexistence of souls, which for some reason have fallen into this world. Translating this myth into Christian vocabulary, Origen sees the soul as a fallen spirit. He supports this view by turning to the two stories of creation that appear in Genesis. Following the duality of those stories, Origen says that there are actually two creations—a point made earlier by Philo of Alexandria. In the first narrative in Genesis, God "made" the human being, while in the second God "shaped" that being. The first then refers to the original creation of intellectual reality, and not to the body. In another of his writings, Origen says:

> It is our inner being, which is incorporeal, invisible, incorruptible and immortal, that has been made after the image of God, and therefore it is thus that the image of God is to be interpreted. Let no one imagine that it is in the flesh that humanity has been made after the image of God, for this would fall into the egregious error of claiming that God has human flesh and form. (*Homilies on Genesis* 1.13; PG 12:55)

This is why the first story in Genesis—when the man, the male, had not yet been created—says that God made the human being "male and female." What this means is that in that original pure intellectual creation there were no gender differences. Origen interprets the words "male and female" as an allegory: "The inner, incorporeal human being is made of spirit and soul, of which the first is masculine and the latter is feminine. When these two are in joined in harmony they produce children, but which is meant a good will, a sound understanding, and valuable thoughts. These fill the earth and rule over it" (ibid. 1.15; PG 12:158).

However, that originally purely intellectual or spiritual creation did not remain as such. Some of those intellects that God had created "cooled off," or strayed from God. As a consequence, they have fallen and become souls. Since they did not all fall to the same degree, some of them are now human souls and others are demons. Among those that are human souls, some have been given a male body and some a female body.

On this basis, Origen develops an entire philosophy of history in which all that is taking place, and the final result of the work of Christ, is the restoration of fallen intellects to their original purity. However, it is important to stress that Origen does not claim this to be a doctrine that all should accept, but only a personal speculation which others must examine and judge: "Our statement, however, that the understanding is converted into a soul, or whatever else seems to have such a meaning, the reader must carefully consider and settle for himself, as these views are not to be regarded as advanced by us in a dogmatic manner, but simply as opinions, treated in the style of investigation and discussion" (*Princ.* 2.8.4; *ANF* 4:288–89).

All human history, from the creation of this material world to its final consummation, is a process whereby God is restoring souls to their original condition as pure spirits or intellects. In this history, each must go through a process of sanctification. Part of that process brings the good works that the Holy Spirit produces in humans. But also part of it is a purification as if by fire, just as illness results in fever, but fever itself is part of a process of healing. It is of this that the Bible speaks when it refers to hell. Hell is not a place of permanent punishment, but a place where souls are purified so that they may be able to return to their original condition. Ultimately salvation is universal, for the essence of salvation is being subject to God. "The end of the world, then, and the final consummation, will take place when every one shall be subjected to punishment for his sins; a time which God alone knows, when He will bestow on each one what he deserves. We think, indeed, that the goodness of God, through His Christ, may recall all His creatures to one end, even His enemies being conquered and subdued" (*Princ.* 1.6.1; *ANF* 4:260).

Origen believes this will be the case because the end must be like the beginning, and original perfection must be restored. If at the beginning there were only pure intellects, the same will be true at the end. But if we remember that one of the main characteristics of intellects is freedom, the logical consequence is that there may well be other worlds, other falls, and other restorations before and after the present one.

WORKS ON THE BIBLE

The works of Origen that have drawn most interest are his volumes *Against Celsus* and *On First Principles*. And those aspects of his thought that have provoked most discussion are his daring speculations. However, Origen always thought of himself as a student of the Bible. This is clear when one looks first at the *Hexapla* and then at his numerous and extensive commentaries. The *Hexapla* was an edition of the Old Testament in six parallel columns. The first was the Hebrew text, followed then by another column transliterating the Hebrew into Greek, and then other columns, each including a different Greek translation. In some cases, when other translations were available, there were more than six columns. In order to signal the differences and relationships among the various texts, Origen employed a series of symbols that had been developed earlier by Alexandrine scholars to use in their study of classical texts. Given the enormous size of this work, which may have been some seven thousand pages, it is probable that it was never copied in its entirety and that therefore it had very little circulation. The complete text existed only in Caesarea, where Origen had produced it and where later scholars such as Eusebius of Caesarea and Jerome had access to it. That copy seems to have been destroyed during the Arab invasions in the seventh century, and all that remains of the *Hexapla* are fragments discovered among the manuscripts in various libraries.

Although the *Hexapla* has earned Origen the title of forerunner of textual criticism, his original purpose was different. We see this in a letter that Origen wrote to Sextus Julius Africanus, who had come to Alexandria following Origen's fame. Julius wrote to Origen, pointing out that in his commentary on Daniel, Origen included the episode of Susanna, which does not appear in the original Hebrew text. Origen answered that it is not only this passage that does not appear in the Hebrew text, but also, in the same book of Daniel, the episodes of Bel and the Dragon, and many others in books such as Esther and Job. While Origen defends the presence of such passages in the canon and their authority, he also explains that in the *Hexapla*, which he compiled mostly for his own use,

> I make it my endeavour not to be ignorant of their various readings, lest in my controversies with the Jews I should quote to them what is not found in their copies, and that I may make some use of what is found there, even although it should not be in our Scriptures. For if we are so prepared for them in our discussions, they will not, as is their manner, scornfully laugh at Gentile believers for their ignorance of the true reading as they have them. (*Ep. Afr.* 5; *ANF* 4:387)

The reason why Origen devoted so much time to this vast work was that he saw it as a tool for his ultimate purpose, which was to study Scripture and comment on it. Most of his commentaries have been lost, and we know of them only through references and quotations from later writers. Among many others, this includes commentaries on Genesis, Psalms, Isaiah, Lamentations, Ezekiel, and the minor prophets, as well as on several books in the New Testament: Luke, Galatians, Ephesians, and several other epistles. Approximately a third of his commentaries on Matthew and John are still extant. We have much more of his commentary on Romans, but this only in a Latin text, which is not completely trustworthy, for here once again the translator Rufinus seems to have felt free to amend the texts.

As one reads these commentaries, it is clear that—yet in a great variety of manners—Origen applies what he says in *On First Principles* regarding biblical interpretation. There, seeking to overcome the difficulties posed by a literal reading of many biblical passages, he says that Scripture may be read at three different levels:

> The individual ought, then, to portray the ideas of holy Scripture in a threefold manner upon his own soul; in order that the simple man may be edified by the "flesh," as it were, of the Scripture, for so we name the obvious sense; while he who has ascended a certain way [may be edified] by the "soul," as it were. The perfect man . . . [may receive edification] from the spiritual law, which has a shadow of good things to come. For as man consists of body, and soul, and spirit, so in the same way does Scripture, which has been arranged to be given by God for the salvation of men. (*Princ.* 4.1.11; *ANF* 4:359)

The historical, literal, or "corporeal" meaning of the text is not to be simply ignored, for it has much to teach. But whenever that meaning is contrary to the divine nature or to the rest of Scripture, it must be left aside in order to seek the true spiritual teaching of a passage.

At any rate, what a discerning reader ought to seek in the Bible is its moral and spiritual teachings, which generally correspond to what Origen calls the second and third levels of meaning—although this tripartite scheme does not seem always to apply, for on occasion Origen seems to imply that there is a single symbolic meaning, and at some other times he finds a wide variety of such spiritual meanings.

The result of this is that the most common interpretation of Scripture is allegorical, and this became a hallmark of Origen's hermeneutics. Just as for a long time pagan commentaries on classical Greek literature had employed allegory in order to find hidden teachings in the works of Homer and others, now Origen employed the same method both to find teachings in sacred texts and to refute those who criticized those texts because much was found in them that did not seem to be worthy of the God of Christians.

The passages in which Origen applies this principle of multiple levels of meaning are numerous. One example may be what he says about the story of Noah and the ark. On approaching this story, Origen announces that he will be interpreting it at several different levels: "As we consider the story of the ark that God ordered Noah to build, we must first deal with the story as it is told, then with the questions that many have posed, seeking answers in what we have learned from our forebearers. Having done that, we can finally rise from the literal narrative to an allegorical and mystical understanding of the spiritual meaning of the text, trying to deal with anything that may be mysterious as the Lord guides us" (*Homilies on Genesis* 2.1; PG 12:161). Origen then proceeds to inquire about a long series of details regarding the ark, such as what its shape was, how many tiers it had, how its wood was joined, and many others. Referring to previous interpreters, but without quoting them, he also raises the question of how so many animals were to be fed for an entire year, and how to keep wild and ferocious beasts away from tame and domesticated ones. Finally, still at the historical or literal level, Origen points out that according to Genesis it was God who closed the door of the ark, and he explains that this was so that it could be sealed from the outside and water could not enter.

Origen affirms and defends this literal meaning. Responding to the objections of the followers of Marcion, who said that this could not be a true word of God because it was impossible to ship so many animals in a single vessel, Origen refers to ancient Egyptian knowledge and theories, attempting to show that what the passage says is not impossible.

But then he moves to what he really finds interesting. The flood is a sign of the end times, when once again all of God's enemies will be destroyed. The ark is a sign of salvation within the church. But this is not enough for Origen, who then moves on to give a supposedly spiritual significance to various details in the text:

> Those who are saved in the church are like the people and animals that were saved in the ark. Since advancement in the faith and merits are not the same in all, the ark does not place them all together. There are two lower decks and three above. Also in the church progress is uneven, even though all belong to the church by the same faith, having been washed in the same baptism. The few who lead a rational life, ruling themselves and teaching others, are like those who are saved with Noah and are close to him, just as the true Noah, our Lord, has few close friends, children, and relatives. These receive his word and wisdom. They have the higher deck in the ark. In the lower levels there are many irrational and ferocious beasts whose wrath has not been bound by the beauty of faith—and here too some are above others for, while being irrational, they remain innocent and open-hearted. As we then rise through the various decks of the ark, we finally come of Noah, whose name means Just, and is Jesus Christ. (Ibid.; PG 12:170)

But Origen is not satisfied with this. Every feature of the ark has a spiritual meaning. The solid pieces of wood are those church leaders who remained firm in spite of every threat. Origen defends this interpretation by affirming that, in Scripture, trees and their wood are a sign of wisdom and firmness. In the spiritual ark, firm and wise leaders are like the boards that face the fury of the elements. The tar employed to caulk the ark is the purity and innocence that make it possible for these firm boards to remain sealed. As to the dimensions of the ark, Origen undertakes a lengthy discussion as to the meaning of width, length, and depth in Scripture. He comes to the conclusion that the 300 cubits of length are 3×100. The rational number par excellence is 100, and it therefore refers to the rational creature. Yet this 100 does not exist out of itself, but is rather the work of the Trinity. Hence the 300. The 50 cubits of width are a reference to forgiveness, for according to the law there was a general forgiveness every 50th year, when those who had sold their properties received them back, and slaves were returned to freedom. Therefore Christ, as the spiritual Noah and in his perfect ark, which is the church, saves humankind from destruction.

This should suffice to show how far Origen's allegorical interpretation is able to carry him. Each word, each number, and each detail have a hidden meaning that only the enlightened can discover. Just as here Origen declares that the planks and various numbers have a specific meaning, elsewhere he affirms that the word "horse" means strength, and that wherever we encounter the word "cloud," we are to understand that God is speaking.

In brief, Origen's biblical commentaries show him as a person of great erudition and an equally vast imagination so that, while he is able to quote Scripture repeatedly and in detail, what he says about it is not exactly what the text says, but what Origen sees in it. This has led some scholars to declare that, for Origen, the Bible itself is like a great puzzle whose solution only Origen knows.

OTHER WORKS

Although his commentaries and homilies are most of what is still extant of Origen's vast production, we must remember that he also wrote more practical treatises on subjects such as prayer and martyrdom. He also carried on a vast correspondence, of which only two letters remain. One of them is the already-quoted letter to Sextus Julius Africanus, and the other is a letter to Gregory the Wonderworker, to which we shall refer in the next chapter.

The significance of Origen's work is enormous. His impact may be seen throughout the history of Greek theology. But his venturesome speculations and his frequently exaggerated allegorical interpretations resulted in a situation in which, while much theology still bears his imprint, much of that very theology rejects Origen's teachings.

11

Other Greek Authors

Origen's impact on Eastern theology was such that throughout the third century most Greek writers were either his followers or his critics.

GREGORY THE WONDERWORKER

One of Origen's most distinguished disciples was Gregory the Wonderworker, or Gregory Thaumaturgus. Among other works, he wrote a *Panegyric to Origen* in which, after describing his mentor's teaching methods, he tells the story of how divine Providence took him to Caesarea, where he met Origen. On the basis of what he says in this work, as well as from other sources in ancient literature, it seems that Gregory was a native of Neocaesarea in Pontus. His original name was apparently Theodore, but after his baptism he came to be known as Gregory. His family was part of the middle aristocracy of the area. A high functionary had forced Gregory's brother-in-law to move to Beirut and serve him. After some time, the brother-in-law was able to send officers to Neocaesarea to bring his wife to Beirut. Gregory, who by then was interested in the study of law, decided to travel with his sister and a brother, partly because he wished to protect her, and partly because there was in Beirut a famous law school. But upon arriving in Caesarea, the group met Origen, who immediately captivated them. As Gregory tells the story, they were "drawn towards him by the power of his reasonings, as by the force of some superior necessity" (*Paneg.* 6; *ANF* 6:27). Gregory's family was pagan, but for some time he had been in quest of a higher truth. At any rate, his meeting with Origen and his teachings led Gregory to Christianity. He tells of this experience as follows:

> And thus, like some spark lighting upon our inmost soul, love was kindled and burst into flame within us,—a love at once to the Holy Word, the most lovely object of all, who attracts all irresistibly toward Himself by His unutterable beauty, and to this man, His friend and advocate. And being most mightily smitten by this love, I was persuaded to give up all those objects or pursuits which seem to us befitting, and among others even my boasted jurisprudence. (*Paneg.* 6; *ANF* 6:28)

Apparently Gregory made this speech around the year 238, as he was readying to leave Caesarea and return to Neocaesarea. Shortly thereafter he became bishop of this city and was quite successful in its evangelization. So many miracles and marvels were associated with his name that he came to be known as Gregory the Wonderworker. Shortly after his death, Gregory of Nyssa wrote a *Life of Gregory* recounting many of his reputed miracles. In this work, the younger Gregory included a declaration of faith that came to be one of the most oft-quoted writings of the Wonderworker:

> There is one God, the Father of the living Word, *who is His* subsistent Wisdom and Power and Eternal Image: perfect Begetter of the perfect *Begotten*, Father of the only-begotten Son. There is one Lord, Only of the Only, God of God, Image and Likeness of Deity, Efficient Word, Wisdom comprehensive of the constitution of all things, and Power formative of the whole creation, true Son of true Father, Invisible of Invisible, and Incorruptible of Incorruptible, and Immortal of Immortal, and Eternal of Eternal. And there is One Holy Spirit, having His subsistence from God, and being made manifest by the Son, to wit to men: Image of the Son, Perfect *Image* of the Perfect; Life, the Cause of the living; Holy Fount; Sanctity, the Supplier, *or Leader*, of Sanctification; in whom is manifested God the Father, who is above all and in all, and God the Son, who is through all. There is a perfect Trinity, in glory and eternity and sovereignty, neither divided nor estranged. Wherefore there is nothing either created or in servitude in the Trinity; nor anything superinduced, as if at some former period it was non-existent, and at some later period it was introduced. And thus neither was the Son ever wanting to the Father, nor the Spirit to the Son; but without variation and without change, the same Trinity *abideth* ever. (*Life of Gregory* 4.72; *ANF* 6:7)

The very fact that Gregory of Nyssa chose this document to quote fully is a sign that one of the main problems we have in trying to recover the work of Eastern Christian writers from this point onward is that during the fourth century, the time of Gregory of Nyssa, Eastern theology was overwhelmed by debates regarding the Trinity. This led authors during the fourth century to read the writings of their predecessors in the third century, looking above all for what they had said on the Trinity. Likewise, copyists gave preference to the writings dealing with that subject. As a result, as we study the work of Christian writers after Origen, we are generally limited to the documents that seemed to be most important during the Trinitarian debates. This is part of the reason why Gregory of Nyssa preserved the Wonderworker's declaration of faith.

Partly for the same reason, two theological treatises of Gregory the Wonderworker have survived. The first, *To Theopompus*, deals with "the impassibility and passibility of God." The second, *To Philagrius*, deals with the consubstantial existence of the persons of the Trinity.

The first of these two treatises is a dialogue that has come to us in a Syriac translation. Gregory says that on the way home he met a certain Theopompus, who asked him if God is impassible. Gregory gave him a quick answer, but his interlocutor was not content with this, followed him home, and there asked for more details. Briefly stated, the problem is that divine impassibility would seem to make God incapable of responding to human passions and events. As a dialogue develops, Gregory argues that God's will is not limited by impassibility as humans understand it. God's sovereign power is such that the impassible can share human passions. Obviously, what is at stake here is the possibility of the incarnation, in which God comes to participate in the passions and sufferings of humanity. As Gregory says:

> Those who want to find fault with this supreme wisdom and this will, hidden in its majesty from everyone; who deny the surpassing power of that God by whose death impassibility was extended to all men; who mock God's arrival at death, and do not understand that the surpassing brightness of his coming must be contemplated with the eye of their mind; and who therefore suppose that this incomprehensible and inconceivable arrival of God at death, without corruption, is a foolish story—these are stuck in darkness in their erroneous understanding, destined to death and corruption. For on account of [God's] impassibility he has no part in mortality, and because of his immortality he can fearlessly tread death underfoot. (Gregory Thaumaturgus, *Life and Works*, ed. Thomas P. Halton, trans. Michael Slusser, Fathers of the Church 98 [Washington, DC: Catholic University of America Press, 1998], 160)

Gregory continues his argument by pointing out that in Greek history there are many who offered their life for a great cause and are now admired. Even without needing the admiration of others, this is what God does. The glory of God is not only in power and impassibility, but also in a power that, joined with divine love, which makes it possible for God to join human pain. In brief, Gregory tells Theopompus that he must not think that God "is turned towards himself and wallows in himself, with the result that he does nothing and allows others to do nothing" (Slusser, 170). And the dialogue then ends with a word of praise for the incarnate God:

> He came therefore, O happy one, Jesus came, who is king over all things, that he might heal the difficult passions of human beings, being the most blessed and generous one. But yet he remained what he is, and the passions were destroyed by his impassibility, as darkness is destroyed by light. He came therefore, he came in haste, to make people blessed and rich in good things, immortals instead of mortals, and has renewed and re-created them blessed forever. To him who is the glorious king be glory forever. Amen. (Slusser, 172–73)

The authorship of the much briefer *To Philagrius*, which has also come to us in a Syriac translation, is debated: some scholars attribute it to Gregory of Nyssa, and others to Gregory Nazianzen. Apparently Philagrius, of whom no more is known, wrote Gregory to ask how the one true God could be Father, Son, and Holy Spirit. Gregory is not willing to accept an easy solution that "the substance undergoes a passion of division corresponding to the application of the names" (*To Philagrius* 3; Slusser, 175). There is only one divine substance, but this is no reason to reject the tripartite formula of "Father, Son, and Holy Spirit." To explain this, Gregory refers to ideas that exist within the mind. These ideas are all different, but each of them is the totality of the mind. "For as no division or cleft is conceived of between mind and idea and soul, so neither is cleft or division conceived of between the Holy Spirit and the Savior and the Father" (*To Philagrius* 3; Slusser, 176–77). After adding several other examples, Gregory explains that his treatise is brief because those with full understanding need no more.

Finally, before leaving Gregory the Wonderworker, one must note that we also have from his pen a paraphrase of the book of Ecclesiastes and a letter commonly known as his *Canonical Epistle* because it is included among the canons of the Eastern church. This epistle, whose addressee is unknown and was probably another bishop, was written when a Germanic invasion brought chaos to the area. There were some whose consciences were uneasy because when they were prisoners of the invaders, they had eaten meat sacrificed to idols. Some felt that women who had been raped by the invaders were defiled. And Gregory's main concern was that some took the opportunity of the circumstances to become rich at the expense of others. Gregory's epistle deals with these various issues, declaring that, according to Deuteronomic law, a woman who has been raped bears no guilt. And, basing his argument on the apostle Paul, Gregory affirms that the prisoners who had eaten meat from the sacrifices were blameless. Much more serious is the case of those who have profited from the invasion to take what was not theirs. "This is a thing which can be averred only of men who are impious and hated of God and of unsurpassable iniquity" (*Canonical Epistle* 2; *ANF* 6:18). Such people, and others who have equally practiced malice, must be disciplined and punished by the church. This is the reason for Gregory's epistle, seeking to lead a colleague to know what he (Gregory) is doing about those who have committed such sins, so that Gregory's own practice may serve as a guide for his colleague. Gregory recommends that those who profited from the invasion and worked with the invaders for the death or sacking of others must be excluded from the church, where they will not even be accepted as "hearers" until a synod gathers to decide on the matter. Those who took people's homes, if they confess their sin and restore what they stole, may be included among the penitents. And at any rate those who kept the commandments and did not take what was not theirs should not expect any particular reward, for they simply did what is expected of a true believer.

SEXTUS JULIUS AFRICANUS

Little is known of the life of Sextus Julius Africanus. He was born in Jerusalem (at that time called Aelia Capitolina) to a pagan family and remained a pagan for most of his life. He served as a soldier under Alexander Severus and apparently gained the respect of the emperor, who entrusted him with creating a library for his use. When the legions of Alexander Severus invaded the kingdom of Edessa, Sextus Julius Africanus accompanied them. Apparently there he met King Abgarus (Abgar), the earliest Christian ruler on record. Nothing is known about Africanus's conversion. We know that he went to Alexandria, seeking wisdom. There he became a disciple of Origen. The already-mentioned letter from Africanus to Origen is one of two of his letters that have been preserved. The other is known to us in fragmentary fashion because Eusebius of Caesarea quoted it extensively.

In that second letter, addressed to a certain Aristides, Africanus discusses the apparent disagreement between the genealogies of Jesus as they appear in Matthew and in Luke. Africanus offers an interesting solution. He claims that the differences are explained on the basis of the ancient tradition in Israel that, if a man dies without leaving sons, his wife should join the brother of the deceased in order to provide heirs. Those who were born from such unions bore the name of the deceased, but were also children of the brother who had taken his place. Africanus believes that this explains the differences between two genealogies.

Africanus's most important work was a *Chronicle* in which he told the history of humankind up to his own time. This writing, of which only fragments remain, was based on the notion that the Savior had come 5,500 years after creation. Following that scheme, Africanus records parallel events that were taking place at each time, not only in Israel, but also throughout the Hellenistic world. The longest extant fragment, several pages long, refers to what was taking place in Persia at the time of Jesus' birth. Although he seems to have known something about Persia and its religion, Africanus is most interested in the reaction of persons when they saw the star announcing the birth of Jesus, and in the sending of the magi with gifts for the child.

FIRMILIAN OF CAESAREA

Firmilian, widely respected bishop of Caesarea in Cappadocia, was also an admirer and disciple of Origen. According to Eusebius of Caesarea and Jerome, Firmilian invited Origen to visit him, and then he went to see the famous scholar in Caesarea of Palestine. According to Jerome, Firmilian remained with Origen in Palestine for quite some time. He also seems to have played an important role in the debates and the synodical decisions surrounding the teachings of Paul of Samosata.

Unfortunately, all that remains of his writings is a letter that he addressed to Cyprian of Carthage—to whom we shall devote another chapter. According to this letter, it was written in response to another from Cyprian to Firmilian, which has been lost. Thus Firmilian's letter is included in Cyprian's epistolary, as number 74 in some editions and 75 in others. The subject of the letter is a debate regarding the validity of baptism received from heretics. Stephen, the bishop of Rome, had affirmed that such baptism is valid and that therefore heretics who had been baptized in the name of the Father, of the Son, and of the Holy Spirit and decided to join the church were not to be rebaptized. Cyprian and the bishops of North Africa rejected that position, and therefore Stephen had broken communion with them. In his letter, Firmilian supports Cyprian and assures him that the same is the position of the bishops of Cappadocia. He also complains that, while there has always been room for different opinions within the church, now Stephen has allowed that diversity to lead to schism:

> But that they who are at Rome do not observe those things in all cases which are handed down from the beginning, and vainly pretend the authority of the apostles; any one may know also from the fact, that concerning the celebration of Easter, and concerning many other sacraments of divine matters, he may see that there are some diversities among them, and that all things are not observed among them alike, which are observed at Jerusalem, just as in very many other provinces also many things are varied because of the difference of the places

and names. And yet on this account there is no departure at all from the peace and unity of the Catholic Church, such as Stephen has now dared to make; breaking the peace against you, which his predecessors have always kept with you in mutual love and honour. (Cyprian, *Ep.* 74 [75].6.1; *ANF* 5:391)

DIONYSIUS OF ALEXANDRIA

The most distinguished of Origen's successors in Alexandria was Dionysius, commonly known as "the Great." Dionysius was born into a pagan family in Alexandria, and his conversion, as described by his biographers, is extraordinary. As they say, he remained a pagan throughout his youth until he had a vision from God telling him to study the writings of heretics in order to refute them and defend the doctrines of the church. At that point the bishop of Alexandria was Heraclas, and Origen was not yet facing the conflicts that would eventually make him move to Caesarea. Therefore, Dionysius studied both with Heraclas and with Origen. When Origen left, Dionysius was put in charge of catechetical work. When Heraclas died, Dionysius became bishop of Alexandria.

Unfortunately, most of the writings of Dionysius have been lost. What remains is mostly the result of the admiration of Eusebius of Caesarea, who devoted to Dionysius an entire book of his *Church History*, quoting him extensively. We also have quite a few of his quotations preserved by Athanasius, although they refer mostly to the correspondence that took place between Dionysius of Alexandria and Dionysius of Rome regarding the doctrine of the Trinity.

Dionysius was a faithful follower of Origen's allegorical method. This became clear when an Egyptian bishop by the name of Nepos wrote a *Refutation of the Allegorists*. In it he argued that "the promises to the holy men in the Divine Scriptures should be understood in a more Jewish manner" (Eusebius, *Church History* 7.24.1; *NPNF*[2] 1:218). This gave rise to a controversy in which Dionysius came to the defense of his Alexandrine teachers and their allegorical interpretations. The result was an extensive discussion of his writing *On the Promises*, in which Dionysius refuted the arguments of Nepos and others. Although this has been lost, we have extensive quotes from Eusebius. Here Dionysius tells of a prolonged meeting that took place in the Egyptian region of Arsinoe, where there was great opposition to allegorical interpretations. Apparently the conversation was friendly and respectful, for Dionysius declares, "I rejoiced over the constancy, sincerity, docility, and intelligence of the brethren, as we considered in order and with moderation the questions and the difficulties and the points of agreement. And we abstained from defending in every manner and contentiously the opinions which we had once held, unless they appeared to be correct" (Eusebius, *Ch. Hist.* 7.24.8; *NPNF²* 1:218).

Since part of the debate had to do with the interpretation of the Revelation of John, Dionysius wrote extensively on the subject, coming to the interesting conclusion that Revelation must have hidden meanings, even though he himself could not fathom them: "But I could not venture to reject the book, as many brethren hold it in high esteem. But I suppose that it is beyond my comprehension, and that there is a certain concealed and more wonderful meaning in every part" (Eusebius, *Ch. Hist.* 7.25.4; *NPNF²* 1:218).

This leads him to discuss the authorship of Revelation, which produces the following conclusion:

> Therefore that he was called John, and that this book is the work of one John, I do not deny. And I agree also that it is the work of a holy and inspired man. But I cannot readily admit that he was the apostle, the son of Zebedee, the brother of James, by whom the Gospel of John and the Catholic Epistle were written.
>
> But I am of the opinion that there were many with the same name as the apostle John, who, on account of their love for him, and because they admired and emulated him, and desired to be loved by the Lord as he was, took to themselves the same surname, as many of the children of the faithful are called Paul or Peter. (Eusebius, *Ch. Hist.* 7.25.14; *NPNF²* 1:309–10)

Several other fragments of letters and biblical commentaries by Dionysius are quoted by later authors. The most important of these are four books that he wrote to the bishop of Rome, also called Dionysius. Apparently someone had declared that when Dionysius of Alexandria refuted patripassionism, he had made an excessive distinction between the Father and the Son, appearing not to believe in the full divinity of the Son. When Dionysius of Rome heard about this, he inquired about the matter from Dionysius of Alexandria. The latter's answer, at least in the quotations preserved, is clear. Athanasius reports:

> "For never was there a time when God was not a father." And this he acknowledges in what follows, "that Christ is for ever, being Word and Wisdom and Power. For it is not to be supposed that God, having at first no such issue, afterwards begat a Son, but that the Son has His being not of Himself but of the Father." And a little way on he adds on the same subject, "But being the brightness of light eternal, certainly He is Himself eternal; for as the light exists always, it is evident that the brightness must exist always as well. For it is by the fact of its shining that the existence of light is perceived, and there cannot be light that does not give light." (Athanasius, *On the Opinion of Dionysius* 15; *NPNF²* 4:182)

This correspondence between Dionysius of Alexandria and Dionysius of Rome took center stage in the fourth century, with its high interest precisely in the relationship among the three divine persons. For that reason, Athanasius quoted Dionysius of Alexandria extensively.

OTHER SUCCESSORS OF ORIGEN

The impact of Origen and his work was enormous. Besides those already mentioned, several other writers in the third century continued his work, while others criticized and attacked it. In Alexandria itself, Theognostus succeeded Dionysius as director of the catechetical school. His writings have been lost, but he seems to have been a faithful follower of Origen. Pierius, whom some considered a lesser Origen, wrote a lost *Life of Pamphilus*, a man whom many considered to be an outstanding follower of Origen. Toward the turn of the century, Bishop Peter, who apparently had been a teacher in the famous catechetical school of Alexandria, criticized Origen in a series of works, but only very short fragments thereof remain. The above-mentioned Pamphilus, originally from Beirut, went to study in Alexandria under Pierius and then settled in Caesarea, where he took up the task of keeping and augmenting the library that Origen had left. That library was the main source for the work of Eusebius of Caesarea.

During the third century, the main opponents of Origen and his teachings were Paul of Samosata and Methodius of Olympus. No complete work of Paul has survived, and most of the remaining fragments seem to be spurious. At any rate, it is clear that Paul opposed Origen both for his allegorical interpretations and for the manner in which he and most Eastern bishops understood the divinity of the Son. According to Paul, instead of speaking about Jesus Christ as the incarnate Word of God, one should speak of Jesus as a human being in whom the power of God dwelled. In both of these points he seems to have been a precursor of the Antiochene school that would flourish in the next century.

Much more remains of the work of Methodius of Olympus, although very little is known of his life. Some say that he was bishop of Tyre and others say of Lycia. It is almost certain that he died as a martyr early in the fourth century. His one work that has been preserved in its entirety is the *Banquet of the Ten Virgins*, or *Symposium on Chastity*. This is a dialogue, in imitation of Plato, whose main purpose is to exalt virginity as a moral value. According to Methodius, at the beginning God ordered that people multiply because the earth was empty. This is also why polygamy, the marriage of siblings, and other such practices that are now prohibited were allowed. Finally, virginity "was sent down to men from heaven, and for this reason it was not revealed to the first generations" (*Symp.* 1.2; *ANF* 6:311). His work is also interesting because most of those speaking are women. It all ends with a long hymn by a woman named Thecla, while the others respond as a chorus.

The other works of Methodius subsist only in fragmentary fashion. It is here that he criticizes the exegetical method of Origen and his purely spiritual eschatology, which seems to leave no room for the resurrection of the body. Methodius also rejects Origen's most extreme ideas, such as the preexistence of souls. But even so, Methodius is like Origen in basing much of his thought on Platonic philosophy.

Quite apart from the work of Origen, although sometimes employing some of his methods, late in the third century and early in the fourth, literature began appearing against Manicheism. The founder of this religion, Manes, lived in Persia in the third century, and already by the year 280 his faith was expanding westward, into the Roman Empire, as well as toward the east, where it subsisted at least until the thirteenth century. Manicheism was essentially a dualistic religion, holding that there are two principles, light and darkness. Both are eternal, and neither of them can be finally destroyed. Human souls are sparks of light trapped within the darkness of the body. By the late third century, particularly in Egypt, Christians began writing against such teachings. Theonas, bishop of Alexandria from 282 until his death in 300, produced the most ancient writing against Manicheism that has survived, although rather than a refutation of Manicheism, it was a warning against it.

Shortly thereafter, probably very early in the fourth century, Alexander of Lycopolis, of whom little is known, also wrote against Manicheism. Some authors say that he was bishop of Lycopolis, while others simply say that this was the city of his residence. He wrote a treatise *Against the Manichaeans*, in twenty-six chapters. After an exhortation of "Christian philosophy" in the first chapter, he employs the remaining twenty-five chapters in refuting Manicheism on the basis of Platonic philosophy.

Finally, although originally written in Syriac and not in Greek, we must mention the *Debate between Archelaus and Manes*, which survives only in a complete version in Latin and a partial one in Greek. According to this document, Archelaus was bishop of a city in Mesopotamia where a Christian by the name of Marcellus practiced such works of charity that he became famous in the area. When this reached the ears of Manes in Persia, he decided to recruit Marcellus for his own teachings and wrote to him. But Marcellus insisted that Manes should come to him. Finally, there was a debate between the two. Most of the document takes the form of a series of acts or minutes of this debate, which took place in the presence of a panel of judges. Manes expounds his doctrines in detail, and Archelaus refutes them.

As Manes was on his way back to Persia, he stopped in another city and again sought to convince Christians there to follow his teaching. The bishop of that city wrote to Archelaus, who came to his help, and a new debate took place. Scholars do not agree as to the historicity of this document. Most consider it a fictitious debate that never took place; others insist on its possible historicity. At any rate, this is one of the oldest summaries that we have of Manichean teachings and how Manicheans sought to interpret Christianity in such a way that it would fit into the teachings of Manes. Also, even though the original Syriac text has been lost, this is one of the oldest documents signaling a growing body of Christian literature in Syriac.

12

Cyprian of Carthage

HIS LIFE

Throughout the third century, Christian Latin theology was centered in North Africa. Hippolytus, whom we have already discussed, lived in Rome but wrote in Greek. It was during the third century that Rome began producing its first theology in Latin, as we shall see when we come to the works of Novatian. And there is no doubt that the foremost theologian writing in Latin in the third century was Cyprian, bishop of Carthage in North Africa.

Cyprian seems to have been born in that city, around the year 200, to an aristocratic pagan family. He received an excellent education, which would later serve him well in his theological and pastoral writings. Very little is known of his youth, and what we know of the rest of his life, beyond what can be seen in his writings themselves, is drawn from the *Life of Cyprian*, by his disciple Pontius, that begins precisely with Cyprian's conversion. The *Octavius* of Minucius Felix and the writings of Tertullian seem to have convinced Cyprian of the error of paganism. Around the year 245, when Cyprian was some forty-five years old, he was baptized. Three years later he was elected bishop of Carthage. When that happened, we are told, he sold many of his possessions in order to give the proceeds to the poor.

THE IDOLS ARE NOT GODS

Probably the earliest extant writing of Cyprian is *The Idols Are Not Gods*, a brief piece written shortly after his conversion. Some scholars doubt that it is actually the work of Cyprian, for his biographer Pontius, who includes a list of

Cyprian's works, does not mention it. At any rate, this work is based on what Tertullian and Minucius Felix had written on the same subject. According to Cyprian, in the beginning the present gods were simply outstanding kings, to whom statues and temples were erected. They are absolutely powerless. If on occasion they seem to be able to produce an apparent miracle, this is not due to their power, but rather to the demons that employ them in order to deceive humans. This writing is also very negative toward Jews, for Cyprian says:

> First of all, favour with God was given to the Jews. Thus they of old were righteous; thus their ancestors were obedient to their religious engagements. Thence with them both the loftiness of their rule flourished, and the greatness of their race advanced. But subsequently becoming neglectful of discipline, proud, and puffed up with confidence in their fathers, they despised the divine precepts, and lost the favour conferred upon them. (*Idols* 10; *ANF* 5:468)

TESTIMONIES TO QUIRINUS

His new obligations as a bishop led Cyprian to write the most extensive of his works, *Testimonies to Quirinus*, in three books. This is a collection of biblical passages applied mostly to polemics against Judaism, seeking to show that Jesus was the promised Messiah. There is little new in this work, for Cyprian seems to be simply continuing and expanding what other Christians had done before him. Since the series of passages from the Old Testament that various Christian writers employ are very similar, scholars believe that there were books of biblical "testimonies" intended to prove the main tenets of Christianity. Later Cyprian would repeat a similar exercise in *To Fortunatus*. The last book of Cyprian's *Testimonies to Quirinus* changes its focus and deals with the practical life of believers rather than with anti-Jewish polemics. It is mostly a series of teachings and principles of conduct based on various biblical passages. This book is important because it is the earliest extant list of such testimonies and also because it includes quotations not only from the Old Testament, but also from the New. Yet it is not very original, for the biblical quotations themselves take a large part of the text, and their interpretations simply follow what others had done before.

TO DONATUS

The treatise *To Donatus* is an autobiographical testimony in the form of an epistle. Cyprian speaks of the conversation he had with his friend Donatus in the quiet of the garden. Not only is the atmosphere placid, but also the language is simple, for Cyprian begins by declaring,

> In courts of justice, in the public assembly, in political debate, a copi-
> ous eloquence may be the glory of a voluble ambition; but in speak-
> ing of the Lord God, a chaste simplicity of expression strives for the
> conviction of faith rather with the substance, than with the powers, of
> eloquence. Therefore accept from me things, not clever but weighty,
> words, not decked up to charm a popular audience with cultivated
> rhetoric, but simple and fitted by their unvarnished truthfulness for
> the proclamation of the divine mercy. (*Don.* [*Ep.* 1] 2; *ANF* 5:275;
> here his *Epistles* are numbered by *ANF*)

Cyprian begins by referring to the time when "I was still lying in darkness and gloomy night, wavering hither and thither, . . . knowing nothing of my real life, and remote from truth and light" (*Don.* 3; *ANF* 5:275). He then turns to a description of the sad condition of the world and of Roman culture and society: the roads full of thieves, seas infested with pirates, and frequent and cruel wars. And the disorder is such that it has become the accepted order of society, for "murder, which in the case of an individual is admitted to be a crime, is called a virtue when it is committed wholesale" (*Don.* 3; *ANF* 5:277). The catalog of ills in private as well as public life continues, to the point that what the world values is in fact worthless:

> In respect of what you regard as honours, . . . what you count affluence
> in riches, what you think power in the camp, the glory of the purple in
> the magisterial office, the power of licence in the chief command,—
> there is hidden the virus of ensnaring mischief, and an appearance of
> smiling wickedness, joyous indeed, but the treacherous deception of
> hidden calamity. Just as some poison, in which the flavour having been
> medicated with sweetness, craftily mingled in its deadly juices, seems,
> when taken, to be an ordinary draught, but when it is drunk up, the
> destruction that you have swallowed assails you. (*Don.* 11; *ANF* 5:278)

Near the end of this work, Cyprian calls Donatus to leave aside the uncertainty and the disorder of the world and join a different order:

> Hence, then, the one peaceful and trustworthy tranquillity, the one
> solid and firm and constant security, is this, for a man to withdraw
> from these eddies of a distracting world, and, anchored on the ground
> of the harbour of salvation, to lift his eyes from earth to heaven; and
> having been admitted to the gift of God, and being already very near
> to his God in mind, he may boast, that whatever in human affairs
> others esteem lofty and grand, lies altogether beneath his conscious-
> ness. He who is actually greater than the world can crave nothing, can
> desire nothing, from the world. (*Don.* 14; *ANF* 5:279)

ON THE DRESS OF VIRGINS

At approximately the same date, Cyprian wrote one of his most influential works, *On the Dress of Virgins*. When he took on the responsibilities of a bishop, Cyprian was concerned that some of the women who were consecrated for the service of God as virgins were still overly concerned about their dress, their appearance, and their jewels. He comments: "What have they to do with earthly dress, and with ornaments, wherewith while they are striving to please men they offend God?" (*Dress* 5; *ANF* 5:431). He therefore laments: "The Church frequently mourns over her virgins; hence she groans at their scandalous and detestable stories; hence the flower of her virgins is extinguished, the honour and modesty of continency are injured, and all its glory and dignity are profaned" (*Dress* 20; *ANF* 5:435).

The same subject appears also in Cyprian's correspondence. In one of his letters, addressed to a certain Pomponius who seems to have been a bishop in a nearby city, Cyprian notes the gravity of some of the reports he has received from Pomponius: "Those virgins who, after having once determined to continue in their condition, and firmly to maintain their continency, have afterwards been found to have remained in the same bed side by side with men; of whom you say that one is a deacon; and yet that the same virgins who have confessed that they have slept with men declare that they are chaste" (*Epistles* 61; *ANF* 5:357). Cyprian insists that the chastity required of virgins is not satisfied with a technical definition of virginity, but requires absolute purity. He believes that virginity is a great blessing for women who consecrate themselves to it, as well as an eschatological sign of the future to which all believers look.

Referring to the curses in Genesis, he tells the consecrated virgins: "You are free from this sentence. You do not fear the sorrows and the groans of women. You have no fear of child-bearing; nor is your husband lord over you; but your Lord and Head is Christ, after the likeness and in the place of the man" (*Dress* 22; *ANF* 5:436). And the eschatological dimension appears further on in the same paragraph: "That which we shall be, you have already begun to be. You possess already in this world the glory of the resurrection. You pass through the world without the contagion of the world; in that you continue chaste and virgins, you are equal to the angels of God" (*Dress* 22; *ANF* 5:436).

THE RESTORATION OF THE FALLEN
AND *THE UNITY OF THE CHURCH*

Some of the most important writings of Cyprian were the result of the persecution of Decius, which began the year after Cyprian became a bishop.

The imperial decree ordered all to offer sacrifice to the gods and to have a document proving that they had done so. After a long time of peace, when it seemed that martyrdom would be but a remote possibility, many Christians hurried to obey the imperial decree. Others bribed an officer in order to buy a document without actually sacrificing to the gods. Some remained firm at first, but eventually gave way to fear of torture and offered the required sacrifice. Among those who remained firm, some simply fled or hid from the authorities, while others were in prison and tortured, but did not die, and still others suffered martyrdom. Cyprian, recently elected as a bishop, followed the path of flight—although not an absolute flight, for he simply went to a secluded place outside the city and there continued directing the life of the church through an abundant correspondence. Since there had been some dissension when Cyprian was elected, the discontented now criticized him for hiding at a time of persecution.

The persecution did not last long, and early in 251 Cyprian returned to Carthage, where he convoked a synod to determine what should be done with those who had fallen, usually called the "lapsed" (*lapsi*). While Cyprian was still in hiding, some of the lapsed wished to return to the church and sought the blessing of the "confessors" to do so. "Confessor" was the title given to those who had remained firm in the faith even amid torture but had survived. Some of these confessors were willing to give the lapsed certain documents absolving them and restoring them to the communion of the church. Cyprian, first from exile and then in Carthage, insisted that it was necessary to establish an order that all would follow, and that the restoration of the lapsed was not up to the confessors, but should rather be in the hands of the established authorities of the church. But his own position was difficult, for he had hid while the confessors were suffering for their faith. A presbyter named Novatus and a deacon named Felicissimus argued that the confessors were more saintly and therefore had more authority than Cyprian, and on that basis they broke with the bishop and accepted back into the communion of the church those lapsed who had been forgiven by confessors. The result was a schism within the church of Carthage. Meanwhile, as we shall see in another chapter, something similar was happening in Rome, resulting in what is usually called the schism of Novatian.

These events—the debate over the lapsed and the resulting schisms—led to some of Cyprian's most important writings. There is no doubt that the most influential among these is *On the Unity of the Church*, which Cyprian wrote to deal with the double challenge of schism as it had appeared in Carthage itself and in Rome with Novatian.

Cyprian saw the schismatic spirit as one of the most insidious ways in which the Enemy attacks Christians. According to him, it is not only the open attack on the faith by persecution that must be feared, but also even more the veiled attack of the Enemy to undermine love and faith in the church. "Those whom he cannot keep in the darkness of the old way, he circumvents and deceives by the error of a new way" (*Unity* 3; *ANF* 5:422). If the church is the bride of Christ, "whoever is separated from the Church and is joined to an adulteress is separated from the promises of the Church." Therefore, "he can no longer have God for his Father, who has not the Church for his mother" (*Unity* 6; *ANF* 5:423). Confessors are to be admired, but one must remember that they have not yet attained glory itself. A confessor may give a bad example and in that case ought not to be followed. This is precisely what happens when some confessors encourage schism.

Chapter 4 of this treatise presents serious problems both as to the text itself and as to its translation and meaning. There are two different versions. The longer of these includes most of what the briefer one says, but then also has some important additions. These underscore the authority of Peter among the apostles, therefore implying the primacy of Peter's successors in Rome. The point at issue is whether these references to the authority of the bishop of Rome were part of the original text or are a later addition. Some suggest that both versions are the work of Cyprian, who first produced the shorter text and then the longer one, in response to the schism that was taking place in Rome. Others argue that the original text is the longer one and that it was Cyprian himself who, as a result of his disagreements with Bishop Stephen of Rome, eliminated the references to Peter that seemed to imply Roman supremacy. Most likely the original text is the briefer one, to which some interpolations bolstering the authority of Rome were later added. At any rate, Cyprian does affirm that "the rest of the apostles were also the same as was Peter, endowed with a like partnership both of honour and power; but the beginning proceeds from unity" (*Unity* 4; *ANF* 5:422). What most interests Cyprian is not the relative authority among bishops in various cities, but the unity of the church, which is to be manifested in the unity of the episcopacy: "And this unity we ought firmly to hold and assert, especially those of us that are bishops who preside in the Church, that we may also prove the episcopate itself to be one and undivided. Let no one deceive the brotherhood by a falsehood: let no one corrupt the truth of the faith by perfidious prevarication. The episcopate is one, each part of which is held by each one for the whole" (*Unity* 5; *ANF* 5:422–23).

About the same time when he was composing this treatise, Cyprian was writing another dealing with the same problem from a different angle, the matter of the lapsed in times of persecution. This is *On the Lapsed*, or *On the Fallen*. Cyprian opens his writing by rejoicing in the peace that the church now enjoys and also praising the confessors:

> We look with glad countenances upon confessors illustrious with the heraldry of a good name, and glorious with the praises of virtue and of faith; clinging to them with holy kisses, we embrace them long desired with insatiable eagerness. The white-robed cohort of Christ's soldiers is here, who in the fierce conflict have broken the ferocious turbulence of an urgent persecution, having been prepared for the suffering of the dungeon, armed for the endurance of death. Bravely you have resisted the world: you have afforded a glorious spectacle in the sight of God; you have been an example to your brethren that shall follow you. (*Lapsed* 2; *ANF* 5:437)

While Cyprian bewails the persecution and the sufferings of his flock, he also says that persecution itself has come as a result of the lack of faith and disobedience of believers, who have been occupied with collecting wealth and earning the respect of the world. When the test of persecution came, there were those whose very actions proved that they needed to be tested: "They indeed did not wait to be apprehended ere they ascended, or to be interrogated ere they denied" (*Lapsed* 8; *ANF* 5:439). Some went so far as to invite others to follow their evil example. Some, in order to hold on to their goods, obeyed the imperial edict. "Their wealth fettered them like a chain" (*Lapsed* 11; *ANF* 5:440). But now that persecution had passed, some were too ready to accept the fallen without further ado:

> As if the storm of persecution had raged too little, there has been added to the heap, under the title of mercy, a deceiving mischief and a fair-seeming calamity. Contrary to the vigour of the Gospel, contrary to the law of the Lord and God, by the temerity of some, communion is relaxed to heedless persons,—a vain and false peace, dangerous to those who grant it, and likely to avail nothing to those who receive it. They do not seek for the patience necessary to health, nor the true medicine derived from atonement. Penitence is driven forth from their breasts, and the memory of their very grave and extreme sin is taken away. The wounds of the dying are covered over, and the deadly blow that is planted in the deep and secret entrails is concealed by a dissimulated suffering. Returning from the altars of the devil, they draw near to the holy place of the Lord, with hands filthy and reeking with smell, still almost breathing of the plague-bearing idol-meats. (*Lapsed* 15; *ANF* 5:441)

Cyprian's purpose in all this is to make sure that the process of restoring the fallen will follow a certain uniform order, and that it be placed in the hands of the properly established authorities of the church, rather than in those of the confessors. As a further argument to bolster his position, he gives a series of anecdotes of people who dared take communion without being properly restored by the authorities of the church and have suffered for it. For instance, a woman who had presented the sacrifice to the gods and then received communion by stealth suffocated and died amid violent convulsions. On the basis of all of this, Cyprian calls the fallen to return to the church through the established authorities: "He who has thus made atonement to God; he who by repentance for his deed, who by shame for his sin, has conceived more both of virtue and of faith from the very grief of his fall, heard and aided by the Lord, shall make the Church which he had lately saddened glad, and shall now deserve of the Lord not only pardon, but a crown" (*Lapsed* 36; *ANF* 5:447).

The same concern over the necessity to establish uniform and fair principles for the restoration of the fallen may be seen in several of Cyprian's letters. Among many examples, one may quote *Epistles* 11 (17 in other lists), where Cyprian, while acknowledging the need to love the lapsed, insists on the order that is required to restore them to the communion of the church:

> That you bewail and grieve over the downfall of our brethren I know from myself, beloved brethren, who also bewail with you and grieve for each one, and suffer. . . . Yet I hear that certain of the presbyters, neither mindful of the Gospel nor considering what the martyrs have written to me, nor reserving to the bishop the honour of his priesthood and of his dignity, have already begun to communicate with the lapsed, and to offer on their behalf, and to give them the eucharist, when it was fitting that they should attain to these things in due course. (*Ep.* 11; *ANF* 5:292)

FACING THE PLAGUE

Two other issues are central in Cyprian's works: the plague that swept North Africa in the mid-third century, and the matter of whether those who have been baptized by heretics and returned to the church should be rebaptized.

The results of the plague were disastrous in many ways. There was an enormous mortality rate, to the point that the dead were piled on the streets and no one dared bury them for fear of contagion. The economic and social upheaval was far-reaching. Authorities were incapable of preventing the looting of abandoned homes. Once again pagans affirmed that the reason for all these calamities was that the ancient gods had been abandoned, and therefore Christians should be blamed for them. Finally, believers allowed themselves to be carried away by the prevailing mood, losing hope, abandoning the ill, and even participating in the looting. All of this required Cyprian's attention and action.

He responded to what was being said regarding the abandonment of the ancient gods as the cause of the prevailing evil in the treatise *To Demetrianus*. Who this Demetrianus was is not known. Apparently he was a civil functionary, or perhaps a priest for one of the ancient gods. According to Cyprian, it was the "railing and noisy clamour" of Demetrianus that led him to write this response. For some time Cyprian preferred to ignore what seemed to be senseless ravings, but eventually he decided that he must refute them. He based his argument on what many ancient writers had said, that the world was aging, that therefore it was not as healthy as it used to be, and that this may be seen in the calamities of the time: "You must in the first place know this, that the world has now grown old, and does not abide in that strength in which it formerly stood; nor has it that vigour and force which it formerly possessed" (*Demetr.* 3; *ANF* 5:458). If Christians are to be blamed for the signs of the world's aging, the elderly could also blame them because they are no longer as strong as they used to be, nor are their hearing and sight as sharp as they once were.

Furthermore, the evil that all are witnessing is also the result of the manner in which society in general has broken the commandments of God. People rebel against God by doing as they please, and Cyprian comments:

> And you wonder or complain in this your obstinacy and contempt, if the rain comes down with unusual scarcity; and the earth falls into neglect with dusty corruption; if the barren glebe hardly brings forth a few jejune and pallid blades of grass; if the destroying hail weakens the vines; if the overwhelming whirlwind roots out the olive; if drought stanches the fountain; a pestilent breeze corrupts the air; the weakness of disease wastes away man; although all these things come as the consequence of the sins that provoke them, and God is more deeply indignant when such and so great evils avail nothing! (*Demetr.* 7; *ANF* 5:459)

Cyprian insists that the pagan idols are not gods. If sometimes they seem to be so, this is not because of them, but rather the work of demons that employ them. The powerlessness of demons may be seen in people whom Christians exorcise, for when the demons leave them, they wail.

Turning then to legal matters, and taking an argument from Tertullian, Cyprian points out the implicit contradiction in the manner in which the state deals with Christians: "Make your election of one of two alternatives. To be a Christian is either a crime, or it is not. If it be a crime, why do you not put the man that confesses it to death? If it not be a crime, why do you persecute an innocent man?" (*Demetr.* 13; *ANF* 5:461).

Finally, Cyprian stresses the contrast between the values of pagans and the life of Christians, and he invites his reader to participate in the same joy and peace: "We do not envy your comforts, nor do we conceal the divine benefits. We repay kindness for your hatred; and for the torments and penalties which are inflicted on us, we point out to you the ways of salvation. Believe and live, and do ye who persecute us in time rejoice with us for eternity" (*Demetr.* 25; *ANF* 5:465).

Cyprian also wrote several other treatises and numerous letters seeking to help his flock respond properly both to persecution and to the plague. *On the Mortality* is a call to the faithful to remain firm and joyful amid the calamities of an aging world. Those who complain that the plague hits Christians as well as pagans must remember that they did not accept Christianity as a way to avoid the evils of this world nor to enjoy a temporal happiness, but rather to attain to an everlasting joy. While Christians are in the present world, they will still be subject to the human condition, and they share in the sufferings of the rest of humanity, just as when a ship sinks, all those in it drown. Therefore Christians are not to fear death, but rather look upon it as a door to eternity.

On the Advantage of Patience is an exhortation to that virtue. Part of it repeats much of what Tertullian had said earlier on patience, and another part is an amplification of a sermon that Cyprian had preached on that subject. *On Works and Alms* calls believers to practice good works of love and particularly to give alms and support the needy even while the plague rages. The rich who employ their goods to benefit the poor invest them properly, and that is not the case of those who simply wish to accumulate wealth, or of those who fear that by helping others they will lose what is properly theirs. It is not correct to claim that one does not help the poor in order to defend the patrimony of one's children and heirs. That is not the preoccupation of a good father, for what a good father should really seek is to have his children learn true wisdom from him. Even in the midst of these very difficult times, believers are obliged to practice love, particularly by supporting and helping the needy.

THE BAPTISM OF HERETICS

Although none of his works deal exclusively with the subject, Cyprian was repeatedly involved in the debate regarding the validity of baptism performed by heretics. Both in the Greek-speaking East and in North Africa it was customary to rebaptize those who came to the church after having received baptism from a heretical or schismatic group. In contrast, in Rome such a baptism was accepted, and those who came from heretical or schismatic groups but had been baptized were received into the church by a simple lay-ing on of hands. This disagreement and the resulting debates occupy several of Cyprian's epistles, including the already-mentioned letter that Firmilian wrote to him (see chap. 11).

Although the first letter in which Cyprian deals directly with the subject dates from the year 255, already earlier, in *On the Unity of the Church*, he had explained his stand regarding baptism received from heretics: "Although there can be no other baptism but one, they think that they can baptize; although they forsake the fountain of life, they promise the grace of living and saving water. Men are not washed among them, but rather are made foul; nor are sins purged away, but are even accumulated. Such a nativity does not generate sons to God, but to the devil" (*Unity* 11; *ANF* 5:425). Cyprian's stance on the baptism of heretics is based on the ecclesiology that he expounds in that treatise. The church, as the bride of Christ, can only be one. It is within the church that the children of God are conceived. Therefore, just as outside the church there is no salvation, so there is no baptism outside the church.

The matter was not the subject of much debate in North Africa. Cyprian himself did not insist that all other bishops had to agree with him on this point. Also, several years earlier, in 220, the bishops of Africa had decided that heretics ought to be rebaptized. For this reason, the conflict regarding the rebaptism of heretics was mostly with the bishop of Rome, Stephen, while in Africa itself there were debates about other subjects regarding the validity of baptism. For instance, some were asking if a baptism is valid when the ill who are apparently at the edge of death ask for baptism and receive it by having water sprinkled over them. This form of baptism was usually called "clinical" baptism, for it took place while the person was in the bed, or *klinē*. Cyprian's answer to that question is that, although others are free to disagree with him, he is ready to accept the validity of such clinical baptisms: "In this point, my diffidence and modesty prejudge none, so as to prevent any from feeling what he thinks right, and from doing what he feels to be right. As far as my poor understanding conceives it, I think that the divine benefits can in no respect be mutilated and weakened; . . . Nay, verily, the Holy Spirit is not given by measure, but is poured out altogether on the believer" (*Epistles* 75; *ANF* 5:400–401).

There certainly are some forms of heretical baptism that no one should accept. Such is the case, for instance, of that administered by the Marcionites, who baptize only in the name of Jesus, because that form of baptism distances Jesus from the Father and the Holy Spirit. In this, the bishops of the East as well as those of Africa and Italy were in agreement. They also agreed that those who had been baptized within the church, left it for a while in order to join heretics, and then returned to the church should not be rebaptized, for their initial baptism was still valid. What was then required was a confession and amendment from error and the laying on of hands by the bishop. What was actually debated was what should be done with those who, originally baptized with water and with the Trinitarian formula, but within a heretical or schismatic group, decided to join the church. Stephen and the other bishops in Italy held that they should not be rebaptized, while Cyprian, following the ancient African tradition, held the opposite.

In the controversy, Cyprian as well other leaders of the African church harshly criticized Stephen. It was possibly to him that Cyprian was referring when declaring that "some of our colleagues would rather give honour to heretics than agree with us" (*Epistles* 70; *ANF* 5:377). And if Stephen claims to have particular authority as a successor of Peter, Cyprian reminds him that Peter himself, when he discussed circumcision with Paul, did not claim any such primacy. In brief, Cyprian's position is clearly summarized in the last paragraph of a long letter that he wrote to a certain Pompey about Stephen and his claims:

> Therefore, dearest brother, having explored and seen the truth; it is observed and held by us, that all who are converted from any heresy whatever to the Church must be baptized by the only and lawful baptism of the Church, with the exception of those who had previously been baptized in the Church, and so had passed over to the heretics. For it behooves these, when they return, having repented, to be received by the imposition of hands only, and to be restored by the shepherd to the sheep-fold whence they had strayed. (*Epistles* 73; *ANF* 5:389–90)

The difference between Roman and African practices was not resolved during Cyprian's lifetime. Slowly the African church accepted Roman custom, and by the fourth century it was customary not to rebaptize heretics who came to the church after having received the baptism with water and in the name of the Father, the Son, and the Holy Spirit.

OTHER WRITINGS

Beyond the works already mentioned, Cyprian produced several others on subjects such as the Lord's Prayer and the evil of jealousy and envy. Also, toward the end of his days, he wrote *To Fortunatus*, which is an exhortation to face martyrdom with firmness and courage. A year after producing this work, Cyprian followed his own instructions when facing martyrdom.

THE LIFE AND MARTYRDOM OF CYPRIAN

One of the reasons why today we are able to know many details of Cyprian's life and to offer an approximate date of most of his works is that deacon Pontius, who was with Cyprian during a good part of his life, wrote a biography of the much admired and already deceased Cyprian. Apparently Pontius came to know Cyprian shortly after the latter was elected bishop. Later, during the time of persecution, they went together into exile. His *Life and Martyrdom of Cyprian* is therefore a valuable source for historians—although, as often happens in such cases, one must take into account that Pontius is seeking to celebrate and exalt Cyprian and therefore tends to say little of the controversies in which he was involved, or of the opposition that he faced from some believers in Carthage and the surrounding areas.

There is also a collection of *Proconsular Acts* that includes the trial, sentencing, and death of Cyprian. It is undoubtedly a very ancient document. And the part of it that deals with Cyprian's witness before the proconsul must have been written almost immediately after the event and shortly before Cyprian's martyrdom, for in one of his letters Cyprian himself refers to that document. The rest of the collection, dealing with the trial and death of Cyprian, may well have been written no more than one or two years after the death of the famed bishop.

WRITINGS FALSELY ATTRIBUTED TO CYPRIAN

As often happens with highly admired people, soon works began circulating that falsely claimed to be Cyprian's. Possibly the most important among them is a confused and confusing treatise *On the Repetition of Baptism*, which seems to have been written in order to soften Cyprian's views on this matter and to make it appear that his conflicts with Rome were not serious. There are also several other later writings that have been erroneously attributed to Cyprian.

13

Other Latin Authors

NOVATIAN

It is interesting to note that the two main theologians who flourished in Rome during the third century clashed with the bishop of that city and became schismatics; therefore to this day the Roman Catholic Church considers them antipopes. In chapter 9 this was the case with Hippolytus. Now we turn our attention to Novatian, who is the first significant Latin Christian author in Rome. As should be evident from the foregoing chapters, during this entire period Christian theology in Latin did not center in Rome, nor even in Italy, but rather in North Africa, which produced, among many others, authors such as Tertullian, Cyprian, and somewhat later, Augustine of Hippo.

Very little is known with certainty about Novatian, who was a contemporary of Cyprian. He had apparently been a pagan and was still a catechumen when he was threatened by a possibly fatal disease. At that time he received a "clinical" baptism, by sprinkling while on the sickbed. There is no doubt that he was respected and admired by many in the church in Rome, particularly for his writings, among which stood a significant essay *On the Trinity*. Then, early in 250, Bishop Fabius died as a martyr, and apparently Novatian hoped to succeed him. But when the election took place on the following year, Cornelius was chosen. This was one of many reasons for a strong enmity between Cornelius and Novatian. Soon their disagreements focused on the issue of what was to be done with the lapsed. Novatian held that only God could forgive those who had denied their faith at the time of persecution, while Cornelius agreed with Cyprian and others that, if the lapsed returned to the church, confessed their sin, and through penance showed the sincerity and firmness of their faith, they could be restored to the communion of the church. Novatian's party, which called itself "the pure," would not accept the policies of Cornelius. Shortly after the election of Cornelius, some of the "pure" elected Novatian as bishop of Rome, and he was consecrated by three other bishops who agreed with him, thus creating a schism. Eusebius of Caesarea has preserved long quotations from a letter that Cornelius sent to the bishop of Antioch in which he accused Novatian, among other things, of not having been firm in the faith after his clinical baptism, of cowardice during the time of persecution, and of allowing himself to be carried away by unmeasured ambition. According to Cornelius, when Novatian gave communion to someone, he would hold their hands and not allow them to take communion, demanding: "Swear to me by the body and blood of our Lord Jesus Christ that you will never forsake me and turn to Cornelius" (quoted by Eusebius, *Ch. Hist.* 6.43.18; *NPNF*[2] 1:289). Novatian died in 258, but the schism continued for four hundred more years, when Novatian's last followers disappeared.

The main extant work of Novatian, and the one that earned him fame as a theologian, was *On the Trinity*. Although some historians place it at a later date, it was probably written before Novatian broke with Cornelius. The purpose of the writing seems to be to refute the tendencies to patripassionism that were making headway in Rome. Its structure follows the main articles of the "rule of faith" that believers affirmed when being baptized, articles that referred first to the Father as creator of all things, then to his Son Jesus Christ, and finally to the Holy Spirit. Although, following the pattern of the baptismal formula, the rule affirmed faith in the Holy Spirit, Novatian has little to say about the Spirit, for the patripassionist controversy had to do mostly with the distinction between the Father and the Son. The first eight chapters of this work deal with the nature and attributes of God, who is transcendent, eternal, ineffable, loving, and creator of all that exists. In chapter 9 Novatian turns his attention to the Son, declaring that "the same rule of truth teaches us to believe, after the Father, also on the Son of God, Christ Jesus, the Lord our God, but the Son of God" (*Trin.* 9; *ANF* 5:618). This Jesus Christ is both human and divine, so that Scripture refers to him as God, but also as human: "Let them, therefore, who read that Jesus Christ the Son of man is man, read also that this same Jesus is called also God and the Son of God" (*Trin.* 11; *ANF* 5:620).

But then, in order to show the difference between the Father and the Son, Novatian declares that, while the first is immutable, the second is not. Commenting on the story of the Tower of Babel, he says that the immutable and omnipresent God could not be the one who descended to see the construction of the tower, for that God is everywhere and can neither ascend nor descend. The one who descended was the Son of God, who is therefore different from the Father. In this passage, as in many others, Novatian bases the distinction between the Father and the Son on the immutability of the former and the mutability of the latter. Therefore here we find the subordinationist tendencies that in the fourth century would lead to Arianism and to the bitter controversies surrounding it.

Regarding the Holy Spirit, Novatian has little to say. What he does say is rather subordinationist also: "Christ is greater than the Paraclete, because the Paraclete would not receive from Christ unless He were less than Christ" (*Trin.* 16; *ANF* 5:625). Thus Novatian conceives of the Trinity as a hierarchy in which the Father is greater than the Son, who in turn is also greater than the Holy Spirit.

Novatian also wrote several works of controversy against the Jews. One of them is extant: *On the Jewish Meats*. Basing his argument on Romans 7:14, Novatian claims that, since the law is spiritual and must not be interpreted in a literal sense, there is no such thing as unclean animals—which would make God the creator of uncleanness. The dietetic laws are in truth metaphorical references to various human behaviors. Animals that chew the cud are considered clean because they teach us that we must constantly chew and rechew the divine precepts. Pigs are declared unclean as a metaphor for those who feed on waste and wallow in the mud. And so on. Thus, if there was a literal meaning to the various dietetic prohibitions, this was simply that gluttony and intemperance must be avoided. Furthermore, all these various laws and practices were simply figures, shadows, or "types" announcing Christ. Once the reality has come, the figures or shadows pointing to them are no longer necessary.

We also have two other works of Novatian that are of less importance. One of them, *On Modesty*, is mostly drawn from the writing of Tertullian on the same subject. The other, *On Spectacles*, is usually included among Cyprian's works; yet for several reasons scholars believe that it was actually written by Novatian. Here, taking most of his material from Tertullian and Cyprian, Novatian decries the pagan and lustful dimensions of theater, and therefore he declares that Christians should have nothing to do with it, be it as actors or as mere spectators.

Finally, in Cyprian's epistolary are three letters (nos. 30, 31, and 36) to Cyprian written by the presbyters, deacons, and confessors of Rome. For a number of reasons, it is believed that these letters were written by Novatian, or at least inspired by him. They are the clearest witness we have of the debates taking place in Rome regarding the restoration of the lapsed, and of how for a time the rigorists in Rome saw Cyprian as a champion for their cause. In one of these letters the rigorist party in Rome—Novatian and his followers—tells Cyprian:

> Where is the divine word left, if pardon be so easily granted to sinners? Certainly their spirits are to be cheered and to be nourished up

to the season of their maturity, and they are to be instructed from the Holy Scriptures how great and surpassing a sin they have committed. Nor let them be animated by the fact that they are many, but rather let them be checked by the fact that they are not few. An unblushing number has never been accustomed to have weight in extenuation of a crime; but shame, modesty, patience, discipline, humility, and subjection, waiting for the judgment of others upon itself, and bearing the sentence of others upon its own judgment,—this it is which proves penitence; this it is which skins over a deep wound; this it is which raises up the ruins of the fallen spirit and restores them, which quells and restrains the burning vapour of their raging sins. (Cyprian, *Epistles* 25.6.2; *ANF* 5:204)

In another epistle we find arguments that clearly express the views of Novatian:

If martyrs become martyrs for no other reason than that by not sacrificing they may keep the peace of the Church even to the shedding of their own blood, lest, overcome by the suffering of the torture, by losing peace, they might lose salvation; on what principle do they think that the salvation, which if they had sacrificed they thought that they should not have, was to be given to those who are said to have sacrificed; although they ought to maintain that law in others which they themselves appear to have held before their own eyes? (Cyprian, *Epistles* 29.2.2; *ANF* 5:307)

ARNOBIUS OF SICCA

North Africa was also the land that saw the flourishing of Arnobius of Sicca, a city in the Roman province of Numidia. Little is known about his youth or his life before his conversion, which took place when he was more than sixty years old. Nor is much known of the rest of his life. When he was a pagan, he was a respected teacher of rhetoric in Sicca. Jerome says that his conversion took place because of a dream in which God showed Arnobius the error and vanity of pagan religion. This account is interesting because in his writing Arnobius himself discredits the value of dreams. Jerome also says that when Arnobius wished to join the church and the bishop was unconvinced regarding his conversion, Arnobius wrote his only extant work, *Against the Heathen*, in seven books. (At a time it was thought that there were eight books, but the so-called eighth book of Arnobius is in fact the *Octavius* of Minucius Felix.) The date of Arnobius's death is unknown, although he seems to have lived long enough to have seen the end of persecution and the new order under Constantine.

Arnobius offers a witness to his conversion in *Against the Heathen*, although he gives neither the date nor the reason for his conversion:

But lately, O blindness, I worshipped images produced from the furnace, gods made on anvils and by hammers, the bones of elephants, paintings, wreaths on aged trees; whenever I espied an anointed stone and one bedaubed with olive oil, as if some power resided in it I worshipped it, I addressed myself to it and begged blessings from a senseless stock. . . . Now, having been led into the paths of truth by so great a teacher, I know what all these things are, I entertain honourable thoughts concerning those which are worthy. (*Heathen* 1.39; *ANF* 6:423)

At the beginning of this work, Arnobius makes it clear that his purpose is to answer the claim that some made that the calamities of the times are due to the advance of Christianity and the resulting abandonment of the ancient gods, who had provided for better times. He says:

Since I have found some who deem themselves very wise in their opinions, acting as if they were inspired, and announcing with all the authority of an oracle, that from the time when the Christian people began to exist in the world the universe has gone to ruin, that the human race has been visited with ills of many kinds, that even the very gods, abandoning their accustomed charge, in virtue of which they were wont in former days to regard with interest our affairs, have been driven from the regions of the earth,—I have resolved, so far as my capacity and my humble power of language will allow, to oppose public prejudice, and to refute calumnious accusations. (*Heathen* 1.1; *ANF* 6:413)

The verbosity of these first lines suffices as a sample of the style of the entire writing. Throughout his work, Arnobius seems to be eager to show his knowledge of classical rhetoric, making constant use of it to such a point that on occasion it is difficult to decipher what he actually means. He also makes frequent use of satire to ridicule his opponents. As a result, his work presents serious difficulties for those who today try to translate it into modern languages while seeking to reflect a style that is alien to their prospective readers.

In the first book, Arnobius begins by rejecting the notion that calamities have become particularly frequent in his time. On the one hand, he reminds his readers that the calamities for which Christians are now being blamed have always existed, and they are still frequent among other people beyond the borders of the Roman Empire. On the other hand, he wonders whether such events are in truth calamities. What actually happens is that we tend to think that anything that bothers us or that we find unsatisfactory is therefore bad. Nature and the elements do not have to bend to human likes or whims, but have their own order. Therefore, "if anything happens which does not foster ourselves or our affairs with joyous success, it is not to be set down forthwith as an evil, and as a pernicious thing" (*Heathen* 1.10; *ANF* 6:416).

Scholars have shown that much of this material has been drawn from Epicurean philosophers.

In the rest of this first book, Arnobius argues that the knowledge of the true God is innate and that it is later human false teachings that have obscured this innate knowledge: "Is there any human being who has not entered on the first day of his life with an idea of that Great Head? In whom has it not been implanted by nature, on whom has it not been impressed, aye, stamped almost in his mother's womb even, in whom is there not a native instinct, that He is King and Lord, the ruler of all things that be?" (*Heathen* 1.33; *ANF* 6:421).

It has also been pointed out that Arnobius's view of the ancient gods is not completely clear. Other Christian writers would say either that such gods do not exist, or that they are in fact demons who act to deceive humankind through the idols that people worship. But on occasion Arnobius seems to think that they may be a sort of inferior gods:

> Are the deities inimical to us alone? To us are they most unrelenting, because we worship their Author, by whom, if they do exist, they began to be, and to have the essence of their power and their majesty, from whom, having obtained their very divinity, so to speak, they feel that they exist, and realize that they are reckoned among things that be, at whose will and at whose behest they are able both to perish and be dissolved, and not to be dissolved and not to perish. (*Heathen* 1.28; *ANF* 6:420)

In his second book Arnobius turns to a refutation of the various objections and accusations against Christianity, particularly the objection of those who say that it is not possible for God to have become incarnate in Jesus Christ. On this point, his main argument is that most pagan gods were actual human beings to whom immortality and other divine powers were attributed, and that therefore it is not inconceivable that God may have come to us in this human being Jesus. Much of this second book is a series of answers to objections that pagans may have to the notion of the divinity, life, and death of Jesus. Arnobius's Christology is what later historians would call a "divisive Christology," meaning a Christology that stresses the difference between the two natures of Christ, attributing some actions to one, and some to the other. Thus, for instance, after placing on pagan lips the rhetorical question of whether God actually hung from the cross, Arnobius answers that it was the humanity of Jesus that hung from the cross: "Who, then, *you ask*, was seen hanging on the cross? Who dead? The human form, *I reply*, which He had put on" (*Heathen* 1.62; *ANF* 6:431).

This second book also includes an interesting passage regarding the nature of souls. Arnobius seems to think that a reason why sinners act as they do is that they are convinced of the immortality of their souls and therefore think that whatever they do will not have great consequences, for their souls will continue living. But according to Arnobius, souls are in fact intermediate beings to which God may or may not grant immortality and life eternal. Souls are not, as some Platonists hold, emanations from God. This is why they do not all think or act in like manner.

The rest of the work deals mostly with a description and refutation of all sorts of beliefs and religious practices. Ironically, what Arnobius wrote in order to refute them has become today a helpful source to understand myths and doctrines that would otherwise have been forgotten.

LACTANTIUS

Arnobius's influence continued through his most famous disciple, Lactantius. Little is known about the life of Lactantius. In his *On Famous Men* (discussed in another chapter) Jerome says that Lactantius was a disciple of Arnobius and that during the reign of Diocletian, which began in 284, Lactantius was invited to teach rhetoric in Nicomedia. He seems to have been a pagan by birth, but nothing is known about his conversion. When the worst of all persecutions broke out by Diocletian's order, Lactantius, who by then was a Christian, decided to leave Nicomedia, where in any case he had not had great success, for the language spoken there was Greek, and he was a pro-fessor of Latin rhetoric. After the Edict of Milan, he tutored Constantine's eldest son, Crispus, who would later be executed by his father's order. This is practically all that is known about the life of Lactantius, who seems to have died around the year 320. Eusebius of Caesarea does not even mention him in his *Church History*.

The two best-known works of Lactantius are *On the Death of Persecutors* and the *Divine Institutes*. The first of these was written after the end of Diocle-tian's persecution, for Lactantius mentions the death of Diocletian, which took place in 315. When he wrote, Constantine and Licinius were still sharing rule over the empire. Since the breach between these two took place in 321, it is possible to date the composition of his work between 315 and 321. At the beginning of this writing, Lactantius rejoices in the end of persecution and announces the main subject of his work:

> Of the end of those men [the persecutors] I have thought good to publish a narrative, that all who are afar off, and all who shall arise hereafter, may learn how the Almighty manifested His power and sovereign greatness in rooting out and utterly destroying the enemies

of His name. And this will become evident, when I relate *who* were the persecutors of the Church from the time of its first constitution, and *what* were the punishments by which the divine Judge, in His severity, took vengeance on them. (*Death of Persec.* 1; *ANF* 7:301)

His story therefore begins with Nero and ends with Diocletian. About Nero, he says that "the tyrant, bereaved of authority, and precipitated from the height of empire, suddenly disappeared, and even the burial-place of that noxious beast was nowhere to be seen" (*Death of Persec.* 2; *ANF* 7:302). Domitian not only was murdered in his own palace, but also, despite all his magnificent public works, had his name erased from Roman annals. Decius, who was no better than a savage beast, died by the hand of barbarians who surrounded and killed him. For that reason he was not even buried, and his naked body was abandoned to be eaten by beasts and birds of carrion. Valerian, captured by the Persians, was employed by King Shapur as a stool on which he trod when mounting his horse. Aurelian was murdered by those closest to him. All of this should have served as a warning to these tyrants, but it had no effect, and so persecution continued.

Lactantius summarizes this story in the first six chapters of his work. The remaining forty-six chapters deal with the persecution and death of Diocletian and his main minions in persecution. This is possibly the most important part of his work, at least for historians, for it is one of our main sources for the persecution during Diocletian's reign and the debates over the matter in the imperial court. As to Diocletian himself, Lactantius claims that his abdication was the result of disillusionment over his many failures, and that he suffered from convulsions and dementia to the point where he refused to eat and died in despair.

The *Divine Institutes* are Lactantius's main and most extensive work. Lactantius seems to have begun the first of the seven books in this work shortly after the beginning of Diocletian's persecution, when he fled into exile. The seventh book was written after the end of the persecution. Therefore Lactantius must have been writing this work for ten or eleven years (from 303 or 304 to sometime after 313).

The first three books of the *Divine Institutes* are a continuation of the long history of Latin-speaking apologists from North Africa that we have already seen: Tertullian, Cyprian, and Arnobius, among others. The first book seeks to prove the falsehood of pagan gods. While Lactantius acknowledges the value of the efforts of those who have abandoned luxury and comfort in order to seek wisdom, he also insists that the human mind is incapable of discovering God's great truths and that therefore divine revelation is necessary.

The truth, that is the secret of the Most High God, who created all things, cannot be attained by our own ability and perceptions.

Otherwise there would be no difference between God and man, if human thought could reach to the counsels and arrangements of that eternal majesty. And because it was impossible that the divine method of procedure should become known to man by his own efforts, God did not suffer man any longer to err in search of the light of wisdom, and to wander through inextricable darkness without any result of his labour, but at length opened his eyes, and made the investigation of the truth His own gift, so that He might show the nothingness of human wisdom, and point out to man wandering in error the way of obtaining immortality. (*Div. Inst.* 1, preface; *ANF* 7:9)

Lactantius then proceeds to provide a list of those who have known something about God, beginning with the prophets of Israel, continuing with poets and philosophers, and moving eventually to the *Sibylline Oracles* and other such witnesses. From them Lactantius draws the main characteristics of divinity, in order then to stress the folly of believing in gods who are merely glorified human beings and whose actions and moral principles leave much to be desired.

The second book, *On the Origin of Error*, continues the subject of the indignity of pagan gods and the folly of worshiping heavenly bodies or idols made by human hands. Nor is one to believe the assertions of soothsayers, augurs, or interpreters of dreams.

While the second book showed that the source of much idolatry and superstition is crass error by the unlearned, in the third, *On False Wisdom*, Lactantius tries to show that polytheism is also partly due to the philosophers, whose mutual contradictions are such that little of what they say is worthy of credit. Therefore, human wisdom is incapable of attaining the final truth:

Here, here is that which all philosophers have sought throughout their whole life; and yet, they have not been able to investigate, to grasp, and to attain to it, because they either retained a religion which was corrupt, or took it away altogether. Let them therefore all depart, who do not instruct human life, but throw it into confusion. For what do they teach? or whom do they instruct, who have not yet instructed themselves? whom are the sick able to heal, whom can the blind guide? Let us all, therefore, who have any regard for wisdom, betake ourselves to this subject. Or shall we wait until Socrates knows something? or Anaxagoras finds light in the darkness? or until Democritus draws forth truth from the well? or Empedocles extends the paths of his soul? or until Arcesilas and Carneades see, and feel, and perceive?

Lo, a voice from heaven teaching the truth, and displaying to us a light brighter than the sun itself. Why are we unjust to ourselves, and delay to take up wisdom, which learned men, though they wasted their lives in its pursuit, were never able to discover. Let him who wishes to be wise and happy hear the voice of God. (*Div. Inst.* 3.30; *ANF* 7:100)

That being the case, it becomes necessary to expound the truth as it has been revealed to Christians. Lactantius begins this task in his fourth book, *On True Wisdom and True Religion*. This fourth book focuses on the person of Jesus Christ, who "was twice born, first in the spirit, and afterwards in the flesh" (*Div. Inst.* 4.8; *ANF* 7:106). Here Lactantius retells the life of Jesus, from his birth to his ascension, showing how the prophets and some of the ancient oracles announced each event in that life.

Here he also reaffirms what had been said earlier by Justin and others about the Son of God and the philosophical doctrine of the Logos: "But the Greeks speak of Him as the *Logos*, more befittingly than we do as the word, or speech: for *Logos* signifies both speech and reason, inasmuch as He is both the voice and the wisdom of God. And of this divine speech not even the philosophers were ignorant" (*Div. Inst.* 4.9; *ANF* 7:107).

Finally, in the last chapter of this fourth book, Lactantius deals with the heresies that have appeared among Christians:

> But since many heresies have existed, and the people of God have been rent into divisions at the instigation of demons, the truth must be briefly marked out by us, and placed in its own peculiar dwelling-place, that if any one shall desire to draw the water of life, he may not be borne to broken cisterns which hold no water, but may know the abundant fountain of God, watered by which he may enjoy perpetual light. Before all things, it is befitting that we should know both that He Himself and His ambassadors foretold that there must be numerous sects and heresies, which would break the unity of the sacred body; and that they admonished us to be on our guard with the greatest prudence, lest we should at any time fall into the snares and deceits of that adversary of ours, with whom God has willed that we should contend. (*Div. Inst.* 4.30; *ANF* 7:133)

The fifth book, *On Good*, deals particularly with the injustice committed against Christians when they are judged without being given an opportunity to be heard. The arguments that Lactantius employs here are clearly derived from Cyprian, Tertullian, and Arnobius. But Lactantius goes beyond them, speaking of an original justice in which there is no private property, and therefore no one deprives another of access to the gifts of nature. The loss of this original justice has led to violence and war, and it will continue to do so as long as people insist on worshiping false gods. If, on the contrary, humankind returns to the true God, such injustices and violence will cease:

> They, therefore, who think that no one is just, have justice before their eyes, but are unwilling to discern it. . . . Learn, therefore, if any intelligence is left to you, that men are wicked and unjust because gods are worshipped; and that all evils daily increase to the affairs of

men on this account, because God the Maker and Governor of this world has been neglected; because, contrary to that which is right, impious superstitions have been taken up; and lastly, because you do not permit God to be worshiped even by a few.

But if God only were worshiped, there would not be dissensions and wars, since men would know that they are the sons of one God; and, therefore, among those who were connected by the sacred and inviolable bond of divine relationship, there would be no plottings. (*Div. Inst.* 5.8; *ANF* 7:143)

It is in the midst of this discussion on justice that Lactantius writes lines that witness to the manner in which Christians, even as late as the fourth century, understood justice and shared their goods:

Some one will say, Are there not among you some poor, and others rich; some servants, and others masters? Is there not some difference between individuals? There is none; nor is there any other cause why we mutually bestow upon each other the name of brethren, except that we believe ourselves to be equal. For since we measure all human things not by the body, but by the spirit, although the condition of bodies is different, yet we have no servants, but we both regard and speak of them as brothers in spirit, in religion as fellow-servants. Riches also do not render men illustrious, except that they are able to make them more conspicuous by good works. For men are rich, not because they possess riches, but because they employ them on works of justice; and they who seem to be poor, on this account are rich, because they are not in want, and desire nothing.

Though, therefore, in lowliness of mind we are on an equality, the free with slaves, and the rich with the poor, nevertheless in the sight of God we are distinguished by virtue. And every one is more elevated in proportion to his greater justice. For if it is justice for a man to put himself on a level even with those of lower rank, although he excels in this very thing, that he made himself equal to his inferiors; yet if he has conducted himself not only as an equal, but even as an inferior, he will plainly obtain a much higher rank of dignity in the judgment of God. (*Div. Inst.* 5.16; *ANF* 7:151)

The sixth book, *On True Worship*, does not deal, as one might expect, with the manner in which one is to worship, but rather with the need of two essential elements for true worship: first, that it be worship to the only true God; and second, that it is also service to the rest of humankind and to the image of God found in it. Here once again Lactantius insists on the need for sharing what one has, of doing good without expecting reward, and of giving to those who will give nothing in return.

Finally, the seventh book, *On the Happy Life*, begins by discussing and rejecting what Stoics on the one hand and Epicureans on the other considered to be a happy life. Full happiness will come in the end times, when God will punish some and reward the rest with eternal life. Before that final time, when God will destroy evil and judge humankind, there will be a thousand years of preparation for the judgment. This will involve a renewal of the world so that the sun will be seven times brighter and the moon will reflect its light. During those thousand years the devil will be bound, but near the end God will free him, and there will be a battle whose result will be the death of those who are evil, and the just will walk in the world replete with bones and dead bodies.

Lactantius closes his work with an invitation and a promise:

> This is our inheritance, which can neither be taken away from any one, nor transferred to another. And who is there who would wish to provide and acquire for himself these goods?
>
> Let those who are hungry come, that being fed with heavenly food, they may lay aside their lasting hunger; let those who are athirst come, that they may with full mouth draw forth the water of salvation from an ever-flowing fountain. By this divine food and drink the blind shall both see, and the deaf hear, and the dumb speak, and the lame walk, and the foolish shall be wise, and the sick shall be strong, and the dead shall come to life again. For whoever by his virtue has trampled upon the corruptions of the earth, the supreme and truthful arbiter will raise him to life and to perpetual light. (*Div. Inst.* 7.27; *ANF* 7:222–23)

Besides these two main works already discussed, Lactantius left a treatise *On Divine Wrath*. There is also a *Summary of the Divine Institutes* that may well be his work, although this is not certain. Equally doubtful is the authorship of two poems frequently attributed to him, one on the phoenix and another on the passion of Jesus.

VICTORINUS OF PETTAU

Victorinus was bishop of Pettau or Petovia in Pannonia, what now is Hungary. The very name "Petovia" has misled some into declaring him bishop of Poitiers, in what is now France. It is difficult to decide whether to classify him among Latin or Greek writers. He apparently knew Greek better than Latin, but most of his many biblical commentaries were written in Latin. Jerome would later declare that his style did not do justice to the content of his works. According to Jerome, Victorinus wrote commentaries on several books of the Old Testament, as well as a refutation of heresies and a commentary on the Revelation of John. Of all of these works, only the commentary on Revelation is extant, in a translation by Jerome from Greek to Latin. We also have a rather extensive fragment of his treatise *On the Creation of the World*.

His interpretation of Revelation is clearly millennialist, reading the entire book as a program or outline of events to come. In some cases this results in novel interpretations. For instance, when discussing the four horsemen that appear in chapter 6 of Revelation, Victorinus does not believe that the first represents any sort of evil, but rather the Holy Spirit:

> The first seal being opened, he says that he saw a white horse, and a crowned horseman having a bow. For this was at first done by Himself. For after the Lord ascended into heaven and opened all things, He sent the Holy Spirit, whose words the preachers sent forth as arrows reaching to the human heart, that they might overcome unbelief. And the crown on the head is promised to the preachers by the Holy Spirit. (*Commentary on the Revelation of John* 6.1; *ANF* 7:350)

OTHERS

A poet of whom very little is known is Commodian. Most scholars are inclined to think that he was from North Africa, but there is no definitive proof for such a claim. Nor can precise dates be given for his life and writings. While some have suggested a date as late as the fifth century, most likely he did write during the third century. Two of his poetical works are extant: *Instructions on Christian Doctrine* and *Apologetic Hymn*. The first of these is a collection of eighty-six poems of varying lengths: the shortest has only six verses, while the longest has forty-eight. Each of these poems is also an acrostic, so that the first letters of each verse spell out a word or a phrase related to the subject of the poem itself. In two poems, those first letters are simply the alphabet. In this work Commodian begins with comments about various ancient gods—Saturn, Jupiter, Mercury, Neptune, Bacchus, and others—and then moves on to give advice to his readers. The first series of advices are addressed to people in various conditions. For instance, the rich are told to be humble, and judges are told to be just and not to bend before demands of the rich. After an attack on Jews, Commodian turns to give more advice to Christians according to their state within the church: catechumens, penitents, those seeking martyrdom, ministers, and so forth.

Commodian's other work, his *Apologetic Hymn*, is a single composition of 530 verses arranged in couplets. The style is more fluid, for here the poet does not force language in order to produce acrostics. As to their content, Commodian simply repeats, now in verse, what many earlier apologists had said. Scholars of Latin poetry make it clear that Commodian was not an outstanding poet. His verses seem to be written not to be read by the intellectual elite, but rather to serve as a means for teaching the uneducated. For that purpose, the use of acrostics and metric rhythm might be useful.

There are also several fragments and anonymous works dating from the late third century. We have, for instance, extensive fragments of a refutation of Novatian's views that may have been written by a certain Asterius Urbanus, perhaps while Novatian was still living. There is an anonymous treatise *On the Repetition of Baptism* that has already been mentioned when discussing Cyprian and seems to have been written by a bishop in North Africa who did not agree with Cyprian and most of his colleagues in the area.

Several of Cyprian's correspondents wrote letters that are still included among his epistles; one of them was Novatian, whom we have already discussed. About several others, little is known beyond what may be learned from their letters to Cyprian and his responses: Celerinus, Lucian, Caldonius, Lucius, Felix. The correspondence between Cyprian and Cornelius is an important indication of the links and tensions that Novatian's schism built between Carthage and Rome. These letters, jointly with the already-mentioned correspondence between Dionysius of Rome and Dionysius of Alexandria, are almost all that remain of the third-century writings by bishops of Rome.

Possibly the most studied writing from the third century, or perhaps from the second, is a fragment discovered by Ludovico Muratori, and therefore known as the "Muratorian Fragment." Quite possibly what we have here is the most ancient of extant canons or lists of books of the New Testament. However, it is difficult to determine its date, which some place even as late as the middle of the fourth century. Its list of books in the New Testament, after the four Gospels and Acts, includes thirteen Epistles of Paul, but not Hebrews; two of John, that of Jude, but not the Epistles of Peter and James; and the Revelation of John. It also includes several books that did not finally remain as part of the Bible: the *Wisdom of Solomon*, the *Revelation of Peter*—whose authority was still debatable, according to the fragment itself—and the Shepherd of Hermas.

Part 4

From Nicaea to Constantinople

Introduction to Part 4

The fourth century brought unexpected changes to the life of the church. During the first decade of that century, the church was facing the worst persecution it had ever known. Early in the next decade, in 313, emperors Constantine and Licinius put an end to persecution. During the next few years everything changed radically. Soon Constantine became master of the entire empire. Although officially he did not become a Christian until he was baptized on his deathbed, Constantine increasingly favored the church. His mother, Helena, sponsored the building of great churches at the sacred places of Christianity. Until recently persecuted, Christianity was now tolerated and even promoted. The process continued to the point that long before the end of the century Christianity was the official religion of the Roman Empire.

It is not possible to survey here all the enormous changes that took place on matters such as worship, the prestige of bishops and other leaders, the rapid disappearance of the catechumenate, the building of great basilicas, and so forth. For our purposes here, the most important point is that the fourth century was the golden age of early Christian literature. Names such as Athanasius, Hilary of Poitiers, Basil of Caesarea, Gregory of Nazianzus, Gregory of Nyssa, Ambrose, Jerome, and many others are ample witness to that fact. Augustine, to whose work we shall turn in part 5 of our study when dealing with the fifth century, also lived a significant part of his life during that golden fourth century.

This did not mean, however, that all the major problems facing the church were solved. In many ways, it was the opposite. The golden century was also a century of iron. While the end of persecution made it possible for Christians from various parts of the world to communicate more easily among themselves, and also for many of them to devote significant time to literary labors, that century was also a time of theological controversy such as the church had never seen before. Without much exaggeration, one may well say that the intellectual life of the church was dominated by controversies surrounding Arianism, with its two climactic points that generally serve as limits to this fourth part of this book, the Council of Nicaea (325) and the Council of Constantinople (381). Between those two points, the years around 362 may be considered a watershed, when new currents developed that would eventually lead to the final rejection of Arianism at the Council of Constantinople. For this reason the present section of our story could well be divided into two subsections, for we shall deal first with Christian literature that was generally produced before that watershed, and then with later Christian literature, still in the fourth century.

Finally, one must insist that the context for the various developments of the fourth century was the radical shift from a persecuted to a favored church. A consequence of this different situation was that the controversies of that century were not limited to theological matters, but had also political dimensions. In exchange for favoring the church, emperors expected its obedience and submission. Repeated intervention by the state and its authorities in the controversies of the time and in other matters that until then had been decided by the church alone did not lead to favorable conditions for reflection and theological discussion. For that reason, many of the great figures that have just been mentioned—Athanasius, Basil of Caesarea, Ambrose, and many others—repeatedly clashed with the emperors and their representatives. Therefore much of their work shows their commitment to the difficult task of retaining the essence of earlier Christian faith and life in radically different and unexpected conditions.

14

Eusebius of Caesarea

THE END OF PERSECUTION

Quite possibly there is no better source to understand the changes that took place in the life of the church early in the fourth century than the life and writings of Eusebius of Caesarea. Eusebius seems to have been born near the year 260, probably in Caesarea in Palestine, where he spent most of his life. Whether his family was Christian or not is not known, although since Eusebius does not speak about a conversion from paganism, most historians are inclined to think that he was born into a Christian family. What is quite clear is that the dominant figure during his youth was the bishop of Caesarea, Pamphilus—to such a point that later Eusebius would call himself "Eusebius of Pamphilus."

Pamphilus was born in Beirut and did most of his studies in Alexandria under the Origenist Pierius, who after the martyrdom of Pamphilus would write his biography, of which several ancient authors speak, but it has not reached our days. When Pamphilus arrived at Caesarea, the bishop placed him in charge of the extensive library that Origen had compiled and left behind, to which Pamphilus then added significantly. For this task he recruited a number of collaborators, among them young Eusebius. After Pamphilus died as a martyr in 309, Eusebius continued the task, and it was this library that later provided much of the material for his famous *Church History*.

In 303, under Diocletian's reign, what Christians would soon call the Great Persecution broke out. Apparently it took some time to reach Palestine, and even then the martyrs in that area were not as many as elsewhere. But one of them was Pamphilus, who was arrested in 307 and killed in 309. Eusebius then wrote a biography of his mentor and included a list of all the documents that Pamphilus was able to collect. Unfortunately, this bibliography, which historians would find quite useful in order to know the development of early Christian literature, has been lost.

How Eusebius managed to survive persecution is not known. Part of the answer may be that the policy during this particular persecution was to seek mostly the leaders of the church, and at that time Eusebius was still a young man. In any case, we know that while Pamphilus was in prison, Eusebius visited him repeatedly, and together they wrote an *Apology of Origen*.

Persecution in Palestine abated after the death of Pamphilus, and in the year 311 Emperor Galerius, jointly with the other three who shared rule of the empire with him, issued a decree of tolerance. This did not put an end to all persecution, for still one of the emperors, Maximinus, continued persecuting Christians. Finally, in February of 313, Constantine and his brother-in-law Licinius issued the famous Edict of Milan, which would change the life of the church forever and which Eusebius quotes:

> When I, Constantine Augustus, and I, Licinius Augustus, came under favorable auspices to Milan and took under consideration everything which pertained to the common weal and prosperity, we resolved among other things, or rather first of all, to make such decrees as seemed in many respects for the benefit of every one; namely, such as should preserve reverence and piety toward the deity. We resolved, that is, to grant both to the Christians and to all men freedom to follow the religion which they choose, that whatever heavenly divinity exists may be propitious to us and to all that live under our government. (*Ch. Hist.* 10.5.4; *NPNF*[2] 1:379)

This edict, and many other imperial actions that followed, radically changed the life of Eusebius as well as of the entire church. Although for some time Eusebius focused on serving as pastor to Christians in Caesarea, where he was now bishop, by then several of his writings were circulating widely, and his fame was such that many requested his counsel or invited him for special occasions.

EUSEBIUS AND ARIANISM

But then, just as persecution passed, theological debates came to the foreground. The most important of these had to do with the Alexandrian presbyter Arius and his doctrine, that the Son was lesser than the Father and not eternal as was the Father. Although Eusebius did not quite agree with Arianism, he did incline in that direction. At any rate, he thought that bishop Alexander of Alexandria had acted improperly and too rashly in dealing with Arius. In response to the growing debate, the bishop of Antioch, who supported the position of Alexander, convoked a synod that excommunicated those who supported Arianism, including Eusebius of Caesarea. Finally, when Bishop Hosius of Cordova, who had been sent by Constantine to try to calm the waters, reported to the emperor that he had not been able to do so, Constantine decided to call a great council of bishops from all the church. This met in Nicaea in July of 325.

Athanasius (studied in the next chapter) has preserved the letter that Eusebius wrote to his congregation, explaining what had taken place at the council, apparently because he feared that many among his flock would think that he had wavered. In that letter Eusebius claims that it was he who suggested to the gathered bishops the baptismal creed that was used in Caesarea, and that this was received by the assembly, although Constantine suggested that the word "consubstantial" (*homoousios*) be added. The result was a creed that may well be the most important document in the history of the church beyond the New Testament:

> We believe in one God, the Father Almighty, Maker of heaven and earth, and of all things visible and invisible.
> And in one Lord Jesus Christ, the Son of God, the only-begotten of the Father, that is, of the substance of the Father, God from God, Light from Light, true God from true God, begotten, not made, of one substance with the Father by whom all things in heaven and on earth were made; who for us humans, and for our salvation, came down from heaven, and was incarnate. Being human, he suffered, and the third day he rose again, and ascended into heaven, and he shall come again, to judge the quick and the dead.
> And in the Holy Spirit . . .

This was followed by several anathemas against various expressions or theological opinions that would contradict what the creed said. But those who declared that there was when he was not, that he was not before he was born, or that he was made out of nothing, or who affirmed that the Son of God is of a different hypostasis or of a different substance, or is created, or can change or be altered—all of these the catholic church declared to be anathema. These anathemas or condemnations were to have equal force with the creed itself and were never lifted. However, the traditional usage of creedal formulas in connection with the liturgy, and particularly with baptism, resulted in their being set aside as inappropriate whenever the creed itself was recited.

With a number of additions and modifications, and without the anathemas at the end, this formula, now known as the Nicene Creed, became the most generally accepted creed in the entire Christian church, much more so than the Apostles' Creed, which is limited to Western churches. Therefore, if what Eusebius tells is the exact truth—which some historians doubt, claiming that he was simply trying to justify his actions before his congregation—Eusebius played an important role in the formulation of the most important Christian creed.

At any rate, Eusebius's reaction to the council itself shows how things were changing for Christians. As Eusebius reports, at the council there were more than 250 bishops, while the presbyters and others accompanying them were much more numerous. Eusebius gives us a glimpse of the overwhelming experience that he and his colleagues had:

> In effect, the most distinguished of God's ministers from all the churches which abounded in Europe, Lybia, and Asia were here assembled. And a single house of prayer, as though divinely enlarged, sufficed to contain at once Syrians and Cilicians, Phœnicians and Arabians, delegates from Palestine, and others from Egypt; Thebans and Libyans, with those who came from the region of Mesopotamia. A Persian bishop too was present at this conference, nor was even a Scythian found wanting to the number. Pontus, Galatia, and Pamphylia, Cappadocia, Asia, and Phrygia, furnished their most distinguished prelates; while those who dwelt in the remotest districts of Thrace and Macedonia, of Achaia and Epirus, were notwithstanding in attendance. Even from Spain itself, one whose fame was widely spread took his seat as an individual in the great assembly. (*Life of Constantine* 3.7; *NPNF*[2] 1:521)

And Eusebius continues:

> Now when the appointed day arrived on which the council met for the final solution of the questions in dispute, each member was present for this in the central building of the palace, which appeared to exceed the rest in magnitude. On each side of the interior of this were many seats disposed in order, which were occupied by those who had been invited to attend, according to their rank. As soon, then, as the whole assembly had seated themselves with becoming orderliness, a general silence prevailed, in expectation of the emperor's arrival. . . . And now, all rising at the signal which indicated the emperor's entrance, at last he himself proceeded through the midst of the assembly, like some heavenly messenger of God, clothed in raiment which glittered as it were with rays of light, reflecting the glowing radiance of a purple robe, and adorned with the brilliant splendor of gold and precious stones. (*Life of Const.* 3:10; *NPNF*[2] 1:522)

These words, and many others along the same lines, have led many to consider Eusebius an opportunistic flatterer. But one must remember that when Eusebius wrote these lines, Constantine had just died, and therefore there was not much to be gained by flattering him. What is clearly true is that Eusebius, enthused by the changes that Constantine brought to the life of the church, tended to overlook the great emperor's many faults. Constantine died in 335, and Eusebius continued his literary and pastoral work, becoming somewhat detached from the continuing theological debates until his death in 339.

THE WORKS OF EUSEBIUS

The literary work of Eusebius began long before the end of persecutions, when he was still working with his admired mentor Pamphilus. The defense of Origen that he wrote in collaboration with Pamphilus, now lost, was one of his earliest works. Apparently a few years earlier he had written *Against Hierocles*, a pagan who claimed that the Pythagorean philosopher Apollonius of Tyana was greater than Jesus. He had also published a collection of prophecies regarding the coming of Jesus.

Around 311, when persecution was still raging, Eusebius published a *Chronicle* in two parts. The first of these is a chronology of universal history as it was known at the time. The second relates that history of the world with the history of God's people, beginning with Abraham. His purpose seems to have been both didactic, offering a holistic view of universal history, and also apologetic, showing the deep roots of Christian faith in the faith of Abraham and his descendants. Although the original Greek has been lost, the entire text still exists in an Armenian translation, and the second half also in a Latin translation by Jerome. At about the same time as the *Chronicle*, Eusebius wrote *On the Martyrs of Palestine*, which in some manuscripts became a sort of appendix to the eighth book of his *Church History*. Later he wrote the *Life of Constantine*, to which he soon added a *Praise of Constantine*. There are also a few of his letters still extant, as well as several essays on biblical subjects. The most interesting among the latter is *Canons of the Gospels*, in which he lists those passages that appear in all four Gospels, those appearing in three or two of them, and finally those that appear in a single Gospel.

Most of Eusebius's work is devoted to apology and history. Besides the already-mentioned *Against Hierocles* and the *Chronicle*, much later he also wrote *Theophany*, of which only a Syriac version is extant and in which Eusebius once again deals with prophecies announcing the coming of Jesus. But his great apologetic work is the yoked set of *Preparation for the Gospel* and *Demonstration of the Gospel*.

Preparation for the Gospel and *Demonstration of the Gospel*

In fifteen books, the *Preparation for the Gospel* seeks, in Eusebius's own words, "to show what Christianity is to those who do not know it." From the very beginning of this work, one notices the strong influence of the long philosophical tradition leading from Plato to Origen, with its emphasis on the value of souls above bodies. Thus, after declaring that "it is important to clarify what is this that we call gospel," Eusebius explains:

The gospel proclaims to all that the great and highest gifts announced in ancient times are now actual and visible to all. It is not a matter of seeking a blind wealth, or leading a miserable and painful existence, nor of what has to do with the body and its death, but rather of that which is crucial to the souls, which have a spiritual nature and to which bodies must be subjected following the soul as a shadow. (*Prep. Gosp.* 1.1.2; PG 21:24)

After this brief summary of what he takes to be the gospel message, Eusebius turns to the various objections and accusations raised against Christianity. But what he seeks to refute is no longer the ignorant slander of earlier times, when people claimed that Christians were given to orgies and various other immoralities. Shortly before the time of Eusebius, Neoplatonic philosopher Porphyry of Tyre had published *Against Christians*, a work in which he employed rational arguments to try to show the error of Christianity. Among other things, for Porphyry Jesus is no longer an imposter, as some had claimed earlier, but rather a great teacher and philosopher whose teachings Christians have perverted. It is partly in response to this that in his *Preparation for the Gospel* Eusebius seeks to show first of all that Christianity is a reasonable faith: "We shall deal with them by means of clear evidence, and not with vacuous arguments. We shall use the same demonstrations that we give those who come to listen to our doctrine and that we employ in controversy with our opponents in more philosophical questions" (*Prep. Gosp.* 1.3.2; PG 21:32).

This promise is followed by several chapters where Eusebius tries to show that deciding to accept Christian doctrine is neither foolish nor irrational. He then turns to religious traditions such as those of the Phoenicians and the Egyptians, from which he says the Greeks have derived many of their beliefs. After a long exposition and refutation of all sorts of myths and religious practices, at the beginning of his seventh book Eusebius finally declares, "The time has come to describe the manner of life of the Hebrews, their philosophy and their piety, which we have come to prefer over those of our own ancestors" (*Prep. Gosp.* 7.1.1; PG 21:508). This is the subject of the seventh and eighth books. The ninth is mostly a long list of quotations showing the religion of Israel and its value. While some of these quotations are drawn from Jewish authors such as Philo, most of them are pagan in origin—and Eusebius even quotes the very Porphyry whom he is refuting. The tenth book follows along the same lines, now trying to show by another series of quotations that the Greeks, including Porphyry himself, have drawn much of their wisdom from the Hebrews. In books 11 to 15, Eusebius focuses first on the Platonic tradition, to which he belongs, in order to show that if properly understood this tradition fits well with Christianity, and once again he includes abundant quotations from Porphyry. He then turns to the old argument of the contradictions of the philosophers, including Plato, but above all Aristotle, whose philosophy he summarizes before the entire work finally ends with the promise of a sequel to *Preparation for the Gospel*:

> Having shown the disagreements among them and their doctrines, and also that the study of nature is not our concern, that it is useless and incomprehensible (and the same could be said of all the false education and learning of which the children of philosophers pride themselves), . . . we shall close this work on *Preparation for the Gospel*. The work that completes this one, the *Demonstration of the Gospel*, will require a different point of departure. We must still respond to what is said against us by those of the circumcision, who claim that, belonging to a different nation and a different race, we take possession of their sacred books and of what they include, even though they were not written by us. (*Prep. Gosp.* 15.62.12–18; PG 21:1408)

At the beginning of *Demonstration of the Gospel*, Eusebius declares that this is the work that he promised at the end of the *Preparation*:

> After much toil to complete my fifteen books on *Preparation for the Gospel*, . . . I shall now take as witnesses those beloved of God who are known all over the world. These are Moses and his successors, who were famous for their holiness, and the blessed prophets and sacred writers. Quoting them I will show how they announced events that would take place in our time. (*Dem. Gosp.* 1, prologue; PG 22:13–15)

The full work consisted of twenty books, of which only ten and some fragments of the rest are extant. After speaking highly in the first book of the writings and faith of the Hebrews, in the second he claims that Jews have abandoned the ancient religion and that this too was foretold by prophets of old. Beginning with the third book, and to the end of the extant material, Eusebius relates each of the main events of the life of Jesus to passages in the Hebrew Scriptures. In the end his work is not so much an apology against Judaism, but rather an attempt to use the Hebrew roots of Christianity to refute Porphyry and other pagans who claimed that Christianity was a baseless new invention.

The *Church History*

However, Eusebius's most famous and valuable work is his *Church History*, in ten books. Although he had written most of this work before the advent of Constantine and the peace of the church, after these events he added eight extra chapters dealing with them, and he corrected what he had written before in view of the new conditions. As in several of his other works, at the very beginning Eusebius declares his purpose:

It is my purpose to write an account of the successors of the holy apostles, as well as of the times which have elapsed from the days of our Saviour to our own; and to relate the many important events which are said to have occurred in the history of the Church; and to mention those who have governed and presided over the Church in the most prominent parishes, and those who in each generation have proclaimed the divine word either orally or in writing.

It is my purpose also to give the names and number and times of those who through love of innovation have run into the greatest errors, and, proclaiming themselves discoverers of knowledge falsely so-called, have like fierce wolves unmercifully devastated the flock of Christ.

It is my intention, moreover, to recount the misfortunes which immediately came upon the whole Jewish nation in consequence of their plots against our Saviour, and to record the ways and the times in which the divine word has been attacked by the Gentiles, and to describe the character of those who at various periods have contended for it in the face of blood and of tortures, as well as the confessions which have been made in our own days, and finally the gracious and kindly succor which our Saviour has afforded them all. Since I propose to write of all these things I shall commence my work with the beginning of the dispensation of our Saviour and Lord Jesus Christ. (*Ch. Hist.* 1.1.1–3; *NPNF*² 1:81)

The entire first volume of the *Church History* is then devoted to the time before Jesus, then to his birth under Augustus Caesar, and what took place during the reign of Tiberius. Here we find the legend that the king of Edessa sent a message to Jesus, who responded with a letter that Thaddeus took to Edessa. The second book deals with the very first days of the church and what took place in Palestine after the ascension of Jesus. It also includes the expansion of Christianity to other places and the very first martyrs. The third book continues with the story and traditions about the apostles, the Jewish rebellion against Rome, and the persecution of Domitian. The fourth book lists the succession of bishops in Rome and Alexandria and tells about various heresies in the second century, about Justin, the martyrdom of Polycarp, and similar matters. The next book provides details about martyrs in Gaul, continues listing the bishops of Rome as well as Jerusalem, describes the early Montanist movement, and so forth. Thus the *Church History* moves along in a fairly clear chronological order, all leading to the tenth book and the end of persecution under Constantine, when, according to Eusebius, "we are now permitted to see and celebrate such things as many truly righteous men and martyrs of God before us desired to see upon earth and did not see, and to hear and did not hear" (*Ch. Hist.* 10.1.4; *NPNF*² 1:369).

Throughout this entire work Eusebius continues the practice we have noticed before, abundantly quoting sources and authorities, often including lengthy paragraphs by other authors. This is one of the many reasons why today Eusebius's *Church History* is the most important source we have for much of the history of early Christian literature. Many authors and works he mentions would have been entirely forgotten if it were not for him. Many of the fragments of lost works that we have been citing throughout these pages are actually taken from the *Church History* of Eusebius.

As any historian, Eusebius had his own agendas and biases. Correcting his work after the peace of the church, Eusebius tries to show that the Roman Empire was established so that someday it could come together with the church. This means, for instance, that Eusebius leads us to think that persecution was due to misinformed Roman rulers, when in truth it seems that the more the rulers knew about Christianity, the more they persecuted it.

In any case, Eusebius and his career are a symbolic bridge that carries us rapidly from the worst persecutions and through the peace of the church, in order to reach a time of bitter theological debates, of which the controversies leading to the Council of Nicaea were only the beginning. The outward peace that the church had attained with the end of persecution was not paralleled by an equal peace among Christians.

15

Athanasius

There was no more important Christian writer in the early years of the fourth century than Athanasius of Alexandria, the great defender of the decisions of the Council of Nicaea. However, in order to understand him and his work, it is necessary to deal also with a vast number of treatises, letters, and other documents, some supporting him and the council, and some attacking them. Several of these writings reflect the doubts concerning the decisions of Nicaea that we have already seen in an important leader such as Eusebius of Caesarea. Others proposed more radical forms of Arianism. Unfortunately, most of these texts have disappeared, and all we have are fragments, often quoted in order to refute them, and a few letters from some of the most important figures in the debate.

ARIUS AND ARIANISM

Since the controversy that occupied a good part of the life of the church during the fourth century revolved around the teachings of Arius, those teachings are a good introduction to the life and writings of Athanasius. Arius's most important writing seems to have been a confession of faith written in verse. All that remains of this are a few quotations, most of them cited by Athanasius in order to refute them. According to an Arian historian, Arius wrote these verses so that, being sung to popular tunes, they would be a means of circulating and promoting his views. We do have three letters of Arius, or at least important portions of each of them.

The first of these three letters was addressed to Eusebius of Nicomedia, who would soon become the great defender of Arianism. In that letter, Arius complains that he and all others who, with him and this Eusebius, were disciples of Lucian of Antioch have been treated unjustly. Referring to his own bishop Alexander of Alexandria, he says:

> He has driven us out of the city as atheists, because we do not concur in what he publicly preaches, namely, God always, the Son always; as the Father so the Son; the Son co-exists unbegotten with God; He is everlasting; neither by thought nor by any interval does God precede the Son; always God, always Son; he is begotten of the unbegotten; the Son is of God Himself. . . . These are impieties to which we cannot listen, even though the heretics threaten us with a thousand deaths. But we say and believe, and have taught, and do teach, that the Son is not unbegotten, nor in any way part of the unbegotten; and that He does not derive His subsistence from any matter; but that by His own will and counsel He has subsisted before time, and before ages, as perfect God, only begotten and unchangeable, and that before He was begotten, or created, or purposed, or established, He was not. (quoted by Theodoret, *Church History* 1.4; *NPNF*[2] 3:41)

The second letter, written shortly thereafter, was addressed to Alexander. This includes Arius's declaration of faith, although expressed less starkly:

> The Son, put forth by the Father outside time, and created and established before the worlds, did not exist before He was born, but, being born outside time before the worlds, came into being as the Only Son of the Only Father. For He is neither eternal, nor co-eternal, nor co-uncreated with the Father, nor has He an existence collateral with the Father, as some say, who postulate two unborn principles. But God is before all things, as being indivisible and the beginning of all. Wherefore He is before the Son also. (quoted by Hilary, *On the Trinity* 4.13; *NPNF*[2] 9:34)

Finally, the third extant letter of Arius was written to Emperor Constantine some two years after the Council of Nicaea. It is rather conciliatory in tone, for it says nothing about whether the Son is eternal or not. An interesting point in this letter is that Arius seems to believe that it is not up to church authorities to restore him to the communion of the church, but up to the emperor, to whom he pleads that "may [I] by your pacific and devoted piety be reunited to our mother, the Church, all superfluous questions and disputings being avoided" (quoted by Socrates, *Church History* 1.26; *NPNF*[2] 2:29).

As already stated, the main promoter and defender of Arianism was Eusebius of Nicomedia. Although there is abundant information regarding his theological opinions, and particularly regarding his many political moves seeking to undo the decisions of Nicaea, all that remains of his many writings are fragments quoted by his opponents and a significant portion of two letters, although the authorship of the second of these is in doubt. The first of these letters was written to Paulinus, bishop of Tyre, shortly before the Council of Nicaea. There Eusebius complains that Paulinus has not come to the support of Arius. The second letter, which claims to be written by Eusebius and Bishop Theognis of Nicaea and is addressed to the main leaders of the Council of Nicaea, implies that Arius has been restored to the communion of the church (which may well not be true) and therefore requests that the two writers of the letter also be readmitted to communion.

Although Alexander of Alexandria and Hosius of Cordova were two of the main protagonists of the process leading to the Council of Nicaea, all we have from either of these two is a few letters. The two that we have from Hosius were written long after the Council of Nicaea and therefore refer more to the debates that took place after the Council, debates to which we shall return in another chapter. The first of the two extant letters from Alexander is a long epistle that he writes to his counterpart in Constantinople (also called Alexander) shortly after the controversy broke out in Alexandria, letting him know about the teachings of Arius, the actions that have been taken against him, and the refusal of Arius to submit to the authority of his bishop and the rest of the church. Against what Arius proposes, Alexander argues that if the Father is eternally a father, he must also eternally have a Son. After claiming that what Arius teaches is a denial of the true divinity of the Son, Alexander tells the bishop of Constantinople that Arius and his followers have the support of three bishops in the area of Syria. (Although Alexander does not give their names, we know from the above-quoted letter from Arius to Eusebius of Nicomedia that the three were Eusebius of Caesarea, Paulinus of Tyre, and Theodotus of Laodicea.)

Alexander's second letter is an encyclical addressed "to our beloved and most honored fellow-Ministers of the Catholic Church everywhere" (quoted by Socrates, *Church History* 1.6; *NPNF*[2] 2:3). Here Alexander reports on the teachings of Arius and the action taken against him. This letter, written a few years before the Council of Nicaea, is an indication of the manner in which the debate was expanding, as Arius on the one hand and Alexander on the other sought support beyond Alexandria itself. It is therefore an important document in seeking to reconstruct the process that led from what was originally a debate within a particular city to the great Council of Nicaea and the ensuing controversies.

One of the main opponents of Arianism at the Council of Nicaea was Marcellus of Ancyra, whose writings have also been lost, except for a letter quoted by Epiphanius. In sharp contrast with Arius, who underscored the distinction between the Father and the Son, Marcellus was more inclined toward Sabellianism, a doctrine that tended to confuse the three persons of the Trinity.

Marcellus was condemned as a heretic and deposed by a council in Constantinople. In his exile he went to Rome, where he met both Athanasius and Julius, the bishop of Rome. In his letter, addressed to Julius, Marcellus complains that some opponents of the Council of Nicaea have attempted to turn back the accusation of heresy against him. To prove his orthodoxy, he includes a declaration of his faith:

> In agreement with Holy Scripture, I believe that there is one God and his only begotten Son, who is always with the Father and has no beginning, but is truly God—not created, not made, but on the contrary always in existence. . . . This Son, this power, wisdom, truly and in fact Word of God, our Lord Jesus Christ, is a power that cannot be severed from God, and by whom all that has been made was made. . . . Sacred Scripture has taught me that the divinity of the Father cannot be distinguished from that of the Son, for if the Son or Word is severed from God Almighty, one would come to the conclusion that there are two gods. (quoted by Epiphanius, *Heresies* 3.72; PG 42:395, 388)

THE LIFE OF ATHANASIUS

With that as background, we can now turn our attention to the outstanding figure in the debate that took place immediately after the Council of Nicaea: Athanasius of Alexandria. Little is known about Athanasius's early life. Since he spoke Coptic, and some of his enemies mocked the darkness of his skin, one may well suppose that he was part of the Coptic population, that is, the ancient Egyptians who had been conquered successively by Greeks and Romans and were now generally marginalized by both government and society. Although details are not clear, in his youth he came into close contact with the monks of the Egyptian desert. Later, in the midst of his struggles, the support of these monks proved to be a great asset. Athanasius must have been some twenty-five years old when the Council of Nicaea convened. He attended as a deacon, serving Alexander of Alexandria. When the latter died, Athanasius was elected to succeed him as bishop of Alexandria. At that time, three years after the council (328), imperial policy was beginning to turn against what had been done in Nicaea, and therefore the life of Athanasius was marked by constant conflict with the authorities and repeated exiles. One of those exiles took him to Rome where, as we have just seen, he met both Bishop Julius and Marcellus of Ancyra, whom he may well have met earlier in Nicaea, as well as others. Without ever having the support of the state, Athanasius continued his long series of exiles and returns until he finally died in Alexandria in 373. During the first years after the Council of Nicaea,

Athanasius became its staunch defender, to such a point that some historians have concluded that in the struggle Athanasius created a so-called Arianism that was different from what Arius originally taught, but was rather a combination of a number of concerns that many had regarding what had been decided in Nicaea.

Later Athanasius came to the conclusion that many among those who opposed the decisions of the great council did so because it seemed to them that, in declaring that the Son is "of the same substance" as the Father, the council had fallen into the Sabellian error of not distinguishing sufficiently among the persons of the Trinity. This led Athanasius to insist less on the exact vocabulary of Nicaea, particularly its anathemas. These declared that any who would say that the Son is of a different "substance" or "hypostasis" from the Father was a heretic. However, after taking into account the concerns of those who criticized the Nicene Council, Athanasius convoked a synod that gathered in Alexandria in 362 and accepted the possible use of different terms in order to affirm both the unity and the distinctions among the three persons of the Trinity.

ANTI-ARIAN WRITINGS

Athanasius's literary work was quite extensive. Furthermore, precisely due to his prestige, at a later time other writings that were not his were attributed to him. As a result, there are quite a few sermons that are said to be his, yet whose authorship is dubious. The same is true of his extensive correspondence, although to a lesser degree, for we do have a number of letters that may be properly attributed to him. Among these, the most famous is the letter that he wrote in 367, following the custom that the bishop of Alexandria would write an encyclical declaring the exact date of Easter for that year. In this letter, Athanasius includes a list of the sacred books of the Bible, which is of great importance for the history of the canon of the New Testament.

Probably the best way to understand the theology and writings of Athanasius is to begin with two works that he wrote before the Council of Nicaea, *Against the Heathen* and *On the Incarnation of the Word of God*. In a way, these two works are a single project, which is why some ancient writers tell us that Athanasius wrote "two books against the Gentiles." These two books, particularly the first, are part of the long line of apologetic works that we have been following since the second century. At the beginning, Athanasius declares that his main purpose is to answer those pagans who mock the cross of Christ and declare that Christians are disciples of an evildoer. According to Athanasius, at the beginning there was only goodness, but human free will opted for evil and falsehood, and this is the origin of idolatry. This is why so many of the ancient gods are themselves evil and immoral, and their worship promotes evil and immorality among humans.

In the second part of this first treatise, Athanasius offers a positive description of what true religion is. Although God is far above and beyond anything human, the path to God is not far away, but is to be found within the soul itself. The soul is by nature rational, and if it were not impeded by evil, it would recognize the image of God in itself. Then looking at nature it would see the hand of the Creator, since "creation, as though in written characters, declares in a loud voice, by its order and harmony, its own Lord and Creator" (*Ag. Heath.* 34; *NPNF*[2] 4:22).

> For who that sees the circle of heaven and the course of the sun and the moon, and the positions and movements of the other stars, as they take place in opposite and different directions, while yet in their difference all with one accord observe a consistent order, can resist the conclusion that these are not ordered by themselves, but have a maker distinct from themselves who orders them? or who that sees the sun rising by day and the moon shining by night, and waning and waxing without variation exactly according to the same number of days, and some of the stars running their courses and with orbits various and manifold, while others move without wandering, can fail to perceive that they certainly have a creator to guide them? (*Ag. Heath*, 35; *NPNF*[2] 4:23)

Athanasius then moves on to the doctrine of the Word of God, who is God's very wisdom through whom all things were made and are ordered. God, "like an excellent pilot, by His own Wisdom and His own Word, our Lord and Saviour Christ, steers and preserves and orders all things" (*Ag. Heath.* 40; *NPNF*[2] 4:25).

This serves as a point of departure for Athanasius's second work, *On the Incarnation of the Word of God*. In its first chapter are words that may well serve as a key to understanding the theological outlook of Athanasius: "The renewal of creation has been the work of the self-same Word that made it at the beginning" (*Inc.* 1; *NPNF*[2] 4:36). What Athanasius means by this is that sin simply an error or a bad decision that can be remedied with mere repentance. Had that been the case, the incarnation of the Word would not have been necessary. The truth is that human beings, initially gifted with a mind after the image of God, instead of following that mind have opted for evil, and the consequence is an inescapable subjection to death and corruption.

> Now, if there were merely a misdemeanour in question, and not a consequent corruption, repentance were well enough. But if, when transgression had once gained a start, men became involved in that

corruption which was their nature, and were deprived of the grace which they had, being in the image of God, what further step was needed? or what was required for such grace and such recall, but the Word of God, which had also at the beginning made everything out of nought?

For His it was once more both to bring the corruptible to incorruption, and to maintain intact the just claim of the Father upon all. For being Word of the Father, and above all, He alone of natural fitness was both able to re-create everything, and worthy to suffer on behalf of all and to be ambassador for all with the Father. (*Inc.* 7; *NPNF*[2] 4:40)

The incarnation of the Word of God has changed everything, so that all of creation is now new. According to Athanasius, what has happened is similar to what takes place when a powerful king visits a city. The visit itself of the king, his presence in the city, brings new order and dignity to the inhabitants of the city. Likewise in the incarnation, "now that He has come to our realm, and taken up his abode in one body among His peers, henceforth the whole conspiracy of the enemy against mankind is checked, and the corruption of death which before was prevailing against them is done away" (*Inc.* 9; *NPNF*[2] 4:41).

Furthermore, since the result of all this is the restoration of the image of God that humans have lost, Athanasius—jointly with many other authors in the Christian East—affirms that "He was made man that we might be made God" (*Inc.* 54; *NPNF*[2] 4:65), by which he does not mean that we become gods, but rather that we come to participate in divine immortality.

Although Athanasius wrote all this before Arianism became an issue, it is clear that from this perspective he could not accept the teachings of the Arians. Adding to this Athanasius's faithfulness to the memory of Alexander, and the impact that the great assembly in Nicaea must have had on the young Athanasius, one can see why throughout the rest of his life his main concern was the refutation of Arianism. At the beginning, this led him to use the term "Arians" for any who opposed or criticized the decisions taken at Nicaea, and particularly its creed. Later he came to soften this position, coming to understand and to accept the reasons why some feared that what had been done at Nicaea was a capitulation to Sabellianism.

Athanasius's main work against Arianism is his *Orations against the Arians*, a collection of four speeches, although general scholarly opinion is that only the first three are really his. At approximately the same time as he was composing these speeches, the middle of the fourth century, he also wrote an *Apology against the Arians* and a *History against the Arians* that once again are really one work in two installments, retelling the course of the entire controversy. These writings, jointly with other minor works of Athanasius, today are one of our main sources to reconstruct the complicated events, the comings and goings, and the varying political conditions of the entire debate on the divinity of the Word of God. Here we see not only the course of the controversy, but also many of the intrigues that took place around Athanasius himself.

The debates regarding the divinity and eternity of the Son soon led to a similar controversy regarding the Holy Spirit. Some were willing to affirm the divinity of the Word or Son of God and to declare him coeternal and consubstantial with the Father, but were not ready to say the same about the Holy Spirit. Athanasius's main intervention in that controversy is to be found in his three letters to Serapion, bishop of Thmuis in Lower Egypt. Around the year 358, Athanasius, in one of his many exiles, first hid near Alexandria but eventually was forced to flee further and take refuge among the monks of the desert in the area of Thebaida, in Upper Egypt. There he received a letter from Serapion, a long-standing ally, who now spoke to him of new concerns. Athanasius replied:

> I was overjoyed in receiving your letter. But upon reading it I was discouraged by the perseverance of those who had earlier decided to oppose truth. My dearest friend, you wrote that you were seriously concerned that some among those who have left the Arians because they blasphemed against the Son of God have now turned against the Holy Spirit, claiming that he is a creature, and is just one among the angels that serve before the throne of God. (*Ep. Serap.* 1.2; PG 26:529, 532)

Athanasius saw this as a new way of rejecting what had been decided in Nicaea, no longer attacking the divinity of the Son, but now that of the Holy Spirit. He continues his letter:

> This is a false attack on Arianism, for in truth they are not struggling against Arianism itself, but against the true faith. Just as the Arians in denying the Son also deny the Father, so do these people by diminishing the Holy Spirit also diminish the Son. And these two groups [the Arians and the new enemies of the Holy Spirit] have divided among themselves the task of opposing truth, so that while some attack the Word, and others attack the Holy Spirit, both groups equally blaspheme against the Trinity. (*Ep. Serap.* 1.3; PG 26:532)

The rest of the letter is a series of arguments supporting the full divinity of the Holy Spirit, many of them stressing Athanasius's main contention, that whoever denies the Holy Spirit also denies the Son and blasphemes against the Father. Near the end of this letter, Athanasius rejoices that it is not only the defenders of Nicaea who reject these teachings, but even the Arians reject them—although in this case not because they are concerned over the divinity of the Holy Spirit, but because they believe that both the Holy Spirit and the

Son are creatures, and not divine. Athanasius calls these people "enemies of the Spirit" (*pneumatomachoi*); for that reason to this day, the word "Pneumatomachian" refers to those who are willing to accept the divinity of the Son, but not that of the Spirit.

The second of these three letters is merely a summary of the first, at the request of Serapion, who had asked Athanasius to write such a summary, so that believers would have a clear and simple response to the Pneumatomachians. The third is a summary of some parts of the first that had not been included in the second.

But Athanasius' literary labors were not limited to the Arian controversy and the divinity of the Holy Spirit. He also wrote several biblical commentaries: on Genesis, Psalms, Ecclesiastes, and the Song of Solomon. All that remains of these are fragments quoted by later authors. In any case, probably the most influential writing of Athanasius was not one of his careful theological treatises on Trinitarian relations, but rather his *Life of Antony*.

THE *LIFE OF ANTONY*

The *Life of Antony* was written in 357, a year after the death of the famous ascetic, and its purpose was simply to let his life and teachings be known, particularly by those beyond the area of Egypt—at least, this seems to follow from the heading of the Latin version, which declares that this life was addressed "to the brethren in foreign lands." No matter whether that was the case or not, there is no doubt that the *Life of Antony* provided a significant stimulus for the development of monasticism in the West. According to Athanasius, Antony was born within a relatively well-to-do "Egyptian" Christian family, which probably means that they were Copts. When he was still young, following the example of the apostles, he decided to abandon everything and lead a life of poverty in the desert. There he was faced with great struggles, for

> the devil, who hates and envies what is good, could not endure to see such a resolution in a youth, but endeavoured to carry out against him what he had been wont to effect against others. First of all he tried to lead him away from the discipline, whispering to him the remembrance of his wealth, care for his sister, claims of kindred, love of money, love of glory, the various pleasures of the table and the other relaxations of life, and at last the difficulty of virtue and the labour of it; he suggested also the infirmity of the body and the length of the time. In a word he raised in his mind a great dust of debate, wishing to debar him from his settled purpose. (*Life Ant.* 5; NPNF² 4:196–97)

In his retreat, Antony insisted on solitude, not allowing visits or other distractions, and he was in constant struggle with demons, as Athanasius tells us. The first part of the *Life* deals mostly with these struggles, with Antony's temptations, and with his final victory. Athanasius summarizes:

> And so for nearly twenty years he continued training himself in solitude, never going forth, and but seldom seen by any. After this, when many were eager and wishful to imitate his discipline, and his acquaintances came and began to cast down and wrench off the door by force, Antony, as from a shrine, came forth initiated in the mysteries and filled with the Spirit of God. Then for the first time he was seen outside the fort by those who came to see him. And they, when they saw him, wondered at the sight, for he had the same habit of body as before, and was neither fat, like a man without exercise, nor lean from fasting and striving with the demons, but he was just the same as they had known him before his retirement. And again his soul was free from blemish, for it was neither contracted as if by grief, nor relaxed by pleasure, nor possessed by laughter or dejection, for he was not troubled when he beheld the crowd, nor overjoyed at being saluted by so many. But he was altogether even as being guided by reason, and abiding in a natural state. (*Life Ant.* 14; *NPNF²* 4:200)

The center of the *Life* is a long speech that Antony delivers to the monks—originally in Coptic, Athanasius tells us—on the virtues, attitudes, and practices necessary for monastic life. The central theme of this entire section is the need to renounce all things of the world and a radical change in values:

> Nor let us think, as we look at the world, that we have renounced anything of much consequence, for the whole earth is very small compared with all the heaven. Wherefore if it even chanced that we were lords of all the earth and gave it all up, it would be nought worthy of comparison with the kingdom of heaven. . . . Why not rather get those things which we can take away with us—to wit, prudence, justice, temperance, courage, understanding, love, kindness to the poor, faith in Christ, freedom from wrath, hospitality? If we possess these, we shall find them of themselves preparing for us a welcome there in the land of the meek-hearted. (*Life Ant.* 17; *NPNF²* 4:200–201)

After Antony's long speech, Athanasius tells the story of the rest of his life, his intervention against Arianism, his miracles, his debates on the theme of idolatry, and finally his death.

The impact of this work of Athanasius was enormous. While it was circulating throughout the Eastern reaches of the empire, it was also being translated into Latin, thus allowing the West to learn about Egyptian monasticism. In part due to the fame of this writing, people began thinking that Antony was the founder of Egyptian monasticism, when he probably had a good number of forerunners. At any rate, the *Life of Antony* became the benchmark for what was to be expected of a good monk; it also served as a pattern for later authors who wrote lives of saints similar to the one that Athanasius had written.

THE FATHERS OF THE DESERT

This is possibly the best place to mention ancient literature giving witness to the growing monastic movement, particularly in Egypt. The Antony of whom Athanasius wrote, who therefore came to be reputed as the founder of Egyptian monasticism, was in fact one—certainly the best known—of the many men and women who withdrew to the desert seeking to lead holier lives at a time when the church seemed to be accommodating too readily to the surrounding world. Like Antony, most of those monastics were Copts. Although Antony himself did not grow up poor, many of those who opted for ascetic life in the desert came from the dispossessed class within Egyptian society. The flight to the desert that was taking place was not always motivated by religious or spiritual concerns. Taxes and other burdens on poor Copts were such that many simply abandoned their lands to take refuge in the desert. There, even though living on lands that were not as fertile as those they had left, they could now live better than on the fertile lands that the rich were taking over. The word "anchorite," which now refers to a hermit, originally meant simply "fugitive," so that both the monk who fled society for religious reasons and the peasant who abandoned his lands for economic reasons were "anchorites."

Since most of those who fled to the desert were illiterate, very little is left of those first monks—and even less of the nuns, who in many cases seem to have been twice as numerous as the monks. Antony, coming from a somewhat higher class than the other monks, did write several letters. Athanasius tells us of a correspondence between Antony on the one hand and Constantine and his three sons on the other, who wrote to Antony for some unknown reason. According to Athanasius, Antony did not wish to answer, declaring that for the emperor to write to him was not such a remarkable thing, since God, the greatest ruler of all, had written to humankind through the Law and through God's own Son. On the insistence of other monks, Antony did respond. But whatever he said has been lost.

We do have seven letters that he wrote in Coptic to other monks, which have survived in Greek and Latin translations. These are interesting not only because they allow us a glimpse into monastic life and the relationships among monks, but also because they prove that Athanasius was speaking the truth when he affirmed that Antony had rejected the teachings of Arius. Thus, in his seventh letter (the fourth in other lists) Antony comments on Arianism and declares that its error is partly the result of human pride and of the lack of knowledge of oneself:

> As for Arius, who stood up in Alexandria, he spoke strange words about the Only-begotten: to him who has no beginning he gave a beginning, to him who is ineffable among men he gave an end, and to the immovable he gave movement. *If one man sins against another man, one prays for him to God. But if someone sins against God, to whom should one pray for him?* That man has begun a great task, an unheal-able wound. If he had known himself, his tongue would not have spo-ken about what he did not know. It is, however, manifest, that he did not know himself. (Samuel Rubenson, *The Letters of St. Antony* [Min-neapolis: Fortress, 1955], 211)

Taking part also in a controversy at the time regarding the forgiveness of sins, in a letter to fellow monk Theodorus, Antony says:

> He [God] enjoined me to write to you, disclosing that almost every-where there are many who, although they worship Christ in truth, have sinned after being baptized and [then] weep and mourn. Since He has heard their weeping and mourning, God has wiped out the sins of all those who have acted so, until the day in which this letter is given to you. Read it to your brothers, so that they too might hear it and rejoice. (*To Theodorus*; in Rubenson, *Letters of St. Antony*, 170–71)

Several other letters have been attributed to Antony, but do not seem to be his. They are most likely the work of his disciple Ammonas or some oth-ers among his followers. These provide us a glimpse into monastic ideals at that time. In one of the letters that may well be from Ammonas, there is an interesting exhortation to perseverance:

> You are aware that in the beginning the Holy Spirit leads you to rejoice in spiritual work, for he knows that your hearts are pure. And when the Spirit has given you joy and sweetness, he simply leaves you. This is a sign. He does this with every soul that is beginning the quest for God. He leaves everyone in order to know whether or not they will continue looking for him. (http://www.surco.org/files/Ammonas_0.pdf)

After those early founders, most of their disciples and followers left little writ-ten testimony. An outstanding Egyptian monastic leader was Pacomius, who is credited with having created cenobitic monasticism, one in which monks live in community and no longer as hermits. There is a *Rule* attributed to Pacomius. But over the centuries this document has been so much amended and interpolated that it is impossible to discern how much of it really comes from Pacomius himself.

One of the most erudite monks of those early years of Egyptian monasticism was Serapion of Thmuis, whose correspondence with Athanasius has already been quoted. Apparently Serapion carried correspondence with several others. But most of his letters have been lost. Among those that remain, probably the most valuable is an epistle of consolation and encouragement addressed to the monks in Alexandria, who at that point were sorely tried by the Trinitarian controversies. We also have a collection of short prayers to be employed in various liturgical settings: baptism, confirmation, communion, funerals, and so forth. These are of particular interest for historians of liturgy. But his most important writing was *Against the Manichees*. Although it is not as thorough as Augustine's later treatment of the same subject, it does show exceptional erudition.

From a much later date, we do have the writings of Evagrius Ponticus and of Palladius. But they fall beyond the chronological scope of the present chapter.

Finally, there is a collection of sayings of the most famous spiritual directors of the desert. It is commonly known as the *Sayings of the Fathers*, or as the *Apophthegmata of the Fathers*. In this case once again it is difficult and even impossible to determine what material actually belongs to those to whom it is attributed. The textual history of this document is very complex, and scholars sharply disagree. Furthermore, there are several other similar collections. In one of them sayings are organized according to the initial letter of the name of the monk who is supposed to have proposed them. Another is organized on the basis of the subjects of each saying. Although there is no doubt that these comments originally circulated in Coptic, what is now extant are some translations into other languages, none of them earlier than the end of the fourth century.

16

Latin Writers of
the Early Fourth Century

The fourth century brought to the Latin-speaking West changes similar to those we have already seen in the Greek-speaking East. The Edict of Milan, which put an end to persecution, opened the way both to a vast literary production and to theological debates involving the entire church. Although among these debates the most important was the one concerning the teachings of Arius and his successors, there were several others. But above all it is important to underscore that the new circumstances made the fourth century the golden age of ancient Christian literature.

JULIUS FIRMICUS MATERNUS

The work of Julius Firmicus Maternus is significant as a witness to the great change that took place in the fourth century, and also to the continuity of certain elements that did not disappear. Little is known of his life, although a passing reference in one of his writings apparently indicates that he belonged to the senatorial class and pursued a career in law. At any rate, Maternus grew up in a pagan environment; as he became disillusioned with his legal work, he turned to astrology, with the result that his work in eight books on that subject became a standard textbook for astrologers. This he wrote around the year 336, but some ten or fifteen years later, now a Christian, Maternus wrote a treatise *On the Errors of Profane Religions*.

This treatise, in twenty-nine chapters, may be divided into two sections, the first comprising chapters 1 to 17 and the second section the rest. The first part is a critique of the gods that is quite similar to those we have already found in other Christian apologists. According to Maternus, the gods are frequently immoral and even criminal, thus no more than a reflection of human life and experience. The second part of the work is much more interesting, for here Maternus discusses the religions of his time, particularly the more esoteric ones. As a result, he provides valuable insight for today's study of what historians call "mystery religions." Maternus himself shows that there are similarities between these religions and Christianity, and he explains that such similarities are a wile of the Evil One in order to lead humans astray.

Remarkably, there is an element of continuity between the manner in which Maternus refers to imperial authority before his conversion and the manner in which he mentions it thereafter. When he was writing about celestial bodies and their government of the world, he declared that the emperor, being divine, was not subject to the influence of the stars. Later, writing as a Christian and addressing Constantius and Constans, two of Constantine's sons who at that time shared imperial authority, he speaks of them as instruments of the hand of God in order to establish Christian truth over against the ancient religions. Furthermore, he even proposes the forced conversion of those who insist on the superstitions of their ancestors:

> Most holy emperors, you must uproot, destroy and most severely punish such abomination. . . . Some staunchly refuse to recant, and are going to their own damnation. Help these wretches. Free them lest they die. If God on high has granted you the Empire, it is so that you may heal their wounds. It is better to free them even against their will than allowing that will to lead them to their damnation. (*Errors* 32; PL 12:1048)

HILARY OF POITIERS

The most distinguished Latin Christian writer in the first half of the fourth century was Hilary of Poitiers. He was probably born in that city around the year 310, but little is known about his youth. It is impossible even to say whether he was born in a Christian or a pagan family. At the beginning of his great work *On the Trinity*, he speaks of a conversion. For this reason it has traditionally been thought that he was a pagan until that conversion. Yet in more recent times some have suggested that the references to that conversion are not autobiographical notes, but rather a literary invitation for the reader to seek truth. What Hilary says on the subject may be summarized in his own words:

> My soul was distracted amid all these claims, yet still it pressed along that profitable road which leads inevitably to the true knowledge of God. . . . While my mind was dwelling on these and on many like thoughts, I chanced upon the books which, according to the tradition

of the Hebrew faith, were written by Moses and the prophets. . . .
Thus my mind, full of these results which by its own reflection and the
teaching of Scripture it had attained, rested with assurance, as on some
peaceful watch-tower, upon that glorious conclusion, recognising that
its true nature made it capable of one homage to its Creator. . . . In this
calm assurance of safety did my soul gladly and hopefully take its rest,
and feared so little the interruption of death, that death seemed only a
name for eternal life. (*Trin.* 1.4, 5, 8, 14; *NPNF*² 9:41–42)

There is no certainty regarding the exact date when he became bishop of
Poitiers, although it must have been some time near the middle of the century. Shortly thereafter, he wrote a *Commentary on Matthew*, and then a more
extensive *Commentary on Psalms*. His work *On the Mysteries* deals mostly with
the first six books of the Old Testament and with Hosea. He also wrote a
work on Job that has been lost. In general, his interpretation is typological: he
is interested not only in the words themselves, but above all in the events that
they narrate and the laws they prescribe as types, figures, or announcements
first of all of Jesus Christ, and then also of what the church and its members
are to be. For instance, commenting on the baptism of Jesus, he says:

> In him the economy of a heavenly mystery is revealed. When he is
> baptized, the gates of heaven open, the Holy Spirit is sent and made
> visible as a dove, and thus the fatherly love of God shines on Jesus. . . .
> This shows us that, thanks to what was fulfilled in Christ, after the
> bath in water the Holy Spirit flies to us through the open gates of
> heaven, and we too are blessed with glory, and being adopted by the
> voice of the Father are made children of God. What actually hap-
> pened is an image announcing in truth the mystery prepared for us.
> (*Comm. Matt.* 2.6; PL 9:27)

Hilary's most important writings have to do with the doctrine of the
Trinity and the debate surrounding Arianism. His work *On the Trinity*
was the most complete discussion of the subject in Latin until the time of
Augustine. He also wrote a *Book on the Synods*, which is an important source
for following the course of the debate on Arianism until a general consensus was reached. Hilary also wrote other shorter works against Arianism:
To Constantius, one of Constantine's sons and successors; *Against Constantius and Auxentius*, the latter an Arian bishop of Milan; and *Against Valens
and Ursacius*, Arian bishops in the areas now known as Croatia and Serbia.
While these were carefully crafted theological treatises, they also had political implications, for Emperor Constantius was a staunch defender of Arianism, while Auxentius, Valens, and Ursacius enjoyed imperial favor. These
treatises were the main source of Hilary's many difficulties as well as his
eventual exile from Poitiers.

Returning then to *On the Trinity*, its purpose and structure are expressed by Hilary himself. Immediately after speaking of the peaceful assurance to which we have already referred, Hilary continues:

> There came to light certain fallacies of rash and wicked men, hopeless for themselves and merciless towards others, who made their own feeble nature the measure of the might of God's nature. They claimed, not that they had ascended to an infinite knowledge of infinite things, but that they had reduced all knowledge, undefined before, within the scope of ordinary reason, and . . . denying, under the cloak of loyalty to the One God, the birth of God the Only-begotten. (*Trin.* 1.15–16; NPNF² 9:44)

In other words, what leads Hilary to compose this work is the challenge of Arianism, which would deny the eternity of the Son. To respond to this challenge, Hilary explains that he proposes to write this work in twelve books, which will move progressively toward truth, addressing first those who have less understanding of these things, and eventually reaching the highest levels of understanding of Scripture and doctrine. But in truth Hilary does not always follow the plan that he outlines in the first book, for occasionally, carried away by his enthusiasm or by his interest in a particular biblical passage, he moves ahead of his own intended outline. Still, one can see the progress of the argument. The first three books, after the already-mentioned introductory comments, are basically an exposition of Christian faith, although obviously underscoring the points on which Hilary believes that Arianism strays from proper belief. Then, in the fourth book, Hilary turns more specifically to Arianism, beginning by a detailed discussion of the letter of Arius to Alexander of Alexandria. Finally, as part of his refutation of Arianism, Hilary deals with the Arian interpretation of various biblical passages, which he seeks to refute and correct one by one.

Hilary's *On the Trinity* took several years to compose. Therefore, it is interesting to read it in the light of the process he describes in his *Book on the Synods*, and in conjunction with others of his writings in which one can see his growing involvement in the Arian controversy. Although he was not yet engaged in that controversy when he wrote his *Commentary on Matthew*, already at that point one can see his concern over Arianism. Soon he became deeply involved in the controversy. In 355 Emperor Constantius forced a synod gathered in Milan to declare Athanasius a heretic. Apparently Hilary was not present, but he soon met with the other bishops of Gaul, who declared themselves in favor of Athanasius and in opposition to those who rejected the actions of the Council of Nicaea—among them, Ursacius and Valens. In response to that action, in the following year and under the guidance of the emperor, a synod whose members Hilary called "false apostles" declared that Hilary—who was present but not allowed to defend himself—was a heretic and asked Constantius to condemn him to exile.

That exile, which began in 356, turned out to be of great benefit for the Nicene cause. While in lands foreign to him, Hilary met several bishops who, without being Arian, would not accept what had been done at Nicaea. There he came to realize that the opposition to Nicaea was not a solid block, for it was composed of various groups with different concerns. The most radical claimed that the Son is "different" from the Father. These are now called the *anomoeans*, named from a Greek word meaning "different." Others preferred to set aside what had been done at Nicaea and suggested that, rather than speaking of the "substance" of God, and discussing whether the Son and the Father are of the same substance, what should be affirmed is that the Son is "similar" to the Father. These are known as *homoeans*, named from a Greek word meaning "similar." Ursacius and Valens belonged to this party, and Hilary wrote against them. They sought to prohibit all discussion of the "substance" of God, and therefore their stance seemed to be a slightly veiled attempt to undercut the decisions of the Council of Nicaea.

Finally, most of those who opposed the Nicene formula, that the Son is "of the same substance" as the Father, were ready to say that the Son is of a substance like that of the Father. These were the *homoiousians*, that is, those who proposed the formula "of a similar substance" (*homoiousios*) rather than the Nicene formula "of the same substance" (*homoousios*). For some time the main defenders of the Council of Nicaea—Athanasius and Hilary among them—insisted on the formula "of the same substance" and rejected all other positions as if they were simply various ways of denying the full divinity of the Son. Now both Hilary and Athanasius began to realize that the so-called homoiousians were not opposed to that full divinity, but were concerned that all distinction between the Father and the Son would be wiped out if they were simply declared to be "of the same substance."

In 357, while Hilary was in exile, a synod gathered in Sirmium rejected all that had been done at Nicaea and prohibited any discussion about the "substance" of the Father or of the Son. The reaction was not slow in coming. The strict defenders of the Nicene formula "of the same substance" as well as those who preferred to speak of a "similar substance" saw in this an imposition of extreme Arianism and a radical denial of the divinity of the Son. Upon seeing that the bishops who were now his neighbors, most of whom belonged to the homoiousian party, where aghast at what came to be known as the "Blasphemy of Sirmium," Hilary began a rapprochement with the leaders of that party.

That rapprochement was not easy. Emperor Constantius continued supporting the Arian cause. It was in the midst of those struggles that Hilary composed his treatises against Constantius as well as against Auxentius, Ursacius, and Valens. But Constantius remained firm in his position. Finally, in clear disobedience to the imperial decree, Hilary decided to leave his exile in the Greek-speaking East and return to Gaul. Although the exact date of that return is not known, it is likely that Hilary was already on his way to Gaul when the legions rebelled against Constantius and declared that the emperor was Julian, commonly known as "Julian the Apostate." Shortly thereafter Constantius died and Julian became master of the empire. The new emperor was set on restoring the ancient pagan religion and therefore abandoned Constantius's policy of forcing Christian bishops to agree with him. As a result, the conversations that Athanasius and Hilary had led to a final agreement between the Nicene party and the homoiousians. But this was a long road, and neither Athanasius nor Hilary, who died in 367, was able to see its final solution. That would be the task of the next generation.

It was in this turbulent context that Hilary wrote his twelve books *On the Trinity*. Some words in book 10 seem to indicate that at least the first ten books were written in exile. In them one hears echoes of the difficulties through which Hilary was living while exiled in the East. But there is also a rather extensive section in book 12 in which Hilary discusses and refutes the stance of the Pneumatomachians (on whose stance see chap. 15 on Athanasius). Since this party made most of its inroads in the Greek-speaking East and was scarcely known in the Latin-speaking West, this may imply that Hilary was still in exile when he completed *On the Trinity*.

Having said this, it is important to point out that for Hilary, what he was writing was not merely a rational discourse on a particular doctrine, but rather an integral part of his service to God. Almost at the very beginning, Hilary prays:

> I know, O Lord God Almighty, that I owe Thee, as the chief duty of my life, the devotion of all my words and thoughts to Thyself. The gift of speech which Thou hast bestowed can bring me no higher reward than the opportunity of service in preaching Thee and displaying Thee as Thou art, as Father and Father of God the Only-begotten, to the world in its blindness and the heretic in his rebellion. (*Trin.* 1.37; *NPNF*[2] 9:50)

The same spirit prevails hundreds of pages later, in another prayer at the end of the entire work:

> Keep, I pray Thee, this my pious faith undefiled, and even till my spirit departs, grant that this may be the utterance of my convictions: so that I may ever hold fast that which I professed in the creed of my

regeneration, when I was baptized in the Father, and the Son, and the Holy Spirit. Let me, in short, adore Thee our Father, and Thy Son together with Thee; let me win the favour of Thy Holy Spirit, Who is from Thee, through Thy Only-begotten. For I have a convincing Witness to my faith, Who says, *Father, all Mine are Thine, and Thine are Mine*, even my Lord Jesus Christ, abiding in Thee, and from Thee, and with Thee, for ever God: Who is blessed for ever and ever. Amen. (*Trin.* 12.57; *NPNF*² 9:233)

EUSEBIUS OF VERCELLI

Eusebius of Vercelli merits at least a brief mention, even though all that remains of his work are a few letters, and some of them of dubious authorship. He was born in Sardinia in 283, and after his father died as a martyr, his mother took him to Rome. As a young man, he became a reader in the church of Rome. Later, upon his return to Sardinia, he was elected bishop of Vercelli. When the already-mentioned synod that declared Athanasius to be a heretic met in Milan in 355, Eusebius refused to go along with that decision. This led to repeated public humiliations and then to the intervention of Constantius, who ordered his exile. As an exile, Eusebius went first to Syria, then to Cappadocia, and finally to the Thebaid, in southern Egypt. As in the case of Hilary, the death of Constantius and the accession of Julian to the throne made it possible for Eusebius to return from exile. On the way home, he stopped at Alexandria, where he was present at the already-mentioned synod led by Athanasius in 362. This synod was a turning point in the Arian controversy, for it was there that Athanasius and other defenders of the Council of Nicaea accepted the orthodoxy of the homoiousians—that is, those who preferred to say that the Son was "of a similar substance" as the Father rather than "of the same substance"—as long as they did not undermine the divinity of the Son. This synod also affirmed the full divinity of the Holy Spirit. Eusebius then went to Antioch, where he tried unsuccessfully to put an end to the schism of Meletius. Back in Sardinia, he continued fighting Arianism, particularly by opposing the Arian bishop of Milan, Auxentius, whom we have already encountered.

The most interesting among the extant writings of Eusebius is a letter that he secretly wrote to his flock while in exile, telling them of the rough treatment he and his companions were suffering under an Arian bishop who acted as if he were their jailer, but also rejoicing in God's power and calling his flock in Vercelli to remain firm.

LUCIFER OF CAGLIARI

Like Eusebius of Vercelli, Lucifer of Cagliari was a bishop on the island of Sardinia. Much of his life paralleled that of Eusebius, for he too was exiled for his refusal to accept the decisions of the Arian synod of Milan in 355. After some time in Syria, and then in Palestine, Lucifer, like Eusebius, completed his exile in the Thebaid. These two leaders worked together in resisting Arianism, and there is still extant a letter in which Lucifer tells Eusebius about the synod of Milan in 355. Also like Eusebius, when Lucifer was returning from exile, he stopped in Antioch. But there his attitude was different from that of Eusebius, for while the latter was trying to heal a schism, Lucifer proved inflexible, rejecting not only the true Arians, but also the more moderate party that sought a solution by means of the formula "of a similar substance."

This attitude was typical of Lucifer, who would be one of the most intransigent among the defenders of the decisions of Nicaea. As he saw matters, any who expressed concern regarding what had been done in Nicaea was simply a heretic and must be shunned. His writings are brief treatises in which he vehemently attacks both the emperor and any whom he believed harbored Arian inclinations. One of these treatises, *On Shunning Heretics*, declares that Arians are as idolatrous as pagans, and that this is also true of Emperor Constantius, who defends them. In another, *On Apostate Kings*, Lucifer warns Constantius that his apostasy will not be forgiven no matter how long God's judgment is delayed. When Constantius requested confirmation that it was indeed Lucifer who had written such things, the latter answered with another brief treatise, *That One Is Not to Show Mercy to God's Enemies*. When Constantius himself did not seem to take him very seriously, Lucifer wrote another treatise, even more acerbic, *That One Must Die for the Son of God*. The same tone pervades Lucifer's most extensive work, his two books *In Defense of Athanasius*. This deals mostly with the synod of Milan of 355 and the error and injustice involved in the entire process of convoking and organizing it, as well as in the decision to condemn Athanasius in his absence and without giving him an opportunity to defend himself.

Although these writings remind us of the vehemence of Tertullian, they certainly lack his elegance. This is so much so that historians of the Latin language use the works of Lucifer as a prime example of the development of vulgar Latin in the fourth century. Lucifer himself boasted about his own lack of education.

Lucifer's unflinching opposition to any stance that could be considered Arian in any way, no matter how moderate, led him to see a great apostasy in the synod that Athanasius led in Alexandria in 362, a synod that made room for the more moderate among the critics of Nicaea. The result was a schism that lasted for several decades and whose followers were called Luciferians.

THE *CHRONOGRAPHY OF 354*

In 354, at the request of a rich Roman, someone produced a manuscript that included several writings and data relating to the history and chronology of Rome. The manuscript itself, which apparently was still extant in the eighth century, has been lost. But we do have copies, and this work by a mixture of known and anonymous writers is commonly called the *Chronography of 354*. Among these documents are several that are valuable for reconstructing the history of the church in Rome. Of these the most important is the *Liberian Catalog*, which is a list of popes from Peter to Liberius, who reigned when the list itself was compiled. Another document in this *Chronography* is the earliest indication we have of the celebration of the birth of Jesus in December.

OTHER AUTHORS

Potamius, a contemporary of Eusebius and Lucifer, served as bishop of Lisbon in the mid-fourth century. Apparently sometimes he supported those accepting the Nicene Creed, and at other times the Arians; yet it is impossible to determine the chronological order of his waverings. After the Alexandrine synod of 362 brought about a rapprochement between the Nicene party and its more moderate opponents, Potamius followed that lead. None of his extant works defend truly Arian positions, and only two of them, his *Epistle to Athanasius* and his *Epistle on Substance*, really deal with that controversy.

Much more interesting, but still lacking great literary value, are his two other works, *On Lazarus* and *On the Martyrdom of Isaiah*. They show his penchant for the dramatic and even disgusting. Dealing with the resurrection of Lazarus, Potamius seems to enjoy the most macabre aspects of death and of the corruption of the body, dwelling at length on putrefaction and its signs. And when discussing the martyrdom of Isaiah, an ancient tradition not found in the Bible, he describes in great detail the dismemberment of the prophet.

As was to be expected, little remains of the writings of the early Arians. Most of them have come to us through quotations that others included in their works to refute them. Thus, in his treatise *Against the Speeches of Heretics*, Augustine extensively quotes an Arian sermon in order then to refute it point by point. Besides the works already mentioned, there is a great multitude of writings of apparent Arian inclinations whose authors and dates cannot be determined. Most have subsisted because they were falsely attributed to an orthodox writer. But even so, their influence on later Christian literature was scant.

17

Other Greek Authors
of the Early Fourth Century

Although in recent chapters our attention has focused on the great figures who flourished during the first half of the fourth century—particularly Eusebius of Caesarea, Athanasius, and Hilary—there are many other authors who should at least be mentioned. This was a time of great literary activity among Christians, who now saw themselves free from the constant fear of persecution and also involved in new controversies that were largely due to the growing facility of communications among believers in various areas. But these controversies came to a turning point around the year 360, when first the death of Constantius, then the government of Julian "the Apostate," and finally the Alexandrian synod of 362, provided an opportunity for the clarification of ideas and the development of a new spirit of reconciliation between the most ardent defenders of the Council of Nicaea and those who, while affirming the full divinity of the Son, had reservations about the word "homoousios," "of the same substance."

For these reasons, that date (362) may be seen as a dividing line in Christian theology and literature during the fourth century. Those whom we have studied in recent chapters generally flourished before 362, as did those whom we shall study in the present chapter. We shall then turn to authors who flourished after that date, devoting individual chapters to the most important among them, and finally two chapters to secondary writers, one to those who wrote in Greek and one to those who employed Latin.

EUSTATHIUS OF ANTIOCH

Although the narrative that we have from Eusebius of Caesarea says little about him, one of the main characters at the Council of Nicaea was Eustathius of

Antioch. After serving as a bishop of the city now known as Aleppo, Eustathius was moved to the very important see of Antioch shortly before the Council of Nicaea, perhaps even in that same year, 325. As bishop of Antioch, his participation in the theological debate would be important. According to the ancient historian Theodoret, when Constantine entered the council, Eustathius "crowned the emperor's head with the flowers of panegyric, and commended the diligent attention he had manifested in the regulation of ecclesiastical affairs" (Theodoret, *Ch. Hist.* 1.6; *NPNF*[2] 3:43). Perhaps the reason why Eusebius of Caesarea says little about Eustathius has to do not only with their doctrinal differences, but also with the resentment of Eusebius because the Council of Nicaea placed all of Syria and Palestine under the jurisdiction of Antioch, thereby positioning Eustathius as Eusebius's superior. Immediately after the council, Eusebius began attacking Eustathius, accusing him of Sabellianism, of making the three persons of the Trinity simply three aspects or faces of God.

Shortly after the council, the Arian party began a campaign against the main leaders of that gathering and therefore against Eustathius. Theodoret tells how the Arians disposed of Eustathius. According to Theodoret, Eusebius of Nicomedia and other Arians organized a pilgrimage to the Holy Land whose true purpose was to destroy Eustathius. When, on the way from Constantinople to Palestine, they visited Antioch, Eustathius received them with honors. But when they came to Palestine, they gathered with others among their supporters and planned the downfall of Eustathius. Theodoret says that they convoked a synod that Eustathius attended. Then

> they bribed a low woman, who made a traffic of her beauty, to sell them her tongue, and then repaired to the council, and when all the spectators had been ordered to retire, they introduced the wretched woman. She held a babe in her arms, of which she loudly and impudently affirmed that Eustathius was the father. Eustathius, conscious of his innocence, asked her whether she could bring forward any witness to prove what she had advanced. She replied that she could not. . . . These truth-loving judges condemned him as an adulterer. When the other bishops, who upheld the apostolical doctrines, being ignorant of all these intrigues, openly opposed the sentence, and advised Eustathius not to submit to it, the originators of the plot promptly repaired to the emperor, and endeavoured to persuade him that the accusation was true, and the sentence of deposition just; and they succeeded in obtaining the banishment of this champion of piety and chastity, as an adulterer and a tyrant. (Theodoret, *Ch. Hist.* 1.20; *NPNF*[2] 3:43)

Eustathius was sent into exile, first in Thracia and then in Macedonia. In 343 he was vindicated by a council gathered in Serdica, today Sofia. But by that time he had already died.

Little remains of Eustathius's many works. Among those that are almost entirely lost, there was an extensive treatise *Against the Arians*, and another *On the Soul*, in which he criticized the Platonic understanding of the soul and then accused the Arians of affirming that the incarnate Word did not take the human soul, but only a body. Although most of his correspondence has been lost, what remain, besides a treatise against Origen regarding the biblical story of the witch of Endor, are very many fragments quoted by later writers. Among them, possibly the most important are those taken from his *Homily on Proverbs 8:22*, where Wisdom speaks about its own origin. There are also a number of works by other authors that were attributed to Eustathius after his death.

In his homily on Proverbs 8, of which Theodoret has preserved more than a dozen fragments, Eustathius employs that passage to affirm the eternity of the Word, over against the Arian claim that the Word is a creature. The "Wisdom," or "Sophia," to which Proverbs refers is the same Word who appears in the Gospel of John and who was incarnate in Jesus Christ. According to Eustathius, God "did not create Wisdom or the Word in whom all power dwelt from the very beginning" (Theodoret, *Dial.* 2; PG 18:680).

But Eustathius goes beyond that, for he clearly poses the christological problem that would occupy the main theologians of the following century, leading to intense debate and schisms: the need to affirm at the same time the full and eternal divinity of the Word and his incarnation in a fully human being. He says:

> If the Word was from the beginning with God and with the Father, and if we affirm that all that exists was made by him, then we have to declare that he is the cause of all that has been created. He was not formed in a woman, but is divine by his very nature, existing by itself, infinite and incomprehensible. And this Word was made human, taking form in the womb of the Virgin by virtue of the Holy Spirit. (quoted by Theodoret, *Dial.* 1; PG 18:677)

As we shall see in other chapters, it was not only Eustathius, but also his successors in what eventually came to be called the "school of Antioch," who underscored the need to affirm the full humanity of Jesus Christ, without denying his full divinity. Furthermore, the typically Antiochene image of the Word dwelling in Jesus "as in a temple" is already to be found in Eustathius.

Eustathius is a clear exponent of the Antiochene tradition also in his biblical interpretation. That tradition generally opposed the allegorical interpretation after the style of Origen, which had become standard fare not only in Alexandria but also in other parts of the church. The only writing by Eustathius that is extant as a whole, *On the Necromancy of Origen*, deals with the episode of the witch of Endor. Here he interprets the passage literally, rejecting Origen's allegorical interpretation. What was at stake in this interpretation was the matter of whether Saul had seen Samuel or a demon claiming to be Samuel, for Origen declared that a just man such as Saul could not be in Hades. Over against this position, Eustathius argues that if a person such as Saul could not be in Hades, Jesus himself would not have been able to descend into Hades. Part of what was at stake here was the strong Antiochene conviction that, in order to be fully human, Jesus had to have also a human soul and not just a body, as Origen and many of his followers said.

MARCELLUS OF ANCYRA

Another of the main opponents of Arianism in the Council of Nicaea was Marcellus, bishop of Ancyra, today Ankara, in Turkey. The course of Marcellus's life was similar to that of Eustathius. Having been declared a heretic and deposed by several synods of Arian inclinations, he was also praised and repeatedly restored by the other side. He seems to have died around the year 375. Some six years later, at the Council of Constantinople in 381, now known as the Second Ecumenical Council, some of his teachings were rejected.

It is difficult to know the exact nature of those teachings. Precisely because he was eventually declared a heretic, little of what Marcellus wrote has been kept, although there are many fragments of his works, particularly of his *Against Asterius*, a foremost Arian theologian. Eusebius of Caesarea wrote a treatise *Against Marcellus*, in which he quotes a letter from the latter. Eusebius says:

> I shall begin by the letter he wrote and will refute each false point in his doctrine. He says that he believes in the Father, God Almighty, and in his Son, the only-begotten of God, our Lord Jesus Christ, and in the Holy Spirit. . . . When he says this, I accepted all. . . . But when, leaving aside divine authority, he claims on the basis of a complicated and purely human reasoning that the Father and the Son are not such in the same manner, such speculation is overly daring. (Eusebius of Caesarea, *Ag. Marc.* 1.4; PG 24:753, 756)

In the detailed refutation that follows, it is clear that Eusebius is accusing Marcellus of Sabellianism, as if the Father, the Son, and the Holy Spirit were only three faces or consecutive modes in which God appears at various times. This seems to indicate that Marcellus understood the affirmation that the Father and the Son are of the same substance (homoousios) as a declaration that the distinctions between them are not eternal. For this reason Athanasius seemed to waver in his attitude toward Marcellus, sometimes supporting him and sometimes not.

In the letter that Marcellus wrote to Julius, the bishop of Rome, in defense of his orthodoxy, we have one of the most ancient texts of what would eventually come to be known as the "Apostles' Creed," although there are other similar texts that are much earlier:

> I believe in God the Father Almighty. And in Jesus Christ, his only Son, our Lord, who was born of the Holy Spirit and of the Virgin Mary; was crucified under Pontius Pilate, and buried; the third day he rose from the dead; ascended to heaven, and is seated at the right hand of the Father, from where he shall come to judge the living and the dead. And in the Holy Spirit; the holy church; the forgiveness of sins; the resurrection of the flesh. (quoted by Epiphanius, *Heresies* 72.3; PG 42:385, 388)

BASIL OF ANCYRA

Marcellus was succeeded as bishop of Ancyra by Basil, who was one of the leaders of the homoiousian party, and therefore one of those with whom Athanasius had to negotiate in order to effect a rapprochement between them and the supporters of the decisions of Nicaea. Most of his work has been lost. What remains is some of his correspondence quoted by Epiphanius in order to declare it heretical. Therefore, one has to read that correspondence with the suspicion that quite possibly Epiphanius did not transcribe the entire text faithfully. At any rate, Basil's formula, that the Son is "of a similar substance" to the Father, was accepted by Athanasius and then by others, as long as it was not understood to mean that the Son is less divine than the Father.

DIDYMUS THE BLIND

A much respected and admired figure during the first half of the fourth century was Didymus the Blind, who lived well into the latter half of the century. As his ancient biographer tells, Didymus became blind as a result of a disease when he was four years old. Although this meant that he never went to school, he became a famous scholar. Among his disciples and biographers is the historian Rufinus, who asserts that quite frequently Didymus remained awake at night, like an animal chewing its cud. Another of his disciples, the outstanding scholar Jerome, also shows his admiration:

Didymus of Alexandria, who became blind when he was very young, and therefore was unable to pursue even the most basic studies, showed such a prodigious intelligence that he became knowledgeable in dialectics and even geometry—sciences that require special gifts. He wrote many admirable works: commentaries on all the Psalms, commentaries on the Gospels of Matthew and John, a treatise on doctrines, two books against the Arians and one on the Holy Spirit (which I [Jerome] have translated into Latin), eighteen volumes on Isaiah, three on Hosea which he dedicated to me, and five on Zachariah, upon my request. He also wrote commentaries on Job, and so many others that to deal with all of them would require an entire book. He still lives, and he is more than eighty-three years old. (Jerome, *On Illustrious Men* 109; PL 23:744)

And in the prologue to his translation of Didymus's treatise on the Holy Spirit, Jerome once again, while acknowledging the lack of formal studies or rhetorical training of his mentor, exalts his wisdom. (Jerome's translation of Didymus's *On the Holy Spirit* is particularly valuable, since the Greek original has been lost, and all we have is Jerome's translation into Latin.) Also Athanasius acknowledged the genius of Didymus, for he seems to have made him head of the catechetical school in Alexandria that Origen had directed much earlier.

Being blind, Didymus did not write with his own hand. Some of his biographers say that several of his works were actually notes that his disciples took as he spoke, and that others were simply dictated.

Unfortunately, Didymus followed Origen in some of his most daring theories, such as the preexistence of souls and universal salvation. For this reason the Council of Constantinople that gathered in 553, more than a century and a half after his death, declared him an Origenist and extended to him the anathemas that it pronounced against Origen. Mostly for that reason, not many took the trouble to copy his works, and as a result most of them have been lost. Part of some of the commentaries that until then were lost were rediscovered in the twentieth century, commentaries on the early chapters of Genesis, as well as on Zachariah, Job, and others. (The story of this discovery is interesting. During the Second World War the British occupying Egypt ordered some digging in an abandoned quarry so it could serve as storage. Those who were doing the digging discovered a large number of ancient papyri buried in the rubble. They sold these documents on the black market, and since that time historians and antiquarians have been slowly recovering them.) These documents show Didymus's enormous erudition. In general they follow Origen's allegorical method of interpretation, so that while commenting on any text, Didymus feels free to jump to a vast and sometimes confusing number of other biblical passages, which he relates to the text being studied by means of allegorical interpretations that are often forced or idiosyncratic.

Besides parts of his commentaries, three theological works of Didymus are extant: the already-mentioned treatise *On the Holy Spirit*, a short writing *Against the Manichees*, and his three books *On the Trinity*. This last work was written toward the end of his life, clearly after the (First) Council of Constantinople in 381. It is therefore an important source for understanding how the debate moved from the decisions of Nicaea (325) to this second council, and how difficulties and differences had been resolved. Since this was written after the Council of Constantinople, Didymus not only defends the Nicene formula but also rejects the teachings of those who denied the divinity of the Holy Spirit, a position rejected by that council. In any case, the entire work is mostly a collection of biblical references supporting the decisions of Nicaea and Constantinople.

The treatise *On the Holy Spirit*, which (as stated above) exists only in Jerome's Latin translation, is earlier than *On the Trinity*. It clearly was written before 381, when Ambrose used it as a source for his own work on the Holy Spirit. Most probably it was written near the date of the synod of Alexandria that took place in 362. The purpose of this writing seems to have been to respond to the request of other monks to refute the errors that were circulating regarding the Holy Spirit and to expound the orthodox position. Almost at the very beginning of the book, Didymus says that

> usually what is best for those who are faithful and reverent and have control of their minds is to remain silent regarding an issue being debated, and not to risk the dangers of their own interpretations. But some have plunged into inquiry about celestial matters on the basis not so much of a holy life as of mere daring. They affirm about the Holy Spirit things that are to be found neither in the Scripture nor in the ancient writers of the church. This forces me to respond to the repeated request of the brethren to affirm our understanding of the Holy Spirit on the basis of Scripture, so that those who differ would not be able to deceive others who might not know this fundamental doctrine. (Didymus, *Holy Spirit* 1; PG 39:1033)

After a brief introduction of a few paragraphs, Didymus dives directly into the matter of the Spirit's nature and activity, in order then to move to the relationship between the Holy Spirit, the Father, and the Son, then to affirm the full divinity of the Spirit in relation to the other two persons of the Trinity. There are abundant biblical references and detailed discussions of particular texts. Interestingly, Didymus bases what he says about the divinity of the Spirit not only on the Bible and on rational arguments, but also on the actual work of the Spirit. Just as Athanasius argued that since the new creation is mostly the work of the Son, and this requires a being just as divine as the author of the first creation, now Didymus employs a similar argument for the full divinity of the Holy Spirit. Thus he dictates, "Moving now to complete what has to be said, we can be certain that the Holy Spirit is of the same substance as the Father and the Son for the following reason: just as both the Father and the Son sanctify and purify believers through communion with them, so does communion with the Holy Spirit sanctify and purify them" (Didymus, *Holy Spirit* 53; PG 39:1078).

EUSEBIUS OF EMESA

Eusebius of Emesa was a native of the city of Edessa, in the southeast of what is now Turkey; the common language in that area was Syriac. However, from a young age he learned Greek, and this allowed him to travel and study both in Antioch and in Alexandria. His prestige was such that he was invited to become bishop of Alexandria. But in those turbulent times, Eusebius preferred to continue with his studies, until he became bishop of Emesa, the city now known as Homs in western Syria. According to Jerome, Eusebius was a prolific author; but almost all of his writings have been lost, and all that we have are some fragments of his biblical commentaries and a collection of sermons that he originally preached in Greek, but have survived only in translations into Armenian and Syriac. Eusebius also became known as a mathematician and as an astrologer, although none of his works on such subjects have survived. Such studies created difficulties for him among his flock in Emesa, and apparently for that reason he preferred to spend much time at the service of Emperor Constantius II, whose adviser he became.

Upon reading the sermons of Eusebius, one is captivated by their dramatic tone, by his vision of the cosmic dimensions of the work of Christ, and by his typological interpretation of Scripture. This may be seen in the following paragraph, taken from a sermon on the passion of Christ:

> And now the day of His crucifixion was the day of Adam's transgression.
> God created Adam on the sixth day; and on that day he transgressed.
> On that day too Jesus became obedient and endured His sufferings at
> the sixth hour, when Adam tasted of the fruit; that we should over-
> come in Christ at the same hour that we were overwhelmed in Adam.
> The Tree of Life in the Garden, is the Tree of the Cross. There was
> a woman, through whom sin came into the world; here is a virgin who
> heard Him say: "Behold thy mother." On that day Adam put forth his
> hand for evil; and Jesus spread His holy arms for our good. Adam drew
> near to the tree; and Jesus laid His hands and His feet on the Tree to
> which they were fastened with nails. Adam tasted of the fruit through

lust; and Jesus tasted of vinegar mingled with bitter gall. Adam heard this sentence: The earth shall bring forth to thee thorns and thistles. Our Jesus of His own will was crowned with the thorns of Adam. Adam brought down a curse upon himself; but Jesus who is blessed by them that are condemned, was hanged on the Tree as one accursed. (trans. S. C. Malan [1859], http://www.tertullian.org/fathers/eusebius _of_emesa_sermon_on_passion_02_trans.htm)

18

The Great Cappadocians

A FAMILY AND A FRIEND

Traditionally, historians have referred to the "Three Great Cappadocians." These are Basil of Caesarea, his brother Gregory of Nyssa, and their friend Gregory of Nazianzus. But in truth the great Cappadocians were four, for Macrina, the older sister of Basil and Gregory of Nyssa, played an important role in the life and thought of her brothers.

The parents of Macrina and her brothers were Christian. Their maternal grandfather had died as a martyr during Diocletian's persecution. During that persecution the paternal grandparents abandoned their lands and hid in the forests for seven years, until the end of persecution. Then they returned to their lands, where they had several children. The father of Macrina, Basil, and Gregory—who was also called Basil, like his father and the most famous of his children—was a respected lawyer and professor of rhetoric in the city of Caesarea in Cappadocia, in what is now Turkey. Their mother, Emilia, belonged to the fairly well-to-do class. Basil the father shared his time between his lands and his work in Caesarea having to do with law and rhetoric. The elder Basil and Emilia had at least ten children, some of whom died in infancy. When their son Basil, later known as Basil the Great, was some fourteen years old, his parents sent him to study in Caesarea. There he met a young man by the name of Gregory, and the two would be friends throughout the rest of their lives.

This other Gregory, who came to be known as Gregory Nazianzen or Gregory of Nazianzus, was a son of a bishop and had come to Caesarea to study with his younger brother Caesarius. Sometime later young Gregory and his brother left for Alexandria, where they met Athanasius. But Gregory wished to study in the famous school in Athens, and soon left for that city. Shortly thereafter Basil joined him in that school. Among their fellow students was a young man by the name of Julian, who later became emperor and was known as Julian the Apostate. After completing their studies, Gregory left for Constantinople and Basil returned to Caesarea. There his success as a professor of rhetoric was such that, according to his own brother, he was puffed up with pride, as if he were superior to all the other inhabitants of the city. It was at this point that Macrina intervened, calling her brother to a new life.

MACRINA

Basil's older sister had led a very different life than her brother. While Basil was seeking fame through his undeniable gifts in rhetoric and administration, Macrina had decided to remain single and to devote herself to a life of prayer and austerity. Although we have no writing from her own hand, her younger brother Gregory of Nyssa has left a witness of her and her thought in two works, the *Life of Macrina*, and the *Dialogue on the Soul and Resurrection*. The first of these two is a hagiographic biography that, while saying much about Macrina's holiness, says little about her thought. For this reason, the *Dialogue on the Soul and Resurrection* is much more interesting, for it comes to us as a conversation whose main character is Macrina, and quite possibly the words that Gregory puts on her lips reflect her own thoughts and words.

At the beginning of the dialogue, Gregory says that when he was grieving the death of his brother Basil he went to visit their sister, whom he calls "the Teacher"—a title by which he refers to her throughout the Dialogue. When he saw her, he was even more sorrowful, for it was evident that she was on her deathbed. This leads to a dialogue about life and death in which Gregory simply expresses doubts, questions, and objections, and Macrina responds. The outcome of the conversation is not only an assurance of the immortality of the soul and the resurrection of the body, but also a vast vision of cosmic dimensions. When Gregory asks her what to tell those who become discouraged by the sorrows of life and the world, Macrina tells him what to say:

> It is foolish, good people, for you to fret and complain of the chain of this fixed sequence of life's realities; you do not know the goal towards which each single dispensation of the universe is moving. You do not know that all things have to be assimilated to the Divine Nature in accordance with the artistic plan of their author, in a certain regularity and order. Indeed, it was for this that intelligent beings came into existence; namely, that the riches of the Divine blessings should not lie idle. The All-creating Wisdom fashioned these souls,

these receptacles with free wills, as vessels as it were, for this very purpose, that there should be some capacities able to receive His blessings and become continually larger with the inpouring of the stream. Such are the wonders that the participation in the Divine blessings works. . . . With such a prospect before us, are you angry that our nature is advancing to its goal along the path appointed for us? Why, our career cannot be run thither-ward, except that which weighs us down, I mean this encumbering load of earthiness, be shaken off the soul. (*Soul and Resurrection*; NPNF² 5:453)

BASIL OF CAESAREA

According to Gregory of Nyssa, it was Macrina who convinced their brother Basil that despite all his triumphs and glories, he was following the wrong path. Basil himself says, "Like a man roused from deep sleep, I turned my eyes to the marvelous light of the truth of the Gospel, and I perceived the uselessness of 'the wisdom of the princes of this world,' that come to naught" (*Epistle* 223.2; NPNF² 8:263). As soon as he was able, he received baptism, which he had postponed, and he followed what he understood as the gospel path. Under the influence of Macrina, and probably of others around her, Basil had come to understand that this required an ascetic life. For that reason he spent some time visiting the famous monastic centers in Egypt, Syria, Palestine, and even as far as Mesopotamia. Upon returning from that long journey, he disposed of all his possessions for the benefit of the poor, determining to live in monastic solitude. But, as in many similar cases, the solitary monk was followed there by others who came seeking his direction for a holy life, and the result was a cenobitic monasticism: a monastic life that takes place not in the solitude of a hermit, but within a community of faith. The monks who were part of that community, as well as many visitors—among them Gregory of Nazianzus, who visited him in 358—would pose questions to him, often having to do with concrete situations in monastic life. His answers, apparently some of them written in shorthand by those who were listening, became the basis for the *Rule of St. Basil*. Although there is no doubt that this rule reflects the practices and teachings of Basil himself, it is difficult to determine how much in it comes from him and what was added later. To complicate the matter, there are several different versions of the *Rule*. At any rate, there is no doubt that this document reflects the manner in which Basil understood monastic life and that a good part of it comes from him. And even though some of Basil's other writings contributed significantly to the development of Christian theology, the *Rule* has had a much more direct impact on Christian life, particularly in the Greek-speaking East.

Basil did leave a collection of principles for Christian living: *Moralia*. In this collection, after a brief summary of each principle of Christian life, Basil discusses a series of biblical passages supporting and clarifying it. Thus, for instance, rule number 11, "That judgments of God are not to be taken lightly, but are to be feared even though their result is not immediate," is followed by his five short paragraphs on Matthew 18:28; John 5:14; Luke 13:1–6; Romans 1:28; and Luke 4:25–26.

Among his writings having to do with practical Christian life, the brief treatise that Basil addressed to his nephews, *To the Adolescents*, merits particular attention. It deals mostly with the difficult question of the relationship between pagan culture and Christian faith. Classical literature included myths about the gods and other similar matters that were contrary to Christian teaching. For that reason many Christians refused to attend schools where that literature was taught and thereby deprived themselves of the rhetorical instruction that Basil himself had received and that he found so useful. Pagans also saw the difference between Christianity and pagan culture, for in Basil's time Emperor Julian the "Apostate" ordered that Christians not be allowed to teach classical literature, which they might interpret after their own fashion. Writing to his nephews, Basil claims that "Sacred Scripture, teaching us divine wisdom, leads us to eternal life. But, since our own inability keeps us from the highest thoughts, we must train our spiritual perception by means of the study of profane writings, which are not completely different, and in which we see truth as in a mirror or in a twilight" (*To the Adolescents* 2; PG 31:565).

Like his brother Gregory of Nyssa and his friend Gregory of Nazianzus, Basil took active part in the theological debates of his time, particularly in those leading to the reaffirmation of the Council of Nicaea at the Council of Constantinople that took place in 381, now called the Second Ecumenical Council.

This practical side of Basil's teachings and life is seen most clearly in his 50 sermons and more than 300 surviving letters. These letters are also one of the main sources that we have today for following the controversies surrounding Arianism during the second half of the fourth century. Among the sermons of Basil, some of the most outstanding are his nine homilies on the six days of creation, which he preached during Lent. In them he categorically rejects the allegorical interpretation of the Alexandrians and defends the more literal interpretation that had become normative both in Syria and in Asia Minor. Apparently some criticized the manner in which he interpreted Scripture, without seeking in it hidden allegorical meaning. Basil responded in the last of his nine homilies on the six days of creation:

I know the laws of allegory, though less by myself than from the works of others. There are those truly, who do not admit the common sense of the Scriptures, for whom water is not water, but some other nature, who see in a plant, in a fish, what their fancy wishes, who change the nature of reptiles and of wild beasts to suit their allegories, like the interpreters of dreams who explain visions in sleep to make them serve their own ends. For me grass is grass; plant, fish, wild beast, domestic animal, I take all in the literal sense. (*Homilies on the Hexameron* 9.11; *NPNF*² 8:101)

Probably the most interesting aspect of the sermons of Basil is the manner in which they respond to the difficult economic conditions of the times, when the concentration of wealth and land in a few hands led to poverty and hunger, and even forced some parents to sell their children into slavery. The sermons of Basil repeatedly deal with these circumstances and with the obligation of Christians to respond to them. While preaching from the Gospel of Luke, on the parable about the man who decided to build bigger barns and died that same day, Basil exhorts his hearers: "Remember the goods that you possess are not really yours. They give joy for a short time and then they slip away like water. But in the end you will have to render a detailed account on them" (*Homilies* 6.2; BAC 607:505). And near the end of his homily, he asks the greedy:

Tell me: What is yours? Where did you get it in order to add it to your goods? It is as if someone, having taken a seat in the theater, would then forbid others to come in, as if what was intended for the use of all were only for him. This is what the rich do, for after taking possession of what are common goods, they turn them into private property simply because they took them first. If each took what was necessary to meet their needs and left the rest for the needy, no one would be rich, but also no one would be poor or needy. (*Hom.* 6.7; BAC 657:570)

In another homily, preached during times of drought and famine, he exhorts his audience to understand the enormity of famine and therefore to share what they have:

The sickness of the famished, hunger, produces a terrible suffering. Hunger is the worst of human calamities and the worst form of death. . . . It is a slowly progressing evil that prolongs pain, a disease that calmly awaits in its den, an ever-present death, but always slow in coming. . . . The flesh clings to the bones like a spider's web, the skin loses its color, for the lack of blood produces an ashy appearance. Then the surface of the body turns dark because of its own weakness. . . . The knees will no longer hold. . . . The voice is weak and languid, the eyes sink in their sockets. . . . The empty stomach shrinks. (*Hom.* 8.7; BAC 657:601–2)

Although our interest here is in literature, one must at least mention the manner in which Basil himself sought to respond to such evil not only with words, but also in action. This he did mostly by founding a community designed particularly to benefit the poor. As his friend Gregory of Nazianzus tells us in the *Panegyric to Basil*, also known as Gregory's *Homily* 43:

> Go forth a little way from the city, and behold the new city, the storehouse of piety, the common treasury of the wealthy, in which the superfluities of their wealth, aye, and even their necessaries, are stored, in consequence of his exhortations, freed from the power of the moth, no longer gladdening the eyes of the thief, and escaping both the emulation of envy, and the corruption of time: where disease is regarded in a religious light, and disaster is thought a blessing, and sympathy is put to the test. (*Hom.* 43; NPNF² 7:416)

In that "Kingdom city," *Basileia*, workers were provided work and training, the sick were attended to, and the hungry were fed. Soon this enterprise gained admirers and emulators, so that other similar communities emerged in nearby areas.

Basil's most important works in the field of theology itself are *Against Eunomius* and *On the Holy Spirit*. Eunomius was the main leader of the extreme Arian party in the time of the Cappadocians. Little is known of his early years, but we do know that he became a deacon in 360, two years before the synod of Alexandria in 362 that marks a turning point in Christian theology in the fourth century. Shortly thereafter he became bishop of Cyzicus, a small town in today's Turkey. When the people of the town rebelled against him and expelled him, he took refuge in nearby Constantinople, at that time under Arian control. Not only Basil wrote against him, but also Didymus the Blind, Gregory of Nyssa, and several others. Near the close of the fourth century, his writings were destroyed by imperial decree, so very little remains of his vast literary production. In the controversies of his time, when the opponents of the decisions of Nicaea were divided, Eunomius took the extreme position of the *anomoeans*, declaring that the Father and the Son are of two different substances. This may be seen in a declaration of faith at the end of his only extant writing, his *Apology*:

> There is only one God, unbegotten and without beginning, and there is nothing before him, because nothing can be before the unbegotten. Nor was there anything with him, for the unbegotten is one and only one, a single being with no composition. This is the one and only, always the same, the creator and maker of all things; particularly of

the only-begotten, but also of all the things that he made. Because he begat, created and made the Son before all things, and before all of creation. This he did through his power and might, but not sharing with him his unbegotten substance. God is incorruptible, inseparable, and indivisible, and does not share his substance, nor does he produce another to subsist in him, for only he is unbegotten. God did not create the only-begotten out of his substance, but out of his will. It was also through him that God made the Holy Spirit, the first and greatest of everything else. . . . And after this, through his Son God made all the creatures in heaven and on earth, visible and invisible, corporeal and incorporeal. (*Apol.* 28; PG 30:868)

It was against this extreme Arianism, that declared that both the Son and the Holy Spirit were creatures, and therefore less than God, that Basil wrote *Against Eunomius*. He did not mince words about Eunomius, whom he calls "liar, stupid, greedy, false, and blasphemous" (*Ag. Eunom.* 1.1; PG 29:501). While repeatedly quoting Eunomius, Basil refutes him both by a careful exegesis of various biblical texts that Eunomius and others used to support their position and by a series of philosophical arguments. In these arguments, Basil affirms that Eunomius errs in declaring that the essence of God is being "unbegotten." Once one falls into that error, it obviously follows that the Son, begotten by the Father, cannot share in the divine substance. Basil then moves on to what Eunomius has to say regarding the Holy Spirit as a creature made by God through the Son, and therefore to be included among the "all things" that according to the Gospel of John were made by God through the Word.

The other strictly theological work of Basil is *On the Holy Spirit*. This was written in response to those who criticized the words that Basil employed in the doxology. They would say: "Glory to the Father through the Son and in the Holy Spirit." Basil said and taught his flock to say: "Glory to the Father, with the Son and the Holy Spirit." At the beginning of this extensive treatise, Basil argues that he is not discussing trivialities, for words are important. The importance of even the smallest word is seen in a clear example: "Yea and Nay are but two syllables, yet there is often involved in these little words at once the best of all good things, Truth, and that beyond which wickedness cannot go, a Lie" (*Holy Spirit* 1.1; NPNF[2] 8:2). The rest stresses that our words must pronounce equal glory to the Father, to the Son, and to the Holy Spirit. The doxology that others employ may be understood as if ultimate glory belonged to the Father alone, and not also to the Son and the Holy Spirit. The words that Basil employs clearly show that glory belongs equally to all three, meaning that the three are equally divine.

Basil's work *On the Holy Spirit* was widely influential not only in the Greek-speaking East, but also in the Latin West. Ambrose (to whom we shall return in another chapter) used it as the main source for his own treatise on the same subject—so much so that some sections in Ambrose's work seem to be Latin translations and adaptations of what Basil had said in Greek. Therefore, the work of Basil made a significant contribution to the development and final shape of the doctrine of the Holy Spirit both in the East and in the West.

GREGORY OF NAZIANZUS

Basil's friend and fellow student Gregory was of a very different disposition. While Basil was energetic, facing all difficulties with firm resolution, and sought practical solutions to problems in society and among his flock, Gregory preferred the quiet of a monastic life devoted to prayer, study, and writing. He was still a young man when his father, also named Gregory and bishop of Nazianzus, wished to ordain him as a presbyter so that he might help in pastoral tasks. Gregory refused. When the congregation insisted that he should allow himself to be ordained, Gregory fled, seeking refuge with Basil. Among his sermons, there is one *On Flight*, in which he explains his actions, and we catch a glimpse of his difficulties in dealing with opposition:

> I have been defeated, and own my defeat. . . . As to the cause, either of my original revolt and cowardice, in which I got me away far off, and remained away from you for a time, which perhaps seemed long to those who missed me; or of the present gentleness and change of mind, in which I have given myself up again to you, men may think and speak in different ways, according to the hatred or love they bear me, on the one side refusing to acquit me of the charges alleged, on the other giving me a hearty welcome. For nothing is so pleasant to men as talking of other people's business, especially under the influence of affection or hatred, which often almost entirely blinds us to the truth. (*On Flight* 1; NPNF² 7:204–5)

That episode set the pattern for much of what was to come. Repeatedly, pressed by others, Gregory would accept responsibilities that he would later abandon. The high point of these tendencies took place in Constantinople in 381. Two years earlier, when Arianism still had the support of the state, a small group of Nicene Christians in Constantinople asked Gregory to lead them as their bishop. As a result, in 381, when Emperor Theodosius favored the Nicene cause and convoked the Council of Constantinople, it fell on Gregory—who now had unexpectedly become patriarch of Constantinople— to preside over the assembly. When some questioned his authority to do so, Gregory simply abdicated as bishop of Constantinople. He went to the pulpit and preached an extensive farewell homily that shows his wish to avoid conflicts and enmities:

> Yea by the Trinity Itself, Whom you and I alike worship, by our common hope, and for the sake of the unity of this people, grant me this favour; dismiss me with your prayers; let this be the proclamation of my contest; give me my certificate of retirement, as sovereigns do to their soldiers; and, if you will, with a favourable testimony, that I may enjoy the honour of it; if not, just as you please; this will make no difference to me, until God sees what my case really is. (*Hom.* 42.25; *NPNF²* 7:394)

Then he simply returned to Nazianzus to make certain that an orthodox (Nicene) candidate would become bishop of that city; and he withdrew to a life of prayer and writing, making every effort to stay out of the conflicts in society as well as in the church. His success in this endeavor was such that even the date of his death is unknown.

Most of the extant writings of Gregory are homilies as well as letters and a very extensive collection of poems. The most influential among all these works, and the one that most approaches being a treatise on systematic theology, is his five *Theological Discourses*, which are part of his collection of homilies. These speeches are directed against Eunomius, the already-mentioned leader of the extreme Arian party, whose influence was such that some began calling these Arians "Eunomians." It is mostly due to these five speeches that Gregory is often spoken of not only as "Gregory of Nazianzus," but also as "Gregory the Theologian." In the first of these speeches Gregory establishes the parameters of good theology:

> Not to every one, my friends, does it belong to philosophize about God; not to every one; the Subject is not so cheap and low; and I will add, not before every audience, nor at all times, nor on all points; but on certain occasions, and before certain persons, and within certain limits.
>
> Not to all men, because it is permitted only to those who have been examined, and are passed masters in meditation, and who have been previously purified in soul and body, or at the very least are being purified. For the impure to touch the pure is, we may safely say, not safe, just as it is unsafe to fix weak eyes upon the sun's rays. . . .
> Next, on what subjects and to what extent may we philosophize? On matters within our reach, and to such an extent as the mental power and grasp of our audience may extend.
> Philosophize about the world or worlds; about matter; about soul; about natures endowed with reason, good or bad; about resurrection, about judgment, about reward, or the Sufferings of Christ. For in these subjects to hit the mark is not useless, and to miss it is not

dangerous. But with God we shall have converse, in this life only in a small degree; but a little later, it may be, more perfectly, in the Same, our Lord Jesus Christ, to Whom be glory for ever. (*Hom.* 27.3.9; *NPNF*² 7:285–88)

The second homily of this series deals mostly with what is needed to be able to practice this "philosophizing" about God. This is mostly the practice of virtues as well as a devotion to prayer and meditation. The third of the four homilies treat the Son and his full divinity. They discuss at length the meaning of the word "begotten" when referring to the relationship between the Father and the Son. Here Gregory refutes the views of the Pneumatomachians, who were willing to affirm the divinity of the Son but not that of the Holy Spirit. He explains the relationships within the Trinity by saying that while the Son is "begotten" by the Father, the Holy Spirit "proceeds" from him.

Much of Gregory's direct impact on the life of the church, particularly the Greek-speaking church, was a result of his hymns and poems, of which some four hundred are extant. They were written mostly after he set aside the patriarchate of Constantinople and withdrew to a life of contemplation. In them he follows the metrics and poetic resources of classical Greece, and therefore they are very difficult to translate into the poetical norms of modern languages—which is the main reason why few of Gregory's hymns are found in modern hymnbooks. Some of them are theological poems, particularly about the Trinity and its glory. Since, as historians of liturgy tell us, what is said and done in worship shapes what one believes, the poems of Gregory have shaped the faith and religiosity of the Greek-speaking church throughout the centuries, and this is one of the reasons why he is called "Gregory the Theologian." One of the most famous of his hymns is "Three Lights That Are One." There are also poems about virtues, and some about particular people or even about Gregory himself. One of them is a sort of autobiography whose 1,949 verses are enormously important to understand both the life and theology of Gregory and the controversies of his time.

GREGORY OF NYSSA

Macrina's and Basil's younger brother Gregory was already mentioned in connection with his dialogue with Macrina regarding the soul and resurrection. Since he was much younger than his siblings, they were his main mentors and the ones directing his studies. As Macrina had earlier done with him, Basil sought to convince Gregory to move away from his studies and practice of rhetoric and turn to meditation and the work of the church. Apparently he was married, for there is a letter to him from Gregory of Nazianzus expressing condolences over the death of a beloved woman, who probably was his wife. His brother Basil forced him to accept the bishopric of Nyssa, which was little more than a village, apparently in order to augment the number of orthodox bishops on whom he could count. Although this Gregory did not flee like his friend Gregory of Nazianzus, it was only reluctantly that he agreed to become a bishop, and Basil repeatedly complained about his weakness in administrative tasks and his not being sufficiently firm with his flock. In the entire process of electing Gregory to become a bishop, apparently many outside forces were involved. Emperor Valens supported other candidates of Arian tendencies, and when these were not elected, they sought to hinder the work of Gregory as much as possible. Partly because Gregory did not know how to manage such difficulties, and partly because at that time the political winds were blowing against the Nicene orthodoxy and in favor of Arianism, in 376 an Arian synod deposed him and ordered that he be exiled. After the death of Valens, Gregory was able to return to his church, where he was received with great rejoicing, for his flock seems to have loved him despite his administrative inabilities. After the death of Basil in 379, Gregory became more actively involved in the struggles of those times, apparently seeking to fill the vacuum left by his brother. Jointly with Gregory of Nazianzus, he was a participant in the great Council of Constantinople in 381.

While Basil was an energetic administrator and leader of the Nicene cause, constantly involved in the great controversies and events of his times, and Gregory of Nazianzus was an orator and poet, Gregory of Nyssa was more of a philosopher and a great admirer of Origen. Like the latter, and in sharp contrast with Basil, he practiced the allegorical interpretation of Scripture. Even so, his admiration and respect for his older brother were such that when he wrote a treatise *On the Creation of the Human Being* shortly after the death of Basil, he explicitly sought to follow the literal exegesis of his brother and to restrain his allegorical flights. The same is true of his later *Apology on the Six Days of Creation*. But Gregory himself always preferred allegorical interpretation, by which he was convinced that he could draw a deeper understanding of Scripture than by a more literal interpretation. Thus, for instance, in his *Life of Moses* he makes ample use of allegorical interpretation when commenting on the episode of the burning bush, claiming that the bush itself reminds us that those who withdraw to a life of peace and tranquillity will shine as the bush did and not be consumed, and that the same episode also refers to the mystery of the virgin birth, for just as the fire did not consume the bush, the birth did not destroy the virginity of Mary.

His admiration for Origen and his desire to follow allegorical interpretation as far as possible can be seen in all his other works. Following that method of interpretation, Gregory wrote an extensive study on the titles of the psalms, coming to the conclusion that the entire book of Psalms is like a mystical ladder consisting of five steps through which the soul must ascend. Likewise, preaching on the Song of Solomon, Gregory follows what would eventually become the traditional interpretation, that the entire book is a song of love between the soul and God. Even so, occasionally Gregory is willing to set allegory aside. For instance, in *On the Witch of Endor* he follows the already-mentioned interpretation of Eustathius of Antioch rather than that of Origen.

Gregory also departs from Origen on a number of points of doctrine. This is particularly the case with the preexistence of souls, which Origen had proposed and which by now was clearly opposed to the teachings of the church. Gregory declares that souls are truly preexistent, but only in the mind of God, and he absolutely rejects Origen's speculations about the transmigration of souls. But he does agree with Origen's eschatology in that for him there is no such thing as an eternal punishment, for the sufferings of hell are a way in which spiritual beings—souls, angels, and even Satan—are purified and made part of the final consummation.

Still, on Gregory's writings on Scripture, one must also mention as important examples of his biblical interpretation his eight homilies on the Beatitudes and five on the Lord's Prayer.

In the field of systematic theology or dogmatics, Gregory's most important work was an entire series of treatises against Eunomius. Unfortunately, in the copying and recopying of these writings, they have been intertwined to such an extent that what we now have is a single combination of all of them. His arguments are similar to those of Gregory of Nazianzus, although with greater use of philosophy. In another work, *That There Are Not Three Gods*, he responded to a certain Ablabius, who asked why, if the Father, the Son, and the Holy Spirit are divine, it can be that there are not three gods, just as Peter, James, and John are three different people. Gregory's answer is typically Platonic, arguing that, although Peter, James, and John are three persons, they are all linked by a single human nature. Then, as the answer progresses, Gregory shows that, as he understands them, the distinctions among the three persons of the Trinity have to do with their inner relations. In any case, what results is a clear example of the difference between Western and Eastern understandings of the Trinity: while the East tends to underscore the distinction among the persons, the West tends to emphasize the unity of the Godhead. Also, since a discussion regarding the Trinity had led to the issue of the divinity of the Holy Spirit, Gregory composed a sermon against the Pneumatomachians.

Finally, among the writings of Gregory there is one *Against Apollinaris*. In another chapter we shall return to the teachings of Apollinaris. For the present, let it suffice to say that he understood the incarnation in such a way that the Word or Son of God had taken the place of the rational soul in Jesus, so that his humanity had to do only with his having a human body, while his rational soul was purely divine. Gregory expresses this saying that, according to Apollinaris, "the man who was joined with God does not have his own intellect" (*Ag. Apollinaris*; PG 45:1144). Rejecting such notions, Gregory affirms that Christ was made similar to us in everything except sin. The story of the temptation of Jesus in the desert proves that he had a human rational soul, since the Word of God, being divine, cannot be tempted.

However, Gregory's main theological work was his *Great Catechism*, written, as he says, in order to help those who are to teach others who approach the church. Since such people come from various religious backgrounds, each must be taught according to their particular background: "You will not by the same means cure the polytheism of the Greek, and the unbelief of the Jew as to the Only-begotten God: nor as regards those who have wandered into heresy will you, by the same arguments in each case, upset their misleading romances as to the tenets of the Faith" (*Great Catechism*, preface; NPNF² 5:474).

He then devotes the first four chapters of his catechism to the nature of God. In chapter 3 one finds the interesting affirmation that Christianity has learned from Judaism the singleness of God, and from Hellenism the distinction of persons within the Godhead. Most of the treatise, chapters 5 to 32, is devoted to the mystery of the incarnation, trying to show that it is not irrational, as some claim. Within this context, in chapter 27 Gregory uses an example that seems to be alluding to Apollinaris. Just as someone washing clothes does not pay attention only to the dirt and forget the rest of the garment, in the incarnation God does not assume a human body and forget the soul, which is also a seat of sin. Then, since the purpose of the entire writing is to help those who are to teach catechumens, in chapters 33 to 36 Gregory deals with the sacraments: first, in a more detailed fashion, baptism; and then in chapter 37, the Eucharist. Chapters 38 to 39 return to the subject of the Trinity. Here the argument of Gregory is based on the baptismal rite, which takes place in the name of the Father, of the Son, and of the Holy Spirit.

> Now there have been delivered to us in the Gospel three Persons and names through whom the generation or birth of believers [baptism] takes place, and he who is begotten by this Trinity is equally begotten of the Father, and of the Son, and of the Holy Ghost. . . . For according to the disposition of heart in one who comes to the Dispensation will that which is begotten in him exhibit its power; so that he who confesses that the Holy Trinity is uncreated enters on the steadfast unalterable life; while another, who through a mistaken conception sees only a created nature in the Trinity and then is baptized in *that*, has again been born into the shifting and alterable life. (*Great Catechism* 39; NPNF² 5:507)

Finally, chapter 40 affirms a crucial point that must not be forgotten, that true regeneration takes place only when the person who is being baptized lets go of evil and leads a life according to the teachings of Christ.

This final point leads to a mention of another category among the works of Gregory of Nyssa, dealing mostly with practical and ascetic life. These include exhortations to virginity and to the quest after Christian perfection. Finally, among the works of Gregory there are also several other homilies and speeches as well as some thirty letters.

Although this history deals mostly with the writings of various figures rather than with their theology, before leaving the Great Cappadocians it is necessary to point out that they were the dominant figures in theological discourse in Greek during the second half of the fourth century. It was they who carefully defined the exact meaning and the differences between the Greek terms *ousia* (substance, being) and *hypostasis* (each of the three divine persons), thus leading to the final triumph of Nicene faith at the Council of Constantinople.

19

Other Greek Authors
in the Late Fourth Century

We have taken what happened in Alexandria in 362 as the watershed for our discussion of the fourth century, and the last chapter has been devoted to the Great Cappadocians, who were the dominant figures in Christian theology and literature in the Eastern church at that time. Now, before turning to their contemporaries who wrote in Latin, we must consider those among their contemporaries who also wrote in Greek.

MONASTICISM

In chapter 15 we looked at the beginnings of monastic literature early in the fourth century. However, later in the century some of the great monastic authors flourished. The most famous and one of the earliest ones was Macarius, commonly known as "Macarius the Great." A contemporary of Antony, but probably a bit younger, Macarius—probably of Coptic origin—withdrew from society to live as a hermit in the Egyptian desert. But soon other monks joined him, and a community was formed in which he was known as "the young elder" because his wisdom seemed to belie his youth.

Although several writings have been attributed to Macarius, their authorship is still debated among scholars. Apparently most of them were not written by him, but rather were the product of other monks, some of them called "Messalian" inclinations. This was a movement that seems to have arisen in Mesopotamia in the second half of the fourth century, was repeatedly rejected by church authorities, and eventually also by the Council of Constantinople in 381. Little is known about it. It seems to have been an extreme form of monasticism that insisted on the possibility of attaining a vision of God. Some ancient writers say that members of this movement claimed to be possessed by the Holy Spirit to such a degree that they could see God with their physical eyes. Others tell us that they kept themselves from sleep until they went into a deep slumber and had visions not only of God, but also of demons. Most scholars today think that many of the writings attributed to Macarius, particularly his *Spiritual Homilies*, come from Messalian circles and were attributed to Macarius in order to grant them some authority. If that was the case, it had undoubted success, for the homilies of Macarius were widely circulated, although in some manuscripts the more extreme Messalian passages were omitted.

At any rate, the *Spiritual Homilies* proclaim and propose an absolute purity of life derived from the presence of God:

> Just as when the soul leaves it the body is dead and no longer lives as before, not being able to listen or to walk, when our great heavenly priest, Christ, strikes and kills our life to the world by means of his grace and power, we are dead to all the evil in which we lived before, and no longer hear nor speak nor retain any sort of citizenship in the darkness of sin, for the grace that has entered our lives has expelled from the soul all evil passions. (*Spiritual Hom.* 1.6; PG 34:456)

Without any doubt, the most important monastic author during this second half of the fourth century was Evagrius, commonly known as "Evagrius Ponticus" to indicate his land of origin. Shortly after the Council of Constantinople, Evagrius retired to the Egyptian desert. Before that, he had been a disciple of Basil the Great and Gregory of Nazianzus and had then lived in Jerusalem. In Egypt, he seems to have met Macarius, whose disciple he became.

Evagrius was a prolific author whose work has left its mark on monastic religiosity and practice, particularly in the Eastern church, but also in the Latin West. His main work, *Antirrheticus*, a title that may well be translated as "responses" or "talking back," is a guide for responding to the main eight thoughts or tendencies that lead the soul away from God. This results in a list of eight main sins, a list that later became seven. The title itself suggests that what Evagrius offers is a series of answers to give both the demons and the thoughts that they inspire in the believer. As a source for his answers, Evagrius points mostly to the Psalms, where the poet responds to various temptations, and to Jesus, who in the desert responds to the demon with biblical quotes.

The work presents itself as an answer to a request from a monk by the name of Lucius, a request that has only been preserved in an Arabic translation:

Therefore, I ask your fatherhood to classify the fight against the beings of darkness, and I entreat your holiness to compose for me some clear treatise concerning it and to acquaint me with the demons' entire treachery, which by their own efforts and according to their own undertaking they produce in the path of monasticism. Send it to us, so that we, your friends, might also easily cast off from ourselves those evil suggestions of theirs. (W. Frankenberg, trans., *Talking Back: Antirrheticus* [Collegeville, MN: Liturgical Press, 2009], 45)

Evagrius answers with a letter to which the *Antirrheticus* is attached. Following Lucius's request, he classifies the evil thoughts that the demons engendered into a list of eight. The first of these is gluttony. Taking for granted that his readers already know what gluttony is, Evagrius simply offers a series of sixty-nine biblical references against it. Likewise, he offers biblical answers to the other seven main temptations: fornication, love of money, sadness, anger, listlessness, vainglory, and pride.

The other important work by Evagrius is *The Monastic*, a collection of 150 teachings or pieces of advice for monastic life. The first 100 are addressed to those whose level in monastic life is what Evagrius calls "practical," and the rest to those with deeper understanding, whom he calls "gnostics"; yet he is not referring at all to the ancient heretics who had been given that name, but rather to those who have a higher level of knowledge, thus employing the word "gnostic" in the same sense in which it had earlier been used by Clement of Alexandria and Origen.

Evagrius's dependence on Origen was such that one of the reasons why many of his writings have been lost is that when the Second Council of Constantinople, in 553, rejected several of Origen's views, the prestige of Evagrius himself began declining, particularly in the Greek-speaking church. For these reasons, much of his work that still remains exists only in translations into Latin, Syriac, Armenian, and other languages.

Much of what is known of the first years of Egyptian monasticism we learn from the work of Palladius, who like Evagrius came originally from what is now Turkey. Seeking monastic peace, he first went to Jerusalem and then, a few years after Evagrius, to Egypt. After spending years with Macarius the Great and with Evagrius, his health began declining, and he returned to his native land, where he became a bishop late in the century. He was then involved in the controversy surrounding John Chrysostom (to be considered in another chapter). The work in which Palladius discusses the early history of Egyptian monasticism is his *Historia lusiaca*, which makes him one of the historians and translators who flourished late in the fourth century and early in the fifth (historians and translators to whom we shall return in another chapter).

TITUS OF BOSTRA

The city of Bostra was the capital of the Roman province of Arabia. Christianity seems to have arrived there at a very early date. By the middle of the fourth century, the bishop of that city was Titus. Thanks to church historian Sozomen and to a letter from Emperor Julian, we know that when there were some riots in the city for religious reasons, Titus wrote the emperor and claimed that the source of the riots was not the Christian population of the city, whom he and others were constantly calling to peace, but the rest of the population. Julian's answer was the opposite of what Titus expected, for the emperor wrote to the magistrates of the city, saying that the Christian bishop was falsely accusing them of sedition and that he ought to be expelled from the city. Apparently this was never done, for Titus seems to have remained in Bostra to the end of his days.

The only extant work of Titus, besides a few fragments, is *Against the Manichees*, in four books. We know that it was written after 363, for in it Titus refers both to an earthquake that took place in 362 and to the death of Julian in 363.

The main point of conflict between Christians and Manicheans was the origin and nature of evil. While Manicheans affirmed the existence of two eternal principles, one of good or of light and the other of evil or of darkness, Christians affirmed that there is only one eternal principle, God, and that it is this God who created all things. This is why almost at the beginning of his work, Titus declares that according to the teachings of the church

> we must vigorously affirm that God is not to be blamed for injustices among humans. When we think about how it is that we sin, even though God does not wish us to do so, we are not accusing God, for like him [Mani] we wish to defend him against any such accusation, even the smallest. On the contrary, since we have the correct path of truth both thanks to Scripture and to common sense, we enter into the resulting discussion with full trust, and without any fear we accuse ourselves of such evil things. (*Ag. Manich.* 1.2; PG 18:1069)

APOLLINARIS OF LAODICEA

Apollinaris was somewhat younger than Athanasius, and some fifteen or twenty years older than the Great Cappadocians. He was a native of the city of Laodicea in Syria—not to be confused with the city by the same name in Asia Minor to which the Revelation of John refers. For a long time he was a friend and collaborator both of Athanasius and of the Cappadocians in the defense of the faith proclaimed at the Council of Nicaea. As part of that struggle, he wrote *Against Eunomius* and *Against Marcellus of Ancyra*. Since the former was an Arian, and the second was inclined to Sabellianism—that is, exactly the opposite extreme—Apollinaris followed a middle course between one extreme and the other. His extensive work *Against Porphyry* was widely used in order to respond to the objections against Christianity raised by that famous Neoplatonic philosopher. According to Jerome, his exegetical writings were "innumerable." But practically all of this has been lost, mostly because Apollinaris himself was declared a heretic by the Council of Constantinople in 381, and therefore his works fell into disuse.

As we shall see when we discuss the christological controversies of the fifth century, those controversies actually began earlier, mostly surrounding the Christology of Apollinaris. While he agreed with the Cappadocians regarding the eternal divinity of the Son, he differed from them on the manner in which he understood the incarnation. According to Apollinaris, in the incarnation the eternal Word of God assumed the human body, and dwelt in that body as the rational soul dwells in any of us. In other words, while Jesus' body was human, his mind was exclusively divine. The Cappadocians and many others rejected this, insisting on the need for the incarnation to be the presence of the Word in a full human being.

Even though many of his works disappeared after he was declared a heretic, others are still extant because apparently some of his followers circulated them as if they were the work of respected authors such as Athanasius and Gregory the Wonderworker. Thus we have several brief treatises by him. Also, some of his other writings can be partially reconstructed on the basis of quotations in the works of his opponents, particularly Gregory of Nyssa.

AMPHILOCHIUS OF ICONIUM

A friend and collaborator of the Great Cappadocians, and apparently a relative of Gregory of Nazianzus, Amphilochius collaborated with them in the struggle against Arianism. Apart from his correspondence with the Cappadocians, little remains of his writings. Probably the most important is a letter that he wrote to other bishops as instructed by a synod that met in Iconium and affirmed the full divinity of the Holy Spirit, against the Pneumatomachians.

NEMESIUS OF EMESA

Little is known of the life of Nemesius, who was born late in the fourth century in the eastern city of Emesa, now Homs, in western Syria. Thus, for instance, it is said that he was a physician because he repeatedly quotes the various works of the Greek physician Galen and because the title of his main work, *On Human Nature*, reflects the work of Hippocrates, more than three centuries earlier. There is no doubt that Nemesius was fully acquainted with philosophy, particularly with the Neoplatonic renaissance that was taking place in his own time. His treatise *On Human Nature* is an apologetic work, seeking to show to an educated public that the manner in which Christians understand human nature is not only reasonable, but even agrees with the best of Greek knowledge, both philosophical and medical. Near the beginning of his work, Nemesius says that the human being on the one hand partakes of the nature of physical creation, and on the other surpasses it as a rational being.

> It is well known that man has some things in common with the inanimate creatures, and shares life with the plant and animal creation, while partaking intelligence in common with all beings endowed with reason. With inanimate things he shares a material body mingled of the four elements. With plants he shares not only this but also the faculties of self-nutriment and generation. With irrational animals he shares all these things, and, in addition, a range of voluntary movements, together with the faculties of appetite, anger, feeling and respiration. All these things man and the irrational animals have in common, if not everywhere on equal terms. Finally, by being rational, man shares with the incorporeal rational intelligences the prerogative of applying, to whatever he will, reason, understanding, and judgement. So he pursues virtues, and follows after godliness, in which the quest of every several virtue finds its goal. (*Human Nat.* 1; LCC 4:228–29)
>
> The human being is the goal and culmination of the entire creation. It is for this reason that God did not create it until everything else was prepared. Furthermore, human beings are the link or intermediary between the material world and intellectual beings. Humans were not created immortal, for from the very beginning they needed to eat, and purely intellectual beings do not need physical food. But this human being did have the possibility of attaining perfection by means of moral progress, and therefore was potentially immortal. In order to subsist in the material world, humans need the support of others, and that is the origin of the social order. All of this was derailed by the fall, which had made it impossible for humans truly to serve as a link between the material and intellectual. Among the prerogative of this being who has sinned, there is still that of repentance, which may lead to the immortality not only of the soul, but also of the body. Therefore: When we consider these facts about man, how can we exaggerate the dignity of his place in creation? In his own person, man joins mortal creatures with the immortals, and brings the rational beings into contact with the irrational. He bears about in his proper nature a reflex of the whole creation, and is therefore rightly

called "the world in little." He is the creature whom God thought worthy of such special providence that, for his sake, all creatures have their being, both those that now are, and those that are yet to be. He is the creature for whose sake God became man, so that this creature might attain incorruption and escape corruption, might reign on high, being made after the image and likeness of God, dwelling with Christ as a child of God, and might be throned above all rule and all authority. (*Human Nat.* 10; LCC 4:254–55)

Nemesius then turns to a discussion of the soul and its union with the body. In this entire section he makes abundant use of the surrounding philosophy and of the knowledge and theories inherited from Hellenistic tradition. The body is formed by four elements: earth, water, air, and fire. It is also in this section that he makes ample use of the medical theory of his time, often intertwined with philosophical theories. The same is true of the ensuing long section, dealing with human faculties such as imagination, sight, touch, taste, hearing, and smell. But high above this are the faculties of the intellect, which include judgment, approval, denial, and testing. It is also here that we find Nemesis most clearly expounding the medical theories of his time, affirming, for instance, that memory is located in the cerebellum, while the senses are in the frontal portions of the brain. But there is also in the soul an irrational element that includes first of all the passions. Among these are concupiscence, pleasure, grief, pain, and anger. This irrational part of the soul also includes what could be called vegetative life, that is, nutrition, pulse, breathing, generation, and others.

Then there is also the will, which leads Nemesius to a classification of various human actions, some being voluntary and some not. Involuntary actions are those that take place either out of necessity or unconsciously. In the first there is an external agent, and in the latter the agency is internal. Then Nemesius turns to what could well be called a treatise on ethics, discussing such subjects as which actions are due to ignorance, when that ignorance is culpable, and the place of deliberation in a voluntary action, as well as the matter of how to choose among several possible actions. In this context, Nemesius affirms the freedom of the human will and rejects any form of predeterminism, which includes astrology. Certainly, not all have the same free options. For instance, one cannot say that either the rich or the poor are usually such by their own choosing, for there are many other factors involved in the economic conditions of the person. Yet this does not belie the fundamental fact that humans are mutable by the simple reason that they are creatures, and that they have free will, since this is part of any intellectual nature.

Anyone, therefore, that finds fault with God for not making man incapable of evil, while at the same time being endowed with free-will, is, though he may not know it, blaming God for making man rational, and not irrational. It has to be in one way or the other. Either man must be irrational, or, if he is rational, then liable to act now in one way and now in another, and so he must have free-will. Inevitably, therefore, every nature endowed with reason must also have free-will, and, as part of that same nature, be mutable. (*Human Nat.* 41; LCC 4:419)

Finally, Nemesius devotes the last three chapters of his work to the theme of providence. Here the subject is not so much human nature as the relationship between free will and divine providence. The difference between this second part of the book and the earlier sections is such that sometimes this latter part circulated independently as *On Providence*. Here, making abundant use of Plato, Nemesius enumerates and classifies the various objections to the existence of a divine Providence, and then refutes them. At the end of the entire treatise, Nemesius returns once again to the subject of ethics, dealing with matters such as homicide and greed. Death in itself is not evil, for there is a positive value in a saintly death; but for a sinner death is evil. If someone dies a saintly death by another's action, the death itself may be good, but the other is still a murderer, an evil. And something similar is true of possessions and greed:

> The same arguments . . . apply equally to those who covet and seize other men's goods, for it may very well be that, so far as concerns the people deprived of their possessions, they may be all the better for being relieved of them. Nevertheless, the people who coveted their possessions thereby committed a wrong. For when they committed the theft, they did so out of covetousness, and not with any thought of what might be expedient for their victims. (*Human Nat.* 44; LCC 4:452)

CYRIL OF JERUSALEM

Cyril of Jerusalem became bishop of that city in 348. Since at that time Arianism was in political ascendancy, some ancient historians suggest that Cyril had Arian inclinations, while others defend him. At any rate, it is interesting to note that, even though living at a time when the conflict between Arianism and the faith of Nicaea was at its worst, Cyril sought not to be involved in that conflict, even though the conditions of the time were such that repeatedly, much against his own wishes, he found himself involved in the controversy. All that is still extant of his works are a homily, a letter addressed to Emperor Constantius, and a very valuable series of twenty-three *Catechetical Lectures*, which he dictated in midcentury. In this long series of lectures, Cyril does not mention the debate regarding the consubstantiality of the Son and other related matters, except perhaps only in some very veiled allusions that are subject to various interpretations. We don't know that he attended the Council of Constantinople in 381, where what had been done in Nicaea was reaffirmed and clarified.

The *Catechetical Lectures* are of utmost importance for those who study the history of worship and particularly the history of the catechetical system by which the church prepared the candidates for baptism. In Cyril's time, when people asked for baptism, they were officially added to the list of catechumens, the list of those preparing to receive baptism. After a long period of preparation—during which they attended only the first part of the worship service, the "service of the Word," and not communion, the "service of the table"—they came to the last days of preparation for baptism. This is the context of the *Catechetical Lectures*. Part of their importance lies in being the most ancient document we have that is addressed to the catechumens themselves. Naturally, since doctrinal and practical instruction was always important for the life of the church, from a very early date there were documents designed to serve in that instruction. Such is, for instance, the case of the *Didache* and other documents inspired by it. But those were documents of general instructions, not addressing the catechumens directly. There is also the catechetical speech of Gregory of Nyssa. But this, besides being later than the lectures of Cyril, is not directed at the catechumens themselves, but at their teachers. The same may be said of the slightly later work by Augustine *On the Instruction of the Unlearned*. Therefore, Cyril's *Catechetical Lectures* are one of the most ancient writing addressing the catechumens themselves.

Thanks to information gleaned from other ancient authors, it is possible to know something about the place and time of the year in which these lectures were delivered. It was in the great basilica that Constantine had ordered to be built at the place now called the Holy Sepulchre and at that time called Church of the Resurrection. We also know that they were delivered during Lent. In Palestine what was then called Quadragesima and we now call Lent lasted six weeks, while in other areas it lasted seven. The introduction to the entire series as well as the first eighteen of these *Catechetical Lectures* would then have been delivered during the period of fasting and the preparation for Easter Sunday. The last of these eighteen would have been dated on Good Friday, or perhaps on the evening of that Saturday. The next five lectures, numbers 19 to 23, are known as the *Mystagogical Lectures*—that is, lectures on the "mysteries" or sacraments. They were delivered to the neophytes who had just been baptized and were still called "infants." In some editions, the title of *Catechetical Lectures* refers only to the first eighteen, and the rest are considered a separate work. At the end of lecture 18, at any rate, Cyril announces the mystagogical lectures, where the recently baptized will receive greater instruction:

> And after Easter's Holy Day of salvation, ye shall come on each successive day, beginning from the second day of the week, after the assembly into the Holy Place of the Resurrection, and there, if God permit, ye shall hear other Lectures; in which ye shall again be taught the reasons of every thing which has been done, and shall receive the proofs thereof from the Old and New Testaments,—first, of the things done just before Baptism,—next, how ye were cleansed from your sins by the Lord, *by the washing of water with the word,*—and how like Priests ye have become partakers of the Name of Christ,—and how the Seal of the fellowship of the Holy Ghost was given to you. (*Catech.* 8.33; NPNF² 7:142)

The "things that have been done" to which Cyril refers are the baptismal and communion rites, which are precisely the theme of the *Mystagogical Lectures*. Thus, they would be delivered during the week immediately following Easter, from Monday to Friday.

The first three *Catechetical Lectures* are a sort of introduction to the rest, dealing first with themes such as repentance and, very briefly, baptism. The fourth is an outline of the rest. The fifth deals with faith and prepares the way for a more detailed discussion of the teachings of the church. At the end of this lecture, Cyril taught his hearers the creed with which they would be baptized. According to him, the purpose of this creed is to serve as a summary of biblical teaching:

> But in learning the Faith and in professing it, acquire and keep that only, which is now delivered to thee by the Church, and which has been built up strongly out of all the Scriptures. For since all cannot read the Scriptures, some being hindered as to the knowledge of them by want of learning, and others by a want of leisure, in order that the soul may not perish from ignorance, we comprise the whole doctrine of the Faith in a few lines. (*Catech.* 5.12; NPNF² 7:32)

However, much more interesting, and perhaps surprising for modern Christians, are the instructions that Cyril gives his hearers, forbidding them to write these words down and calling them to learn them by heart: "This summary I wish you both to commit to memory when I recite it, and to rehearse it with all diligence among yourselves, not writing it out on paper, but engraving it by the memory upon your heart, taking care while you rehearse it that no Catechumen chance to overhear the things which have been delivered to you" (*Catech.* 5.12; NPNF² 7:32). (The prohibition against teaching these things to the "catechumens," when Cyril himself was teaching them to candidates for baptism, seems to be a contradiction. But these "catechumens" to be baptized on Easter were no longer called such: now they were in a new category of "competent ones," or "those being in process of illumination.")

Following his own instructions, Cyril does not include in his text the actual words of the creed being used in his church. But since the order of the following lectures seems to be the same as this creed, it is possible to reconstruct it in outline, and it turns out to be very similar to the creed adopted in Nicaea in 325, although with some variants. For instance, where the Nicene Creed says, "maker of all things visible and invisible," the creed of Jerusalem seems to have said, "creator of heaven and earth, and of all things visible and invisible." But the most noticeable differences are in the second clause, dealing with the Son. While the Creed of Nicaea uses the typically Nicene words (in Greek) *ousia* and *hypostasis*, the creed that Cyril taught his flock seems to have affirmed the divinity of the Son without using those words. What in Nicaea was "God from God, true God from true God," in Jerusalem was simply "true God." Since Eusebius of Caesarea, near Jerusalem, says he proposed the creed employed in his church to the Council of Nicaea, and that with some additions this became the foundation for the creed of Nicaea; and since what Eusebius proposed seems to have been very similar to the creed that can be reconstructed from Cyril's lectures, one may conclude that this was a traditional formula employed in Palestine even before the Council of Nicaea. At any rate, all these creeds, while differing in details, were sufficiently similar that any Christian who knew one of them could recognize and accept the others—and could also recognize any Arianism or other doctrines departing from them.

The *Mystagogical Lectures*—that is, *Catechetical Lectures* 19–23—are a rich source for the study of Christian worship in Cyril's time. In the first of them, Cyril explains why a detailed instruction regarding the meaning of baptism has been postponed till after baptism:

> I have long been wishing, O true-born and dearly beloved children of the Church, to discourse to you concerning these spiritual and heavenly Mysteries; but since I well knew that seeing is far more persuasive than hearing, I waited for the present season; that finding you more open to the influence of my words from your present experience, I might lead you by the hand into the brighter and more fragrant meadow of the Paradise before us; especially as ye have been made fit to receive the more sacred Mysteries, after having been found worthy of divine and life-giving Baptism. Since therefore it remains to set before you a table of the more perfect instructions, let us now teach you these things exactly, that ye may know the effect wrought upon you on that evening of your baptism. (*Catech.* 19.1; *NPNF²* 7:144)

Cyril then reviews all that took place in the baptismal ceremony. The neophytes were taken to the atrium, or entrance, of the baptistry and were instructed that, facing west, they were to stretch out their hand in a sign of rejecting the powers of evil and say, "I renounce thee, Satan, all your works and pomp, and your service." Then they were taken to the baptismal pool and asked if they believed in the Father, the Son, and the Holy Spirit, being bathed three times in the baptismal waters. Upon exiting from the pool, they were anointed so that now, joined to Christ, the Anointed, they have become "Christians," or anointed ones.

Likewise, Cyril describes the rite of communion. At the beginning of that rite, a deacon gives the officiating presbyter water to wash his hands, as a sign of a pure life. This is followed by the kiss of peace, indicating that all believers are one and all enmity has been set aside. After the kiss of peace, the presbyter says words that we have already encountered in dealing with Hippolytus: "Lift up your hearts," with the congregational response, "We lift them up to the Lord." And the dialogue continues: "Let us give thanks to the Lord," with the response: "It is meet and right so to do." After this traditional dialogue, there is a prayer to the Holy Spirit, asking for his presence and action on the bread and the wine, followed by an intercessory prayer ending with the Lord's Prayer. Then there is an invitation that may be said or sung so that believers may come to partake of communion. They are to receive the bread on the right hand placed over the left, forming the shape of a throne to receive its king, and they will say "Amen." They will then receive the chalice and once again say "Amen." Thus clearly the customs that Hippolytus described much earlier in the church of Rome were also followed in Jerusalem in Cyril's time.

20

Ambrose

HIS LIFE

We now return to the Latin-speaking West, whose outstanding figure during the latter half of the fourth century was Ambrose of Milan. Ambrose was born in the city of Treves shortly before 340. His father, also called Ambrose, was the praetorian prefect who from his capital in Treves ruled over a vast area of western Europe. Our Ambrose was the third child of the prefect. The eldest, Marcelina, would later devote herself to an ascetic life in Rome, where she was consecrated for that life by Bishop Liberius. His brother Satyrus would follow a political career that eventually made him the governor of a province, which he abandoned when Ambrose, having become bishop of Milan, requested his help.

Little is known about the early years of Ambrose beyond some apparently legendary anecdotes told by his biographers. After the death of the elder Ambrose, the rest of the family moved to Rome; there the younger Ambrose completed his basic education, which included literature, rhetoric, and philosophy. However, when he came to philosophy, he was only interested in practical and moral teachings, and not in metaphysical speculations. He also studied jurisprudence, which would be a good starting point for the career in public administration that both he and his brother planned to follow. At that point his religious instructor was a presbyter by the name of Simplician, who became his friend and would later also go to Milan to continue guiding him in doctrinal and theological matters. After spending some three years with his brother in Sirmium, where both practiced law, Ambrose became governor of the province of Emilia-Liguria, with its capital in Milan.

After the inevitable period of doubt and mistrust that followed his arrival, Ambrose won the respect and admiration not only of the population but also of the emperor, and all the signs were that he would have a distinguished political career. At that point the death of Auxentius, the bishop of Milan, came to change his life. Auxentius was an Arian and had become a bishop when Arianism was supported by the government. His death now left the important bishopric of Milan vacant. The election of his successor would be difficult and might even lead to violence, for both the Arians and adherents to the Nicene Creed sought to place one of their supporters on the important episcopal see of Milan. Ambrose attended the election, hoping that his presence would help avoid a riot. Much to his surprise, some say at the suggestion of a child who shouted his name, the people gathered for the election acclaimed their governor as the next bishop.

For Ambrose, that would mean the end of his political career, and therefore he made every effort to avoid becoming a bishop. But the news reached the ears of Emperor Valentinian, who apparently was pleased that the population of Milan wished to have their governor become their bishop; he ordered Ambrose to be made a bishop and, since Ambrose was trying to hide, decreed that anyone offering him refuge would be outlawed.

Ambrose finally agreed to become a bishop, on condition that he would be consecrated only by orthodox bishops. Although he had been raised in a Christian family, he had never been baptized. By that time there was a hierarchy of orders that one must follow before being consecrated as a bishop. In an unheard-of process, Ambrose was baptized on a Sunday in November of 373, and in the next week he was consecutively made a doorkeeper, a reader, an exorcist, an acolyte, a subdeacon, a deacon, and a presbyter. The next Sunday, a week after being baptized, Ambrose was consecrated as bishop of Milan.

For assistance in this unexpected task, Ambrose on the one hand called his former teacher Simplician, who would now help him in further theological studies; and on the other hand his brother Satyrus, who gave up his position as a provincial governor in order to help Ambrose in administrative matters. The presence of Satyrus was for him a source of strength and encouragement. But that happy condition did not last long, for Satyrus died two years after coming to Milan. Profoundly aggrieved, Ambrose went to the pulpit and declared:

> Nothing among things of earth, dearest brethren, was more precious to me, nothing more worthy of love, nothing more dear than such a brother, but public matters come before private. . . .
> To this must be added that I cannot be ungrateful to God; for I must rather rejoice that I had such a brother than grieve that I had lost a brother, for the former is a gift, the latter a debt to be paid. And so, as long as I might, I enjoyed the loan entrusted to me, now He Who deposited the pledge has taken it back. . . . And so the larger the

amount of the loan, so much the more gratitude is due for the use of the capital. (*Death of Satyrus* 1.2; *NPNF*² 10:161)

He would not hide his pain:

> But now, brother, whither shall I advance, or whither shall I turn? The ox seeks his fellow, and conceives itself incomplete, and by frequent lowing shows its tender longing, if perchance that one is wanting with whom it has been wont to draw the plough. And shall I, my brother, not long after thee? Or can I ever forget thee, with whom I always drew the plough of this life? (*Death of Satyrus* 1.8; *NPNF*² 10:162)

As to Simplician and the studies in which he led Ambrose, the new bishop devoted himself assiduously to them. He was never overly interested in metaphysical or theological speculation, but he was profoundly interested in the study of Scripture as well as of the writings of others, in Latin as well as in Greek, who could help him in his ministerial practice as well as in the theological controversies of the time, particularly the struggle against Arianism. All his free time was taken up in study, and years later Augustine of Hippo would express his admiration for Ambrose's study style: in sharp contrast to what others did then, "while reading, his eyes glanced over the pages, and his heart searched out the sense, but his voice and tongue were silent" (Augustine, *Confessions* 6.3.3; *NPNF*¹ 1:91).

But not only Ambrose was in mourning, for the Visigoths were sacking Roman lands, killing many and taking others into captivity. In response to these events, Ambrose ordered that the sacred vessels of the church be melted down so that their precious metals could be used to buy the freedom of captives. As could be expected, many among the Arians criticized him for having done such a thing. Sometime later, Ambrose would say about those events: "I once brought odium on myself because I broke up the sacred vessels to redeem captives. . . . The Church has gold, not to store up, but to lay out, and to spend on those who need" (*Duties of the Clergy* 2.28; *NPNF*² 10:64).

The struggle against Arianism was long and difficult. Although in Spain and Transalpine Gaul Arianism had practically disappeared, there were still strong centers of resistance to the faith of Nicaea toward the east of Milan, particularly in the regions near the Danube. Now many who came from that area, fleeing the invading Visigoths, were Arian. For some time, under the reign of Emperor Gratian, the orthodox faith had the support of the government, and Ambrose became an adviser to the emperor, to whom he addressed his two books *On the Faith*, at imperial request.

But the political situation was complex, for the government of the Western Empire was not only in the hands of Gratian, but also of Valentinian II, who was still very young. Justina, Valentinian's mother, served as regent. Since she was decidedly Arian, she repeatedly clashed with Ambrose. The first conflicts arose around the election of a new bishop for the city of Sirmium, when Ambrose was able to fend off Justina's plan for having an Arian elected as bishop. But then the conflict began to revolve around the issue of the use of churches in Milan. According to law, church buildings were the property of the state, and therefore Justina had the right to do with them as she pleased. Due to the influx of Arian exiles fleeing the Visigothic invasion, and also because Justina herself brought a number of Goths to the court to serve as her personal guards, Arianism was rapidly growing in Milan. When Justina demanded that a church be turned over to the Arians, Ambrose refused, thus starting an open conflict that would last for a long time. The population of Milan resisted the orders of Justina, who was not sure that she could count on the loyalty of many of her troops.

The climax of the conflict came in an episode at the church called the New Basilica, where Ambrose locked himself up with a large number of his flock while soldiers surrounded the church, hoping that eventually those inside would grow tired and desist. Inside, Ambrose and his followers turned to music. At a time when church music was growing ever more complicated, Ambrose had proposed a musical style that was simpler and easier to sing, consisting mostly in antiphonal chants between two choirs. Most of what was sung was the Psalms. Ambrose himself also composed a number of hymns. Although a large number are attributed to him, only four are undoubtedly his, while there are doubts about many, and some are clearly not the work of Ambrose.

Ambrose himself tells the story of events at the New Basilica with some interesting details in a letter that he wrote to his sister Marcelina in Rome. He tells her that the Imperial Council ordered him to surrender the New Basilica, which was the main church in the city. On the following Sunday, while Ambrose was busy with other matters—explaining the creed to candidates for baptism—there was a riot in which a mob attacked an Arian priest. Upon learning this, Ambrose sent a number of his clergy to rescue the Arian priest, and when celebrating communion prayed that there would be no bloodshed. The government responded by punishing the rioters in various ways. Shortly thereafter, Ambrose told Marcelina in a letter, "I was terrified when I learned that they had sent armed men to take the Basilica, for I was afraid that there would be bloodshed and a massacre because some were defending it decidedly" (*Ep.* 20.1; PL 16:997). The next day tension grew. The loyalty of the soldiers, of whom only a minority were Arian, was in doubt. When the soldiers surrounding the church learned that Ambrose had told his flock that they should abstain from communion with them, they broke into the church. Initially, the result was a panic. But the soldiers made clear that they had not come to fight, but to pray. In his sermon, Ambrose commented on what was taking place, using the biblical text "O Lord, now have the Gentiles come into thine inheritance" (Ps. 79:1). As he spoke, the soldiers began abandoning their weapons and joining him. Finally, Ambrose later reported, "I learned that the Emperor had ordered the soldiers to leave the Basilica and also returned the fines that had been collected from the merchants [who had supported me]" (*Ep.* 20.26; PL 16:1002).

From that point onward, in spite of the political vicissitudes of the time, the authority of Ambrose was widely recognized. This reached its zenith after Theodosius became emperor in 379. Relations between Ambrose and Theodosius were not always cordial. Nor can one say that in the conflicts between the two, justice was always on the side of Ambrose. For instance, when in the small town of Callinicus, on the shores of the Euphrates, Christians sacked and burned the synagogue at the instigation of the bishop, Theodosius ordered that the bishop should pay for the reconstruction of the synagogue and that the arsonists be punished. Ambrose intervened, arguing that this would force believers to choose between apostasy and martyrdom. Eventually Theodosius yielded, and the synagogue was not rebuilt nor the arsonists punished. Another event shows that sometimes it was Ambrose who was on the side of justice. There had been a riot in the city of Thessalonica, and Theodosius responded by ordering the slaughter of a good part of its population. In a famous confrontation, possibly exaggerated and dramatized by the chroniclers, Ambrose refused to admit Theodosius to communion until the emperor showed repentance for this grave sin and gave instructions so that no matter how irate he became, such an event would never take place again.

Ambrose died in 397; as some chroniclers say, his death was on the evening of Holy Saturday, which would already be considered Easter morning. His former tutor Simplician succeeded him as bishop. Emperor Theodosius had also died shortly before that.

Ironically, among the many deeds that made Ambrose famous, none was as important as one of which he does not even seem to have been aware. A young professor who had come from Africa to teach rhetoric in Milan, upon hearing of the fame of the preacher, went to listen to him, not to hear what he said, but rather to take note of how he said it. But, to his own surprise, the young professor was captivated by what Ambrose was saying and by the manner in which he interpreted Scripture. He finally decided to accept the faith of his own mother and of Ambrose, a faith that until then had seemed irrational to him. That young professor whom Ambrose baptized, and who never dared to speak at length with the bishop for fear of interrupting his studies and meditation, was called Aurelius Augustinus, but now is generally known as Augustine of Hippo.

EXEGETICAL WORKS

A vast number of Ambrose's writings have survived. Suffice it to say that in Migne's *Patrologia latina* series, in which all the writings prior to Ambrose occupy thirteen volumes, those of Ambrose take up the next five. He wrote numerous commentaries on Scripture. On Genesis, these commentaries include six books *On the Six Days of Creation*, one *On Paradise*, two *On Cain and Abel*, one *On Noah and the Ark*, two *On Abraham*, one *On Joseph*, and another *On the Blessings of the Patriarchs*. Then there are numerous others on the rest of the Old Testament, particularly on Psalms and the Song of Solomon, but also on a number of particular passages and events, such as Elijah's fasting, the episode of Naboth's vineyard, and the sin and repentance of David. Among the deuterocanonical books, he wrote about Tobias and Maccabees. On the New Testament, he left a *Commentary on Luke* in ten books, as well as commentaries on all the epistles of Paul, from Romans to Philemon.

This shows Ambrose's interest in knowing and teaching Scripture, and also his activity as a preacher, for several of these writings bear signs of having been spoken before being written down. For this reason modern authors differ widely in their classifications of the works of Ambrose, some classifying certain works among biblical commentaries, and others listing the same works as homiletical pieces.

At any rate, in his biblical interpretation Ambrose agreed with Clement of Alexandria, Origen, and many others that in a single passage of the sacred text, there are several levels of meaning. Generally, these are at least three. At a basic level, Scripture has a literal or historical meaning, in which words mean exactly what they say. Second, when applying the text to actual life situations, one finds a "moral" meaning that offers directives for living. Finally, there is the higher level of allegorical or "mystical" meaning, pointing to the great mysteries of faith. Thus, for instance, in commenting on the story of the centurion's servant that appears in Luke 7, Ambrose begins by discussing the story itself, then employing it as an example for the present life, and finally taking the entire discussion to what he calls the "mystical meaning":

> What a sign of divine humility, that the Lord of heaven was willing to visit the centurion's servant! . . . He did not do this because he could not heal from a distance, but rather to provide us an example of humility to imitate, teaching us to be deferential with the humble as well us with the great. . . .
>
> As to the mystical meaning, . . . he [the centurion] believed the word and understood that it was by virtue of a power that was not human, but divine, that Christ healed people. He saw the mystery that Christ cannot heal human hearts that are still pagan [but must first come to them]. (*Commentary on Luke* 5.84, 86; BAC 257:270–71)

One can see Ambrose's rhetorical ability in all his works, but particularly in his commentaries and discussions regarding Scripture. This is more so since many of these now-written works were actually prepared as speeches or sermons. As an example of this rhetorical ability, one may quote a passage in which Ambrose comments on the birth of Jesus:

> He has been small, and he has been a child, so that you can be a perfect human. He has been tied in swaddling clothes so that you may be freed from the bonds of death. He has been placed in a manger so that you may be placed on the altars. He has been placed on earth so that you may be among the stars. He had no place in the inn so that you may have many mansions in heaven. (*Comm. Luke* 2.41; BAC 257:109)

One of Ambrose's outstanding sermons deals with the episode of the vineyard of Naboth, in the first book of Kings, chapter 21. The story told there is that King Ahab, under the advice of Jezebel, unjustly took possession of Naboth's vineyard, taking not only his property, but also his life. In his sermon, Ambrose declares that the rich are like a bottomless pit, with an insatiable thirst and hunger into which wealth sinks. According to Ambrose, this is the reason why one speaks of a "man of wealth," which means not that the man possesses the wealth, but rather that the wealth possesses the man. The rich do not know how poor they are, for the more they have, the more they desire, so that no matter what they have, they will always be poor. As they come to possess greater wealth, this does not end their greed, but rather exacerbates it. Ambrose is blunt about it:

> You take the clothing off the naked and dress your walls with it. The naked calls at your door, and you do not even look at him. This naked one begging from you is a human being, and you are worrying about how to obtain better marbles for your floors. The poor ask you for money and receive nothing. You have before you a human being asking for bread, and you put golden bits in the mouths of your horses. You enjoy your jewelry while they do not have anything to eat. The people are hungry and you lock your granaries. The people are clamoring and you exhibit your jewelry. Woe to the one who can save so many lives from death and does not do so! (*On the Vine of Naboth* 12; PL 14:784)

DOGMATIC WORKS

Ambrose's strictly theological or dogmatic writings are fewer than his biblical commentaries, sermons, and speeches. In general they are also less interesting, for Ambrose was much more a preacher than a speculative theologian. As he himself declares,

Men learn before they teach, and receive from Him what they may hand on to others.

But not even this was the case with me. For I was carried off from the judgment seat, and the garb [*infulis*] of office, to enter on the priesthood, and began to teach you, what I myself had not yet learnt. So it happened that I began to teach before I began to learn. Therefore I must learn and teach at the same time, since I had no leisure to learn before. (*On the Duties of the Clergy* 1.1.1; *NPNF*² 10:1)

For the learning that he sought, Ambrose turned primarily to the most important Christian authors who had written in Greek, for he had an excellent command of that language.

Two of Ambrose's most important theological works were written at the request of Emperor Gratian, who wished to learn more not only of Christianity, but specifically of the Nicene faith and its reasons for rejecting Arianism. The first of these two works of Ambrose was *On the Faith*. When the emperor asked him to amplify the two books that he had written, adding material particularly regarding the Holy Spirit, Ambrose did so first by adding three new books to the earlier work, reinforcing his arguments against Arianism. Apparently much of what was added here was taken from previous sermons and lectures, for it has an undeniable oratorical style. Then, to deal with the matter of the Holy Spirit, Ambrose wrote another work, *On the Holy Spirit*, in three books.

Ambrose's arguments against Arianism are mostly drawn from earlier authors, particularly Athanasius and Basil the Great. But he had exceptional ability for summarizing and simplifying such arguments to make them more easily understandable, sometimes at the risk of oversimplifying matters. This may be seen in the following paragraphs, which are the heart of his argument in *On the Faith*:

Now let us consider the disputings of the Arians concerning the Son of God.

They say that the Son of God is unlike His Father. To say this of a man would be an insult.

They say that the Son of God had a beginning in time, whereas He Himself is the source and ordainer of time and all that therein is. We are men, and we would not be limited to time. We began to exist once, and we believe that we shall have a timeless existence. We desire after immortality—how, then, can we deny the eternity of God's Son, Whom God declares to be eternal by nature, not by grace?

They say that He was created. But who would reckon an author with his works, and have him seem to be what he has himself made?

They deny His goodness. Their blaspheming is its own condemnation, and so cannot hope for pardon.

They deny that He is truly Son of God, they deny His omnipotence, in that whilst they admit that all things are made by the ministry of the Son, they attribute the original source of their being to the power of God. But what is power, save perfection of nature?

Furthermore, the Arians deny that in Godhead He is One with the Father. Let them annul the Gospel, then, and silence the voice of Christ. For Christ Himself has said: "I and the Father are one." (*On the Faith* 1.5.34–40; *NPNF*[2] 10:206–7)

The extensive work *On the Holy Spirit*, in which Ambrose responds to a request from Gratian, takes particular aim at the Pneumatomachians—those who accepted the full divinity of the Son but not of the Holy Spirit. In this case as well, Ambrose takes most of his materials from Greek authors, which led curmudgeon Jerome to declare that Ambrose had taken good things from Greek writers and bad things from Latin writers. However, Jerome does not merit much attention on this point, for his prejudice against Ambrose—as well as against any other who might overshadow him—led him to say about Ambrose, "I shall not offer my opinion about him, . . . for I fear if I praise him, I will be accused of lying, and if I criticize him, I will be accused for speaking the truth" (*On Illustrious Men* 124; PL 23:751).

This particular writing by Ambrose was important for the Latin-speaking West, whose theologians had not dwelt much on the doctrine of the Holy Spirit, which had become a central theme of discussion in the Greek-speaking East. In the West, some seem to have thought that the Holy Spirit was simply the Word of God, and others that the Holy Spirit was just a divine power. Ambrose's response to this was to bring into the West the result of earlier discussions in the East. Thus, as by then had become common among Eastern theologians, Ambrose affirms that the Holy Spirit is God and a third person of the Trinity, thus distinct from the Father and the Son.

Another important theological work by Ambrose, *On the Sacrament of the Incarnation of the Lord*, is much briefer. Here he repeats his arguments against Arianism and also rejects the theories of Apollinaris. The treatise itself has an interesting history. Two officers with Arian inclinations had criticized Ambrose for what he had said in a sermon regarding the incarnation. Ambrose announced that he would answer them in public. At the appointed time, the two officers were not there, and Ambrose began speaking about Cain and Abel in order to allow them time to arrive. Finally, when it was clear that they would not show up, Ambrose began dealing with the subject under discussion. Later he learned that they had died in an accident. Ambrose was polishing shorthand notes that someone had taken of his speech when he received a petition from Gratian that he would answer the objections to Nicene ortho-doxy posed by the Arian Palladius of Ratiana, in what today is Bulgaria. Rather than writing a new treatise, Ambrose composed an addendum to what he was about to publish. The most significant element in this treatise, which mostly repeats earlier arguments against Arianism, is its rejection of the teachings of Apollinaris, that in the incarnation the Word of God came to take the place of the human rational soul in Jesus. Ambrose bases his argument on what the Cappadocians had already said: that if the purpose of the incarnation is to save human beings, the Word of God must have become incarnate in a complete human being, particularly since the main seat of sin is the soul:

> He [the Word of God] took on flesh in order later to make it return from the dead. And he also took and received a perfect rational human soul. . . . The very Word of God did not come to join the flesh by taking the place of the soul, but just as he took our flesh he also perfectly took a soul when he assumed human nature. I declare that he assumed the soul, so that he could bless it with the sacrament of his incarnation. (*Sacrament of the Incarnation of the Lord* 7.65, 67; PL 16:834–35)

The treatise *On the Mysteries* is a series of lectures for those who had been recently baptized, similar to the lectures in parallel circumstances by Cyril of Jerusalem. They were delivered beginning on Easter Sunday, explaining to the neophytes the meaning of baptism, confirmation, and communion. At their very opening, Ambrose affirms that for several days he has been preaching about Christian life and that now, after baptism, the time has come to teach the neophytes regarding the "mysteries" of the faith, meaning the sacraments:

> The season now warns us to speak of the Mysteries, and to set forth the purport of the sacraments, which if we had thought it well to teach before baptism to those who were not yet initiated, we should be considered rather to have betrayed than to have portrayed the Mysteries. And then, too, another reason is that the light itself of the Mysteries will shed itself with more effect upon those who are expecting they know not what, than if any discourse had come beforehand. . . .
>
> Open, then, your ears, inhale the good savour of eternal life which has been breathed upon you by the grace of the sacraments. (*Myst.* 1.2–3; NPNF[2] 10:317)

This work is particularly valuable because here we have a description of many of the rites, gestures, and words that were employed in worship at that time.

There is also a treatise under the title of *On the Sacraments* that may or may not be the work of Ambrose. While it is impossible to give a definitive answer to this question, most scholars are inclined to think that Ambrose did indeed produce this work. The difference in style between this writing and others from Ambrose's hand may well have to do with the particular style and interests of whoever took the notes of what Ambrose was saying rather than with Ambrose's style itself. This treatise is very similar to *On the Mysteries*, for it too is a series of lectures addressed to the neophytes on six successive days.

But it includes some details on baptism and communion that are not to be found in the other work.

Finally, among the dogmatic writings of Ambrose, one must mention his two books *On Penance*, whose main purpose is to refute the views of the Novatians. The point of departure of this treatise is that moderation and kindness are to be fundamental characteristics of disciples of Christ and that the Novatians do not practice them. Their insistence on permanently denying communion to any who abandoned the faith in times of persecution is a violation of the essential principle of the Christian faith, which is love. Jesus forgave all sorts of sin, and the church must not block the path to restoration that Jesus pointed out. Anyone who has sinned gravely is not to be abandoned, but rather led to repentance and restored to the Christian community by means of the authority that Jesus gave to his disciples and to the church to restore the fallen.

PRACTICAL AND ASCETICAL WORKS

Most of Ambrose's works on asceticism deal with virginity and with continence for widows who have been consecrated to the Lord. The most important are *On the Virgins, On Virginity, On the Institution of Virgins, Exhortation to Virginity*, and *On Widows*. Among all these writings the most important is the first, which consists of three books that Ambrose wrote to his sister Marcelina, who had been consecrated to virginity long before Ambrose became a bishop. According to Ambrose, the importance of virginity was shown by the Son of God himself becoming flesh through a virgin. Similarly, the church is a virgin whose children are all who believe. This does not mean that marriage is to be undervalued. But one must remember all the difficulties and pain that marriage brings with it. A married woman has the consolation of her children, but also suffers with their problems. These children begin producing discomfort and pain even before they are born, and then they are the cause of even greater pains. Virgins avoid all this, besides being free from greed and ostentation.

Ambrose's great practical work is *On the Duties of the Clergy*. The very title of the book in Latin, *De officiis ministrorum*, shows that Ambrose proposes to write a book similar to Cicero's classical *De officiis*, but addressing the specific tasks and functions of the clergy. This work, published in three books, was apparently based on a series of lectures and instructions that Ambrose delivered to the clergy under his supervision. The use of a title similar to that of Cicero's work shows that Ambrose, while drawing from the teachings of Greco-Roman antiquity, will also seek to show that Christian virtues are far above their pagan counterparts; yet Ambrose does not always mention his pagan sources. At the same time, Ambrose is seeking to substitute the most admired figures of antiquity with better Christian examples.

In the first book, Ambrose establishes a distinction between "ordinary" and "perfect" virtues. In chapter 11 he uses the example of the rich young man to establish this distinction. The man had done all he was obliged to do, but even so, he was not perfect. To be perfect he had to go further and to practice other virtues. This distinction would play an important role in the history of monasticism, which on this basis distinguished between "commandments" that all must obey and "counsels of perfection" to be followed by those who seek perfection. But then Ambrose returns to the four cardinal virtues of classical and Hellenistic thought: prudence, fortitude, temperance, and justice. He discusses each of these in order, reviewing what ancient authors, particularly Cicero, said about them, in order then to redefine them in Christian terms. For instance, while classical authors taught that justice consists in doing no evil to anyone who has not harmed one, gospel teaching goes far beyond that. Therefore, while in ancient jurisprudence the essence of justice was to distinguish between what is private and what is public, and to respect the rights of all others, Ambrose affirms that the Christian God has made all things for the use of all, and that what has made them the private property of a few is greed, and therefore injustice.

In the second book, Ambrose returns to a subject already mentioned in the first, the relationship between happiness and virtue, and between virtue and that which is convenient or useful. People often think that there is a contradiction between what is virtuous and what is convenient or useful because we forget that the final use of all things is eternal life. Therefore, that which seems to be useful or convenient is not so in truth.

Finally, in the third book, Ambrose returns to the subject of a perfection that goes beyond mere obedience to commandments, and he exhorts his readers to seek that perfection. Here, as in the entire work, he looks to Scripture for examples of persons and actions that demonstrate their superiority over pagan virtue.

This may well be Ambrose's most influential book. It certainly is one of the most original, for here he is not translating into Latin what others had said before in Greek, but rather relating Christian faith with the ethical tradition of the Latin world. This work in three books is the first attempt in the Christian West to systematize ethical thought. The themes discussed here had already been taken up by authors such as Tertullian, Cyprian, and others. But now Ambrose systematized them and drew lines both of continuity and of contrast between Christian ethics and their traditional Roman counterpart.

LETTERS

Ambrose's epistolary is of great importance. We have some ninety letters of Ambrose. (This is an approximate figure, for the authorship of a number of letters is not settled.) Some among his letters are addressed to emperors, sometimes responding to letters received from them; others are to his sister Marcelina, letting her know about his conflicts with the Arians, telling her about events such as the discovery of the supposed martyrs Gervasius and Protassius; and many are addressed to other leaders of the church.

The most interesting among these letters is number 51, which Ambrose wrote to Theodosius after the massacre in Thessalonica. Here, with a respectful yet firm attitude, Ambrose points out to the emperor the enormity of his crime and how this resulted from his not restraining his anger; finally he tells the emperor that he will not allow him to take communion until he repents:

> I urge, I beg, I exhort, I warn, for it is a grief to me, that you who were an example of unusual piety, who were conspicuous for clemency, who would not suffer single offenders to be put in peril, should not mourn that so many have perished. Though you have waged battle most successfully, though in other matters, too, you are worthy of praise, yet piety was ever the crown of your actions. The devil envied that which was your most excellent possession. Conquer him whilst you still possess that wherewith you may conquer. Do not add another sin to your sin by a course of action which has injured many.
>
> I, indeed, though a debtor to your kindness, for which I cannot be ungrateful, that kindness which has surpassed that of many emperors, and has been equalled by one only; I, I say, have no cause for a charge of contumacy against you, but have cause for fear; I dare not offer the sacrifice if you intend to be present. Is that which is not allowed after shedding the blood of one innocent person, allowed after shedding the blood of many? I do not think so. (*Ep.* 51.12–13; *NPNF²* 10:451–52)

21

Jerome

HIS LIFE AND HIS CHARACTER

Few among those early Christian writers whom tradition came to call the "Fathers of the church" have been as influential as Jerome. At the same time, few of them have been as irascible and bellicose.

Jerome was born in a small town in the northeastern corner of what now is Italy, in approximately 347, into a Christian family, although not one of profound devotion. When he had completed his basic studies in his native land, his parents sent him to study in Rome, apparently hoping that he would follow a career in politics and administration. There he and a group of friends became interested in Christianity and an ascetic life, and he was baptized shortly after his twentieth birthday. While in the imperial capital, Jerome also began to build what would eventually become a vast library by copying manuscripts of Christian as well as pagan authors. He then left for Treves with his friends and his books, and apparently it was there that he decided to abandon all thought of a lucrative political career and devote himself to study and to asceticism. Later, in Aquileia, he joined a group of friends with similar interests. One of these was Rufinus, who had become his close friend in Rome.

Jerome says that his sojourn in Aquileia was a time of happiness. But for some unknown reason he decided to leave. Years later when Rufinus was in Egypt, Jerome wrote to his friend a letter in which he mentions his departure from Aquileia and says that

> After that sudden whirlwind dragged me from your side, severing with its impious wrench the bonds of affection in which we were knit together, . . . I wandered about, uncertain where to go. Thrace,

Pontus, Bithynia, the whole of Galatia and Cappadocia, Cilicia also with its burning heat, one after another shattered my energies. At last Syria presented itself to me as a most secure harbor to a shipwrecked man. (*Ep.* 3.3; *NPNF*² 6:5)

He also tells Rufinus that in Syria he lost an eye due to a fever. Even so, he continued studying with ever greater zeal. He had decided to devote his life to the study of Scripture, but he continued reading and studying classical writings, Greek as well as Roman. It was probably there, in Antioch, that he went through the inner struggles about which he would write much later in a letter to his disciple and friend Eustoquium:

Many years ago, when for the kingdom of heaven's sake I had cut myself off from home, parents, sister, relations, and—harder still— from the dainty food to which I had been accustomed; and when I was on my way to Jerusalem to wage my warfare, I still could not bring myself to forgo the library which I had formed for myself at Rome with great care and toil. And so, miserable man that I was, I would fast only that I might afterwards read Cicero. After many nights spent in vigil, after floods of tears called from my inmost heart, after the recollection of my past sins, I would once more take up Plautus. And when at times I returned to my right mind, and began to read the prophets, their style seemed rude and repellent. I failed to see the light with my blinded eyes; but I attributed the fault not to them, but to the sun. (*Ep.* 22.30; *NPNF*² 6:35)

Jerome felt overwhelmed by this tension between his Christian faith and pagan letters when, as he says in the same letter, he became critically ill, was thought to be about to die, and had a shattering vision:

Suddenly I was caught up in the spirit and dragged before the judgment seat of the Judge; and here the light was so bright, and those who stood around were so radiant, that I cast myself upon the ground and did not dare to look up. Asked who and what I was I replied: "I am a Christian." But He who presided said: "Thou liest, thou art a follower of Cicero and not of Christ. For 'where thy treasure is, there will thy heart be also.'" (*Ep.* 22.30; *NPNF*² 6:35)

That vision did not lead him to abandon classical letters, which he always continued studying. Nor did he dispose of his library, which he would soon take with him to his desert retreat. But he did become more assiduous in his study of Scripture. And it would be such study that would lead to his fame.

Perhaps as a result of that vision, a little over a year later Jerome left Antioch in order to withdraw to the desert nearby and live as a hermit devoted to an ascetic life and to study. From then on, the desert came to be for Jerome a symbol of an idyllic ascetic life. In one of his letters he exclaims, "O desert, bright with the flowers of Christ! . . . O wilderness, gladdened with God's especial presence!" (*Ep.* 14.10; *NPNF*[2] 6:17). But this is only one side of the coin, for in the same letter to Eustoquium quoted above, he comments:

> How often, when I was living in the desert, in the vast solitude which gives to hermits a savage dwelling-place, parched by a burning sun, how often did I fancy myself among the pleasures of Rome! I used to sit alone because I was filled with bitterness. Sackcloth disfigured my unshapely limbs and my skin from long neglect had become as black as an Ethiopian's. Tears and groans were every day my portion; and if drowsiness chanced to overcome my struggles against it, my bare bones, which hardly held together, clashed against the ground. (*Ep.* 22.7; *NPNF*[2] 6:24–25)

Although he is frequently depicted as a hermit dedicated to solitary study, in fact Jerome lived as a hermit for only some two years. During that time he continued copying books and thus augmenting his library, and he also studied Hebrew. Leaving the desert, he returned to Antioch, where he joined those who defended the strictest Nicene orthodoxy against Arianism—although Jerome was never particularly interested in theological speculations and was content with accepting already-established theological views. In Antioch he continued studying the Bible, partly under the direction of Apollinaris of Laodicea, who would later be declared a heretic by the Council of Constantinople. In one of his letters he says: "At Antioch I frequently listened to Apollinaris of Laodicea, and attended his lectures; yet, although he instructed me in the holy scriptures, I never embraced his disputable doctrine as to their meaning" (*Ep.* 83.3; *NPNF*[2] 6:176).

From Antioch, Jerome set out on further travel. He was in Constantinople in 381, when the gathering now called the Second Ecumenical Council took place there. He took the opportunity to meet several of the most distinguished figures that had gathered in the capital for the council, among them Gregory of Nazianzus, who presided over the first session of that council. Gregory, who followed Origen's methods for biblical interpretation, helped Jerome gain a deeper understanding of those methods. Finally, after fifteen years of absence, Jerome returned to Rome.

In Rome, Bishop Damasus, who admired his writings, made Jerome his secretary. Apparently it was Damasus who first suggested that Jerome should produce a new translation of the Bible into Latin. The Old Latin version of the Old Testament most commonly used at the time was not directly translated from the original Hebrew, but from the Greek version known as the Septuagint, and Damasus wished for a direct translation. During this time in Rome, Jerome made his first attempts in that direction.

Also during this time in Rome, Jerome began a close relationship with a group of devout women who were interested not only in ascetic life, but also in study. One of their leaders was Marcella, who would constantly ask Jerome about Scripture. In response, Jerome would write extensive letters (*Epistles* 23–29, 32, 34, 37, 38, 40–44, and 59). Since Marcella's questions showed her vast learning and often had to do with the meaning of the Hebrew text, Jerome's answers were actually erudite treatises on the text of Scripture. While in Rome, Jerome also established contact with another group of devout women that included Paula and her daughter Eustoquium. We also have several letters that Jerome wrote to these two women, who were not only his disciples but later also his collaborators.

However, while Jerome's collegial relationship with these women was remarkable, he also proved to be rather bellicose in his relations with other men, particularly those who might overshadow him. Jerome soon clashed with several leaders of the church in Rome. Although many attacked and criticized him, Bishop Damasus protected him. But when Damasus died in 384, Jerome found life in Rome ever more difficult.

Finally he decided to leave for the Holy Land. Also Paula and Eustochium left the city with the same goal, and they joined Jerome along the way, perhaps in Cyprus, or perhaps in Antioch. Having arrived at the Holy Land, they set out on a pilgrimage that took them as far as Alexandria, where Jerome was able to meet Didymus the Blind. Didymus added to what Jerome had learned from Gregory of Nazianzus regarding the methods of Origen for the study and interpretation of Scripture.

It was not until 386 that Jerome and his companions finally settled in Bethlehem. Sometime before, Rufinus, Jerome's friend from the time of their youth, had established a monastic community dedicated to study near Jerusalem, and nearby Melania—a distinguished Roman woman with whom Rufinus had established relations similar to those that Jerome had with Marcella, Paula, and Eustoquium—had established a similar community for women. Jerome renewed his friendship with Rufinus, for they were both dedicated to study, and they would borrow books one from the other in order to copy them. Meanwhile, all these communities grew, although those for women grew much more rapidly than those for men.

It was there, in Bethlehem, that Jerome spent the last thirty-four years of his life, dedicated both to his studies and to a vast number of controversies in which he was involved not only because of the turbulent conditions of the time, but also because of his own bellicosity. Finally, shortly after the death of Eustoquium in 419, Jerome died. To his very last days, he continued studying Scripture as previously, and he was commenting on the book of Isaiah when he died.

Jerome's bellicosity, which eventually left him practically friendless among men, was paralleled by great pride. Convinced as he was of his own genius, with good reason, he was always afraid that others would not recognize it. A sign of this is that in his work *On Illustrious Men*, after listing the most important authors and distinguished men who lived before him, Jerome places himself at the end of the list: "I, Jerome, son of Eusebius, . . . have written up to the present year, that is, the 14th of the reign of Theodosius, all that follows: [and here follows a long list of all his works]" (*Ill. Men* 135; PL 23:755–59).

Among the many conflicts in which he was involved, and which cost him most of his friends, two examples stand out: his disputes with Rufinus and with Augustine.

Jerome's friendship with Rufinus was deeply rooted in their youth. For a long time, even at a distance, Rufinus remained Jerome's best friend. In the already-quoted letter in which he tells how he had to leave Aquileia, Jerome addresses Rufinus, who at that time was in Egypt with Melania:

> Oh, if only the Lord Jesus Christ would suddenly transport me to you as Philip was transported to the eunuch, and Habakkuk to Daniel, with what a close embrace would I clasp your neck, how fondly would I press kisses upon that mouth which has so often joined with me of old in error or in wisdom. But as I am unworthy (not that you should so come to me but) that I should so come to you, and because my poor body, weak even when well, has been shattered by frequent illnesses; I send this letter to meet you instead of coming myself, in the hope that it may bring you hither to me caught in the meshes of love's net. (*Ep.* 3.1; *NPNF*[2] 6:4)

When Jerome and his women companions finally settled in Bethlehem, since the communities of Rufinus and Melania were relatively near, the two friends would meet periodically in order to exchange ideas and manuscripts. These were some of the happiest and most productive years in Jerome's life, for it was at that time that he wrote a good number of his works.

But then discord intervened. At the beginning it had to do with Origen and allegorical interpretation. Jerome admired Origen's erudition and his writings about Scripture but would not accept his philosophical speculations about matters such as the preexistence of souls, the universality of salvation, and the like. Rufinus, for his part, not only admired the great Alexandrine teacher but also defended his opinions, which many found offensive. For a number of reasons, a controversy broke out regarding the Origenism that Rufinus and others proposed. Matters were complicated by intrigues both in Jerusalem and in Rome. Although Jerome had never paid much attention to the subject of the controversy, because he was interested in Origen's erudition and not in his theology, he was not able to avoid the debate. The result was a bitter break with the friend of his youth, Rufinus. There were mutual and public accusations. Rufinus wrote an *Apology*, and Jerome responded in kind, but with more vitriol, with an *Apology against the Books of Rufinus*. The ancient friendship disappeared, and the conflict continued escalating until, after eight years of accusations and responses, Rufinus simply decided to pay no attention to whatever Jerome was saying about him.

The clash with Augustine had to do in part with lost letters and gossip, for someone began saying that Augustine had written a book against Jerome, and the letter in which Augustine told Jerome that this was not true never reached its destination. Having received an explanation of the matter from Augustine, Jerome wrote him, accepting his account, but also took the opportunity to let Augustine know of his own authority as senior to Augustine: "It is puerile self-sufficiency to seek, as young men have of old been wont to do, to gain glory to one's own name by assailing men who have become renowned" (*Ep.* 102.2; *NPNF*[1] 1:324). But tensions continued, particularly when Augustine dared criticize Jerome's great work, his translation of the Bible into Latin, a version now known as the Vulgate, to which we shall return. Augustine wrote to Jerome, telling him about a dispute that arose in Africa because Jerome translated the name of the plant that sheltered Jonah as a gourd and not as a vine, as in the ancient Greek translation known as the Septuagint. He also told Jerome, who had learned Hebrew from Jewish teachers, that he did not think Christians should learn how to read the Bible from Jews. He accepted the legend claiming that the Septuagint had been divinely inspired and suggested that, instead of translating the Old Testament from the Hebrew, he should actually translate it from the Septuagint:

> For my part, I would much rather that you would furnish us with a translation of the Greek version of the canonical Scriptures known as the work of the Seventy translators [the Septuagint]. For if your translation begins to be more generally read in many churches, it will be a grievous thing that, in the reading of Scripture, differences must arise between the Latin Churches and the Greek Churches, especially seeing that the discrepancy is easily condemned in a Latin version by the production of the original in Greek, which is a language very widely known; whereas, if any one has been disturbed by the occurrence of something to which he was not accustomed in the translation taken from the Hebrew, and alleges that the new translation is wrong, it will be found difficult, if not impossible, to get at the Hebrew documents by which the version to which exception is taken may be defended. And when they are obtained, who will submit to have so many Latin and Greek authorities pronounced to be in the wrong? Besides all this, Jews, if consulted as to the meaning of the Hebrew text, may give a different opinion from yours: in which case it will seem as if your presence were indispensable, as being the only one who could refute

their view; and it would be a miracle if one could be found capable of acting as arbiter between you and them. (*Ep.* 104.6; *NPNF*[1] 1:327)

Jerome's reaction was fulminating, particularly since what reached him was not Augustine's letter from his own hand, but rather a copy. After claiming that he could not believe that Augustine had said such things, he tells Augustine that he suspected that

> this had not been done by you in a guileless spirit, but through desire for praise and celebrity, and éclat in the eyes of the people, intending to become famous at my expense; that many might know that you challenged me, and I feared to meet you; that you had written as a man of learning, and I had by silence confessed my ignorance, and had at last found one who knew how to stop my garrulous tongue. (*Ep.* 105.2; *NPNF*[1] 1:327)

And then, once again claiming authority because of his age—although in truth he was only a few years older than Augustine—Jerome went on:

> Desist from annoying an old man, who seeks retirement in his monastic cell. If you wish to exercise or display your learning, choose as your antagonists, young, eloquent, and illustrious men, of whom it is said that many are found in Rome, who may be neither unable nor afraid to meet you, and to enter the lists with a bishop in debates concerning the Sacred Scriptures. As for me, a soldier once, but a retired veteran now. (*Ep.* 105.3; *NPNF*[1] 1:327)

The storm abated, and the correspondence back and forth did not continue, although years later Augustine seems to be remembering it when he tells Jerome: "Although in addressing you I consult one much older than myself, nevertheless I also am becoming old; but I cannot think that it is at any time of life too late to learn what we need to know" (*Ep.* 131.1; *NPNF*[1] 1:523).

What finally brought the two back together was the arrival of Pelagianism in Palestine. Although Jerome knew that on matters having to do with Scripture he had an advantage over Augustine, he also had to confess that in theological matters the advantage was Augustine's. Therefore, Jerome set aside his differences with Augustine and consulted him regarding the teachings of Pelagius and how to respond to them.

This entire story draws the profile of a rigid and ill-humored man. But the truth is that sometimes, particularly in his letters—and even more so in those addressed to feminine colleagues—Jerome allows himself a bit of humor. For instance, when a young woman decided to set aside marriage and embrace life as a bride of Christ, Jerome tells her mother, who disagreed with her daughter's decision, that she should not be angry that her daughter had decided to marry the emperor instead of a soldier, telling her that her daughter had done her a great favor, for now the mother was becoming God's mother-in-law!

THE VULGATE

Although a good number of Jerome's works deal with other subjects, the vast majority are the result of his biblical studies. Among them none has been as influential through the ages as his translation of the Bible known as the Vulgate. When Jerome was in Rome at the service of Bishop Damasus, he began revising the Latin translation of the Gospels that was then employed. His first steps were cautious, for he knew that the texts from the Gospels and from the Psalms that were read and repeated in worship could not easily be changed without causing offense. Therefore, during his years in Rome, Jerome corrected in the Gospels and in Psalms only those translations that actually departed from the original meaning, leaving the rest as they were. But at the same time he began to compare various traditional renditions of passages in the Old Testament in order to determine their original meaning. Then, inspired by Origen's *Hexapla*, he began a series of comparisons between the Hebrew text and the Septuagint. Finally he began his translation into Latin from the original languages, Greek for the New Testament and Hebrew for the Old. It is not known exactly when Jerome began this task, or the order and date of the translation of various passages. Apparently the first book he translated from Hebrew was Job. In any case, Jerome did establish a clear distinction between the Jewish canon of the Old Testament, which he accepted, and the canon of the Septuagint, which includes the deuterocanonical books. Finally, toward the end of the first decade of the fifth century, he undertook the task of translating the Bible as a whole.

Although at the beginning some people resisted Jerome's translation, as we have already seen in his correspondence with Augustine, slowly the Vulgate made headway to such a point that it became the official Bible of the entire Latin-speaking church. This was mostly for two reasons. The first was the undeniable erudition of Jerome and his meticulous care to be as faithful to the original Hebrew and Greek as possible. The second was the literary quality of Jerome's translation. Although years earlier he claimed that he had ceased being a Ciceronian, in fact he always continued emulating the style of Cicero and other classical authors. Therefore his translation, besides being careful, was also elegant. This was particularly true of the Psalms, in which Jerome somehow managed the difficult task of translating Hebrew poetry into the canons of Latin poetry without twisting its meaning. The impact of that translation of Psalms was such that to this day one hears echoes of Jerome's work in translations into modern romance languages.

EXEGETICAL WORKS

As we have repeatedly seen, Jerome did not pay much attention to many of the theological debates of his time, and even when he was drawn into them, he did not write much on the subject. His interest lay in scriptural studies, and it was to them that he devoted his life. But it was not simply a matter of studying the existing text. It was also necessary, by means of philological studies, to determine the meaning of the text, and by means of geographical studies to understand the physical circumstances of biblical narratives. Among other things, since he lived in the Holy Land, he spent time speaking with the local inhabitants as well as with Jewish scholars in order better to understand the meaning of the words as well as their physical context.

Jerome's writings on Scripture are incredibly numerous. Many of them did not take the form of a commentary, but rather of extensive letters in which he responded to questions about the text of the Bible. Examples of this are the already-mentioned letters to the women who studied and collaborated with him, as well as another to Damasus regarding the Seraphim that Isaiah saw surrounding the throne of God. The same may be said about his homilies, for many of them are almost word-for-word commentaries on the passage for the day.

As to biblical commentaries in the strict sense, Jerome wrote several: on Genesis, Psalms, Isaiah, Jeremiah, Ezekiel, Daniel, the minor prophets, the Gospels of Matthew and Mark, and several Pauline epistles. To this one must add his extensive book *On the Interpretation of Hebrew Names*, in which he tries to discover the etymology of the proper names of people and places that appear in the Old Testament. When reading these commentaries, one may be surprised to discover that, despite his great admiration for Origen, Didymus, Gregory of Nyssa, and many other allegorical interpreters, Jerome focuses his attention on the literal meaning of the text. Although he generally avoided the theological debates of his time, he would on occasion relate them to his studies. For instance, in commenting on Matthew 26:38, where Jesus says, "My soul is very sad," Jerome alluded to the teachings of Apollinaris, which he rejected by saying: "Let those who imagine that Jesus assumed [only] an irrational soul also explain how he can be sad and know the time of his sadness" (*Comm. Matt.* 26:38; PL 26:205). The value of some of the data that Jerome gives in his commentary and other works of biblical scholarship is such that to this day some of his information is used by biblical scholars.

POLEMICAL AND DOGMATIC WORKS

Since Jerome was not particularly interested in theological debate, and he seldom intervened in it—and also because of his own polemical inclinations—Jerome's works on theology are mostly polemical. Early in his career he wrote a fictitious *Debate between a Luciferian and an Orthodox* in which he sought to refute the teachings of Lucifer of Cagliari. Later he wrote against a certain Helvidius a treatise *Against Helvidius on the Perpetual Virginity of Mary*, and another *Against Jovinian*. The first of these two is particularly interesting because Helvidius had declared that, since Jesus had brothers, Mary herself could not have been a virgin throughout her life. Responding to this, Jerome offered an argument that soon became traditional, yet was in fact a way of evading the literal meaning of the text. According to Jerome, the "brothers" of Jesus are not really such, but rather his cousins.

When the debate on Origenism broke out, and Bishop John of Jerusalem, in whose jurisdiction Jerome lived and who had succeeded Cyril of Jerusalem, took the side of the Origenists, Jerome wrote a bitter and even insulting treatise *Against John of Jerusalem*. Toward the end of his life, when a certain Vigilantius criticized Jerome's community, he also wrote against him. At about the same date he wrote a *Dialogue against the Pelagians*, in three books.

HISTORICAL AND BIOGRAPHICAL WRITINGS

We have had several occasions to refer to Jerome's *On Illustrious Men*, in which he takes up a model that was common in classical Latin literature, but now uses it to deal with the great figures of Christian history.

He also employed the biographical genre for exalting monastic life. Along these lines he wrote three works. The first of them, *Life of St. Paul*, refers not to the apostle but to another monk who, according to Jerome, lived before the Antony whose life Athanasius had written. The *Life of the Slave Malcus* tells the story of two slaves, Malcus and a woman, who escaped from a life of slavery among Bedouins and fled to Antioch, where they led a monastic life and where Jerome came to know them. The *Life of Hilarion* tells the story of a wandering monk.

TRANSLATIONS

Jerome always thought that part of his task was to let the Latin world learn of the biblical studies and the thoughts of the East. Therefore, he produced many translations. Obviously, the best known among these is the Vulgate. But he also translated a good number of Origen's homilies on various biblical passages. Yet, for reasons already explained, he did not translate those works where Origen lets his imagination run wild on doctrinal matters. Toward the end of his life, some Egyptian monks asked him to translate into Latin several writings of Pacomius, or at least attributed to him. Since these writings were in Coptic, the monks translated them into Greek, and then Jerome translated the Greek into Latin. The resulting collection is known as the *Pacomiana latina*. Finally, one may mention his translation of the *Chronicle* of Eusebius of Caesarea, whose original Greek has been lost and therefore is now known only in Jerome's translation.

22

Other Latin Authors
of the Late Fourth Century

By the date we have now reached in the late fourth century, there are so many Christian authors that it is practically impossible to mention all of them. We have already considered the most important among them. It now remains to include a word about a number of other Latin writers who merit at least some discussion.

AMBROSIASTER

Since two chapters back we were studying Ambrose, it may be well to begin this particular chapter about secondary Latin authors by referring to the one usually known as Ambrosiaster, that is, "Star of Ambrose." This is a totally fictitious name, invented in the sixteenth century simply because no one knows who this writer was whose work was attributed to Ambrose from an early date. In other words, his name means that he is a false Ambrose. This is not to say that the author claimed to be Ambrose. What actually happened was that with the passage of time his work, much admired by many and therefore often copied, was incorporated into the corpus of the works of Ambrose.

Nothing is known about Ambrosiaster, not even whether before his conversion he was a Jew or a pagan. His writing shows that he was well acquainted with the various religious practices that existed in Rome; but this does not necessarily imply that he was a pagan, for he may simply have studied these religions as an outsider. The same is true regarding his knowledge of Judaism, which leads some scholars to suggest that before his conversion, Ambrosiaster was a Jew. Some have claimed that he was a high Roman official, others that he was a Jew by the name of Isaiah who then abandoned his faith, and still others have tried to identify him with various authors of the time. But in the end all that we can say about Ambrosiaster is that we know nothing.

Ambrosiaster's main work, which earned him the title "Star of Ambrose," is an excellent *Commentary on the Epistles of Saint Paul*, which was often included among the works of Ambrose. It is the most ancient extant Latin commentary on these epistles, and there is no doubt that both Augustine of Hippo and Pelagius read and studied it. Later, comparing his writing with another that was traditionally included among the works of Augustine, *Questions on the Old and New Testaments*, scholars have come to the conclusion that this too comes from Ambrosiaster.

The *Commentary on the Epistles of Saint Paul* is a detailed and carefully ordered commentary on all the epistles of Paul, from Romans to Philemon. One does not find here the allegorical flights of Origen and other Alexandrian scholars. Ambrosiaster's purpose is to make sure that his readers can understand the literal meaning of the text. Occasionally he pays particular attention to a phrase that may be difficult to understand, and at other times he makes general commentaries on a longer passage. For this reason he has been associated with the Antiochene school, which was always more interested in the literal or historical meaning of biblical texts than in possible allegorical interpretations. This does not mean, however, that Ambrosiaster avoided relating the passages he was studying to theological matters, particularly to the heresies that were circulating at the time.

As an example of this way of commenting on the sacred text, one may quote the words of Ambrosiaster in the preface to his commentary on Corinthians:

> Paul had remained in Corinth for eighteen months teaching the Corinthians the word of God. For this reason he deals with them with loving affection and great trust, sometimes warning them about something, and sometimes speaking harsh words of condemnation, as if they were his own children. He wrote to them for many reasons: First, there were faithful believers who formed parties, some claiming that they followed Paul, some Peter or Apollos rather than Christ. Paul has harsh words for them. . . . Second, the Corinthians were being attracted by the wisdom and eloquence of the world, so that even though they declared that they were Christians, they were led astray by philosophical notions contrary to Christianity. Third, they were angry and frustrated because Paul had not visited them. Fourth, they had allowed a fornicator to remain within the community of the church. Fifth, Paul felt the need to remind the Corinthians of what he had told them in a previous letter. Sixth, they would deceive one another, and when they fought, they had recourse to pagan courts. Seventh, although Paul had the right to receive economic support, he refused to do so in order not to leave room for false apostles. Eighth, heretics were beginning to sow confusion regarding marriage. Ninth,

Paul wished to insist on the need to remain faithful to what he had taught them. Tenth, Paul was giving them necessary instructions regarding virgins. And there were other reasons beyond these that will become clear in the commentary itself. (*Comm. Epistles of Saint Paul*, preface; PL 17:193)

The other work that scholars attribute to Ambrosiaster is *Questions on the Old and New Testaments*. The study of this particular work involves serious difficulties, for it has come to our time in three different versions of varying length and in which the questions posed are not always the same. Scholars do not agree as to how much of this is actually the work of Ambrosiaster and how much comes from a later compiler. There are also some other documents and fragments that some scholars attribute to Ambrosiaster, while others do not.

As to his theology, probably the most interesting note is his insistence that justification does not come through the law, but only through faith in Christ. This is similar to what Augustine would say later and is one of many signs that Augustine had read and studied the commentaries of Ambrosiaster.

EGERIA

In the year 379 or shortly thereafter—that is, near the time of the Council of Constantinople—a remarkable woman was traveling through biblical lands and leaving a detailed account of her journeys and experiences. When this account was discovered late in the nineteenth century, it was at first attributed to a French woman named Sylvia. But later studies seem to indicate that she came from the region of Galicia, in the Iberian Peninsula, and that her name was Egeria. All we know of her is her name and what she lets us know in her report of her travels. We do not even know who accompanied her, although she wrote in the plural, thus indicating that she was part of a group of pilgrims.

Egeria's travels took her far from her native Iberia, for after visiting Palestine she went to Sinai, then on to Egypt, and eventually back to Syria, where she went as far as the Euphrates, and to Edessa. When she finally reached Constantinople, she sent her "sisters" in Iberia the story of her travels and experience. Quite possibly these "sisters" were nuns, although they may also have been simply sisters in Christ, or even just sisters by blood. Although both the beginning and the end of the document have been lost, what remains is enormously interesting.

The extant portion of Egeria's account begins after she had already traveled much and finally came to Mount Sinai. She recounts:

As we moved along, we came to a certain place where the mountains through which we were travelling opened out to form an immense valley, vast, quite flat, and extremely beautiful; and across the valley there appeared Mount Sinai, God's holy mountain. . . . We had to cross this valley in order to be able to climb the mountain. This is the vast and very flat valley where the children of Israel tarried during those days when the holy man Moses climbed the mountain of God; and he was there for forty days and forty nights. This is also the valley where the calf was made, and to this day its location is shown, for a large stone set there stands on the very spot. Furthermore, at the head of this same valley is the place where God spoke twice from the burning bush to the holy man Moses as he was grazing his father-in-law's flocks.

And here was our route: first, we would climb the mountain of God, because on the side from which we were approaching the ascent was easier; and from there we would descend then to the very head of the valley where the bush stood, because the descent from the mountain of God was easier there. (*Egeria: Diary of a Pilgrimage*, trans. G. F. Gingras [New York: Newman Press, 1970], 49–50)

The narrative continues. Egeria says that climbing the mountain was not easy, for it was an almost vertical ascent, but that they were able to climb with the help of the monks of the area, and that when they finally arrived at the top, they found a holy man and several priests with whom they celebrated communion after reading the entire story of Moses and the mountain.

Finally, coming down from the mountain range, Egeria says that they reached the burning bush, which "still lives and produces offshoots." In the entire narrative, Egeria does not write only about her religious experiences, but also about the places she visited, their topography, their flora, and so forth. Also upon arriving at each place, she records who welcomed them and how they lived. Since most of these were monastics not only in cities such as Jerusalem and Antioch, but also in remote areas of Arabia and Mesopotamia, this document is also an important source for the history of monasticism. Upon reaching Edessa, Egeria tells the story of the supposed correspondence between Jesus and King Abgar (see above, chap. 4) and adds the legends that she heard regarding the miraculous powers of the letter from Jesus. For instance, she says that once when the Persians attacked Edessa, the king took the letter of Jesus to the city gates, and its radiance blinded the enemy.

What historians find most interesting in this document is what Egeria says regarding worship, particularly in the city of Jerusalem. After listing the particular times for prayer and the ceremonies that took place in the holy sites, Egeria describes Sunday worship; she declares that it follows the same usages that are customary "everywhere" on the Lord's day, an indication that what was done at that time in the far lands of Galicia from which Egeria hailed was very similar to what was done in Jerusalem. Furthermore, besides writing about daily hours of prayer and about Sunday worship, Egeria offers an account of what took place on special days such as Epiphany. When she comes to Lent, she writes down what was done each day of the week. On the last week before Easter, which she calls the "Paschal Week," and in the East was the "Great Week," the narrative abounds in details of great interest. And then she also adds important data regarding other special times such as Ascension Day and Pentecost.

Egeria's narrative is also an important source for the history of the catechumenate, the process of preparation for baptism. She says that eight weeks before Easter the priest would receive and write down the names of all catechumens. The following day, in a sort of court presided by the bishop, candidates for baptism were individually presented, and the bishop inquired about their life and customs from those who knew them. If any were found lacking, the bishop would tell them they must straighten their ways before they could be baptized. After five weeks in which there were three daily hours of instruction on Scripture, they were taught the Nicene Creed and its meaning. At the beginning of Holy Week each candidate had to come individually before the bishop and then recite the creed in public and in the bishop's presence. After their baptism, neophytes received a special instruction in which the bishop explained to them the meaning of the ceremonies in which they had just taken part. This special instruction only the baptized—the neophytes as well as those who had been baptized earlier—could attend. Those who were still catechumens had to wait until their baptism in order to attend. Since among the people some spoke Greek and some Syriac, this teaching was offered in Greek, and someone translated it into Syriac.

Unfortunately, the conclusion of Egeria's account has been lost, and the last we hear from her is that "on the fourth day . . ."

RUFINUS OF AQUILEIA

We have already referred to Rufinus of Aquileia, particularly in connection with his friendship and conflicts with Jerome. These conflicts had to do mostly with Origenism, which Rufinus defended and Jerome rejected. In 345 Rufinus was born near the city of Aquileia, in Italy. After being raised in a Christian family and receiving an excellent education, he embraced monastic life, and it was then that he and Jerome became friends. Next he spent some time in Egypt, where he was captivated by Didymus the Blind. It was this time in Egypt that made him both an expert in and an admirer of Origen's works.

Rufinus came to be known mostly as a translator from Greek into Latin. First, he translated the *Apology of Origen* written by Pamphilus of Caesarea, and then he translated Origen's main work on systematic theology, *On First Principles*. It was the publication of this translation that provoked his clashes with Jerome, for Rufinus seemed to imply that Jerome shared his admiration for Origen. That first disagreement was soon complicated by a tangled web of lost letters, commentary and gossip by friends and enemies, and several other factors. Even so, Rufinus never accepted all the teachings and theories of Origen, for, as he says in his translation of *On First Principles*, he felt free to correct Origen on those points where he seemed to stray from orthodoxy.

Besides these products, Rufinus also translated several of Origen's commentaries on Scripture, as well as many of his homilies. To these he added translations of works of other authors such as Basil the Great, Gregory of Nazianzus, and Evagrius Ponticus.

His original works were fewer. In the field of biblical hermeneutics, he wrote a treatise on *The Blessings of the Patriarchs*. His *Commentary on the Creed of the Apostles* is an important resource for reconstructing the evolution of the ancient Roman creed that eventually became the Apostles' Creed. He also wrote a continuation to Eusebius's *Church History*, which ended in the year 324, and now Rufinus continued the account up to 395, when Emperor Theodosius died. This became an example for other later authors who, as we shall see further on, sought to continue the work of Eusebius of Caesarea.

DONATISM

Although the great subject of theological debate during the fourth century was Arianism, other issues also led to literary production. The most important of these was the restoration of those who had abandoned the faith in times of persecution. As we have seen, this was the spark that provoked the schism of Novatian in third-century Rome. The matter became much more important when the Edict of Milan ended persecution, and many who had abandoned the faith for fear of persecution now wished to return to the church. Although there were similar debates elsewhere, the most virulent and the one leading to the most important schism took place in the Latin-speaking provinces of North Africa. In this case, the great action against faith that the lapsed had committed was that, following Diocletian's orders, they had turned over the Scriptures to be destroyed by the government. For this reason, these lapsed were called *traditores*: those who gave over, or gave up, Scripture. Since one of the main opponents against the easy readmission of the *traditores* was Donatus, those who followed him came to be known as Donatists.

On the basis of their theology, Donatists underscored the value of martyrdom, and therefore several of the "acts of martyrs" of the fourth and fifth centuries bear signs of the Donatist convictions of their authors.

One of the main leaders of Donatism was Parmenian, the Donatist bishop of Carthage. He wrote five books *Against the Church of the Traditores*, besides commentaries on Psalms and letters. Although his work has been lost, some of his arguments can be reconstructed thanks to the refutations of Tyconius and Optatus of Milevis, and somewhat later of Augustine of Hippo.

Tyconius was an interesting figure, for while holding Donatist convictions he did not share the more extreme position of Parmenian, against whom he wrote several works. As a result, he was excommunicated by the Donatists. This did not lead him to embrace the opposite side, but simply to withdraw from all organized parties and devote himself to study. His main extant work is a strange *Book of the Seven Rules*, dealing with principles for biblical interpretation—although, rather than hermeneutical rules, these principles are mostly a series of theological affirmations that must always be taken into account when interpreting Scripture.

Quite possibly Tyconius's most influential work was his *Commentary on Revelation*, part of which has been lost. Its importance is that this was one of the main sources that Augustine employed in *The City of God* to develop the central thesis of the existence of two cities.

Optatus of Milevis was the main anti-Donatist writer before the time of Augustine. He wrote seven books *Against the Calumnies of the Donatists*, also called *Against Parmenian*. Part of this work is historical in nature, for Optatus reviews the origin of the schism in order to show that the supposedly pure Donatists were just as culpable as the *traditores* whom they condemned. As to the church, Optatus affirms that it must necessarily be universal, and that therefore a church limited to a particular area, as that of the Donatists, cannot be a true church. Furthermore Donatists, who claim to be so pure, repeatedly commit atrocities against those who disagree with them. Thus, much of the debate had to do with the use of force in matters of religion, for on the one hand Optatus berated the violence of the Donatists and on the other hand justified imperial intervention to suppress them. It in only in the fifth book that Optatus finally comes to the crucial point of the controversy: whether the validity and efficacy of the sacraments, particularly of baptism, depend on the purity of those administering them. Optatus's argument is simply that the one acting in the sacrament is not the minister, but God, and that it is a gross error to claim that the sin of a minister has the power to impede God's action. Finally, near the end of the work, Optatus returns to the theme of the violence and rapine committed by the Donatists.

While this was going on in North Africa, across the Mediterranean, in Europe, the Novatian schism that had begun a century earlier still continued. Bishop Patian of Barcelona sought to refute the Novatian argument that the church, being the body of Christ, has to be pure and exclude all sinners from its bosom. As Optatus in North Africa against the Donatists, in Spain now Patian, writing against the Novatians, summarizes the history of the movement he opposes. He then moves on to a series of passages in Scripture dealing with the forgiveness of sins. In discussing these matters, he establishes a sort of hierarchy of sins and sinners, thus seeking to respond to the Novatian contention that the church is too ready to forgive sinners.

PRISCILLIANISM

The case of Priscillian and his followers is one of the most confused and shameful episodes in the history of the church in the fourth century. It is confused, because Priscillian was accused of so many heresies, and so wide a variety of them, that it is difficult to determine the exact nature of his doctrines. It is shameful in part because at the heart of the entire process were envy and calumny, but also because in the end Priscillian and his followers were decapitated—the first time we learn of someone being executed on a charge of heresy.

All agree that Priscillian was extraordinarily gifted, particularly in oratory. Most contemporary witnesses, including most of those who called him a heretic, say that he led a pure and exemplary life. The main source for our knowledge of the events surrounding Priscillian is what Sulpitius Severus says near the end of his *Sacred History*. There Sulpitius depicts Priscillian as "a man of noble birth, of great riches, bold, restless, eloquent, learned through much reading, very ready at debate and discussion" (*Sacred History* 2.46; *NPNF²* 11:119). According to Sulpitius, Priscillian's beliefs originated in the East, mostly in Egypt, and were generally gnostic.

It is very unlikely that Priscillian was really a gnostic or, as others claimed, a Manichean. What is certain is that he was energetic, firm in his convictions, and devoted to an ascetic life. He was repeatedly accused of Encratism—that is, of deriding marriage as a sin—and it is possible that some of his assertions made him vulnerable to such accusations. What is clear is that some bishops, perhaps angered because Priscillian's austerity put them to shame, accused him of heresy. Others rallied to his support and made him bishop of Avila. When his enemies finally managed to have him declared a heretic, Priscillian went to Italy to seek support from Damasus and Ambrose, the bishops of Rome and Milan. But neither would give him such support, apparently out of a conviction that at least some of Priscillian's views were indeed heretical. After returning to Spain, Priscillian became a subject of bitter debates between his defenders and his detractors. Eventually, after many vicissitudes, Emperor Maximus, who had usurped the throne, condemned him to death under an accusation of immorality and practicing magic. Even the bishops who had persecuted him were horrified when they learned what had been done to him. Several of those who earlier had denied their support to Priscillian, including Ambrose, expressed their disgust, and his main accusers were deposed. But the precedent was already set, and eventually it would become common practice for church authorities to turn heretics over to the "secular arm" for their punishment.

When it comes to the history of literature, the case of Priscillian and his followers is equally confusing. Jerome says that he knows several of the writings of Priscillian. But all that has survived is a confusing mass of documents that seek to defend Priscillian and some of his views, yet whose authorship is impossible to determine. The only extant writing that clearly was the work of Priscillian is his *Canons on the Epistles of Paul*, which is a sort of introduction to Pauline theology, presented in nine fundamental points, each of them followed by a series of quotations from Paul. Among other books that may or may not be the work of Priscillian there is a *Book to Damasus*, which seems to have been presented to the bishop of Rome when Priscillian sought his support. The *Apologetic Book* defends the orthodoxy of Priscillian and his followers, listing and then rejecting a long list of heresies of which they were accused. Possibly the most interesting in this entire corpus is the *Book on the Apocrypha and the Faith*, whose author asserts that not all books inspired by the Holy Spirit are part of the canon. According to this document, although the apocryphal books include many heresies and errors, this is mostly due to interpolations made by heretics in order to claim authority for their doctrines. However, the books themselves may well have been inspired by the Holy Spirit. Apparently the purpose of this writing is not to defend the apocryphal (deuterocanonical) books themselves, but rather to affirm the continued activity of the Holy Spirit and therefore the inspiration of Priscillian and his followers.

23

Christian Literature in Other Languages

Although the vast majority of extant ancient Christian literature was originally written in Greek or Latin, there are also numerous writings in other languages such as Syriac, Armenian, and Coptic. Many of these are translations, most often from the Greek, and for this reason in earlier chapters we have repeatedly referred to ancient Christian literature originally written in Greek, but that exists also, sometimes only, in translations into these languages. Unfortunately, this literature has not been sufficiently studied for several reasons. The most important is that, as a consequence of the theological debates of the fifth century, and also of political circumstances, there was a growing distance between the churches that spoke Greek and Latin on the one hand and those that spoke other languages on the other hand. As a result, the Greek-speaking "Orthodox" often considered those other churches heretical. Those that did not accept the decisions of the Council of Ephesus in 431 they dubbed "Nestorian," and those that did not accept the decisions of the Council of Chalcedon they considered "Monophysite." Also, many of these churches continued suffering persecution in their own lands, and therefore could not produce a literature comparable to that of the Greek- and Latin-speaking churches. Finally, the languages themselves in which this material was written are not as commonly known as Greek or Latin, and therefore fewer people are able to study it in their original languages—a difficulty which I confess I share, finding myself in this chapter discussing writings in languages that I cannot read. But even so, this ancient literature in diverse languages is also valuable and allows us to see the roots of churches that subsist to this day, although frequently ignored in the West.

SYRIAC LITERATURE

For several centuries Syria and its capital, Antioch, were one of the main centers of Christianity, as may be seen already in the Acts of the Apostles. Although the vast majority of literature from that area is written in Greek, there are also many signs that Christianity soon made headway among the Syriac-speaking population. One of these signs is that Tatian's *Diatessaron* was soon translated into Syriac and for several centuries was the preferred text of the Gospels in much of the region. Also, just as Christianity expanded westward by means of Greek and Latin, its eastward expansion was generally in Syriac. This was so much so that apparently the earliest Christians in India spoke Syriac.

Bardesanes flourished as early as the end of the second century and the early years of the third. His name means "son of the Daisan," a river near the ancient city of Edessa. Apparently it was there that Bardesanes was born to an aristocratic family with connections to the king of the city. There is one work of his—or perhaps of one of his disciples—called *Book of the Law of Nations*. This takes the form of a dialogue between Bardesanes and one of his disciples on the subject of the freedom of the will, involving the stars and their influence on human life.

Various ancient authors provide contradictory information regarding Bardesanes: he was first an orthodox Christian and then a gnostic; he was first a gnostic and then a Christian; he founded the sect of the "Bardesanites"; it was not he, but his son, who created that sect; and so forth. Certainly, sometime after his death there was a Bardesanite movement with strong dualistic tendencies. What is not clear is the relationship between Bardesanes himself and the Bardesanites. Apparently Bardesanes did not clarify his thought, or his thought varied. By the beginning of the fourth century, Aphrahat commented that the thought of Bardesanes was as fluid as the waters of the Daisan, after which he was named.

The two great Christian Syriac writers at the end of the fourth century were Aphrahat and Ephraim. The first was born at the border between the Roman and the Persian Empires. He was bishop of a city in inner Syria that at that time was under Persian rule. For that reason, and for the significance of his work, he was known as "the Persian sage," even though he wrote in Syriac, not in Persian. It was not until the tenth century that scholars in the area rescued his writings and brought them back to light.

Twenty-three pieces of Aphrahat's writings are extant. Some are homiletical in nature, others are epistolary, and still others are theological treatises. All of them jointly are usually called his *Demonstrations*. The first twenty-two of them are organized following the Syriac alphabet, each beginning with a different letter in that alphabet. The last one, which relates the gospel and the work of Jesus with the fruit of the vine, is clearly not part of the same collection. From the text itself, we know that this last piece was written in 345. The others seem to have been written some nine years earlier. The original Syriac text of the *Demonstrations* was lost until it was rediscovered in the nineteenth century.

Aphrahat's style is both elegant and simple, taking examples from daily life and thus making his points accessible to the unlearned. This may be seen in the very first of his *Demonstrations*, written in response to a disciple who asked him to explain more about the nature of faith. He told him:

> Faith is compounded of many things, and by many kinds is it brought to perfection. For it is like a building that is built up of many pieces of workmanship and so its edifice rises to the top. And know, my beloved, that in the foundations of the building stones are laid, and so resting upon stones the whole edifice rises until it is perfected. . . . And now hear concerning faith that is based upon the Stone, and concerning the structure that is reared up upon the Stone. For first a man believes, and when he believes, he loves. When he loves, he hopes. When he hopes, he is justified. When he is justified, he is perfected. When he is perfected, he is consummated. And when his whole structure is raised up, consummated, and perfected, then he becomes a house and a temple for a dwelling-place of Christ. (*Demonstrations* 1.2–3; *NPNF*[2] 13:345–46)

Somewhat younger than Aphrahat was Ephraim, commonly known as Ephraim Syrus, or Ephraim the Syrian. He was born early in the fourth century in Nisibis, a city at the disputed border between Rome and Persia. When the Council of Nicaea met in 325, Ephraim was present as a companion to the bishop of Nisibis. When the Persians took over the area, Ephraim took refuge in Edessa, where he seems to have ministered to other refugees until his death in 373. Jerome includes him in his list of "illustrious men," and historian Sozomen says:

> Ephraim the Syrian was entitled to the highest honors, and was the greatest ornament of the Catholic Church. . . . His style of writing was so replete with splendid oratory and with richness and temperateness of thought that he surpassed the most approved writers of Greece. If the works of these writers were to be translated into Syriac, or any other language, and divested, as it were, of the beauties of the Greek language, they would retain little of their original elegance and value. The productions of Ephraim have not this disadvantage: they were translated into Greek during his life, and translations are even now being made, and yet they preserve much of their original force,

so that his works are not less admired when read in Greek than when read in Syriac. (Sozomen, *Church History* 3.16; *NPNF*[2] 2:295)

Ephraim's literary production was quite extensive. Some ancient authors declare that he wrote on almost every book of the Bible. However, only his commentary of Genesis remains in its entirety. This is followed by the commentary on Exodus up to chapter 22. Most of the rest is lost or remains only in very fragmentary form. From his extant writings it is clear that Ephraim was not inclined to allegorical interpretations, although occasionally he offers an allegorical reading of a text. On this score he seems to represent the emerging Antiochene school, with its emphasis on the text itself and its literal meaning and its avoidance of allegorical flights of interpretation.

Ephraim was above all a poet. Many of his works are written in verse. Apparently some were intended to be said aloud and are therefore poetical homilies. But also many of his poems have a liturgical purpose, to be sung during worship. In this type of liturgical singing, normally a cantor would sing the stanzas, and the choir or the congregation would respond with a repeated phrase. To this day, many churches sing some of his hymns.

COPTIC LITERATURE

Christianity expanded rapidly into the inner regions of Egypt, where the common language was Coptic and where Coptic Christian literature arose. First there were a number of translations, mostly of parts of Scripture, but also of gnostic texts originally written in Greek. Such was the case of the ample corpus of gnostic texts in the Nag Hammadi Library, named after the place where it was discovered. There were also translations of some apocryphal books such as the *Acts of Andrew*, the *Acts of Pilate*, and others. As we have repeatedly seen, there are a number of ancient Christian documents originally written in Greek that have survived only in Coptic translations.

Ancient chroniclers affirm that Hieracas, who led a monastic community in the Nile Delta, was the first Christian to write original works in Coptic. He wrote several hymns and a commentary on the six days of creation. But all that remains of his work are a number of fragments of dubious authorship.

The most important Christian writer in ancient Coptic was Schenoudi, who lived at the end of the period we are now studying or early in the next. According to ancient legends, he died near the year 450, when he was 118 years old. He certainly was present at the Council of Ephesus in 431. Most of his works are letters and homilies.

OTHER LANGUAGES

During the period we are studying, Christianity made headway among the Goths, mainly through the work of Ulfilas, or Wulfila, whose name is Gothic for "wolf cub." Ulfilas developed an alphabet with which to write the Gothic language, and he either translated or had others translate the Bible into Gothic. This translation was apparently used in parts of Spain as late as the seventh century. But all that remains of it are a number of fragments, some of them rather extensive.

During this period Christianity advanced also into Ethiopia. However, all the Christian works that remain from those early years are translations of some books of the Bible, including some that the church at large did not include in its canon, such as *Enoch* and *Jubilees*.

In the Roman provinces of North Africa, near ancient Carthage, the old Punic language of the Carthaginians was still spoken, although strongly influenced by Berber. It was mostly among Punic speakers that Donatism made its greatest advances, particularly the more radical branch of Donatism, the Circumcellions. But the only Punic Christian writing that remains is to be found in funerary inscriptions.

PART 5
The Fifth Century

Introduction to Part 5

While theological controversies played an important role during the fourth century, they would become a dominant feature during the fifth. Particularly in the East, Nestorianism and Monophysitism took center stage, and much of the theological literature, particularly in Greek, dealt with it. Differences and disagreements between the Eastern Greek-speaking church and the Latin West were growing. Imperial intervention in theological matters became ever more frequent. The invasions of the Germanic peoples and others brought new challenges, particularly in the West. While in the East the ancient Roman Empire, now known as the Byzantine Empire, would last for another thousand years, in the West the supposed empire was but a shadow that officially disappeared in 476. Therefore, imperial interventions, whose importance was great in the East, hardly affected the theology of the West. But at the same time the Western church had to face the difficult task of reconstructing what had been destroyed by the invasions and adapting to new conditions and an emerging new culture.

This does not mean, however, that there were no great Christian authors during the fifth century. The last years of the fourth century, and the early fifth century, saw the flourishing of the greatest and most influential of all Western theologians: Augustine of Hippo. Somewhat later, in midcentury, Leo the Great not only brought new prestige to the Roman see but also produced some of the best homilies of antiquity. The East produced one of the greatest preachers in the entire history of the church, John Chrysostom, and there were also outstanding historians, poets, and exegetes.

24

Chroniclers and Historians

Just as we began our discussion of the fourth century by discussing Eusebius of Caesarea, so is it now appropriate to begin our discussion of this new century by referring to the chroniclers and historians who tell us of the events of those times, and who are also an important source for much of what we know of other authors. Several of them modeled their works after their predecessors, particularly the *Church History* of Eusebius of Caesarea—to which Rufinus had added two books, bringing it up to 395—and Jerome's list of *Illustrious Men*.

SULPITIUS SEVERUS

Sulpitius Severus was born to a relatively wealthy family in Aquitania near the year 360, and for a time he led a distinguished legal career. When his wife died, he decided to take up a life of contemplation, partly inspired by his mother-in-law, Basula. In his pursuit of the contemplative life, he found support and inspiration in Martin of Tours, and it was thanks to the writings of Sulpitius that Martin became famous. The best-known and most influential of the works of Sulpitius is his *Life of St. Martin*, a relatively brief book in twenty-seven chapters, which include the famous story that when Martin saw a naked beggar shivering in the cold at the gate of the city of Amiens, since he had nothing else to give him, he tore his cape into two pieces and gave half to the beggar. As Sulpitius tells the story, while he slept that night, Martin saw the Lord dressed in half a cape and saying to him, "Inasmuch as you did it to one of the least of these my brothers, you did it unto me."

There are also other writings by Sulpitius about Martin. Three of them are dialogues in which he compares the virtues of Martin with those of the

Egyptian monks. There are also three letters in which he defended Martin against those who accused him of heterodox inclinations, and then also told of his death. In the third of these letters, addressed to his mother-in-law, we find an interesting complaint that Basula did not respect his privacy and even circulated what he had written for his own use or for only some others to read:

> If it were lawful that parents should be summoned to court by their children, clearly I might drag you with a righteous thong before the tribunal of the prætor, on a charge of robbery and plunder. You have left me no little bit of writing at home, no book, not even a letter—to such a degree do you play the thief with all such things and publish them to the world. If I write anything in familiar style to a friend; if, as I amuse myself I dictate anything with the wish at the same time that it should be kept private, all such things seem to reach you almost before they have been written or spoken. Surely you have my secretaries in your debt, since through them any trifles I compose are made known to you. (*Ep.* 3; *NPNF*[2] 11:21)

However, this seems to be simply a friendly complaint, for Sulpitius says he is unhappy that Basula has learned of a letter that he wrote to a deacon by the name of Aurelius (his second epistle) telling him about the death of Martin, and now she wants him to do likewise for her—which Sulpitius gladly does.

In spite of his interest in Martin, Sulpitius's most extensive work is his *Sacred History*, in two books. The entire first book and more than half of the second deal mostly with biblical history. The entire history of the church up to Constantine is summarized in a very few pages, in four chapters. Then he devotes two chapters to Helena, Constantine's mother, and twelve to the Arian controversy. Finally, in chapter 46 of the second book, we come to the time of Sulpitius himself, and the last six chapters deal with Priscillianism. This is the most important part of the entire work, for he undoubtedly knew that story more directly and is one of the main sources through which we learn of it.

PAULUS OROSIUS

Another outstanding historian late in the fourth century and early in the fifth was Paulus Orosius. He was born near the year 380, apparently in what is today the city of Braga, in Portugal. These were difficult times in that area, due both to Priscillianism and to the invasions of the Suevi. Little is known of his youth, although he obviously had an excellent education. He tells us about some of his adventures:

> I am referring to the time when I found myself facing some barbarians
> whom I had never seen. As they attacked me, I avoided them. When
> they finally caught me, I mollified them. Even though they were not
> believers, I begged them. Being their prisoner, when a sudden fog
> appeared, I escaped under its cover. They were almost able to grab
> me. I tell this so that others may know of it and be moved. At the same
> time I am quietly pained that those who hear me have no idea what
> it was like, and I am disturbed by the insensibility of those who have
> no understanding of what these sufferings were. (*Histories against the
> Pagans* 3.20; PL 31:830)

Eventually his travels took him to North Africa, where he met Augustine,
and to the East, where he also met Jerome. Three of his works are extant. Of
lesser importance are his *Apologetic Book against Pelagius* and a *Commonitory
[Warning] to Augustine against the Errors of the Priscillianists and the Origenists*.
Augustine responded to this latter work with his own *Book to Orosius against
the Priscillianists and the Origenists*. But there is no doubt that his most important work is *Histories against the Pagans*, in seven books. The first six tell the
story of humankind from Adam to Augustus Caesar. The last covers the entire
period from the birth of Jesus to the time of Orosius himself.

The exact date when Orosius wrote his *Histories* is unknown. It seems to
have been during the second decade of the fifth century, around 416. Shortly
earlier Rome had been sacked by the Goths (August 24, 410), which had
shaken the world and had given credit to the claims of some pagans that Rome
had fallen because it had abandoned its ancient gods. Augustine had asked
Orosius to respond to such claims. Thus, in a way, the *Histories* of Orosius
are an attempt to respond to the same accusations that later led Augustine to
write his great work, *The City of God*.

This particular work of Orosius is the earliest attempt to retell the story of
humankind as it was then known from a Christian perspective. The wide scope
of his vision may be seen in the early chapters of his first book, where Orosius
gives geographic data about the context in which a human history takes place.
Thus, he says that Asia goes as far as the "Eastern Ocean," where the river
Ganges flows; as to be expected, his descriptions of the Mediterranean world
are much more detailed and better informed than those of distant lands. It is
also interesting to see that in this entire work, while refuting the opinions of
pagans regarding the fall of Rome, Orosius shows respect and appreciation
for the achievements of humankind even apart from faith in Christ.

In Orosius's vision of history, empires succeed one another. Thus, he
speaks first of the Babylonian Empire, then of the Macedonian, of the Car-
thaginian, and finally of the Roman Empires. Quite naturally, within that vast
vision Orosius gives particular attention to events related to his native Hispania. Also, apparently in order to show how ephemeral all human empires

are, Orosius seems to be particularly interested in the defeats and sufferings of the conquered. With a strong sense of irony, as a refutation of those who claim that ancient times were better than the present, Orosius comments about the times of Xerxes:

> Those were beautiful times that we miss! Calm days that now seem so bright for us who now live in darkness! Days in which in a short time, led by three successive kings, a single country was able to produce nine million men who died. And, what can we say about poor Greece that defeated that great horde and in doing so was itself destroyed? . . .
> What does this lead us to think, but that even though people might not like them, all times are good, or perhaps that there were never really good times? (*Histories* 2.1; PL 31:775)

Later in this work, commenting on the Germanic invasions, Orosius says that even though these have produced violence and rapine, this is not new, for what the barbarian invaders now do in Hispania was done earlier by the Romans. This is then followed by a long catalog of violence and usurpation among Romans. Therefore, the notion that the world was happier when Rome worshiped the ancient gods, or that it was these gods who made Rome great and happy, is sheer error. And later on, by way of conclusion, Orosius declares that he would accept what was said about the negative impact of Christianity if any are able to prove that indeed there was a better time. Since Christianity came, furthermore, many wars, numerous political disorders, and much cruelty have been averted. And then he finishes his work with some words to Augustine, who had requested that he write it:

> Blessed father Augustine, as you requested, and with the help of Christ, I have shown as clearly and briefly as I could the passions leading to sin and the punishment that comes from it, the struggles of the world in sharp contrast with the will of God, from the very beginning to this day. But I have made a distinction between Christian times and the confused and faithless earlier age, so as to show the beneficial presence of Christ in our time. . . . As to the worth of what I have done, you will have to decide, for you are the one who requested it. If you decide to publish it, it will be your decision, as will be also the case if you decide to destroy it. (*Histories* 7.43; PL 31:1174)

GENNADIUS

The third Latin historian whom we are to consider is Gennadius. Although Gennadius composed several works, little remains of them. Hardly anything is known of his life beyond the information that he gives at the end of his collection *On Illustrious Men*, where, following Jerome's example, he includes himself: "I, Gennadius, a presbyter in Marseille, wrote a book against all heresies, five against Nestorius, ten against Eutyches, three against Pelagius, and one on the millennium in the Revelation of John. The latter, accompanied by a letter regarding my faith, was addressed to blessed Gelasius, bishop of the city of Rome" (*On Illustrious Men* 97; PL 58:1120). Apart from the work just cited, all that remains of these books are a number of fragments. However, there is among the writings traditionally attributed to Augustine one under the title *On Church Doctrines* that many scholars believe was written by Gennadius.

Reading these two works one comes to the conclusion that Gennadius was part of a movement that, while not accepting the doctrines of Pelagius, was not willing to accept those of Augustine, and therefore it is often called "semi-Pelagianism." We know that what is today southern France was the main center for that movement, and Gennadius himself lived in Marseille.

SOCRATES SCHOLASTICUS

While both Sulpitius Severus and Paulus Orosius wrote in Latin, there were also important historians who wrote in Greek. Three among them stand out: Socrates Scholasticus, Sozomen, and Theodoret of Cyrus. Since the latter was also an important theologian and interpreter of Scripture, he is discussed in chapter 30 (below).

Socrates is commonly known as Socrates Scholasticus in order to distinguish him from the famous Athenian philosopher of the same name. Others call him simply "Socrates of Constantinople." Little is known of his life. He was born in Constantinople around the year 380, or slightly later, and spent most of his life in that city, perhaps with some interludes in nearby lands, such as Cyprus and Thessaly. The date of his death is unknown, although it must have been after 449, the ending point of his *Church History*. In this work Socrates seeks to bring the work of Eusebius of Caesarea up to date. Therefore, he begins in 323, which is the ending point of Eusebius's *Church History*. Socrates's work is divided into seven books, each of them dealing with one of the main emperors during that time.

Like Eusebius, Socrates was not particularly interested in the fine points of various theological positions, although he did accept the decisions of the church at large on such matters. This is partly due to the desire to be impartial in his narrative, perhaps also in part to his lack of clarity as to the fine theological debates of the time, but mostly because he was a person of irenic spirit who was convinced that the details of doctrine should not lead to the bitter controversies of his days. Quite possibly he had in mind the debates that were taking place around him regarding Monophysitism when, commenting on the earlier debates that took place after the Council of Nicaea (325), he says:

> So that while they occupied themselves in a too minute investiga-
> tion of its import, they roused the strife against each other; it seemed
> not unlike a contest in the dark; for neither party appeared to under-
> stand distinctly the grounds on which they calumniated one another.
> Those who objected to the word *homoousios*, conceived that those
> who approved it favored the opinion of Sabellius and Montanus; they
> therefore called them blasphemers, as subverting the existence of
> the Son of God. And again the advocates of this term, charging their
> opponents with polytheism, inveighed against them as introducers of
> heathen superstitions. (*Ch. Hist.* 1.23; *NPNF*[2] 2:27)

His attitude regarding various ceremonies and practices was similar. He describes several of them, making it clear that not all are in agreement and that it is not necessary to opt for one option and reject all others. Thus, for instance, commenting on the date of Easter, which was still being debated, he says that none of those participating in that debate had any reason to be so obstinate. He personally prefers what is being done in Rome as well as in the entire Western church and in much of the East. According to him, when Quartodecimans claim that their practices are directed by the apostle John, they cannot prove it, and the opposite party is also unable to prove their claim that they are following what was taught by Peter and Paul. Also, it is custom-ary in Rome to fast for three weeks before Easter Sunday, where elsewhere the fasting period lasts six weeks—that is, about forty days if one does not count Sundays, which cannot be days of fasting, but of celebration. The same is true in matters of abstinence, for some abstain from some foods, and others abstain from others.

Socrates has sometimes been accused of Novatian tendencies. He certainly spoke favorably of the moral integrity of Novatian and other leaders of his movement. He also had a rigorist inclination himself. But his positive words regarding Novatianism are most likely the result not of his being a part of that movement, but rather of his desire to be fair and impartial.

SOZOMEN

Sozomen, whose full name was Salaminus Hermias Sozomenus, was born in the region of Gaza early in the fifth century. His family had been pagan until his grandfather was converted. Since the family had financial resources, Sozomen's grandfather, and then his parents, provided financial support for monasticism in the area, and it was apparently among those monks that young Sozomen began his studies. Then he studied law in the famous school of Berytus (now Beirut) and then went to Constantinople to practice law. He died there in 450. He was already a mature man when he began writing a church history that, like Socrates's, began where Eusebius of Caesarea had ended. While most of his *Church History* is extant, the last part of the ninth book, in which Sozomen proposed to bring his story up to the year 439, has not survived.

Sozomen's main source for his *Church History* was the already-discussed work by the same title of Socrates Scholasticus. More than two-thirds of his material makes use of information provided by Socrates, sometimes even employing the same words and phrases. Furthermore, the structure of Sozomen's work is similar to that of Socrates, for he too organizes his narrative following the history of the emperors. Thus, the first two books deal with the time of Constantine, the third with Constans, the fourth with Constantius, the fifth with Julian, the next with Valens, and the last three with Theodosius, Arcadius, and Valentinian III. And, like Socrates, Sozomen does not seem to be overly interested in theological debates, particularly those having to do with fine points of disagreement.

What then was Sozomen's purpose in writing this work? Was he simply plagiarizing what Socrates had said? Some respond affirmatively to this question, but there are some significant differences between the two historians. While Socrates seems to think of history as a succession of high points and low ones, in which good times are followed by bad times, in order then to return to the good times, Sozomen seems to think that there is progress in history. Certainly, there are difficult times and setbacks. But in general God is leading history to its culmination, and a historian is able to see this.

The other important point in which there is a difference between Sozomen and Socrates is the vision of the relationship between church and state, particularly with regard to progress in history. Socrates was more interested in the history of the church itself and used the reigns of various emperors as a framework within which to tell his story. Therefore, the goal of the history that Socrates told is the faithfulness of the church, in which peace and concord must reign. For Sozomen, there is a close connection between the faithfulness of the church and that of rulers. When there are good rulers, there are good times for the church, leading not only to the flourishing of the church, but also to its greater faithfulness. Evil rulers bring about corruption in the church, and even though among the faithful may be some who resist the evil influences of government, most of the church succumbs to them. Therefore the final goal of history—toward which all seems to be moving, according to Sozomen—is the existence both of an ideal government and a church that, influenced and supported by such a government, will also be faithful and obedient.

Beyond all this, much of the contribution of Sozomen is in his interest in the missionary expansion of Christianity, not only throughout the Roman Empire, but also beyond its borders. It is thanks to him that we have some important data regarding the beginnings of Christianity in other places. As he says near the beginning of his work, "I have had to deliberate whether I ought to confine myself to the recital of events connected with the Church under the Roman government; but it seemed more advisable to include, as far as possible, the record of transactions relative to religion among the Persians and barbarians" (*Ch. Hist.* 1.1; *NPNF*[2] 2:241).

25

Augustine

In the entire history of the church, there is no figure who can compare with Augustine of Hippo. The impact of his writings and theology may be felt even today, sixteen centuries after his life, particularly in the various branches of the Western church, Catholic as well as Protestant. Apart from Paul and other biblical writers, no other Christian author is quoted as often as Augustine, and this by theologians as diverse as Thomas Aquinas, Luther, and Calvin.

HIS LIFE: THE *CONFESSIONS*

In sharp contrast with many of the authors we have been studying, the life of Augustine is fairly well known. This is partly due to his own importance, partly to the work of his friend and companion Possidius, who wrote a *Life of Augustine* shortly after his death, and partly because Augustine himself told much about his early years in his *Confessions*.

If it were only for Possidius, we would know little about Augustine's internal struggles before his conversion, for Possidius summarizes Augustine's early life in few words, some of them not entirely accurate:

> Augustine was born in the city of Tagaste, in the province of Africa, from honorable Christian parents [which is not quite true, for Augustine's mother was a Christian, but his father was converted later]. They were part of the municipal curia, and under their guidance and support he was well instructed in human letters, that is, the so-called liberal arts. At first he taught grammar in his birthplace, and then rhetoric in Carthage, in Rome, and in Milan. . . . In the latter city the bishop was Ambrose, a priest beloved of God, outstanding leader among the

greatest men of the time. Jointly with the faithful, Augustine attended church in order to listen to the sermons that Ambrose preached frequently, and listened to him attentively. For some time in Carthage, he had been contaminated by the errors of the Manichees when he was a youth, and therefore he was particularly interested in all that was said for or against that heresy. The liberating love of God touched the heart of the bishop so that he would deal with the matters pertaining to the Law with which Augustine was struggling. Slowly that heresy disappeared from his spirit, and being confirmed in the Catholic faith, he was consumed by a burning desire to learn and come to a better understanding, so that on Easter he could receive the purification of holy baptism. (Possidius, *Life of Augustine* 1; PL 32:34–35)

What Possidius summarizes in these few words Augustine himself tells us in the first nine books of his *Confessions*. These "confessions" are not, as one might understand that word today, a litany of sins for which he asks forgiveness. They certainly include many examples of Augustine's sins and his expressions of profound contrition; but what Augustine wishes to confess in this work is the providential mercy of God that has guided him through a long and difficult spiritual pilgrimage. The result is a spiritual autobiography that is unparalleled in ancient literature, Christian as well as pagan. The central thesis of the work is expressed by Augustine himself in words in the very first chapter that have become famous: "For Thou hast formed us for Thyself, and our hearts are restless till they find rest in Thee" (*Conf.* 1.1; *NPNF*[1] 1:45).

As Possidius says, Augustine was born in Tagaste, in North Africa. His father, Patrick, was an officer in the city government. His mother, Monica, of Punic (North African) stock, was a devout Christian. Augustine was very young when his parents noted his exceptional gifts and, with the help of a wealthy friend, provided an excellent education for him, first in Tagaste itself, then in the nearby city of Madaura, and finally in Carthage. There he took a concubine, whose name is not known but whom he seems to have loved dearly. They had a son, whom they named Adeodatus. During that time he also became interested in the teachings of the Manicheans. In those teachings he sought an answer to the doubts he had, particularly regarding the origin of evil. But in the end he was disappointed. For a time he dabbled in the agnostic views of the philosophers who were then called the "academicians." During the entire process Monica continued encouraging him to accept Christianity, which Augustine felt was incompatible with the best of classical antiquity and with the philosophy he had studied.

Later, referring to those days in Carthage and to his inner struggles, Augustine would ask: "And where was I when I was seeking Thee? And Thou wert before me, but I had gone away even from myself; nor did I find myself, much less Thee" (*Conf.* 5.2.2; *NPNF*[1] 1:80). And later he adds: "Out of the blood of my mother's heart, through the tears that she poured out by day and by night, was a sacrifice offered unto Thee for me" (*Conf.* 5.7.13; *NPNF*[1] 1:83).

It was thus that he arrived at Milan in order to teach rhetoric. Pursuing his career in that field, he went to listen to Ambrose, not because he was interested in what Ambrose said, but because Ambrose was a famous speaker, and Augustine wished to see how he employed rhetoric. Unexpectedly, what he heard Ambrose say began solving some of his difficulties with Christian faith:

> For although I took no trouble to learn what he spake, but only to hear how he spake (for that empty care alone remained to me, despairing of a way accessible for man to Thee), yet, together with the words which I prized, there came into my mind also the things about which I was careless; for I could not separate them. And whilst I opened my heart to admit "how skillfully he spake," there also entered with it, but gradually, "and how truly he spake!" (*Conf.* 5.14.24; *NPNF*[1] 1:88)

Augustine further explains that what most helped him in Ambrose's preaching was that he could now understand Scripture in such a way that it was compatible with the best of Platonic philosophy, and thus to overcome some of the great intellectual difficulties that Christian faith had posed for him.

He still had some doubts. Regarding that faith, he says that it "did not appear to me to be vanquished; nor yet did it seem to me to be victorious" (*Conf.* 5.14.24; *NPNF*[1] 1:88). But a greater obstacle than any doubt was the difficulty that Augustine had in abandoning the pleasures of the world. Following the example of his mother and of many whom he saw around him, he was convinced that in order to be a true Christian, one had to lead an ascetic life. By then Monica had forced him to abandon his concubine. Now it seemed necessary to abandon all the desires and values of the world. Therefore, although he had his name added to the list of catechumens in Milan, he was not baptized. His struggle was no longer between belief and disbelief, but between willing and not willing.

It was then, when Augustine was most tormented by his inner struggles, that the famous episode in the garden in Milan took place, when in his anguish he heard the voice of a child who said, "Take and read, take and read." Hearing in these words a personal call, Augustine took a codex he had at hand and read in the Epistle to the Romans: "not in reveling and drunkenness, not in debauchery and licentiousness, not in quarreling and jealousy. Instead, put on the Lord Jesus Christ, and make no provision for the flesh, to gratify its desires" (Rom. 13:13–14). At that point he finally made a decision and happily went to tell his friends and his mother.

The *Confessions* then turn to a joyful time of retreat with his mother and friends in a villa that a friend had in Cassiciacum, near Milan. He then was baptized by Ambrose and left for Tagaste with his mother and friends. A series of circumstances forced them to remain in Italy for some time, and it was there that Monica died, full of joy for the conversion of her son. After telling of his last experiences with Monica and his pain in having lost her, but also of his consolation in their common faith, Augustine leaves the autobiographic tone of the *Confessions* and turns his attention to the subjects of memory and time, always in connection with his own experience and with the providential presence of God in his life. While scholars still debate whether Augustine's *Confessions* is the earliest spiritual autobiography, historians of philosophy in general agree that Augustine's discussion of time at the end of this work is the first systematic analysis of time, with few forerunners in classical philosophy.

Although Augustine does not continue his autobiography beyond the point of his conversion and baptism, it is possible to reconstruct the rest of his life, thanks to his many epistles, other information gleaned from the rest of his works, and the already-mentioned biography by Possidius. Very briefly, after the death of Monica, Augustine and his friends went on to Africa and, after spending some time in Carthage, returned to Tagaste, where they established a sort of monastic community devoted not only to prayer, but also to meditation and to philosophical and doctrinal discussion. Some three years later, when Augustine was visiting the city of Hippo in order to discuss with a friend the community that he had founded in Tagaste, Bishop Valerius had him ordained, much against his will.

This began a new stage in the life of Augustine, marked by repeated controversies with Manicheans, Donatists, Pelagians, and pagans. These controversies were the occasion for the vast majority of his writings. Finally, in August of 430, when the Vandals were besieging the city of Hippo, Augustine died.

FIRST WRITINGS

Augustine did not wait until his baptism to begin writing on Christianity. The way he understood it, the life that he had now accepted would combine a moderate asceticism with the ideal of ancient philosophers of "productive idleness." What Augustine sought when withdrawing to Cassiciacum with his mother and friends was to devote himself to meditation and to discussion regarding truth. It is no coincidence that his first work was *Against the Academicians*, in three books. "Academicians" was the name given to ancient thinkers who had come to the conclusion that, if there is such a thing as truth, it is far beyond human reach. That position had been attractive to Augustine after his disappointment with the teachings of the Manicheans. If Manicheism had no answer for Augustine's questions, this would seem to indicate that truth was unreachable. Therefore, in *Against the Academicians* Augustine tried to show that, even though absolute truth belongs only to God, the human mind is capable of conceiving truths.

Augustine dedicated this treatise to Romanianus, the wealthy friend of the family who had supported his first studies, apparently in order to show him that he had not wasted his money and that his having abandoned a career in rhetoric was not a failure, but a victory. It takes the shape of a conversation between Augustine and his companions in Cassiciacum.

Responding to the skepticism of the academicians, Augustine points out that there are at least two sorts of truth that are indubitable. The first includes those truths that are purely intellectual and apply always and everywhere. If some object that when one dreams, one believes that what one sees is truth, and then discovers that it is not, Augustine answers, "That three times three makes nine, and that this is the square of intelligible numbers, is absolutely true, even if all humankind is snoring" (*Ag. Acad.* 3.11.25; BAC 21:193). But even beyond these universal truths, the mind knows another sort of truth. In this regard, Augustine declares, "I see no way in which an academician can refute one who says: 'I know that this seems white to me'" (*Ag. Acad.* 3.11.26; BAC 21:193), for even though the thing itself may not be white, that it appears white to this person is still true.

Shortly thereafter Augustine composed another treatise, also in the form of a discussion with his friends, *On the Happy Life*. Here, after showing that only communion with God can make a human being happy, Augustine quotes the conclusion of Monica, who was part of the discussion: "Such is no doubt the happy life, for it is a perfect life, and as we believe, we can rapidly be led to it on the wings of a firm faith, a joyful hope, and a burning love" (*Happy Life* 4.35; BAC 10:665–67).

In his two books *On Order*, Augustine poses the problem that had always caused him grave concern and whose answer he had not found among the Manicheans, that is, the problem of the existence of evil and its origin. Augustine's answer, which he would later amplify, is that evil is not a substance, and that no substance is in itself evil, for evil is rather a disorder affecting substances that are themselves good. In this book one also finds words that Augustine addresses to Monica and do not seem to fit with what he says elsewhere about women: "Women philosophized in ancient times, and I very much like your philosophy" (*On Order* 1.11.31; BAC 10:723).

Soliloquies, a work in two books, expands on the theme of truth that Augustine had discussed earlier in *Against the Academicians*. It is presented as a dialogue between Augustine and reason, and most of it is devoted to establishing the nature of truth and the various sorts of truths. The treatise *On the Teacher*, also written in those early days, is a dialogue between Augustine and his son, Adeodatus, also on the nature of truth and how to reach it. It opens with a discussion on words as signs and their relationship with the signified, in order to come to the conclusion that "it is not the sign that makes us know something, but rather the knowledge of the thing that shows us the value of the word, that is, what the sound signifies" (*Teacher* 10.34; BAC 21:741). And this in turn leads Augustine to affirm what Justin and others had said earlier regarding the Word as the source and foundation of all knowledge: "We understand the many things coming to our intelligence not by consulting the outer voice that we hear, but rather by consulting the inner truth that reigns in the mind. Words may interest us to consider. But that truth that is considered and teaches is Christ, who according to Scripture dwells in a human being as the immutable Power and the eternal Wisdom of God" (*Teacher* 12.34; BAC 21:745).

Also during that time in Cassiciacum, Augustine began refuting Manicheism, which he had earlier followed, in part seeking to call to truth those who through him had fallen into error. This is the purpose of *On the Customs of the Catholic Church and of the Manichees* and of his first exegetical work, *On Genesis against the Manichees*, as well as of two other treatises that he began writing in Cassiciacum but did not finish until after his ordination: *On Free Will* and *On True Religion*.

In all these early treatises of Augustine, written shortly after his conversion, one notices speculative interests similar to those of the Platonic philosophers whom Augustine admired and whose methodology he followed. After all, apart from the need to correct the Manichean errors that he once held, Augustine was mostly interested not in teaching the church, but rather in seeking truth by means of spiritual and intellectual exercises after the pattern of the philosophers, but now inspired also in his recently affirmed the faith.

But then, when visiting the city of Hippo, and when he least expected it, he found himself forced to receive ordination. Now he had officially become a shepherd of God's flock, and therefore his writings should center on that task rather than on philosophical speculation, although he never abandoned the latter. The result was a vast number of writings that soon spread throughout the Christian world and began giving him such stature that even today he is recognized as one of the greatest theologians of the church. As in the case of other pastors, much of the literary work of Augustine after his ordination consisted of sermons, letters, commentaries, and other writings on Scripture, and above all refutations of what he was convinced were some of the errors circulating in his time.

EXEGETICAL AND HOMILETICAL WORKS

As a pastor, Augustine was convinced that his main task was to help the people of God understand Scripture, and it was to that task that he would devote most of his literary labors. Some five hundred of his sermons are extant. (This is an approximate number, for some that have been traditionally attributed to him may not be his, and there are also numerous fragments of anonymous sermons that may well be his.) The nature of the sermons varies, for some seem to be based on shorthand notes taken while being preached, and others have signs of having been polished by him, perhaps on the basis of such shorthand notes.

To that huge number of sermons one must add his *Expositions on the Psalms*, long commentaries on each of the psalms that were originally spoken out loud, and occupying several volumes in any of their various modern editions. One also notes a homiletical character in his commentary on the First Epistle of John, as well as in the first fifty-four of his *Tractates on the Gospel of John*.

As if this were not enough, Augustine also produced several biblical commentaries. Without mentioning all of them, it should suffice to say that these include several works, some of them quite extensive, on Genesis: *On Genesis against the Manichees*, *On Genesis to the Letter*, *Questions on the Heptateuch*, and others. As to the New Testament, he wrote, besides the already-mentioned works on the Gospel and the First Epistle of John, two books *On the Sermon on the Mount* and four others refuting those who questioned the authority of the Gospels by pointing out the differences among them. Within the Pauline corpus, he produced two works on Romans and one on Galatians. Also within this category of biblical interpretation, he wrote *The Mirror of Scripture*, which is a summary of the divine commandments, taken from the Bible, and generally following the order of the canon. Also, when consulted on matters of Scripture, Augustine collected a number of his responses in two books of *Questions of the Gospels*.

Finally, around the year 397, shortly after being made bishop of Hippo, Augustine began writing on the methodology to be followed in the study and interpretation of Scripture. The title by which this work is now known, *On Christian Doctrine*, does not do justice to the content of this book. This is so because its first part is devoted to a discussion regarding the nature of truth and its relationship with words seeking to express it. But the book as a whole is a manual on homiletics and hermeneutics. For some reason that is not altogether clear, Augustine abandoned that project for a while, then only completed it much later. In his *Retractations*, to which we shall return, Augustine declares, "When I found the unfinished books on Christian doctrine, I decided to finish them rather than leaving them as they were and leaving that task to others" (*Retract.* 2.4.1; BAC 168:53).

In the prologue to this work, written after completing it, Augustine spells out his purpose:

> There are certain rules for the interpretation of Scripture which I think might with great advantage be taught to earnest students of the word, that they may profit not only from reading the works of others who have laid open the secrets of the sacred writings, but also from themselves opening such secrets to others. These rules I propose to teach to those who are able and willing to learn, if God our Lord do not withhold from me, while I write, the thoughts He is wont to vouchsafe to me in my meditations on this subject. (*Chr. Doctr.*, prologue 1; *NPNF*[1] 2:519)

And then, in words addressed to those who thought that they did not need such a guide for interpreting the Bible, he says in words still pertinent today:

> But now as to those who talk vauntingly of Divine Grace, and boast that they understand and can explain Scripture without the aid of such directions as those I now propose to lay down, and who think, therefore, that what I have undertaken to write is entirely superfluous. I would such persons could calm themselves so far as to remember that, however justly they may rejoice in God's great gift, yet it was from human teachers they themselves learnt to read. (*Chr. Doctr.*, prologue 4; *NPNF*[1] 2:519)

In the rest of his work, after insisting on the need for knowing all that God has taught not only Christians, but also the great thinkers among the pagans, Augustine offers one of the earliest Christian treatises on the art of preaching combined with the science of interpretation.

DOGMATIC WORKS

While studying and commenting on Scripture, Augustine also produced several more systematic works. Shortly after being ordained, he wrote *On the Faith and the Creed*, which he decided to publish only on the insistence of his friends. Also, at that level of basic introduction to a life of faith, he later wrote the *Enchiridion*, or handbook on the Christian life, which became one of the most widely read books during the Middle Ages, and which is sometimes also called *On Faith, Hope, and Charity*.

His *Two Books to Simplician on Various Questions* are addressed to Simplician, the theological mentor and successor of Ambrose. Later Augustine would declare that in writing this treatise, possibly around the year 398, he did not sufficiently stress the importance of grace as the beginning of faith. For this reason, this particular treatise is valuable for an understanding of the process that took Augustine to his positions against Pelagianism.

Augustine's most important systematic work is *On the Trinity*. Writing this treatise took several years. As Augustine himself says, he was in the middle of book 12 and in no hurry to complete the work when, "having kept them so long that the patience of those who ardently wished to have them ran out, they were stolen when they were still not as polished as I would have preferred before publishing them" (*Retract.* 15.1; BAC 39:115; see also *Ep.* 174; BAC 99:553). This forced him to complete the fifteen books in which the work was finally published.

Augustine offers a summary of what he intends to do in each of the books of this work (*Trin.* 15.3.5; BAC 39:835–39). The first seven books are a summary of what by that time had already become generally accepted Trinitarian doctrine. The rest of the work is much more original, characterized by the many analogies that Augustine employs to illustrate and interpret the mystery of the Trinity. The best-known of these analogies, and probably the most appropriate, is the one comparing the unity of the one God to the unity of the mind, in which there is memory, understanding, and will:

> Since, then, these three, memory, understanding, will, are not three lives, but one life; nor three minds, but one mind; it follows certainly that neither are they three substances, but one substance. Since memory, which is called life, and mind, and substance, is so called in respect to itself; but it is called memory, relatively to something. And I should say the same also of understanding and of will, since they are called understanding and will relatively to something; but each in respect to itself is life, and mind, and essence. And hence these three are one, in that they are one life, one mind, one essence; and whatever else they are severally called in respect to themselves, they are called also together, not plurally, but in the singular number. But they are three, in that wherein they are mutually referred to each other; and if they were not equal, and this not only each to each, but also each to all, they certainly could not mutually contain each other; for not only is each contained by each, but also all by each. For I remember that I have memory and understanding, and will; and I understand that I understand, and will, and remember; and I will that I will, and remember, and understand; and I remember together my whole memory, and understanding, and will. For that of my memory which I do not remember, is not in my memory; and nothing is so much in the memory as memory itself. Therefore I remember the whole memory. Also, whatever I understand I know that I understand, and I know that I will whatever I will; but whatever I know I remember.

> Therefore I remember the whole of my understanding, and the whole of my will. Likewise, when I understand these three things, I understand them together as whole. For there is none of things intelligible which I do not understand, except what I do not know; but what I do not know, I neither remember, nor will. Therefore, whatever of things intelligible I do not understand, it follows also that I neither remember nor will. And whatever of things intelligible I remember and will, it follows that I understand. My will also embraces my whole understanding and my whole memory whilst I use the whole that I understand and remember. And, therefore, while all are mutually comprehended by each, and as wholes, each as a whole is equal to each as a whole, and each as a whole at the same time to all as wholes; and these three are one, one life, one mind, one essence. (*Trin.* 10.11.18; *NPNF*[1] 3:142–43)

This was one of Augustine's most influential works since it is the basis on which many theologians during the Middle Ages wrote about the Trinity. In particular, the manner in which Augustine sees in the human mind and in other creatures certain analogies to understand the Trinity led medieval theologians to develop an entire hierarchy of being, each one bearing the seal of the Trinity that had created it, although in various degrees: images, similitudes, vestiges, and even shadows. And the above-quoted analogy of the human mind—a mind that is only one, but is at the same time memory, intellect, and will—became the most common Trinitarian analogy in Western theology.

Augustine was never fully satisfied with this work. In 416, when he had just completed it, he wrote to Aurelius, the bishop of Carthage, complaining that he had been forced to write with more haste than he intended: "If I had been able to follow my plan, the views would have been the same, but the books themselves would be clear and simpler" (*Ep.* 174; BAC 99:555). This dissatisfaction was not due only to the haste with which he had to finish the work, but also to his conviction that the mystery of the Trinity is such that whatever human beings can understand of it falls far short. Therefore, at the end of book 15 we find a prayer that expresses the humility of the theologian before the subject he faces:

> When, therefore, we shall have come to Thee, these very many things that we speak, and yet come short, will cease; and Thou, as One wilt remain "all in all." And we shall say one thing without end, in praising Thee in One, ourselves also made one in Thee. O Lord the one God, God the Trinity, whatever I have said in these books that is of Thine, may they acknowledge who are Thine; if anything of my own, may it be pardoned both by Thee and by those who are Thine. Amen. (*Trin.* 15.24.51; *NPNF*[1] 3:228)

POLEMICAL WORKS: MANICHEISM

A large part of Augustine's writings sought to refute ideas and doctrines with which he disagreed. In some cases that purpose is relatively subtle, as in *On the Trinity*, which was in part provoked by the inroads that Arianism, though defeated in the Greek East, was making in the West as a result of the Germanic invasions. But there are many others that are openly polemical and show Augustine's struggles in defense of what he took to be the true faith, particularly against three main enemies: Manicheism, Donatism, and Pelagianism.

Augustine's first polemical works were directed against the doctrines and practices of the Manicheans. One reason was that Augustine himself had followed them, and now he felt the need to correct the views not only of Manicheans in general, but also of particular individuals with whom he has shared those beliefs. This is why, almost immediately after his conversion, he wrote *On the Customs of the Catholic Church and of the Manichees, On Genesis against the Manichees, On Free Will*, and *On True Religion*.

Those early works were followed by many others against the same adversaries. The treatise *On Two Souls* argues against the Manichean theory that in human beings there are two souls, one coming from God and another from the principle of evil. The *Debate with Fortunatus* is a report of a debate between Augustine and a Manichean leader by that name. *Against Adiamantus* responds to the argument of one of the most celebrated Manichean leaders, who had produced a long list of contradictions between the New and the Old Testaments that was highly respected and celebrated among Manicheans. Another foundational writing among Manicheans was a letter from its founder, Mani, that served as the basis of instruction for new converts. Augustine refuted it in *Against a Letter of Mani*. The treatise *On Free Will*, in three books, tries to show the senselessness of the Manichean view that the destinies of the good soul and the evil soul are predestined, and that a human being can do nothing out of one's own accord. To these should be added several letters, sermons, and other treatises against various Manichean leaders and against views such as the duality of the human soul, the contrast between the two Testaments in the Bible, the nature of the final consummation, and so forth.

Yet throughout these controversies Augustine always returns to the main concern that for a time attracted him to Manicheism: the problem of evil. How can one attribute to a good God the numerous evils that exist in the world? The Manichean answer was simple: there is evil in the world because there are in fact two eternal principles, one of good and one of evil. Augustine deals with the subject again and again, but possibly most clearly in his treatise *On the Nature of Good*. He wrote this in 405, and two decades later, in his *Retractations*, he would summarize it as follows:

The book *On the Nature of Good* addresses the Manicheans. It shows that God is by nature immutable and is also the highest and sovereign good, and also that all other natures, be they spiritual or corporal, come from God, and that all, simply because they are natures, are good.

It also explains what evil is and whence it comes, and shows how many goods Manicheans attribute to an evil nature, and how many evils they attach to the good. This error makes them think of good and evil as two natures. (*Retract.* 2.9; BAC 21:977)

Augustine's argument in this book is based on a radical monotheism. There is nothing that does not come from God:

All life both great and small, all power great and small, all safety great and small, all memory great and small, all virtue great and small, all intellect great and small, all tranquillity great and small, all plenty great and small, all sensation great and small, all light great and small, all suavity great and small, all measure great and small, all beauty great and small, all peace great and small, and whatever other like things may occur, especially such as are found throughout all things, whether spiritual or corporeal, every measure, every form, every order both great and small, are from the Lord God. (*Nat. Good* 13; *NPNF*[1] 4:353)

This means that Augustine cannot accept the apparently easy solution of the Manicheans, that good things are produced by the principle of good, and evil ones by the principle of evil. It also means that all that exists, being God's work, is good. The mere fact of existing is good. Furthermore, all that exists has a degree of beauty and of order. What, then, is evil? Evil is not a substance or thing, for every substance proceeds from God. Evil is rather the corruption of a good substance or nature in such a way that its goodness and beauty are diminished. "No nature, therefore, as far as it is nature, is evil; but to each nature there is no evil except to be diminished in respect of good" (*Nat. Good* 17; *NPNF*[1] 4:354).

POLEMICAL WORKS: DONATISM

While Augustine's writings during the first years after his conversion dealt mostly with his own meditations and with his refutation of Manicheism, his ordination led him to pay more attention to the main conflict dividing the church in North Africa: Donatism. This is not the place to summarize the history and teachings of Donatism. Let it suffice to say that it arose at the end of the last persecution, claiming that those who had not been absolutely firm at a time of persecution were now unworthy of administering the sacraments, and that any who had communion with them became equally unworthy. In consequence, the only true church was that which rejected any who had any contact with anyone who accepted the ministrations of an impure church.

During his youth, Augustine does not seem to have been much concerned about Donatism, even though until shortly before his birth most of the population of Tagaste had been Donatist, and apparently some of Augustine's relatives were still part of that movement. But now that he had become first a pastor and then a bishop, Augustine had to pay greater attention to the faith of his flock, to the unity of the church, and to the question of whether the validity of sacraments depended on the purity of those who administered them.

Augustine's first intervention in the controversy was his *Song against the Donatists*, with 20 stanzas of 12 verses each, a total of 240 verses, and each verse with two hemistichs. Like the Arians before them, Donatists had composed popular songs by which they spread their teachings. In his youth, as a student of rhetoric, Augustine had composed several poems after the pattern of Virgil, poems that were well received but have been lost. Now he composed this psalm in which each stanza began with a letter of the Latin alphabet and therefore is often known as Augustine's *Abecedary*. At the end of the poem the church, like a loving mother, invites her children to return to her. While good as a teaching tool, this poem has not been highly praised by students of classical Latin poetry.

For several years Augustine did not write much about Donatism. What finally led him to write more extensively against Donatism was a letter in which Parmenian, the Donatist bishop of Carthage, challenged the affirmation of Tyconius that the church is by nature universal and that therefore Donatism, which is limited to North Africa, cannot claim to be the true church. Augustine responded in the year 400 with a treatise *Against Parmenian's Epistle*, in which he began by rejecting the Donatist claims regarding the origins of the movement, in order then to move to a more detailed discussion of the church, which by its very nature must be willing to receive sinners.

Augustine's most important work against Donatism is *On the Unity of the Church*. His point of departure in this treatise, as well as in much of his controversy with the Donatists, is the importance of the church as the body of Christ. He says:

> In his fullness Christ has both a body and head. The head is the only-begotten Son of God, and the body is his church. They are husband and wife, one in the flesh. Any who do not agree with sacred Scripture regarding the head are not part of the church, even though they may be where it is. Likewise, any who agreeing with sacred Scripture

regarding the head break away from the unity of the church, are also not within it, because they withdraw from the body of Christ. (*Unity Ch.* 4.7; BAC 30:661)

Then Augustine offers a vast series of biblical texts that he employs against Donatism and presents following approximately the order of the canon of the Bible. Finally, in chapter 17 he begins his own refutation of Donatism. What he believes to be the weak point of Donatism is that in order to accept what Donatists say, one has to believe that all the churches founded by the apostles are no longer true churches, and that the true church exists only in Africa, from whence it must now go to the rest of the world.

> It would be absolute madness to claim that the preaching of the gospel to all nations is to come not from the churches founded by the apostles and their work, but that, since those have perished, their rebirth and the conversion of the rest of the Gentiles will come out of Africa through the followers of Donatus. I suppose that this is so ridiculous that they themselves would laugh at such a notion. And yet, it is only by affirming such a thing, which would make them blush, that they have anything to say. (*Unity Ch.* 17.44; BAC 30:735)

According to Augustine, what the Donatists say regarding the origin of the controversy is not true, for most of the accusations against the leaders of the church are false, and some Donatists have sinned as much as those whom they condemn. The visible church must always include wheat and tares, and deciding who is wheat and who is tare is not up to humans, but to God. Furthermore, based on what Optatus of Milevis said earlier, Augustine affirms that in the sacraments, as for instance in baptism, there are three parties present: first the Trinity, then the person receiving the sacrament, and also the one administering it. This is also the order of importance of the three parties. A sacrament is a work of the Trinity for the benefit of those receiving that sacrament; it does not depend on the virtue of the one administering it. If it were not so, if baptism were dependent on the virtue of the ministry, since degrees and forms of virtue vary from person to person, "there would be almost as many baptisms as there are those baptizing" (*Unity Ch.* 25.59; BAC 30:763). Therefore the faithful can rest assured that the sacraments they receive are valid even though those administering them may be unworthy.

Finally, Augustine tackles the complaints of Donatists regarding imperial actions against them and at the same time recalls the violent actions of the extreme Donatists, the Circumcellions, against the church that they oppose. Regarding the latter form of violence, even if what they say about the church were true, "an illegal punishment for illegal actions, and keeping people away from what is illegal by means equally illegal, is not right" (*Unity Ch.*

20.54; BAC 30:755). As to the emperors and their actions against Donatism, Augustine affirms that crimes committed by the Donatists must be punished, although with a measure of Christian mercy. And he adds, "As to ourselves, even as God allows others to do so, we do not wish to have even the lightest laws of repression employed against you, except in order to keep the Catholic Church free from your terror" (*Unity Ch.* 20.55; BAC 30:759).

POLEMICAL WORKS: PELAGIANISM

Augustine's third great and ongoing polemic was with the followers of Pelagius, an austere and devout man, probably a monk, from the British Isles. There is no doubt that his personal holiness made him highly respected and admired. He was in Rome when he read and was distressed by some words of Augustine in his *Confessions*: "Give what Thou commandest, and command what Thou wilt" (*Conf.* 10.29.40; NPNF¹ 1:153). What Augustine meant by these words is that the commandment of God can only be obeyed through the grace of God. Pelagius saw in this a great error, for it would imply that if one does not obey a divine commandment, it is because one has not received from God the necessary grace. This led to a debate between Pelagius and the bishop of Rome, who defended what Augustine had said. After that debate, as the Goths approached Rome, Pelagius left for Africa, where Augustine was at the time. But, as Augustine himself reports, his concern over Donatism did not give him the opportunity to converse with Pelagius, who shortly thereafter left for the East. There for a time Pelagius found support, but eventually his teachings were rejected by the Council of Ephesus in 431.

Although there is no doubt that Augustine had good reason to reject the teachings of Pelagius, one must point out, first, that it was not Pelagius but his disciples Celestius and Julian of Eclanum who most strongly opposed Augustine's teachings. And second, that what Pelagius actually taught is often simplified by saying, for instance, that he insisted on justification by works and not by faith. But Pelagius was a careful student of Paul's epistles and wrote a *Commentary on Romans* showing that this was not his position, for commenting on Romans 5:1 he says, "None are saved by their own merits, but all are equally saved by the grace of God" (trans. Theodore de Bruyn, *Pelagius's Commentary on St. Paul's Epistle to the Romans* [Oxford: Clarendon Press, 1993], 89). The debate was not over the value of works, but rather about the place of grace in Christian obedience.

Augustine's writings against Pelagianism are many. Among the earliest are two treatises addressed to a tribune by the name of Marcellinus, who shortly before had represented the emperor by presiding over a synod that took place in Carthage and rejected the teachings of Celestius. Marcellinus was concerned because some claimed that he had erred, and he wrote to Augustine asking for advice. The first of the two treatises with which Augustine responded is *On Punishment and the Forgiveness of Sins*. But still Marcellinus was concerned that in that first treatise Augustine had affirmed that even though it is possible in this world to reach the point where one is free from all sin, this has only been achieved by Jesus Christ. Augustine's second treatise defends that point. Later, in 415, some monks sent to him Pelagius's work *On Nature*, to which Augustine responded with *On Nature and Grace*, refuting Pelagius in moderate and respectful tones.

Much more important for the development of the controversy was the treatise *On the Grace of Jesus Christ and Original Sin*, written some three years later, in 418, in response to the works of Pelagius seeming to deny that grace is absolutely necessary for every moment in the Christian life. Responding to what Pelagius had said, Augustine affirmed that according to Pelagianism, "the grace and help of God does not come to us for each act, but really consists in free will or in law and teaching." Furthermore,

> in the books which he has published on the freedom of the will, and which he mentions in the letter he sent to Rome, [one finds] no other sentiments than those which he seemingly condemned. For that grace and help of God, by which we are assisted in avoiding sin, he places either in nature and free will, or else in the gift of the law and teaching; the result of which of course is this, that whenever God helps a man, He must be supposed to help him to turn away from evil and do good, by revealing to him and teaching him what he ought to do, but not with the additional assistance of His co-operation and inspiration of love, that he may accomplish that which he had discovered it to be his duty to do. (*Grace of Jesus Christ and Original Sin* 1.3.3; *NPNF*[1] 5:218)

This will turn out to be the main issue in the controversy: when humans do good, do they do so simply out of their own decision, or do they do it because the grace of God leads them to it, cooperating with them?

By this time Augustine's controversy was beginning to focus on Julian of Eclanum, whose position was much more radical and bellicose than that of Pelagius or his earlier disciples. From that point onward, Augustine's main works in the controversy were directed against Julian. These include *Against Two Epistles of the Pelagians*, *Against Julian the Defender of the Pelagian Heresy*, and *Incomplete Work against Julian*. The first of these consisted of four books that Augustine sent the bishop of Rome, who had forwarded to him two letters that he had received, one from Julian and another from a group of Pelagian bishops. The second is a refutation, point by point, of a work in four books that Julian had published. The third was one of Augustine's last writings, for he was working on it when he died.

But the controversy was not limited to the positions of Augustine on one side and the Pelagians on the other. Soon others, particularly in southern France, while rejecting the doctrines of Pelagius, also had difficulties with those of Augustine. They are commonly called "semi-Pelagians," and we shall be discussing them in the next chapter. It was in response to them that Augustine probably produced some of his most careful writings on the subject under discussion, the place of grace in salvation and the Christian life, along with related subjects such as predestination and free will. Among these works of Augustine, two stand out: *On Grace and Free Will* and *On Rebuke and Grace*, which he completed three years before his death.

The reason for these writings was a controversy that began among the monks of Hadrumetum, in what today is Tunisia, about whether what Augustine declared regarding the primacy of grace in salvation canceled human free will. In order to settle the matter, two monks were sent to consult Augustine himself, and he answered not only with two letters, but also with the treatise *On Grace and Free Will*. This did not end the difficulties, for the monks still had doubts, and in an attempt to respond to those doubts, Augustine wrote *On Rebuke and Grace*. It is in these two works, jointly read, that we see Augustine's final position on the relationship between grace and free will.

At the very beginning of the first of these two treatises, Augustine briefly states the main subject under discussion:

> With reference to those persons who so preach and defend man's free will, as boldly to deny, and endeavour to do away with, the grace of God which calls us to Him, and delivers us from our evil deserts, and by which we obtain the good deserts which lead to everlasting life: we have already said a good deal in discussion, and committed it to writing, so far as the Lord has vouchsafed to enable us. But since there are some persons who so defend God's grace as to deny man's free will, or who suppose that free will is denied when grace is defended, I have determined to write somewhat on this point to your Love, my brother Valentinus, and the rest of you, who are serving God together under the impulse of a mutual love. . . . (*Grace and Free Will* 1.1; *NPNF*[1] 5:443–44)

Free will must be affirmed, because without it there would be no sense in God giving commandments. If God commands, it is because we have the freedom to obey or not to obey. And it is also necessary to affirm grace, because without it humans can do nothing.

Now, do the many precepts which are written in the law of God, forbidding all fornication and adultery, indicate anything else than free will? Surely such precepts would not be given unless a man had a will of his own, wherewith to obey the divine commandments. And yet it is God's gift which is indispensable for the observance of the precepts of chastity. . . . In order, however, that this victory may be gained, grace renders its help; and were not this help given, then the law would be nothing but the strength of sin. (*Grace and Free Will* 8; *NPNF*[1] 5:447)

This means that grace is present both at the beginning and throughout the Christian life: "He [God] operates, therefore, without us, in order that we may will; but when we will, and so will that we may act, He co-operates with us. We can, however, ourselves do nothing to effect good works of piety without Him either working that we may will, or co-working when we will" (*Grace and Free Will* 33; *NPNF*[1] 5:458).

In this entire matter it is important to note that, while Augustine insists that grace is the point of departure for salvation, he would not agree with what later Protestant Reformers would say, that salvation is not by merits, but only by grace. For Augustine, on the contrary, grace makes it possible for humans to obtain the merits by which they are saved.

Augustine explains this more fully in *On Rebuke and Grace*, where there are four stages or different conditions in which Augustine sees human freedom at work. As Augustine explains in this treatise, before the fall humans had freedom both to sin and not to sin; after the fall, the second form of freedom was lost, so that there was still freedom to sin. Grace restores the freedom not to sin, although not all the time, so that in the present condition believers have the freedom both to sin and not to sin. Finally, at the consummation of all things, there will only be freedom not to sin. Augustine summarizes all this as follows: "Therefore the first liberty of the will was *to be able not to sin*, the last will be much greater, *not to be able to sin*; the first immortality was to be able not to die, the last will be much greater, not to be able to die; the first was the power of perseverance, to be able not to forsake good—the last will be the felicity of perseverance, not to be able to forsake good" (*Rebuke and Grace* 33; *NPNF*[1] 5:485).

Since those who are in the state of not being able not to sin are incapable of coming out of that state, it is necessary for the grace of God to take the initiative. This is why, as Augustine says above, grace first operates on those who do not believe and then cooperates with them so that they may be able to do good and attain salvation. For the same reason, Augustine affirms that grace is irresistible, for otherwise sinners, not having the freedom not to sin, would necessarily resist and reject it. And this is also the main reason for Augustine's affirmation of predestination. Since only those who receive that first grace can be saved, and that gift depends on the sovereign will of God, those who receive that grace will be only those who have been predestined for it.

THE *CITY OF GOD*

Among the many works of Augustine, none is more encompassing than the *City of God*. Its initial motivation was the fall of Rome, taken and sacked by the Visigoths in 410. Among those who mourned that tragedy were some who claimed that Rome had lost its ancient power because it had abandoned the gods that made it great. Therefore it was necessary to abandon Christianity and to return to the ancient religions, a religion that by now Christians called "paganism," that is, the faith of the rude and unlettered *pagani*. In view of that pagan interpretation of the fall of Rome, Augustine felt that a refutation was necessary. Very shortly after completing the *City of God*, Augustine commented about his purpose in writing it:

> Meanwhile, Rome was destroyed by the invasion and flood of the Goths, led by Alaric. People who worshiped many false gods, whose name now is that of pagans, seeking to blame Christianity for this destruction, began blaspheming against the true God with unparalleled bitterness. Therefore I, burning in zeal for the house of God, decided to write these books on the *City of God* against such blasphemies and errors. This work took me several years, for a thousand other urgent matters interrupted it. (*Retractations* 43.1; BAC 171–172:56)

The "several years" to which Augustine refers here were in fact thirteen, from 413 to 426. Although Augustine says that this delay was due to his many other obligations, it was also due to the vast scope of the project, which was not simply a response to pagan claims, but actually became an entire retelling and reinterpretation of most of history, biblical history as well as Roman history.

In order to refute what pagans were saying, Augustine makes use of the image of two cities that had been employed earlier, among others, by the Revelation of John and by Tyconius. In words often quoted, Augustine bases these two cities on two "loves" or principles of action:

> Accordingly, two cities have been formed by two loves: the earthly by the love of self, even to the contempt of God; the heavenly by the love of God, even to the contempt of self. The former, in a word, glories in itself, the latter in the Lord. For the one seeks glory from men; but the greatest glory of the other is God, the witness of conscience. The one lifts up its head in its own glory; the other says to its God, "Thou art my glory, and the lifter up of mine head." (*City of God* 14.28.1; *NPNF*[1] 2:282–83)

Augustine himself explains that out of the twenty-two books of this work, the first ten seek to prove both that it is not true that the pagan gods brought about Roman prosperity, and that the present evils have nothing to do with such deities. The remaining twelve books of the work may be divided into three sections: books 11–14 deal with the origin of the two cities, the next four (15–18) with their histories, and the last four (19–22) with their ends. The result of this outline is that Augustine devotes extensive sections in the first books to the history and myths of the Romans, and the rest of the work then begins with creation and continues biblical history with the fall, an entire book summarizing history from the times of Noah to the prophets, and then another from the prophets to Christ. This includes also a long section in which Augustine offers a chronological parallelism between the history of Rome and biblical history. In the last books there are frequent repetitions of things said before. For instance, on the theme discussed above, the scope of free will at various stages in human history, Augustine says:

> Neither are we to suppose that because sin shall have no power to delight them, free will must be withdrawn. It will, on the contrary, be all the more truly free, because set free from delight in sinning to take unfailing delight in not sinning. For the first freedom of will which man received when he was created upright consisted in an ability not to sin, but also in an ability to sin; whereas this last freedom of will shall be superior, inasmuch as it shall not be able to sin. This, indeed, shall not be a natural ability, but the gift of God. (*City of God* 22.30.3; *NPNF*[1] 2:510)

Within this scheme, Augustine divides history into seven ages, paralleling the six days of creation and the seventh of rest. Then, at the end of this vast work, he declares that he wishes he could have been much more explicit regarding the various details on the six ages parallel to the six days of creation:

> But there is not now space to treat of these ages; suffice it to say that the seventh shall be our Sabbath, which shall be brought to a close, not by an evening, but by the Lord's day, as an eighth and eternal day, consecrated by the resurrection of Christ, and prefiguring the eternal repose not only of the spirit, but also of the body. There we shall rest and see, see and love, love and praise. This is what shall be in the end without end. For what other end do we propose to ourselves than to attain to the kingdom of which there is no end? (*City of God* 22.30.5; *NPNF*[1] 2:511)

THE *RETRACTATIONS*

Early in the present chapter it was pointed out that in his *Confessions* Augustine left us an unprecedented work, a spiritual autobiography by which it is possible to reconstruct much of his early life. Thanks to that work, we know the doubts and anguish that eventually led Augustine to conversion. Now, toward the end of his days, shortly after completing the *City of God*, Augustine wrote another unusual work, the *Retractations*. Just as when dealing with the *Confessions* it was necessary to explain that this did not mean, as we might understand, a retelling of a litany of sins, now in dealing with the *Retractations* it is also necessary to point out that this does not mean that Augustine is retracting in the sense of taking back whatever he said earlier. It is more of a revisiting of all that he had written up to that point and retracing the path that he had followed, placing each work in its context and explaining something about its purpose. Certainly, when he finds something he wrote on which he has now changed his mind, he acknowledges and corrects his former error. For instance, he rejects the notions regarding the preexistence of the soul with which he flirted during his youth. But what is most significant about this work is that in it Augustine offers us an unprecedented history of the path that led him from the garden in Milan to the *City of God*.

26

Figures Surrounding Augustine

Although Augustine lived both at the end of the fourth century and the beginning of the fifth, it was in the fifth century that his impact dominated Western Christian literature. His stature was such that there are few Christian Latin writers in the fifth century that are not his defenders, opponents, or at least questioners.

PELAGIUS AND HIS FOLLOWERS

In the preceding chapter we already spoke of Pelagius and his main followers, for it is impossible to follow Augustine's literary production without taking into account the opponents whom he is addressing in many of his works. As we have seen, one of Augustine's main concerns during his later years was the challenge of Pelagianism.

Pelagius produced abundant literature, but most of it has been lost. For those works still extant, it is difficult to determine who truly is the author. Furthermore, apparently some among the Pelagians preferred to remain anonymous, for at the high point of the controversy Jerome complained that that Pelagians did not take responsibility for what they said by attaching their names to their writings. And the matter becomes even more complicated because throughout the manuscript tradition, some writings of Pelagius or of his followers were attributed to others, some even to Augustine.

Therefore, although several writings are clearly the work of Pelagius, there are many others whose authorship is still debated. Among those that can be definitively attributed to him, the most important is the already-mentioned *Commentary on the Thirteen Epistles of Paul*. Upon reading this book, is clear that, although quite often Pelagius has been depicted as an ignorant fanatic, in fact he was a careful student of Paul, even though his understanding of the Pauline doctrine of grace was diametrically opposed to that of Augustine. There is also a rather long *Book on the Hardening of Pharaoh's Heart*. These two works, as well as several homilies and treatises attributed to Pelagius, seek to interpret difficult passages in Scripture in the light of other passages, particularly those of the same author or body of literature. Thus, for instance, on the matter of the hardening of Pharaoh's heart, Pelagius quotes an enormous number of biblical passages trying to show that the justice and love of God are such that one must not interpret what is said in Exodus regarding Pharaoh's heart in any way that contradicts the justice and love of God.

Among the dogmatic works of Pelagius, those written against Augustine stand out. One of them is the treatise *On Nature*, which affirms that human nature is such that by its own power it is able to obey the divine commandments and abstain from sin. Two other works written in refutation of Augustine were *On the Possibility of Not Sinning* and *On Free Will*. Of these last two works, only fragments remain, mostly as quotations within Augustine's writings.

Among the writings attributed to Pelagius that may or may not be his, the most interesting is *On the Rich*, which argues that society should not be divided between the rich and the poor. God's purpose is that all be "poor" in the sense of having all that is necessary and no more. Any who have more than that are rich, and their wealth is actually dispossessing the poor of what they need in order to live. Therefore, having the just measure of goods is a gift of God, who has provided such goods for the use of all; but excessive goods are a sin and a violation of the divine purposes.

As we saw in the chapter regarding Augustine, his most frequent opponent in the Pelagian debate was not Pelagius himself but some of his followers, particularly Celestius and Julian of Eclanum. The former left Rome, fleeing the Visigoths, and for a time settled in Carthage, where his doctrines were not welcome among Augustine and his colleagues. He was particularly accused of denying that Adam's sin was transmitted to his descendants and therefore that it was not to free them from that sin that children were to be baptized. All that remains of his writings are quotations either in treatises refuting him or in the acts of synods that condemned his teachings.

The case of Julian is similar, for also of him we only have fragments quoted in order to refute them. His first intervention in the controversy took place when the bishop of Rome, Zosimus, issued an encyclical letter against Celestius. After being rejected in Carthage, Celestius had now returned to Rome. In this epistle Zosimus rejected Pelagianism and urged all the bishops of Italy to agree with him in that position. Julian refused, asking Zosimus for further explanations, and thus began a literary debate whose main participants were Julian himself, Zosimus, and Augustine. According to Julian in his *Four Books against Turbantius*, Augustine's claim that original sin is transmitted from Adam and Eve through physical procreation leads to a contempt for the body similar to that of the Manicheans, and that therefore Augustine, even after having written abundantly against Manicheism, still retained some of the views that he had learned in his youth from the Manicheans.

Besides these three authors, and the works that are clearly theirs, there are many anonymous documents with clear Pelagian connections that have survived only because they have been attributed to writers such as Augustine or Ambrose.

JOHN CASSIAN

Little is known of Cassian's youth. He clearly benefited from an excellent education, and therefore it is likely that his family had means. Although the date of his birth is unknown, he was apparently born in Marseille around the year 360 and thus was a contemporary of Augustine. He was still a young man when he embraced monastic life in Bethlehem. After spending some time there, he and a companion decided to visit Egypt in order to explore the depths of monastic life. There he met some of the most distinguished Egyptian monks and spent several years visiting the most remote places where monastics sought to hide from the world. From Egypt he went to Constantinople, where he was ordained a deacon by the patriarch of that city, John Chrysostom. When, as we shall see later, John Chrysostom was deposed and persecuted by imperial authorities, Cassian was sent to Rome as a representative of Chrysostom's cause. How long he remained in Rome is unknown. In any case, there he met an archdeacon by the name of Leo, who would later become bishop of that city and come to be known as Leo the Great. It was Leo who later, on the basis of Cassian's knowledge of the debates that were raging in the East, urged him to write against Nestorius.

After his sojourn in Rome, Cassian settled in Marseille, where he founded two monasteries, one for men and another for women. By that time monasticism had begun to make headway in the West, particularly north of Marseille, in the valley of the Loire, where many sought to follow the examples of Martin of Tours and Hilary of Poitiers. Now, in Marseille, Cassian soon became the accepted leader not only of the monastery of St. Victor, which he had founded, but of the entire monastic movement in the area, attracting people from distant places who would come to St. Victor in order to learn about monastic life, just as Cassian had done earlier in Egypt.

While he was in St. Victor, Cassian wrote his two most important works, both on monastic life. The first one, in twelve books, is known by the extensive title of *On the Cenobitic Institutions and on the Remedies against the Main Principal Evils*, but more commonly simply as *Cenobitic Institutions*, that is, institutions for monks who live in community rather than in solitude. Here Cassian applied to Western monastic life much of what he had learned earlier in Syria and Egypt, although adapting it to Western culture and uses. The first four books deal mostly with the organization of monastic life. The subject of the first is the dress or habit of monastics, the second and third deal with the hours and practices of prayer, and the fourth describes the novitiate through which candidates to monastic life must pass in order to make certain that they have true monastic vocation. The rest of the work is guidance as to how monastics are to avoid the eight great evils: gluttony, fornication, greed, anger, listlessness, laziness, vainglory, and pride. Given the difference between the first four books and the other eight, sometimes the latter circulated by themselves under the title of *On the Eight Principal Evils*.

Cassian's second work of monastic life is his series of twenty-four *Conferences* or *Collations*, which take the shape of conversations with some of the best-known leaders of Egyptian monasticism. There is some connection between these *Conferences* and the *Cenobitic Institutions*, for in writing the latter Cassian was already planning to write the former as an appendix or series of clarifications regarding what he was saying in the *Institutions*. Taken together, both works show Cassian's ability to communicate to the West what he had learned in the East, although at the same time applying it within a different context. It is also important to note that in the *Conferences* are several statements that seem to be rejecting Augustine's views on grace. For this reason Cassian is often called a semi-Pelagian. For instance, in the third conference we find the following words:

> Thus, the divine protection never leaves us, but is always present. The love of the Creator for his creatures is such that his providence not only works with us, but even goes ahead of us. . . . And, when this providence sees in us the beginning of an inclination of the will towards the good, it strengthens, illumines, and moves us so that we may go forward unto salvation, increasing what God had placed in us or what God sees growing within us as a result of our own efforts. (*Conferences* 13.8; PL 49:912–13)

In passages such as this Cassian on the one hand seems to affirm, with Augustine, that it is God who initiates a person's inclination toward the good, but on the other hand he also leaves the door open to Pelagianism in declaring that God sees good growing out of human efforts.

These two writings by Cassian made an enormous impact on Western monasticism. Although it is frequently said that it was Benedict of Nursia who gave shape to Western monasticism, one must not forget that when Benedict wrote his *Rule*, almost a hundred years after Cassian's death, he repeatedly acknowledged his debt to Cassian. Thus the Benedictine rule instructs its followers that they should read the *Conferences* of Cassian.

Finally, there is Cassian's one work on systematic theology, written at the behest of Leo the Great: *On the Incarnation of the Lord against Nestorius*. It is not a particularly profound work nor one that is carefully structured, but it is interesting because here Cassian suggests that there is a connection between Nestorianism and Pelagianism, for—at least according to Cassian's understanding—the former affirms that Jesus has been joined to God for reason of his merits, and this comes close to Pelagianism. Thus, although Cassian has often been dubbed a semi-Pelagian, here we see him clearly rejecting the teachings of Pelagius and his followers.

PROSPER OF AQUITAINE

During the last years of Augustine's life, and immediately after his death, his most decided defender against Pelagianism was Prosper of Aquitaine. Little is known of the life of Prosper. He certainly received an excellent education, for his usage of both Latin and Greek is exemplary. Although he hailed from Aquitaine, he settled in Marseille, where he admired the monastery of St. Victor that Cassian had founded. But he did not join that monastery or any other. For some time he had already been living in Marseille when, shortly before Augustine's death, the objections of the semi-Pelagians to Augustine's teachings began to appear. Prosper wrote to Augustine, letting him know of his concern over the matter, and Augustine answered by sending him two works that had originally been a single one, *On the Gift of Perseverance* and *On the Perseverance of the Saints*. Shortly after Augustine's death, Prosper began taking steps so that the Roman see would take action against semi-Pelagianism. Partly as a result of this, Pope Celestine wrote the bishops in Gaul, warning them about semi-Pelagianism. This warning did not seem sufficient for Prosper, who returned to Marseille in order to refute the teachings of those who seemed to be denying Augustine's teachings, particularly Cassian. After the latter's death, Prosper returned to Rome, where he began writing on subjects other than simply the defense of Augustine. Among other things, some ancient chroniclers affirm that he worked with Leo on the famous *Dogmatic Epistle to Flavian*, commonly known as *Leo's Tome*, that played a crucial role at the Council of Chalcedon.

Prosper's literary work was vast and varied. Besides his correspondence with both Augustine and Rufinus at the beginning of his controversy with Cassian and his followers, shortly before Augustine's death he wrote a poem of over a thousand verses regarding Pelagianism, semi-Pelagianism, and their relationship. To this were added several works on the same subject. Among them the most discussed at the time was *On Grace and Free Will against the Collationists*, meaning those who studied the *Collations [Conferences]* of Cassian. Also, following the example of some we have studied in earlier chapters, Prosper wrote an extensive *Chronicle* from creation to the year 455; to this *Chronicle* others later added appendices, continuing the narrative.

However, his most important work, even though some scholars question its authorship, is *The Call of All Nations*, which is the first systematic Christian discussion of the salvation of the Gentiles, or nonbelievers. It seems to have been the product of Prosper's mature years. While earlier he had been a faithful follower of all that Augustine had said regarding grace and predestination, as years passed he began moderating his position. The problem he had to face was that, on the one hand, he wished to affirm what Augustine had said, that the beginning of faith (the *initium fidei*) is the result of the grace of God, not of human effort; and on the other, he did not wish to lead that affirmation to its ultimate consequences, that those who are lost are such because God has not predestined them to receive that initial grace. Prosper was convinced of the universal salvific will of God, that God wishes all to be saved. But that being the case, how is it that some do not receive that grace that they need as the beginning of faith? Prosper himself poses the problem succinctly at the beginning of his work:

> A great and difficult problem has long been debated among the defenders of free will and the advocates of the grace of God. The point at issue is whether God wills all men to be saved; and since this cannot be denied, the question arises, why the will of the Almighty is not realized. When this is said to happen because of the will of men, grace seems to be ruled out; and if grace is a reward for merit, it is clearly not a gift but something due to men. But the question again arises: why is this gift, without which no one can attain salvation, not conferred on all, by Him who wills all to be saved? Hence there is no end to discussions in either camp so long as they make no distinction between what can be known and what remains hidden. (Prosper, *Call of All Nations* 1.1; ACW 14:26)

Similarly, at the beginning of the second book Prosper reiterates the three points that he believes it is necessary to affirm, even though we might not see how they can be reconciled:

First, we must confess that God wills all men to be saved and to come to the knowledge of truth. Secondly, there can be no doubt that all who actually come to the knowledge of the truth and to salvation do so not in virtue of their own merits but of the efficacious help of divine grace. Thirdly, we must admit that human understanding is unable to fathom the depths of God's judgments, and we ought not to inquire why He who wishes all men to be saved does not in fact save all. For if we do not search into what we cannot know, then we shall have no difficulty in reconciling the first point with the second, but we shall be able to preach and to believe them both with the security of an undisturbed faith. (Prosper, *Call of All Nations* 2.1; ACW 14:89)

Throughout the entire work Prosper struggles with these three irreconcilable principles. His general conclusion is that God gives all a general grace, and to others a special grace through which they can respond positively to the grace previously offered. Naturally, this does not solve the difficulty, and in the end Prosper simply has to affirm the inscrutability of the divine designs. Since it is impossible to penetrate the mystery of such designs, all we can do is to affirm at the same time that God wishes all to be saved, and that those who are indeed saved are such by the grace of God. In the end, Prosper's conclusion is what he already stated at the very beginning, that one must acknowledge the "distinction between what can be known and what remains hidden."

However, the significance of this writing by Prosper is not in what he says regarding grace and free will, but rather in his interest in the destiny of those who have not heard the gospel. One may well say that this is an unavoidable question when reading Augustine's *City of God*. When one looks at human history in the wide terms in which Augustine does, one immediately seeks the action of God, the city of God, among the many peoples who have had no opportunity to hear the gospel message. Now Prosper, when posing the question of the call to those nations, is expanding the vision of the church beyond its traditional horizons. Historically, it was a time when the Roman Empire still existed in theory, but was no longer a political reality, for the various Germanic rulers, even though declaring themselves to be subjects of the empire, were in truth independent. Thus, in the following lines one finds echoes not only of Augustine and the *City of God*, but also of an emerging political order:

But the grace of Christianity is not content with the boundaries that are Rome's. Grace has now submitted to the sceptre of the Cross of Christ many peoples whom Rome could not subject with her arms; though Rome by her primacy of the apostolic priesthood has become greater as the citadel of religion than as the seat of power.

It may be true that, just as we know that in former times some peoples were not admitted to the fellowship of the sons of God, so also to-day there are in remotest parts of the world some nations who have not yet seen the light of the grace of the Saviour. But we have no doubt that in God's hidden judgment, for them also a time of calling has been appointed, when they will hear and accept the Gospel which now remains unknown to them. Even now they receive that measure of general help which heaven has always bestowed on all men. (Prosper, *Call of All Nations* 2.16–17; ACW 14:120–21)

VINCENT OF LERINS

In the year 434, giving only the pseudonym of "Pilgrim," someone published an influential treatise under the title of *Commonitory*, that is, *Warning*. Some sixty years later Gennadius, discussed in chapter 24, affirmed that this "Pilgrim" was actually Vincent, a monk in Lerins, near Marseille, and to this date scholars agree with his assessment. Since the monastery in Lerins was at that time a center of semi-Pelagianism, it is commonly said that such was the position of Vincent. In fact, the *Commonitory* does not affirm semi-Pelagian doctrine, but it clearly is written against Augustine and those who held his views on grace and predestination.

Originally Vincent wrote two separate works, or two parts of a single project. But the second part was stolen, and Vincent, instead of rewriting it, simply added at the end of the part that he still had a summary of the second part. For that reason, chapters 29 to 33 are in fact a summary of a commonitory that is not extant. But this summary does not say much that is different from the first part of the work.

As it has reached our time, the book has thirty-five chapters. Already in the first two, "Pilgrim" not only announces the purpose of his writing but also hints at his answer. As to the first, he says that his purpose is not to be an "author" (a creator) but simply to repeat what he has heard and received from the ancients and must be preserved. As to the second, Vincent says that

all possible care must be taken, that we hold that faith which has been believed everywhere, always, by all. For that is truly and in the strictest sense "Catholic," which, as the name itself and the reason of the thing declare, comprehends all universally. This rule we shall observe if we follow universality, antiquity, consent. We shall follow universality if we confess that one faith to be true, which the whole Church throughout the world confesses; antiquity, if we in no wise depart from those interpretations which it is manifest were notoriously held by our holy ancestors and fathers; consent, in like manner, if in antiquity itself we adhere to the consentient definitions and determinations of all, or at the least of almost all priests and doctors. (Vincent, *Commonitory* 2; NPNF² 11:132)

The three main principles at the beginning of this quotation, "what . . . everywhere, always, by all"—*quod ubique, quod semper, quod ab omnibus*—are commonly called the "Vincentian canon" and since that time this has been repeatedly used against any doctrine that might look different or innovative. Vincent has no admiration or respect for those whom he considers heretics, calling the Pelagians "frogs, fleas, and flies." But at the same time he affirms that the divine providence uses them in order to test the church and to help it refine and strengthen its faith.

Vincent is certain that the final authority in matters of faith is Scripture. But he is also aware that all the main ancient heretics claimed to base their teachings on Scripture, and that even the devil quotes the Bible in order to tempt Jesus. This is because one can interpret a single text in various ways, and therefore we need to have certain principles of judgment regarding any interpretation. Therefore, even though Scripture is the final source of authority, the criterion that is to be used in judging any doctrinal interpretation is that it upholds, or at least does not contradict, what has been believed everywhere, always, and by all. For that reason, toward the end of his writing, Vincent says that the constant practice of the church has been to defend the faith on two foundations: the authority of the sacred canon and the tradition of the church. As is well known, in the Protestant Reformation this became an important point of contention between Catholics and Protestants.

This does not mean, however, that doctrine does not evolve. Vincent knows that, through the centuries that have passed between the times of Jesus and his own, the church has been refining its doctrines and making them more precise, as with the doctrine of the Trinity. Yet this does not mean that new doctrines are being invented, but rather that doctrine is growing and evolving in the same way in which the human body grows and develops. As the body grows, differences appear between what it used to be and what it now is; but it is still the same body. Likewise, the evolution of doctrines is necessary and valuable, for it is a way in which the meaning of the faith is better understood. But such evolution must not be such that it becomes a new reality rather than a development of what was already there. Thus, just as the body grows and the arm of an adult is not the same as that of a child, so also do doctrines grow when facing new tests, thus coming to a better understanding, although in essence they remain the same.

OTHER AUTHORS

Since as time goes by the number of Christian writers increases, in the present chapter we have only been able to discuss the most outstanding. But there are a few others who must at least be mentioned.

Marius Mercator clashed with Celestius in Rome, and after that he wrote copiously in defense of Augustine and against Pelagianism. The most significant extant pieces by him are two warnings, or commonitories, the first against Celestius and the second against both Celestius and Pelagius. Rather than original works, both writings are a summary of the teachings of Pelagianism and the actions that various church bodies have taken against them.

Quodvultdeus was a bishop of Carthage who fled when the Vandals conquered North Africa. Several of his sermons are extant. Two of these are explanations of the Nicene Creed in relation to the baptism of neophytes, like sermons of others we have seen before. The rest is a series of repeated warnings against Arianism, which had never been a real threat in North Africa but was now brought in by the Vandals, who were Arians. His *Book of the Promises and Predictions of God* is much more interesting. Here he reviews biblical history in 153 chapters, frequently interpreting the significance of that history by means of typology, so that past events are promises and announcements of the advent and work of Jesus.

Salvian of Marseille (ca. 418–ca. 472), although originally from the north of Gaul, went south to Marseille with his wife and daughter and for a time practiced an ascetic life within the family. Eventually, apparently by common agreement, he and his wife separated in order to lead celibate lives. He first joined the monastery in Lerins, where Vincent resided, and then moved to St. Victor, which Cassian had founded. It was there that he apparently spent the rest of his life. Although we have the titles of several of his works, only two of them, plus some letters, have come to our days. The first of these two, *On Greed*, is noted for its elegant and sometimes overly refined style. Its main theme is possessions, all of which are in truth mere loans from God and must be shared with the needy. Such sharing is just as necessary for a holy life as any other virtue or practice. The second work, *On the Government of God*, seeks an explanation as to why God has allowed the Germanic invasions and all their destruction. Salvian's answer is that, rather than blaming God for what has happened, believers must understand that the reason why the barbarians were able to conquer them was their own infidelity. That infidelity was such that Salvian repeatedly declares that one does not find among barbarians the same injustices that exist in a supposedly Christian civilization, implying that the barbarians are morally above most Christians.

An element in Augustine's thought that would eventually become generally accepted, but at the time led to controversy, was his affirmation that the soul is incorporeal. Faustus of Riez (ca. 410–ca. 495), who eventually became head of the famous monastery in Lerins, wrote a treatise *On Grace and Free Will* in which he argued that only God is incorporeal and to claim that the human soul is incorporeal is to confuse the creatures with their Creator. Responding to this, Claudianus Mamertus (?–473), in his *Condition of the Soul*, came to the defense of Augustine, arguing that, if the human soul is to be capable of bearing the image of God, it must be incorporeal, as God is.

It is also important to point out that the fifth century saw a great flourishing of Christian poetry. As early as the New Testament, we find poetic passages that seem to have been sung by early Christians, jointly with translations of the Hebrew psalms. Then there are similar passages in some of the authors that we have already discussed. Clement of Alexandria, Claudianus, and Ambrose also wrote some hymns and poems.

A fairly common practice in antiquity was to combine isolated verses from famous classical poets, joining them to create a poem with a different meaning. Such compositions, called "centos," or "centones," did not have great literary merit but were employed as a means to memorize lessons. Christians also used such compositions. The most important of these was the work of Petrona Proba, a relatively well-to-do Roman woman who composed a cento of almost seven hundred verses summarizing all biblical history. It is to her and others like her that Jerome refers with pejorative and misogynous words. After quoting her, he says:

> The chatty old woman, the doting old man, and the wordy sophist, one and all take in hand the Scriptures, rend them in pieces and teach them before they have learned them. Some with brows knit and bombastic words, balanced one against the other philosophize concerning the sacred writings among weak women. Others—I blush to say it— learn of women what they are to teach men; and as if even this were not enough, they boldly explain to others what they themselves by no means understand. (*Ep.* 57.7; *NPNF*[2] 6:59)

In the fifth century Christian poetry reached its highest point in antiquity in the person of Aurelius Prudentius (348–ca. 412). He was a native of Spain, though to this day there are several places in that land claiming the honor of being his birthplace. Since in his writings he never speaks of his conversion, most probably he was born within a Christian family. He received an excellent education, particularly in classical Roman literature. For some time he followed a career in politics, coming to occupy important positions next to Emperor Theodosius. Late in the fourth century he abandoned that career in order to devote himself to an ascetic life and to Christian poetry. He published a collection of his poems in 405, and after that date he disappears from history. Fortunately, that collection includes a preface and an epilogue that help us understand more of his life and his goals. In the preface he says:

I am now 57 years old, the end is approaching, and in my old age God is pointing to the coming day. . . .

Twice I governed over noble cities holding the reins of law, and did justice, to the pleasure of the good and the fear of the evil. Finally the liberality of the prince [Theodosius] placed me within the military structure, next to him. (Preface 1–3, 17–22; BAC 58:5–7)

Although written in Latin, most of the poems of Prudentius have Greek titles, in imitation of what had also been done by several classical Latin poets. The title of the first collection is *Cathēmerion*, which could roughly be translated as "for each day." The first six of the twelve poems in this collection are to be sung at particular times of the day: when the rooster crows, in the morning, before dinner, after dinner, at the lighting of lamps, before going to sleep. The other six are to serve on particular occasions, such as days of fasting, Christmas, Epiphany, and so forth.

The second collection, *Apotheōsis*, sometimes called *On the Godhead*, is actually a single poem of more than a thousand verses defending Trinitarian doctrine against various heresies.

This is followed by *Hamartigenia*, "the origin of sin," where, in almost a thousand verses, he takes up the problem that had so worried young Augustine and comes to the conclusion that all that God has created is good, but it is the soul that out of its own will does evil. Most of this poem takes the form of a debate and refutation of Marcion, who had proposed the existence of two gods as a way to explain evil.

The fourth piece, almost as extensive as the two previous ones, is *Psychomachia*, "the struggle of the soul." Here Prudentius depicts a battle between the soul and paganism. This is followed by two books, also in verse, *Against Symmachus*, who had proposed to bring the altar of the goddess Victory back into the Senate. The *Peristephanon*, "about Stephen," includes fourteen hymns to various martyrs and saints.

The *Dittochaeum*, a title on whose meaning scholars disagree, is so different from the rest that some believe it is not by Prudentius. It is a collection of forty-nine stanzas whose original purpose seems to have been to serve as inscriptions to a series of paintings for an unknown church building. The first twenty-four stanzas refer to the Old Testament, from Adam and Eve to King Hezekiah. Number 25 is about the Annunciation. The other twenty-four refer to the New Testament, from Bethlehem to Revelation. This structure seems to indicate that the author intended to place the first twenty-four on the wall at one side of the church, the twenty-fifth at the center, perhaps in the apse, and the other twenty-four on the other side. If this conjecture is true, these verses were written for a church dedicated to the Annunciation.

The hymns of Prudentius soon began being used in worship, particularly in the Breviary that Benedictines and other monastics employed in their prayers. Partly for this reason, Prudentius was the most influential Latin poet throughout the Middle Ages. In later times, since Latin poetry is very different from modern poetry, he fell into disuse. Even so, some of his hymns still make their way into modern hymnals. The most famous of these is:

> Of the Father's love begotten,
> Ere the worlds began to be,
> He is Alpha and Omega,
> He the source, the ending He.
>   (Trans. J. M. Neale, in *The Presbyterian Hymnal*
> [Louisville, KY: Westminster / John Knox Press, 1990], #309)

27

Leo the Great

HIS LIFE

Leo was born in Rome or nearby late in the last decade of the fourth century. He spent most of his life in the ancient capital, where he died late in 461. Little is known about his life before he was elected bishop of Rome. We know that he was much involved in the life of that church and that he was profoundly concerned over the theological debates that at that point were raging both in the East and the West. In the West the main issues were still Pelagianism and Donatism, which continued being strong in Africa, as well as Priscillianism, which was making headway in Spain. In the East it was the time of the great christological controversies leading to the Councils of Ephesus (431) and Chalcedon (451). Leo was interested in all these matters long before he became a bishop, encouraging the production of works refuting notions that he considered heretical. For instance, as we have already seen, he was still an archdeacon when he asked John Cassian to write a refutation of the Christology of Nestorius.

The time and place where Leo lived presented difficult circumstances. He was still a teenager when, under the command of Alaric, the Visigoths took and sacked the city of Rome. The decline of the old empire was evident everywhere. Since the north of the Italian peninsula was now divided among various invaders, the emperors left Rome in order to seek refuge in Ravenna or elsewhere on the southern tip of the peninsula, from where they could easily flee to Constantinople.

Leo was bishop of Rome when the Huns, led by Attila, invaded the area. His hordes seemed unstoppable: after taking and sacking the cities of Aquileia, Milan, and Pavia, they marched on Rome. Emperor Valentinian III had fled to Ravenna, and all seemed lost, for the city was practically defenseless. It was then decided to send an embassy to Attila under the leadership of Leo, who was accompanied by two of the most prestigious leaders of the city. What took place between Leo and Attila is not known. Some suggest that Leo warned Attila that, if he sacked the holy city, his destiny would be the same as Alaric's, who thirty years earlier had done the same and died almost immediately. At any rate, Attila not only spared Rome but also marched north, leaving Italy.

Something similar happened four years later, although this time the result was not the same. The Vandals, led by Genseric, took the city and demanded a huge ransom. Even so, the Roman populace saw the efforts of their bishop and credited him with having convinced the Vandals to treat the conquered with a measure of mercy.

In the midst of all this, Leo was still working for the benefit of the church. When the Eastern church was divided by the debate over Monophysitism, Leo intervened by writing a famous letter, which would eventually be endorsed by the Council of Chalcedon in 451, the same year in which Leo faced Attila.

Leo's conciliatory spirit was manifested also when the old debate regarding the date of Easter flared up once more. Over a hundred years earlier, the Council of Nicaea (325) had decided to reject the claims of the Quartodecimans and celebrate Easter always on a Sunday. Then, given the difficulty in the calculations involved, and since Alexandria had long been noted for its astronomical studies, it was decided that the patriarch of Alexandria, aided by the astronomers of the city, would set the date on which the church would celebrate Easter each year, then circulate that information to the rest of the church. While Leo was bishop of Rome, some other bishops in the West began questioning the manner in which Alexandria calculated the date of Easter; but Leo calmed the waters, arguing that it was more important to keep unity than to enter into controversies over dates.

Leo died late in 461, after having served as bishop of Rome for twenty-one years. He was soon dubbed "the Great," a title by which he is still known.

HOMILIES

Leo was not a prolific writer like Augustine or Jerome. What we have from him are almost a hundred homilies and a slightly larger number of letters. As is frequently the case, there is no absolute certainty as to how many and which of these homilies and letters are truly his. But there is general consensus regarding most of them. There is also a document by the name of *Leo's Sacramentary*, which seems to have no real connection to him.

Some of Leo's homilies are among the best literary and theological jewels of Christian antiquity, although others are not of the same quality. The first five of his collection of homilies do not rise to the same literary level as the rest, but they are interesting because they tell about his own election to the episcopacy and his tasks and special occasions. The next six (6–11) deal with collections for the poor. In them Leo reaffirms what the church had thought for a long time, that alms and support for the needy are an essential element of Christian faith.

It is beginning with homily 12 that we see Leo's adeptness at joining the dates and celebrations of the church with doctrines that he thought were important to affirm, and doing this with unique eloquence. Although Leo did not preach them in that order, most of the editions of his sermons organize them following the liturgical year, so that, after the eleven already mentioned, the next nine deal with Advent, followed by ten on Christmas, eight on Epiphany, twelve on Lent, and so on up to Pentecost. This is followed by other homilies dealing with other religious feasts, with fasting, and with the Beatitudes. Given the importance of its particular subject, the entire collection closes with homily 96, dealing with the much-debated subject of the two natures in Christ.

A good example of the manner in which Leo joins the dates in the liturgical calendar with theology is his first homily on Christmas. While reading this homily, it is important to remember that Leo is preaching at a time when the church is rent by debates regarding the union of the two natures of Christ. When we read it while keeping that in mind, we see the skill with which Leo intertwines the liturgical date with the faith of the people in such a way that they may be instructed on profound and important theological subjects:

> Our Saviour, dearly-beloved, was born to-day: let us be glad. For there is no proper place for sadness, when we keep the birthday of the Life, which destroys the fear of mortality and brings to us the joy of promised eternity. No one is kept from sharing in this happiness. There is for all one common measure of joy, because as our Lord the destroyer of sin and death finds none free from charge, so is He come to free us all. Let the saint exult in that he draws near to victory. Let the sinner be glad in that he is invited to pardon. Let the gentile take courage in that he is called to life. For the Son of God in the fulness of time which the inscrutable depth of the Divine counsel has determined, has taken on him the nature of man, thereby to reconcile it to its Author: in order that the inventor of death, the devil, might be conquered through that (nature) which he had conquered. And in this conflict undertaken for us, the fight was fought on great and wondrous principles of fairness; for the Almighty Lord enters the lists with His savage foe not in His own majesty but in our humility, opposing him with the same form and the same nature, which shares indeed our mortality, though it is free from all sin. . . .

Therefore the Word of God, Himself God, the Son of God who "in the beginning was with God," through whom "all things were made" and "without" whom "was nothing made," with the purpose of delivering man from eternal death, became man: so bending Himself to take on Him our humility without decrease in His own majesty, that remaining what He was and assuming what He was not, He might unite the true form of a slave to that form in which He is equal to God the Father, and join both natures together by such a compact that the lower should not be swallowed up in its exaltation nor the higher impaired by its new associate. Without detriment therefore to the properties of either substance which then came together in one person, majesty took on humility, strength weakness, eternity mortality: and for the paying off of the debt, belonging to our condition, inviolable nature was united with passible nature, and true God and true man were combined to form one Lord, so that, as suited the needs of our case, one and the same Mediator between God and men, the Man Christ Jesus, could both die with the one and rise again with the other. (*Hom.* 21.1–2; *NPNF*² 12:128–29)

This homily, and many others like it, show why Leo was so concerned about a particular christological doctrine that has circulated in the East and now seems to him to be threatening the very core of Christian faith.

The same combination of liturgical times with faith and doctrine may be seen in the first of his homilies on the resurrection of the Lord:

Since, therefore, by our forty days' observance we have wished to bring about this effect, that we should feel something of the Cross at the time of the Lord's Passion, we must strive to be found partakers also of Christ's Resurrection, and "pass from death unto life," while we are in this body. For when a man is changed by some process from one thing into another, not to be what he was is to him an ending, and to be what he was not is a beginning. But the question is, to what a man either dies or lives: because there is a death, which is the cause of living, and there is a life, which is the cause of dying. Let the old sink, that the new may rise. . . . We must die, therefore, to the devil and live to God: we must perish to iniquity that we may rise to righteousness. . . . We must greatly rejoice over this change, whereby we are translated from earthly degradation to heavenly dignity through His unspeakable mercy, Who descended into our estate that He might promote us to His, by assuming not only the substance but also the conditions of sinful nature, and by allowing the impassibility of Godhead to be affected by all the miseries which are the lot of mortal manhood. (*Hom.* 71.1–2; *NPNF*² 12:182)

The homilies of Leo, most of them fairly brief, have repeatedly been used through the centuries in order to help Christians join their worship and devotion with the doctrines of the church. Several of them appear in the Breviary.

EPISTLES

Scholars are in general agreement that at least 123 of the epistles attributed to him were actually written by Leo. Many of these letters are administrative in nature, referring to matters within the life and organization of the church. Thus, for instance, number 4 deals with some of the possible impediments to ordination, such as being a slave, having remarried, or being a moneylender. Among the administrative or practical matters discussed in number 12 is the question of the status of a consecrated virgin who has been raped by barbarian invaders. (On some of these issues, the attitude of Leo leaves much to be desired.) Number 14, to the bishop of Thessalonica, discusses how bishops are to be selected and how they ought to behave. Also, several letters try to refute doctrines that Leo considered heretical, such as Priscillianism (no. 15). And many others, such as number 16, deal with matters of worship such as how and when baptism is to be administered. That wide variety of subjects makes Leo's epistolary that much more valuable to historians.

However, this epistolary becomes particularly interesting as we seek to understand Leo's participation in the Monophysite controversy. His letter number 20 was written in June of 448 in response to the leading proponent of Monophysitism, Eutyches, who had written to him complaining that Constantinople had become a hotbed of Nestorianism and that he was a defender of orthodoxy. As we know from other sources as well as from the later course of the controversy, Eutyches and those who supported him were staunch opponents of Nestorianism, which asserted that in Christ the actions of one nature were to be adjudicated to one person and the actions of the other nature to another person. In 431 the Council of Ephesus had rejected Nestorianism, for if the union of the two natures is not real, it is hard to see how events such as the crucifixion of Jesus can be more than the tragic and unjust execution of a man. But in rejecting the excessive distinction between the humanity and the divinity in Jesus Christ, and emphasizing the two natures, there was always a danger that the divine nature would overwhelm and eclipse the human. This was why many considered the teachings of Eutyches heretical, particularly since he apparently affirmed that there were two natures before the incarnation, but that after the incarnation there was only one nature in Christ, the divine.

When the bishops gathered at Constantinople declared that Eutyches had erred, he wrote to Leo and other important bishops, telling them about the injustice that he felt had been committed concerning him. Leo received not only this letter but also another from Flavian, the patriarch of Constantinople, telling him about the procedure and reasons why the teachings of Eutyches had been rejected. Rather than hastening to judgment, Leo asked Flavian for more details. Finally, after much correspondence, Leo became convinced that the matter was important and that Flavian was right. It was then that he wrote his famous letter number 28, also known as his *Dogmatic Epistle*, or as *Leo's Tome*.

In this letter, Leo begins by explaining to Flavian why at the beginning he lent an ear to the communication from Eutyches but has now settled his mind: "What before seemed concealed has now been unlocked and laid open to our view." Now he understands that Eutyches is to be counted among those who "stand out as masters of error because they were never disciples of truth" (*Ep.* 28.1; *NPNF*[2] 12:39). Referring now to the acts of the synod that had taken place in Constantinople, he says:

> But when during your cross-examination Eutyches replied and said, "I confess that our Lord had two natures before the union: but after the union I confess but one," I am surprised that so absurd and mistaken a statement of his should not have been criticised and rebuked by his judges, and that an utterance which reaches the height of stupidity and blasphemy should be allowed to pass as if nothing offensive had been heard: for the impiety of saying that the Son of God was of two natures before His incarnation is only equalled by the iniquity of asserting that there was but one nature in Him after "the Word became flesh." (*Ep.* 28.6; *NPNF*[2] 12:43)

Leo expresses his opinion in words that would soon become normative for the orthodox understanding of the incarnation:

> Without detriment therefore to the properties of either nature and substance which then came together in one person, majesty took on humility, strength weakness, eternity mortality: and for the paying off of the debt belonging to our condition inviolable nature was united with passible nature, so that, as suited the needs of our case, one and the same Mediator between God and men, the Man Christ Jesus, could both die with the one and not die with the other. Thus in the whole and perfect nature of true man was true God born, complete in what was His own, complete in what was ours. And by "ours" we mean what the Creator formed in us from the beginning and what He undertook to repair. For what the Deceiver brought in and man deceived committed, had no trace in the Saviour. Nor, because He partook of man's weaknesses, did He therefore share our faults. He took the form of a slave without stain of sin, increasing the human and not diminishing the divine: because that emptying of Himself whereby the Invisible made Himself visible and, Creator and Lord of all things though He be, wished to be a mortal, was the bending down of pity, not the failing of power. . . . For both natures retain their own proper character without loss: and as the form of God did not do away with the form of a slave, so the form of a slave did not impair the form of God. (*Ep.* 28.3–4; *NPNF*[2] 12:40–41)

At the risk of surpassing the limits of a history of literature in order to enter the history of the church and its doctrines, it is important to say a word about the later significance of this letter. The controversy regarding the teachings of Eutyches came to such a point that Emperor Theodosius II decided to call a council that should meet at Ephesus in 449. Theodosius appointed Dioscorus, patriarch of Alexandria and a decided enemy of Flavian, to preside over that council. He also instructed that the main theologian among those who opposed Eutyches, Theodoret of Cyrus, should not be allowed to speak at the council. Thus, even before the council convened, its decision was predetermined. At the meeting itself the letter of Leo was not allowed to be read, and Flavian was mistreated in such a way that he died a few days later.

Leo would not accept what he called the "robbers' synod" (*latrocinium* instead of *concilium*) of Ephesus. There was nothing he could do, for the emperor supported what had been done at Ephesus. Then, quite unexpectedly, Theodosius died and circumstances changed. It was possible then to call a new council, which gathered in 451 in the city of Chalcedon, which faced Constantinople across the Bosporus. Leo wrote to the new emperor, suggesting that Leo's delegates should preside over the assembly, and this request was granted. Even though the two papal legates presided over the gathering, it was in fact an Eastern council, for these two were the only representatives of the West. When Leo's letter that the Ephesian Council of 449 had suppressed was read, it received general approval. Although there are indications that many in the East did not wholly agree with Leo, his letter came to have an authority parallel to that of the Definition of Faith issued by this council, and the definition itself was often read in the light of Leo's letter.

When one considers Leo's literary output as a whole, one sees in it parallel emphases. In his sermons, Leo relates the essential doctrines of the faith with liturgical dates and occasions, and at the same time with the daily life of believers. In his letters, even though many are concerned mostly about administrative matters, Leo relates those matters with the doctrinal issues and with the practices of those who are to lead in worship. Thus, although he is called "the Great" mostly by reason of his administrative abilities and his success in his embassy before Attila, in fact his greatness must be found primarily in the manner in which he combined faith with practice, and worship with both.

28

John Chrysostom

While Augustine was writing works that would leave an indelible print on all Western theology, in the Greek-speaking East John Chrysostom was taking the Christian pulpit to its highest peak. As in the case of Augustine, we could have included Chrysostom in the fourth century, for both were luminaries guiding the passage from one century to the next. Even so, Chrysostom belongs in the fifth century because it was then that his work reached its zenith, and also because his life and writings are best understood within the context of the political vicissitudes and the controversies that were dividing the Eastern church during the fifth century.

HIS LIFE

"Chrysostom" was not his birth name, which was simply John. The title of "Chrysostom," meaning "golden mouthed," was given to him shortly after his death. But this fit so well with who he was that it soon was used as it is today, as if it were actually part of his name.

John was born in the middle of the fourth century in Antioch, where his father was an officer of the Roman army. But his father died shortly after his birth, and John was raised by his mother, Anthusa. Rather than marrying again, Anthusa devoted herself to raise and educate her child. Like Augustine to his mother, Monica, John was always extremely grateful to Anthusa—which has led several modern authors to compare the two mothers and their relationships with their two sons. The great difference is that John never seems to have gone through a period of rebelliousness or search after faith, as did Augustine. As far as we know, he never suffered an angst such as Augustine describes in his *Confessions*. But, like Monica, Anthusa soon became aware of the exceptional gifts of her child and made every effort to enhance his education. The high point of that education came when John began studying under the direction of Libanius, the most famous speaker in the entire Roman Empire. The fame of Libanius was such that the most cultured and powerful people in the empire, whenever they had the opportunity, would go to hear him speak. Fortunately, Libanius lived in Antioch, and therefore John did not need to leave Anthusa in order to pursue his studies. He was twenty years old when he began studying with Libanius and continued with him for two years.

Libanius was still a follower of paganism even though by then the ancient religion had lost most of its vitality, and the ancient Greek poets were not read any longer in order to follow their religion and their gods, but rather to learn from their elegance of style. Until shortly before this time, many Christians thought that they should neither study nor teach classical letters, full as they were of stories about the ancient gods. Now, even though things had changed, Libanius was still a faithful follower of the ancient gods, and for him literary studies were also religious exercises. Later John would comment that this famous professor with whom he studied was extremely superstitious. But in spite of those differences, John learned from Libanius the best use of Greek in all its ancient beauty and elegance, and this was one of the reasons why he would later come to be known as "Chrysostom." It was also in that school that John befriended Theodore of Mopsuestia, whom we shall meet in another chapter.

That Chrysostom remained faithful to his Christian faith even though his teacher was a convinced pagan does not mean simply that he continued professing Christianity. It was also that he would not allow the values of his teacher to dull his own. Libanius was convinced that rhetoric and the beauty of language were the greatest gifts of the gods to humankind. He was also proud of his abilities and encouraged his disciples to boast of theirs. But Chrysostom would not allow himself to be led by such views, and later, when he was generally admired, he sought to place things in their proper order, declaring that love is much more important than oratory. Preaching on the Gospel of Matthew, he said that

> if oratory were taken away, our life will be nothing the worse; for indeed even before this, it had continued a long time; but if thou take away the showing of mercy, all is lost and undone. And as men could not sail on the sea, if harbors and roadsteads were blocked up; so neither could this life hold together, if thou take away mercy, and compassion, and love to man. (*Hom. on Matt.* 52.5; *NPNF*[1] 10:325)

And in an earlier passage he declared that even if he had

> the polish of Isocrates, the gravity of Demosthenes, the dignity of
> Thucydides, and the sublimity of Plato, . . . I pass by all such mat-
> ters and the elaborate ornaments of profane oratory; and I take no
> account of style or of delivery; yea let a man's diction be poor and his
> composition simple and unadorned, but let him not be unskilled in
> the knowledge and accurate statement of doctrine. (*On the Priesthood*
> 4.6; *NPNF*[1] 9:67)

Firm as he was in his Christian faith, John had his name added to the list of
catechumens and after the usual time of preparation was baptized. After completing his studies with Libanius, for some time he pursued a career in law,
which at that time was the main use for rhetorical studies. But he was always
attracted to monastic life, and he decided to withdraw from society and live
as a monk. These purposes were thwarted when he told his mother, who, as
he tells the story, "took me into her own private chamber, and, sitting near
me on the bed where she had given birth to me, she shed torrents of tears."
Chrysostom then records what his mother said, reminding him of her twenty
years as a widow devoted to her son, and finally imploring:

> Only in return for all these benefits I beg one favor: do not plunge
> me into a second widowhood; nor revive the grief which is now laid
> to rest: wait for my death: it may be in a little while I shall depart. . . .
> When, then, you shall have committed my body to the ground, and
> mingled my bones with thy father's, embark for a long voyage, and set
> sail on any sea thou wilt: then there will be no one to hinder thee: but
> as long as my life lasts, be content to live with me. (*On the Priesthood*
> 1.5; *NPNF*[1] 9:34)

Chrysostom did as she asked. Rather than leaving for a remote place, he
remained at home, where he began leading the disciplined life of a monk.
When Anthusa died, Chrysostom and three friends left to live as monks in the
nearby mountains. But six years later he decided that God was not calling him
to such a life, and he returned to the city. There, much against his will, he was
ordained as a priest, and the city for the first time heard him preach. Soon his
fame was such that when the episcopal see of Constantinople was vacant, the
emperor secretly sent his agents to Antioch, where they kidnaped the famous
preacher in order to make him bishop or patriarch of Constantinople. It was
there that Chrysostom's fame reached its high point as people would come to
hear him from all over the empire.

However, the tasks of a bishop were much more than preaching. Chrysostom was well aware of the complicated politics within the court and how
these were reflected in the life of the church. After concentrating first on the

life and customs of his own clergy, Chrysostom undertook the difficult task of seeking to reform the life of the entire city, particularly of its high classes. Soon his conflicts with the imperial court were such that Chrysostom was sent into exile. The result was a protest of such magnitude that the government was forced to pardon the exiled bishop and invite him to return to the city. But this did not end the conflicts, and Chrysostom was once again sent into exile. The resulting riots led to a fire that destroyed the famous cathedral of Saint Sophia. But this time, rather than allowing Chrysostom to return to the city, the government decided to exile him to a much more remote place, to which he was traveling when he died in 407.

TREATISES ON ASCETICISM AND OTHER TOPICS

Chrysostom is known mostly as a preacher, and the vast majority of his writings are sermons or speeches. Yet before becoming famous as a preacher, Chrysostom had written several treatises. Later he continued writing about subjects as varied as the education of children, virginity, and suffering. Two of his early works were motivated by the decision of his friend Theodore, who would later become bishop of Mopsuestia, to abandon monastic life for the sake of an attractive woman. At that time Chrysostom still believed that the highest vocation of any believer was the monastic life, and he wrote two exhortations *To Theodore after His Fall*. He was convinced that what Theodore had done was a great sin, and he appealed to his friend with visions of hell, comparisons with the Ninevites, and calls to repentance. The tone of both treatises may be seen at the very beginning of the first:

> Now perhaps I shall seem to say what is incredible to some who now witness thy desolation and overthrow; for on this account I wail and mourn, and shall not cease doing so, until I see thee again established in thy former lustre. . . . For if the devil had such great power as to cast thee down from that pinnacle and height of virtue into the extremity of evil doing, much more will God be able to draw thee up again to thy former confidence; and not only indeed to make you what you were before, but even much happier. (*To Theodore after His Fall* 1.1; NPNF[1] 9:91)

It is more difficult to date most of Chrysostom's minor writings. Some of them deal with suffering and adversity and how to overcome them. When he was already patriarch of Constantinople, he wrote on the virtue of virginity, and particularly against the practice of the *virgines subintroductae*, women consecrated to virginity who lived under the same roof as men equally consecrated to a celibate life. Also, partly reflecting his experience with his mother and partly out of his own ascetic tendencies, he wrote encouraging widows to abstain from remarriage. He composed another treatise, *On Vainglory and the Education of Children*, in which these two subjects are joined, speaking first of vainglory as the root of many evils, to the point that some people seek to gain more than they need while others die of hunger and still hide their need. But the cause of vainglory is that it has been planted in people since childhood. Therefore, a new form of discipline is required in which, while respecting children, they are also ruled by laws and principles. This treatise, which later became relatively popular, does not seem to have been very influential in the time of Chrysostom or immediately thereafter, for only a few ancient manuscripts have been preserved.

His work in six books *On the Priesthood* has been much more influential. Here Chrysostom presents a dialogue between himself and his friend Basil when both were elected bishops. There has been much debate as to who this Basil was, for the tone of the treatise itself seems to indicate that he is a fictional character. Also, many argue that the manner in which Chrysostom deals with his supposed friend, even mocking him to the point of cruelty, is an indication that Basil never existed. Finally, Chrysostom refers to him in such terms that if he were a real person, it would be difficult to understand why he never mentioned him in any of his other writings and sermons. On the other hand, others argue that this writing offers so many details about Chrysostom's life that most of it must be true. An example of this is that here Chrysostom, in a very detailed fashion, reports his conversation with his mother when he considered becoming a monk and she objected.

No matter whether truth or fiction, the writing begins by speaking of a close friendship between Basil and Chrysostom, and how this friendship was strained when Basil decided to become a monk and Chrysostom was still tied to the world. While Basil called him to become a monk, Anthusa pulled in the opposite direction. Much later they heard that there was a project to make both of them bishops. Basil asked Chrysostom to decide together what they would do, and Chrysostom agreed. But Chrysostom did not consider himself worthy of that position and was certain that Basil was. When the time came for their consecration, Chrysostom hid, and Basil was made a bishop against his will, agreeing simply because he was convinced that Chrysostom was doing likewise. When he learned that Chrysostom had hid, Basil was angry and sought out his friend in order to tell him so. The scene that Chrysostom depicts is surprising: "I laughed for joy. . . . But when he saw that I was delighted and beaming with joy, and understood that he had been deceived by me, he was yet more vexed and distressed" (*On the Priesthood* 1.6; NPNF[1] 9:35).

Basil is angry not only because he has been deceived, but also because he would have difficulty explaining the events to any who question him, and will have nothing to say against those who mock him for the deception or those who accuse him of seeking to become a bishop for his own vainglory. His complaints are extensive and emotional, for this is the friend whom he has trusted for many years.

Chrysostom's answer is surprising. In a long speech, he tells his friend that he deceived him for a good purpose, and that deception is not bad, for it is through deception that great generals attain victories and great physicians get their patients to follow their instructions. He even goes as far as declaring that the apostle Paul deceived those who would read his letters and that he did so for their own good.

This takes us to the second chapter of the work, where Chrysostom explains to Basil that the reason why he deceived him was that he was convinced that Basil had the faith, gifts, and attitudes necessary to practice the priesthood, while he did not have them. A good pastor has to be wise in caring for souls, firmly correcting the flock and at the same time punishing them with moderation and love. Finding and guiding straying sheep is not a task that all can perform. Therefore Chrysostom says that the reason why he hid was that he did not wish to place those who had elected him in a bad position. And he deceived Basil because he was convinced that his friend was indeed called to this ministry.

The third book deals mostly with the reason why Chrysostom had rejected such an ordination. He did not do so in order to be able to continue a career following the ambitions of the world, but rather because he had great respect for the priesthood. His own idea of pastoral functions is so high that he does not consider himself worthy of them.

Yet here one finds words that reflect Chrysostom's strong anti-feminine prejudice: "The divine law indeed has excluded women from the ministry, but they endeavor to thrust themselves into it; and since they can effect nothing of themselves, they do all through the agency of others; and they have become invested with so much power that they can appoint or eject priests at their will: things in fact are turned upside down" (*On the Priesthood* 3.9; *NPNF*[1] 9:49).

This is part of a long list of requirements and impediments for pastoral duties that are the reasons why Chrysostom considers himself unworthy of such a calling. The path of ministry is not to be followed because of ambition or vainglory, for a pastor is to serve others and not to be served by them. A pastor must be as wise as if he had a thousand eyes. In consequence, the life of the pastor is much more difficult than the life of a monk. Furthermore, while it is relatively easy to practice an outward moderation in order to control the body in the sight of others and of oneself, it is much more difficult to practice an inner mortification, setting aside all the natural inclinations of the soul.

And then there is also another argument based on the indignity with which the office is tarred, for elections within the church are such that they themselves are a denial of the faith:

> Come, then, and take a peep at the public festivals when it is generally the custom for elections to be made to ecclesiastical dignities, and you will then see the priest assailed with accusations as numerous as the people whom he rules. For all who have the privilege of conferring the honor are then split into many parties; and one can never find the council of elders of one mind with each other, or about the man who has won the prelacy; but each stands apart from the others, one preferring this man, another that. Now the reason is that they do not all look to one thing, which ought to be the only object kept in view, the excellence of the character; but other qualifications are alleged as recommending to this honor. (*On the Priesthood* 3.15; *NPNF*[1] 9:53)

The fourth book is remarkable for its harsh words about the punishment deserved by those who have undertaken the pastoral ministry unworthily. Those who elect a priest for unworthy reasons will be punished. And then Chrysostom returns to the matter of the abilities necessary: having ease of speech; knowing how to combat heresies and other enemies of the faith; deeply understanding the laws of logic and dialectics. Paul was an example of all this, and Chrysostom calls his readers to develop the same qualities.

The fifth book is one of the best and oldest manuals on homiletics that have survived. John, who would eventually be called Chrysostom for his golden speech, stresses the need to study in preparation for preaching and to work out carefully what one is to say. In all this, it is important to avoid seeking popularity by preaching what the audience would like. This is one of the reasons why a preacher has to know what he is saying and why he is saying it, for otherwise his strongest words can be set aside as a result of ignorance or even mocked. At the same time, a preacher must respect those who criticize him, even if they have no reason to do so. In all this, one must be very careful, for those who are used to being praised develop a sort of hunger for praise itself and will become envious particularly when they hear others being praised.

Finally, the sixth book returns to the initial subject of the discussion, for Basil thought that by having him ordained, Chrysostom had deprived him of the higher life of contemplation and asceticism. But Chrysostom surprises him by declaring that an active life is to be preferred and is even more difficult than a life of contemplation. It is easier to practice virtue when one is alone than when one lives in the midst of a community and is responsible for others. At this point Chrysostom includes a question by Basil and a response that is worthy of careful consideration:

Basil: Dost thou then think this to be a great thing? and dost thou fancy that thou wilt be saved when thou art not profitable to any other? Chrysostom: Thou hast spoken well and nobly, for I am not myself able to believe that it is possible for one who has not labored for the salvation of his fellow to be saved. (*On the Priesthood* 6.10; *NPNF*[1] 9:79)

HOMILIES ON SCRIPTURE

If he had written only the treatises already discussed, Chrysostom would be considered an important Christian author. But it was his sermons that made him shine above all others. They not only gave him fame, but also the very name of "Chrysostom."

Most of Chrysostom's homilies are part of a long series of sermons in which he preaches in detail and in order on a book of the Bible. Although most of his homilies deal with the New Testament, there are also several series on the Old. After preaching a series of nine homilies on Genesis, Chrysostom preached another series of sixty-seven homilies on the same book. Although he never preached a series on the Psalms by order, we do have fifty-eight sermons on Psalms. This series on Psalms is usually counted among his homilies, although there are indications that he never preached them and that they were rather carefully written and thus profound commentaries that he was developing as a basis for preaching. Apart from Genesis and Psalms, Chrysostom neither preached nor seems to have planned to preach a series on other books of the Old Testament, although we do have a number of sermons, some of them part of a small series, on some of those other books. Thus, there are five sermons on the history of Hannah, and three on David and Saul. The case of Isaiah is somewhat more complicated, for we do have six of his sermons on that book, but there is also a commentary on Isaiah that exists only in Armenian and may well be his.

It was to the New Testament that Chrysostom paid most careful attention. We have 90 homilies on Matthew, 88 on the Gospel of John, 55 on Acts, 32 on Romans, 74 on Corinthians, 24 on Ephesians, 15 on Philippians, 12 on Colossians, 16 on the two Epistles to the Thessalonians, 28 on the two Epistles to Timothy, 6 on Titus, 3 on Philemon, and 34 on Hebrews. There is also a detailed verse-by-verse study of Galatians that may well have been written in preparation for preaching on that book.

In all these homilies Chrysostom's hermeneutics is typically Antochene. At this point it is important to acknowledge the difference between the sort of exegesis that was typical of Antioch and that which prevailed in Alexandria. For people in Alexandria, ever since the times of Clement and Origen, a good interpreter of Scripture was one who was able to read it following allegorical methods similar to those that were employed by the interpreters of classical pagan literature. In contrast, in Antioch the tradition prevailed of beginning by a careful study of the literal meaning of the biblical texts, then having resource to allegory only in rare cases when the text itself required it. This meant that one should not take separate words from here and there, nor isolated verses in order to weave them with others and thus create meanings that are not truly found in the text itself of Scripture. In Antioch, on the basis of that literal and historical reading of Scripture, it was also customary to see in past events some signs of what was to come. This is particularly true of the manner in which the Old Testament was read, finding in it events that are "types" or "figures" of the advent, life, and work of Jesus.

This is why several of the series of homilies by Chrysostom begin with an explanation regarding the context in which a particular book of the Bible was written. Thus, for instance, before launching into his extensive series of homilies on the Corinthian correspondence, Chrysostom begins by explaining what sort of place Corinth was:

> As Corinth is now the first city of Greece, so of old it prided itself on many temporal advantages, and more than all the rest, on excess of wealth. And on this account one of the heathen writers entitled the place "the rich." For it lies on the isthmus of the Peloponnesus, and had great facilities for traffic. The city was also full of numerous orators, and philosophers. . . . Now these things we have mentioned, not for ostentation's sake, nor to make a display of great learning: (for indeed what is there in knowing these things?) but they are of use to us in the argument of the Epistle. (*Hom. 1 Cor.*, preface; *NPNF*[1] 12:1)

Chrysostom then refers to the time that Paul spent at Corinth and to some of the events that took place there. (Oddly, he places in Corinth some events that actually took place in Ephesus.) Then he explains the specific circumstances of the letter, the doubts that some Corinthians had, who were some of the main characters, and other similar matters. It is only after he has explained all this that he finally turns to the first verse in the letter in order to preach on it.

The first homily deals only with the first three verses in the epistle, studying them carefully and explaining their meaning at the same time that he relates it to the circumstances in Corinth and the reasons for the letter. From that point on, whenever in order to understand the meaning of a particular passage it is important to remember the conditions prevailing in Corinth, the questions that Christians there were posing, and other similar matters, Chrysostom takes the time to explain these matters in order to clarify the original and literal meaning of the passage. For instance, when he comes to chapter 8, which deals with food sacrificed to the idols, Chrysostom carefully explains the nature of the problem and why Paul responds as he does. As he himself says, "It is necessary first to say what the meaning of this passage is: for so shall we readily comprehend the Apostle's discourse" (*Hom. 1 Cor.* 20.1; *NPNF*[1] 12:111). He then goes on to explain the practice of sacrificing meat to the idols and eating it, and the issues this raised for Christians in the city.

The same sort of historical introduction appears in most of the other series of homilies. In these introductions Chrysostom also takes time to explain the place of the book that he is discussing within the entire Bible and its history. For instance, when beginning his series of ninety homilies on the Gospel of Matthew, he explains the relationship between the two Testaments as well as the similarities and differences among the four Gospels, finally turning to the genealogy that opens the first of the Gospels.

Chrysostom's style in these homilies is worthy of consideration. On the one hand, he clearly shows that he is a master of the Greek language. He uses it in all its purity and beauty, to such a degree that his style is comparable to that of the best ancient classical writers. But at the same time one notes that he is constantly relating directly with his audience. There are abundant puns that would delight his audience. In some cases the rhythm itself is such that it would help those who heard to remember what he had said. The homilies are replete with illustrations and examples taken from daily life. Such is the case in the opening homily on Matthew, where Chrysostom captivates his audience by telling them that they are going to enter into a beautiful city. It is the heavenly city, high above any human city, and yet seems to draw from many believers only a passing interest. In words that remind us of the manner in which today people are interested in every minor event in the life of a star singer and pay little attention to more important news, Chrysostom says:

> But thou knowest exactly the affairs of the world, as well new as old, and such too as are quite ancient; thou canst number the princes under whom thou hast served in time past, and the ruler of the games, and them that gained the prize, and the leaders of armies, matters that are of no concern to thee; but who hath become ruler in this [heavenly] city, . . . thou hast not imagined even as in a dream. And the laws that are set in this city thou wilt not endure to hear, nor attend to them, even when others tell thee of them. How then, I pray thee, dost thou expect to obtain the blessings that are promised, when thou dost not even attend to what is said?
>
> But though never before, now, at any rate, let us do this. Yea, for we are on the point of entering into a city (if God permit) of gold, and more precious than any gold. (*Hom. Matt.* 1.16–17; *NPNF*[1] 10:7)

As to the subjects of Chrysostom's preaching, while he takes quite seriously his exegesis of the biblical texts, in commenting on them Chrysostom includes frequent and sometimes long digressions on some of his favorite themes, such as the sin of vainglory, luxury in dress, the temptations of the circus or the theater, the value of virginity and chastity, and many others. But possibly the subject that most frequently appears, and certainly the one that gained him the enmities that eventually led to his exile and death, is the responsibilities of the rich toward the poor. Chrysostom is so passionate about this subject that sometimes, in the middle of a diatribe on it, he asks his audience to forgive the vehemence of his words. Thus, commenting on the ninth chapter of Paul's First Epistle to the Corinthians, he depicts the rich in words that may be quite offensive:

> "Yea," saith one, "let the moth eat, and let not the poor eat; let the worm devour, and let not the naked be clothed; let all be wasted away with time, and let not Christ be fed; and this when He hungereth." "Why, who said this?" it will be asked. Nay, this is the very grievance, that not in words but in deeds these things are said: for it were less grievous uttered in words than done in deeds. . . . What madness is this? (for a madness it is, and plain distraction,) to fill your chests with apparel, and overlook him that is made after God's image and similitude, naked and trembling with cold, and with difficulty keeping himself upright.
>
> "But he pretends," saith one, "this tremor and weakness." And dost thou not fear lest a thunderbolt from heaven, kindled by this word, should fall upon thee? (For I am bursting with wrath: bear with me.) (*Hom. 1 Cor.* 21.5; *NPNF*[1] 12:123)

And in another sermon in the same series, in one of many digressions that seem quite disconnected with the passage itself, he says:

> Wherein, I ask, differs the rich man from the poor? Hath he not one body to clothe? one belly to feed? In what then hath he the advantage? In cares, in spending himself, in disobeying God, in corrupting the flesh, in wasting the soul. Yea, these are the things in which he hath the advantage of the poor: since if he had many stomachs to fill, perhaps he might have somewhat to say, as that his need was more and the necessity of expense greater. But even "now they may," saith one, "reply, that they fill many bellies, those of their domestics, those of their hand-maidens." But this is done, not through need nor for humanity's sake, but from more pride: whence one cannot put up with their excuse. (*Hom. 1 Cor.* 40.6; *NPNF*[1] 12:248)

OTHER HOMILIES

Although quite naturally all of Chrysostom's homilies are based on his exegesis of Scripture, those that have just been mentioned are series of studies and sermons whose unity lies in the orderly reading of a particular book or section of Scripture. But also among his homilies are others that deal with specific subjects and are united by a theme rather than a particular section of Scripture.

Along these lines, one may mention his series of eight sermons *Against the Jews*, in which his concern does not seem to be so much the Jews themselves as the attraction that some of the practices and feasts of Judaism had for Christians—which in any case does not avoid his expressing the prejudices against Jews that were circulating at the time.

There is also a series of homilies *On the Statues* that Chrysostom preached when he was still in Antioch and a riotous mob destroyed the statues of the emperor and other notables. All feared the wrath of the emperor, whose vengeance they awaited. Chrysostom preached these sermons seeking both to strengthen his hearers before the impending disaster and reminding them of the evil practices and attitudes that had led to their difficulties. The last homily in this series celebrated the imperial pardon that the bishop of Antioch and others had obtained.

Also, while in all of his sermons Chrysostom underscores the moral principles of Christianity, some are devoted exclusively to a particular aspect of this theme. One of them, *On Almsgiving*, emphasizes once again the duties of those who have resources toward those who do not have them. Another, *Against the Games of the Circus and the Theater*, warns against the violence and the licentious customs that such spectacles not only accept but also promote.

As was to be expected, Chrysostom also preached homilies whose subject is a particular occasion in the church year, particularly the Nativity, Epiphany, and Holy Week. There are also homilies addressed to those who are preparing to receive baptism. They include beautiful metaphors for the renewal that takes place in baptism, but also much moral and even moralizing teaching on subjects such as the dress of women.

Few of Chrysostom's sermons are strictly doctrinal, even though in many of them there are extensive passages regarding Christian doctrine. His twelve homilies dealing directly and specifically with doctrinal matters are refutations of the extreme Arianism that was still circulating at the time. But besides this attack against doctrines that had already been rejected by most Christians, Chrysostom did not use the pulpit to criticize or refute those with whose doctrines he disagreed.

Finally, some of Chrysostom's sermons offer unexpected vistas on the life and tensions of the time. Besides the already-mentioned homilies on the destruction of the statues in Antioch, there are two dealing with Eutropius. This powerful man in Constantinople had long been the main instigator of the government's opposition to Chrysostom. When Eutropius fell from imperial grace, he fled to the church, where he received sanctuary while clinging to the altar. The first of Chrysostom's two homilies dealing with this matter was preached in the presence of Eutropius and dealt mostly with the vanity of worldly glories. The second was preached when Eutropius, attempting to flee from the safety of the church, was captured and killed. Under the same category one may include the two sermons that Chrysostom preached in connection with his own exile in 403—the first of these, before departing for exile, and the second upon his return.

As we come to the end of this chapter on the greatest among all Christian preachers in antiquity, it may be well to close it in the same manner in which he concluded many of his homilies, with a doxology combining an invitation to faith and obedience with the proclamation of the glory of God:

> Knowing therefore these things, let us flee from the evil banquets of luxury and cleave to a spare table; that being of a good habit both of soul and body, we may both practice all virtue, and attain the good things to come, through the grace and mercy of our Lord Jesus Christ, with Whom to the Father, with the Holy Ghost, be glory, power, and honor, now and ever, and world without end. Amen. (*Hom. 1 Cor.* 39.18; *NPNF*[1] 12:243)

29

The Alexandrians

NEW CIRCUMSTANCES

As we have repeatedly seen throughout the course of this history, there were always differences in emphases and perspectives among Christians in the early church, even the most orthodox. From an early date Western Christianity, as it developed in the Latin-speaking areas of the Roman Empire, tended to relate its faith to the traditional Roman interest in law and therefore to underscore the moral dimensions of Christianity rather than more speculative matters. From this perspective, with its emphasis on law, the saving work of Jesus consisted above all in paying the debt that humankind had contracted by reason of sin. One sees indications of this tendency in the work of Tertullian, but particularly in other Western theologians who came after him. At about the same time, in Alexandria, which had become the center of Greek philosophy, there was a strong interest in relating the faith with the best of classical philosophy. From this perspective, the outstanding element in the work of Jesus is that he taught eternal truths and revealed the will of the Father. And there was also, mostly in Syria but also to an extent in Asia Minor, a third perspective for which what was important about the work of Jesus was that he assumed humanity in order to free all humankind from its subjection to sin and death.

During the early centuries, such differences did not lead to schisms or to acrimonious disagreement. But toward the end of the fourth century, and certainly in the fifth, things changed, particularly in the Eastern Greek-speaking church. This was partly due to political reasons. The patriarchs of Alexandria and Antioch vied for supremacy. Since there was now in the East a third patriarchate, Constantinople, the struggle between Alexandria and Antioch often centered on whether the patriarch of Constantinople would be a partisan of one or the other of the two ancient great sees.

Now in the fifth century, theological differences between Alexandria and Antioch centered on the person of Jesus Christ and how to understand the presence and union in him of both divinity and humanity. This is not the place to discuss the subtleties of various christological positions that developed at the time, or the course of the controversies and the political maneuvering involved. (I have discussed the first of these two subjects in the book *A History of Christian Thought*, and the second in *The Story of Christianity*.) Let it suffice to say, regarding the events themselves, that it was this debate that led to the Council of Ephesus in 431, to the council in the same city in 449 that Leo the Great dubbed "a robbers' synod," and finally to the Council of Chalcedon in 451. The bitter debates did not end with that council, but continued for centuries, leading to schisms that still exist. As to the history of theology, and particularly of Christology, for the present let it suffice to say that Alexandrian Christology was what later scholars have called "unitive," while Antiochene Christology was "disjunctive." This means that what most concerned the Alexandrians was the unity of the person of Jesus Christ, even when this might seem to diminish or eclipse his humanity. In contrast, Antiochene Christology sought to make sure that the complete humanity of Jesus Christ was affirmed, and therefore sought to understand the union between the divine and the human in such a way that the humanity remained intact. Since quite often this was done by establishing a strong distinction or even a barrier between the divine and the human in Jesus Christ, the word "disjunctive" has become a standard way of describing it.

For the history of literature, which is our concern here, the main consequence of these new circumstances is that a good portion of the extant Christian Greek literature from the fifth century is highly polemical and sometimes even virulent. As each side sought to refine its position in response to critiques from its adversaries, the result was that Christology became increasingly subtle, less practical, and ever more difficult to relate to the Jesus who appears in the Gospels.

THEOPHILUS OF ALEXANDRIA

The beginnings of the debate may well be in the conflict between Theophilus of Alexandria and John Chrysostom. As we have seen, the latter was much more interested in preaching and in justice among Christians than in theological subtleties. But Chrysostom hailed from Antioch, and therefore when he was raised to the patriarchate of Constantinople, this caused great jealousy and resentment in Alexandria. Theophilus, the patriarch of Alexandria, soon became Chrysostom's main enemy, and the cause of many of his difficulties and sufferings. It was Theophilus who repeatedly accused Chrysostom not only of heresy, but also of sedition against imperial authority. It was also he who in 403 presided over a meeting known as the "Synod of the Oak," which declared Chrysostom a heretic and had him exiled.

Even in the writings of his defenders, Theophilus does not appear to be an admirable person. In his actions there is a good dose of political ambition and shady maneuvering. As an Alexandrian, he was a staunch defender of Origen until Origenism came under attack, at which point he became a decided opponent of the position he formerly held. On his initiative a synod gathered in Alexandria in 401, over which he presided, declaring Origen's teachings to be heretical. But even so, when a few years later he learned that Synesius of Cyrene, who had the imperial ear, had been made bishop of Pentapolis in Syria, he declared his support, even though Synesius was well known for defending some of the most extreme Origenist positions: for instance, he affirmed the preexistence of souls and the eternity of the world, while rejecting the doctrine of the resurrection of the body. But now this did not seem important to Theophilus because Synesius, besides being politically influential, was his personal friend.

Little remains of the writings of Theophilus. Besides some homilies, we have a few letters and fragments of others. Most of them include repeated attacks on his enemies, both in the theological and in the political arenas. He also wrote a treatise in which he proposed to set the dates of Easter for an entire century beginning in 380. He sent it to Emperor Theodosius, hoping that his proposal would be accepted as part of the imperial calendar, thus increasing the prestige both of Alexandria as an episcopal see and of Theophilus himself. But the emperor did not agree.

Several of the extant letters of Theophilus are simply the continuation of the established tradition that the bishop of Alexandria would write a circular letter on each Easter. Others are part of a brief correspondence with Jerome. The only one of his homilies still extant in the original Greek deals with the final judgment. Three others, as well as some fragments, exist only in an ancient translation into Coptic. His main work, a detailed attack on Origen, has been lost.

CYRIL OF ALEXANDRIA

Theophilus died in 412, and two days later his nephew Cyril succeeded him as patriarch of Alexandria. Cyril was much more careful than his uncle in his theological positions and much more scrupulous in his theological maneuvers. He was present at the Synod of the Oak that condemned Chrysostom, and his opposition to Antiochene theology was just as firm as Theophilus's. Therefore, although at first he did not center his attention on his opposition to Antiochene theology, he refused to add the name of Chrysostom to the dyptichs in Alexandria until 417, thus ten years after the death of the famous preacher. (In the church the word "dyptich," which originally referred to any writing on two hinged tablets, had come to mean the list of people for whom prayer was raised at communion. The action of erasing a name from the dyptichs was tantamount to breaking communion with that person.) But even so, for sixteen years the new patriarch of Alexandria focused his attention mostly on biblical studies and controversies against Arianism, Apollinarism, and other doctrines that the church had already rejected. He also wrote an extensive work *Against Julian*, of which only about a third is extant, but what remains is still a fairly large work in ten books.

Writings Not Related to the Nestorian Controversy

It was not until 428 that Cyril's focus of attention shifted away from biblical commentaries. It has correctly been said that if the Nestorian controversy had not eclipsed his hermeneutical works, Cyril would be highly respected as a commentator on Scripture. His early works show great literary ability, particularly in their style, and make him a master writer among Christian authors. From among his commentaries on the Old Testament, two are extant, one on Isaiah and the other on the Minor Prophets. They are extensive and detailed works in which Cyril studies the biblical text, frequently verse by verse. There are also fragments, and from these and various other sources we know that he also wrote commentaries on Kings, Psalms, Proverbs, the Song of Solomon, Jeremiah, Daniel, and Ezekiel. On the New Testament, he wrote a commentary on John, another on Luke—although this is actually a series of homilies, of which more than 150 have survived, mostly in Syriac translations—and a commentary on Matthew, of which only some fragments are extant. Of these, the *Commentary on John* seems to be the earliest: although clearly reflecting Alexandrine theology, there are no direct allusions here to Nestorius or to the controversy surrounding him. On the other hand, as is clear from extant fragments, the *Commentary on Matthew* was written after 428, when the controversy began.

Apparently during those early years Cyril's main concern was the refutation of Judaism and Arianism. The earliest among his extant works is *On the Worship of God in Spirit and in Truth*. It is a (probably fictitious) dialogue between Cyril and a certain Palladius. Despite its title, this is not a discussion of worship, but rather of the relationship between Christianity and the

Hebrew Scriptures. Palladius is concerned because Jesus says both that he has not come to abolish the law and that he has come to establish worship in spirit and truth. It is difficult to see how to deal with these two apparently contradictory sayings at once. Cyril's answer is based on the typological hermeneutics that we have found repeatedly. God certainly ordered worship as it is described in the Old Testament. But those practices and ceremonies were only a sign, figure, or "type" of what was to come. Thus the error of the Jews is not in believing that God did indeed establish the ancient ceremonies, but rather in not understanding that now that the reality has come, its sign or announcement is no longer necessary.

Cyril also dealt with the interpretation of the Old Testament in another of his works, *Glaphyra*, "beautiful things." This is a series of commentaries on various passages of the Pentateuch, particularly Genesis and Exodus. At the beginning of this writing we find words clearly showing that Cyril is an heir to Origen and to those who, after the great Alexandrian teacher, saw several levels of meaning in Scripture. He says, "We shall begin by explaining historical events in a useful and proper way. But we shall also draw out from that narrative what is a type or shadow, looking at it in a way that takes into account the mystery of Christ, and points to it" (*Glaphyra* 1.1; PG 69:16).

In all of these early writings of Cyril, there is a combination of literal, typological, and allegorical interpretations. Like Origen, Cyril frequently declares that the biblical text has a literal meaning that should not be set aside, but also a deeper allegorical and spiritual meaning.

As an example of this sort of interpretation, one may quote what he says in his *Commentary on the Twelve Prophets* regarding the words of Micah: "If the Assyrians come into our land and tread upon our soil, we will raise against them seven shepherds and eight installed as rulers. They shall rule the land of Assyria with the sword, and the land of Nimrod with the drawn sword; they shall rescue us from the Assyrians if they come into our land or tread within our border" (Mic. 5:5–6). After explaining who the Assyrians were and why Nimrod's name appears, Cyril says:

> Interpreting this verse, we see once again that its meaning goes beyond obvious material matters and rises to a higher level, so that the literal image makes clear what is taking place spiritually. Thus, when the prophet says "Assyrian," he is not referring only to those who come from Babylon, but actually to the very creator of sin, Satan. In short, the tireless host of demons opposes all that is holy and besieges the holy city, which is the spiritual Zion, the Church of the living God, an image of the spiritual Jerusalem. . . .
>
> Thus, when saying "the Assyrians come into our land," he is referring to the hostile and unfettered powers that struggle against the

saints. . . . Probably what the prophecy says about numbers seven and
eight refers to the people of God—first to those who live before the
incarnation, then to those who lived during it, and finally to those of
us who came later. We must take into account that before the incarnation, in the Law of Moses, rest on the seventh day received particular
attention. But it was a time of figures and shadows. The whole body
of the holy prophets were raised as a guide to faith and the knowledge
of God. But then the Only-begotten came and suffered on the cross
for our benefit, so after defeating the powers of hell, he came back to
life on the eighth day. . . .

We see the hosts of demons being destroyed by Christ so that
they would no longer oppress the earth under the sun, as before the
incarnation. Now they are in their proper place, held back by the
good conduct of the saints, and therefore excluded from the land of
the saints, who therefore can live peacefully, and thus do what pleases
God following the path that He illumines. (*Comm. Twelve Proph.*,
Mic. 5:5–6; PG 71:718–19)

Cyril uses this as part of his answer to the challenge that Judaism still
raised. At the same time, he was also concerned over the persistence of Arianism, which had now come to extreme expressions. This can be seen in
his entire *Commentary on St. John*, where Cyril begins commenting on the
words "in the beginning was the Word" in the prologue of that Gospel:
"There can be nothing before the beginning, unless we change the meaning of the very word 'beginning.' . . . Therefore, one cannot say that the
Only-begotten has any beginning that is in any way related to time. The
Only-begotten exists before all ages. For the same reason his divinity will
not allow him to have an end, for he shall always be the same" (*Comm. John*
1.1; PG 73:24–25).

Cyril and the Nestorian Controversy

Leaving aside the details of the early development of the controversy, one
may say that it began in 428 and centered on the question of whether it was
legitimate to call Mary the *Theotokos*, "Mother of God." Since this title may
create confusion among modern readers, it must be clarified. What was at
stake was not primarily the dignity of Mary, as today when one speaks of Mary
as "Mother of God." The issue was christological, and the debate concerned
to what degree the union of divinity and humanity in Jesus Christ is such that
one can ascribe to the divinity whatever can be said of the humanity. Literally, the Greek word *Theotokos* does not mean "mother of God," but rather
"bearer of God." In other words, the question was not so much about Mary
as it was about whether one can say that the one who was born from her is

God. Naturally, the manner in which one responds to this question has to do with the differences that have repeatedly been noted between the unitive Christology of the Alexandrians and the disjunctive one of the Antiochenes. For the former, what was most important was the absolute union of divinity and humanity in Jesus Christ. That unity must be such that anything one can say about the man Jesus is also said about God. Thus, one must affirm that God was born in Bethlehem and walked in Galilee, even though this does not imply that God did not exist before being born in Bethlehem nor that when he walked in Galilee he was absent from the rest of the world. This principle that whatever can be said about the humanity of Jesus must be said also about his divinity has come to be known as the "transference of properties" or, in the traditional Latin phrase, the *communicatio idiomatum*. By virtue of the incarnation, according to this principle, the divine and human are so joined in Jesus Christ that whatever one says of the one may be said of the other. Therefore, the declaration that Mary is Theotokos, or that God was born from her, is perfectly orthodox.

In contrast with that position, the disjunctive Christology of the Antiochenes sought to safeguard the complete humanity of Jesus by establishing a distinction between that humanity and his divinity in such a way that some things may be said about the one, and some about the other. As we shall see in our next chapter, up to that time Antiochene theologians had not expressed doubts about the title of Theotokos as applied to Mary. Yet Nestorius was concerned about it, and as patriarch of Constantinople he supported those who objected to that title.

It was news from Constantinople that led Cyril to write his most influential theological works, all directed against Nestorianism and in defense of the title Theotokos, although, ironically, in all of his works before the beginning of that controversy that title appears only once. Upon learning of the opposition of Nestorius to the practice of calling Mary Theotokos, Cyril wrote several letters, at first most of them addressed to the Egyptian monks, warning them about the errors of Antiochene theology. He also wrote a work in five books *Against the Blasphemies of Nestorius*, although this is a title given to this writing at a later time, for the work itself does not address Nestorius personally, but only tries to refute his doctrines. From the beginning Cyril clearly expresses his objections to the christological views prevalent in Antioch:

> They tear apart the unity of the one Lord Jesus Christ, dividing him into two different sons, denying God the Word the sufferings of the flesh. . . . Furthermore, there is another important consideration having to do with us who live on earth and for whom the Word of God took flesh and became human. Had he not been born like us

according to the flesh, had he not shared in the same conditions of which we share, he would not have been able to free human nature from the sin of Adam, nor would he have been able to undo the corruption of our bodies, nor could he have put an end to the curse from the first woman. (*Ag. Blasph. Nestorius* 1.1; PG 76:17, 21)

Since Cyril is not concerned only over the titles that may be given to Mary, but also and above all over the unity of the incarnate Lord, after devoting the first book to the defense of the title of Theotokos, in the other four he deals mostly with the dangers of an excessive distinction between humanity and divinity in Jesus Christ.

At the same time, Cyril took practical action against Nestorius and his Christology. He addressed to Emperor Theodosius II a treatise *On the Proper Faith*, warning him about the teachings of Nestorius, for he feared that the emperor, living in Constantinople, would be influenced by the patriarch of the city. He also wrote directly to Nestorius. In his first letter, upon hearing that Nestorius was annoyed by what Cyril had said and done, Cyril wrote to tell him first of all that it was Nestorius, and not Cyril, who created the controversy, and also that Nestorius must not blame Cyril personally for having intervened, for the discussion has become widespread, and even in Rome Bishop Celestine is concerned. Nestorius responded with an angry letter, threatening Cyril with grave consequences. He also made certain that preaching in the great cathedral of St. Sophia would focus on the matter and explicitly reject the title of Theotokos. In response, Cyril moved to obtain as much support from others as he could and wrote Nestorius, telling him that he had been misinformed, but at the same time reaffirming and underscoring the essential elements of Alexandrian Christology, while complaining that Nestorius had sheltered certain heretics who had fled from Alexandria. He then wrote a third letter in which he called on him to "leave aside the absolutely evil and distorted doctrines that you now hold and in their place affirm the Orthodox faith that the holy apostles and evangelists bequeathed to the church" (*Third Letter to Nestorius*; PG 77:53). And at the end of the letter he demands that Nestorius accept and affirm a series of twelve anathemas. From the point of view of the history of literature, the contrast between these twelve anathemas and what Cyril had written before the Nestorian controversy is remarkable. What had earlier been a clear and elegant style now becomes heavy, lacking in elegance, and often difficult to understand. These twelve anathemas, which became crucial in the rest of the controversy, were these:

1. If anyone does not affirm that Emmanuel is true God, and that therefore the Virgin is mother of God, . . . let him be anathema.

2. If anyone does not affirm that the Word of God the Father has been sub-stantially united to flesh and is one Christ jointly with his own flesh, who is both God and human, let him be anathema.

3. If anyone divides the hypostases of the one Christ after the union, join-ing them only as a conjunction . . . and not as a true union, let him be anathema.

4. If anyone divides in the Gospels and in the apostolic writings what is said about Christ, . . . and ascribes it to two persons or subjects so that some things may be applied to the human separately from the Word of God, and others only to the Word of God the Father, let him be anathema.

5. If anyone dares say that Christ is an inspired man rather than the true God and the Only-begotten Son, who became flesh and shared in our flesh and blood, let him be anathema.

6. If anyone dares say that the Word of God the Father is the God of Christ or his Lord, rather than affirming that this one Christ is at the same time divine and human, because Scripture affirms that the Word of God became flesh, let him be anathema.

7. If anyone says that the man Jesus was under the control of God the Word, and that to the glory of the Only-begotten something else is to be added that is not the Only-begotten himself, let him be anathema.

8. If anyone declares that the human being assumed in Christ is to be wor-shiped jointly with God and with the Word . . . rather than worshiping Emmanuel with a single worship and a single act of praise because the Word has been made flesh, let him be anathema.

9. If anyone says that the one Lord Jesus Christ has been glorified by the Spirit, so that it is by the power of the Spirit as something alien received from another that Christ is capable of acting against the demons and per-forming miracles upon humans, rather than saying that the Spirit by which he performed miracles belongs to the same Christ, let him be anathema.

10. Divine Scripture affirms that Christ has been made high priest. . . . Therefore, if anyone says that it is not the very Word of God who has been made our high priest and apostle in becoming flesh and human like us, but speaks also about a man born of woman who is not the Word, . . . let him be anathema.

11. Whoever does not affirm that the flesh of the Lord gives life, and that this flesh is that of the very Word of God the Father, but says that it actually belongs to someone different who has been joined to him by reason of merit, or simply because divinity dwells in him, . . . let him be anathema.

12. If anyone does not affirm that the Word of God suffered in the flesh, was crucified in the flesh, tasted death in the flesh, and has come to be the first begotten from among the dead because as God that he is life and gives life, let him be anathema. (*Explanation of the Twelve Chapters*; PG 76:296–312)

However, it is not only because of its style that this third letter to Nesto-rius and the accompanying anathemas are a turning point in the life of Cyril. The Council of Ephesus, convened in the hope of reaching an agreement on the point at issue, had the contrary effect. In the end there were two councils gathering at Ephesus, one presided over by Cyril and the other by John of Antioch, each condemning the other and declaring its leaders to be heretics. Since an agreement was not reached, imperial authorities intervened, and for a while the leaders of each side were in prison. This led to a process of negotiation and forced reconciliation and to a Formula of Reunion in 433. For some time, Cyril had to tone down his positions. This may be seen in his *Explanation of the Twelve Chapters*, whose main purpose was to convince the authorities and some more moderate bishops who criticized the anathemas that their purpose was simply to reject the excesses of Nestorius. In order to do so, he does much of what today we would call "double-talk."

The apparent reconciliation between Cyril and the Antiochene theologians would soon break down. On a visit to Jerusalem in 438, Cyril noted the influence in that area of some Antiochene theologians even before Nestorius. These were particularly Diodore of Tarsus and Theodore of Mopsuestia, who will be discussed in our next chapter. After returning to Alexandria, Cyril began writing against these two men, who were highly respected among the Antiochenes. Toward the end of his life he wrote an important treatise, *Christ Is One*, in which he once again made use of his stylistic ability; this treatise is considered not only his most mature work but also his most elegant. Although directed against Nestorius, this work repeatedly accuses Diodore and Theodore of being the true forerunners and creators of Nestorianism. Cyril died in 444, shortly after completing this treatise, but this and others among his writings contributed to a prolonged and heated controversy that more than a hundred years later would lead to the Second Council of Constantinople (553), which rejected the works and teachings of Diodore and Theodore as well as those of Ibas of Edessa. But this would take us far beyond the limits of the present chapter.

AN ONGOING TRADITION

The council of 451 was simply one more landmark in the long history of Alexandrian theology. When, in that Council of Chalcedon, the most extreme Alexandrians were condemned and their leader Dioscorus was deposed, this did not spell the end of the Alexandrian christological tradition. Many in Egypt considered the Council of Chalcedon an imperial imposition, and therefore among the Coptic people of the land, Dioscorus became a great hero. Soon the Coptic Church broke away from the rest of the church, naming its own patriarch of Alexandria. In response, the imperial church called these Copts "Monophysites." From Egypt, that form of Monophysitism passed on to Ethiopia. Something similar happened in some areas of Syria, where another Monophysite church arose. Armenia, one of the areas where Christianity had taken root in a very early time, was invaded by the Persians precisely as the Council of Chalcedon was being convoked and therefore was not represented there. Also, even though the Byzantine Empire promised help, such help never arrived, and the church in Armenia also became Monophysite. These various churches have continued existing up to this day.

30

The Antiochenes

Early in the preceding chapter we summarized some of the theological and political reasons for friction between Alexandria and Antioch. As we saw, the conflict between John Chrysostom and Theophilus of Alexandria was mostly due to those tensions. Chrysostom is indeed the best known and most influential expression of the Antiochene school and its theology, even though he did not attack Alexandrian theology as vigorously as the other Antiochenes. Already during the lifetime of Chrysostom, there were other Antiochenes whose theological positions, expressed in fairly radical ways, provoked the ire and the attacks of Alexandrian theologians. Furthermore, even from a much earlier date, while the Arian controversy was still raging, there were notable differences between Antiochene and Alexandrian theologians. At that time the great teacher of the Antiochene school of theology was Lucian, and this is why Arius, upon being condemned by Alexander of Alexandria, wrote to those whose support he expected, calling them "fellow Lucianists." But Lucian wrote little, and what he did write has been lost. We do know that he dedicated himself to the detailed study of the Greek text both of the Old Testament and of the New, and he insisted on the literal meaning of such texts. But, since we cannot say much about Lucian, the earliest author of the christological school of Antioch whom we can study is Diodore of Tarsus.

DIODORE OF TARSUS

When John Chrysostom and Theodore of Mopsuestia—whom we shall discuss later in this chapter—decided to devote themselves to monastic life, they did this under the direction of the already-famous Diodore, who would later become bishop of Tarsus. Although Diodore wrote abundantly, all that we have from him is his *Commentary on Psalms 1–51*. Historian Socrates Scholasticus tells us that he "wrote many treatises, in which he limited his attention to the literal sense of scripture, avoiding that which was mystical" (*Ch. Hist.* 6.5; *NPNF*² 2:138). But the loss of his work seems to have begun quite early, for already in the fifth century historian Sozomen, referring to Diodore, reports, "I have been informed [that he] left many books in his own writings in which he explained the significance of the sacred words and avoided allegory" (*Ch. Hist.* 8.2; *NPNF*² 2:399). In any case, among the fragments that have been preserved we find Diodore declaring, "We prefer the historical over the allegorical."

Diodore was a representative of the school of Antioch not only in that which refers to biblical interpretation, but also in his Christology. He was a firm opponent of Alexandrian Christology, which seemed to him to undo or obscure the full humanity of Christ. In response, Cyril of Alexandria wrote a book against both him and Theodore of Mopsuestia, claiming that what Nestorius taught was simply the continuation of the teachings of Diodore and Theodore. As a result, years after his death Diodore was declared a heretic— which is one of the reasons why his works have been lost. This is particularly tragic since Diodore had been one of the great defenders of Christianity against the campaign of Emperor Julian to restore paganism.

THEODORE OF MOPSUESTIA

Little is known of the life of Theodore of Mopsuestia, and much of what ancient documents tell us about him was written either to defend him or to accuse him of heresy. He was born near the year 350 and died around 428. Theodore was a contemporary and a friend of John Chrysostom, with whom he was a fellow student under Libanius. Together with John, he turned to monastic life under the direction of Diodore of Tarsus. When he temporarily abandoned that life, Chrysostom wrote *To Theodore after His Fall* (on which see chap. 28). Theodore was little more than forty years old when he became bishop of Mopsuestia, a position that he occupied until his death.

Theodore's writings dealt mostly with the interpretation of Scripture, and therefore he was frequently known as "the Interpreter." One of his main works was a commentary on Genesis, now lost. Fortunately, a century later John Philoponus quoted him so extensively that it is possible to reconstruct much of the lost commentary. There are also extant fragments of his writings on Exodus, Judges, and other books of the Old Testament. In spite of such serious losses, we still have his *Commentary on the Twelve Prophets* and his *Commentary on Psalms.* There is also a Syriac translation of his *Commentary on the Gospel of John*, and a Latin version of his *Commentary on Paul's Lesser Epistles.* Only fragments remain of his commentary on the four main epistles of Paul.

Apart from his exegetical writings, the main extant work of Theodore is a series of sixteen *Catechetical Homilies* that follow an order similar to that of Cyril of Jerusalem on the same subject. They were rediscovered early in the twentieth century in a Syriac version. Jointly with Cyril's and other similar works, these homilies are a valuable source for understanding both the catechesis and the baptismal and eucharistic liturgies of the time. There also are many quotations from his works on the subjects that were then debated; but such quotations, often recorded by his enemies, do not provide a trustworthy or balanced view of his theology.

Back on the subject of Theodore's work as a biblical interpreter, one can say that his *Commentary on Psalms* is a good example of his exegetical method, which is essentially historical. Since he was convinced that David was the author of all the psalms in the book of Psalms, he tried to place them within the context of the life and time of David. When some of the psalms obviously refer to events or conditions of later dates, Theodore simply declares that David was prophesying about the future.

His exegetical method is most clearly seen in his *Commentary on the Twelve Prophets* and may be illustrated by contrasting the different ways in which Cyril of Alexandria and Theodore interpret the first verses of Joel. After acknowledging that Israel was repeatedly invaded, Cyril says:

> If you wish to find a moral meaning in these stories you do not err. This means that the soul is frequently attacked by passion and is on the verge of losing every virtue. It falls under these repeated attacks by reason of its indifference, and this is why the prophet says: "What the cutting locust left, the swarming locust has eaten. What the swarming locust left, the hopping locust has eaten, and what the hopping locust left, the destroying locust has eaten." The evil and unclean powers that attack our mind so and endlessly chew on it harm us as much as any disease. (*Comm. Twelve Prophets,* Joel 1:4; PG 71:332–33)

In contrast, on the same passage Theodore comments:

> He wishes to warn them of the coming evil in a symbolic manner. As usual, those who come later are worse than the earlier ones. The king of Assyria, Tiglath-Pileser [III], came as a locust, and destroyed much of what you had. Then came Shalmaneser, as another locust eating what remained. He was followed by Sennacherib, like a new locust who did great damage among the twelve tribes of Israel. And then as another epidemic came the attack of the Babylonians, who took the people of Judah into slavery. (*Comm. Twelve Prophets,* Joel 1:4; PG 66:213)

The contrast between these two interpretations shows the nature of Theodore's exegetical method, which is historical and cleaves to the text as much as possible. He often speaks of the "mythologists," who are ignorant of both sacred and profane history, do not understand what they are reading, and therefore give it whatever meaning pleases them. This must have been more clearly explained in his unfortunately lost treatise *Against the Allegorists*. We do know, however, that he allowed for a distinction between the ignorant "mythologists" and the allegorists, who do have knowledge, but instead of employing it to understand the text itself, use it to go after hidden mystical meanings.

NESTORIUS

Antiochene Christology led to the tragic story of Nestorius, who became patriarch of Constantinople in 428. Since for a long time Alexandrians and Antiochenes had vied for the possession of that important post, the mere fact that Nestorius was an Antiochene was sufficient reason to expect the Alexandrians to oppose him. But such opposition came to a head as Nestorius exaggerated the emphases of Antiochene Christology and thus made himself vulnerable to accusations from the Alexandrians. The debate centered on the title of Theotokos as given to the Virgin Mary. As already stated, the issue was not so much one of Mariology as it was one of Christology, focusing on the nature of the union of divinity and humanity that took place in Jesus Christ. The Alexandrians' unitive Christology led them to insist that all that can be said about the humanity of Christ can also be said about his divinity. On their part, the Antiochenes, seeking to safeguard the full humanity of Jesus, held that it was necessary to separate his humanity and his divinity, so that the former will not be overwhelmed by the latter. In other words, what was being discussed was what theologians call the *communicatio idiomatum*: the possibility of transferring what is said about one of the two natures to the other. The question was this: The one who was born of Mary, was he God, or not? The Alexandrians said "yes," but Nestorius insisted that rather than saying that God was born of Mary, one must say that it was Christ who was born of Mary. While this was a clear consequence of Antiochene Christology, Nestorius was going further than his predecessors, for Antiochene theologians such as Theodore of Mopsuestia had clearly stated that the one who was born from Mary was God.

Leaving aside the theological subtleties and the political maneuvers involved in the controversy, we may say that Nestorius was declared a heretic by the Council of Ephesus in 431. Since John, the patriarch of Antioch, defended him and presided over a rival council, the debate was long and difficult. At the end Antiochenes and Alexandrians agreed that Nestorius had erred and was correctly deposed, and Nestorius himself was forced to retire first to a monastery in Syria and later to a distant oasis in the Egyptian desert.

In that entire process, for a number of reasons having to do with his own political advisers as well as with Cyril's maneuvers, Emperor Theodosius II was firmly opposed to Nestorius. In 435, four years after the Council of Ephesus, an imperial order was issued to the effect that all the works of Nestorius must be destroyed and that they were not to be read, copied, or preserved. It is therefore not surprising that most of what Nestorius wrote has been lost. We know, for instance, that he wrote a treatise *Against the Theopaschites*, that is, the Alexandrians who claimed not only that God was born in Jesus, but also that God had suffered in him. Of his many sermons, apparently only four have survived, mostly because they were erroneously included among the sermons of John Chrysostom. There are also some of his letters, not only in their Greek original, but also in Latin and in Syriac translations. Given their suppression within the Roman Empire, many of Nestorius's followers sought refuge beyond its borders, where Syriac was commonly spoken. For this reason, most of what survives of the writings of Nestorius exists only in Syriac translations.

Late in the nineteenth century a Syriac translation of Nestorius's last work, *The Bazaar of Heraclides*, was discovered. He wrote this late in 451 or early in the following year. In 451, the Council of Chalcedon met, and the Antiochenes had a partial victory in that some of the extreme Alexandrian positions were condemned. Dioscorus, the patriarch of Alexandria who had succeeded Cyril, fled before being declared a heretic. When Nestorius wrote the *Bazaar*, he seems to have known of the flight of Dioscorus, but not of the final decision of the council. However, he was convinced that the news from Chalcedon vindicated him. In the previous year, Theodosius had died in an accident, and Nestorius was also convinced that this was a divine punishment. The extant Syriac translation of the *Bazaar* seems to have been produced around 535.

At the beginning of this manuscript the translator into Syriac tries to explain the strange title of the writing, saying that it is a "bazaar of spiritual knowledge." As to "Heraclides," the translator supposes that it must have been somebody who lived near Damascus and was famous for his virtues and impartiality. This is followed by an outline in which the translator summarizes the content of the entire work:

> Now in the first place he [Nestorius] composed one dissertation wherein he speaks of all the heresies against the Church and of all the sects that exist concerning the faith of the three hundred and eighteen [the Council of Nicaea], arguing valiantly against those who are of greatest repute among them. And in the second part he assails Cyril,

putting before [everything else] the inquiry touching the judges and the accusation of Cyril. And the third [contains] his own defense and the comparison of their letters; and with this he finishes the first book. But the second book he divides into two parts: the defence and the refutation of the blame for the things on account of which he was anathematized; and in the second [part he recounts that which took place] from [the time] when he was anathematized until the end of his life. (*Bazaar of Heracleides*, proemium [ed. G. R. Driver, Oxford: Calendon, 1925], 5–6)

Here it is not necessary to enter into the details of Nestorius's Christology, for it is a subject having to do with the history of Christian thought, which I have discussed elsewhere. As literature, the *Bazaar* is a diatribe mostly against Cyril, but also against Emperor Theodosius II. As to Cyril, Nestorius complains that he was never allowed to defend himself, for Cyril had decided beforehand that he was his enemy. On the Council of Ephesus, he says:

If then he [Cyril] was on the bench of judges, what indeed shall I say of the bench of judges? He was the whole tribunal, for everything which he said they all said together, and without doubt it is certain that he in person took the place of a tribunal for them. For if all the judges had been assembled and the accusers had risen in their place and the accused also likewise, all of them would equally have had freedom of speech, instead of his being in everything both accuser and emperor and judge. He did all things with authority, after excluding from authority him who had been charged by the emperor, and he exalted himself; and he assembled all those whom he wanted, both those who were far off and those who were near, and he constituted himself the tribunal. And I was summoned by Cyril who had assembled the Council, even by Cyril who was the chief thereof. Who was judge? Cyril. And who was the accuser? Cyril. Who was bishop of Rome? Cyril. Cyril was everything. (*Bazaar of Heracleides* 2.1, p. 132)

And Nestorius ends his book with bitter words about Theodosius II, implying that all the misfortunes of that emperor and of the empire itself were at least partly due to the injustices done against Nestorius not only by Cyril and Theodosius, but also by Leo the Great, who even though holding the correct doctrine did not come to the aid of Nestorius:

As you know, you first saw the death of the ruler's daughter, and then saw the great demon of adultery take possession of the Empress with perverse insult. And you saw that the cities of Africa and Spain . . . and even Rome itself were sacked by the Vandal barbarians, . . . and soon will the barbarian come back to Rome, and then Leo, who certainly held to the correct doctrine, but agreed to the injustices committed against me without examination or trial, with his own hands will have to turn the sacred vessels of the sanctuary into the hands of the barbarians. . . .

As for me, I have suffered the torments of my life as if they were only of one day. And now that the time comes for me to be undone [to die] I daily ask God for me to be dissolved, for my eyes have seen the salvation of God. Oh, desert, rejoice over me! You are now my adopted father where I live, you are my mother in my exile, and after I die you will keep my body unto the resurrection thanks to the will of God. Amen. (*Bazaar of Heracleides* 2.2, pp. 379–80)

IBAS OF EDESSA

Another of the main exponents of Antiochene theology was Ibas, who became bishop of Edessa in 435, thus four years after the Council of Ephesus. His election was disputed, and eventually he was accused of heresy before Theodosius II. His main extant work is a letter that he wrote to a certain Mari in Persia, about whom little is known, but who seems to have headed the church in that land. This letter, written in 433, when, thanks to the Formula of Reunion, a certain measure of peace had temporarily been reached between the Alexandrians and the Antiochenes, defended the position of the Antiochenes, and also had harsh words for the role and actions of the Alexandrians, particularly of Cyril, at the Council of Ephesus. In the process that led to the "robbers' synod" of Ephesus in 449, this letter was often employed by the enemies of Ibas as proof of his heresy. In that council of 449, completely controlled by Dioscorus and by Emperor Theodosius II, the main Antiochene theologians were declared heretics and deposed. This included, besides Ibas, Theodoret of Cyrus, another of the main exponents of Antiochene theology.

THEODORET OF CYRUS

There is no doubt that the outstanding scholar and theologian within the Antiochene tradition after Theodore of Mopsuestia was Theodoret of Cyrus. Born in Antioch late in the fourth century, Theodoret was an avid scholar from his youth: he was well versed not only in Greek and Syriac, but also in Hebrew, and probably could also deal with Latin. He claims to have been a disciple of both Theodore of Mopsuestia and Diodore of Tarsus, although quite likely this does not mean that he had a direct relationship with them but rather that he learned from them by reading their writings. He was some thirty years old when he was elected bishop of Cyrus, a small city in Syria.

There he had a distinguished career as an administrator and as shepherd of his flock.

Theodoret was meeting with other nearby bishops in Antioch when letters arrived from Cyril and from Celestine, the bishop of Rome, regarding the teachings of Nestorius. The bishops gathered in Antioch wrote to Nestorius, urging him to accept the term Theotokos, which was at the heart of the controversy. Scholars consider quite likely that this letter was written by Theodoret. But then Cyril published his *Third Letter to Nestorius*, with its twelve anathemas. Both in tone and in content this amounted to a declaration of war on Antiochene theology. John, the bishop of Antioch, forwarded Cyril's anathemas to Theodoret and asked him to refute them. Theodoret wrote a *Refutation of the Anathemas of Cyril* and sent it to John with a cover letter. In that letter he spoke of his anguish at seeing the church divided, and also of the damage that the flock was suffering because of what he considered Cyril's errors. Theodoret tells John:

> I am desolate upon reading the anathemas that you have sent me asking that I refute them in writing, and make clear their heresy. It pains me to think that someone who has been made a shepherd, and has been placed in charge of such a great flock in order to heal the sick sheep, is himself ill, and seeks to infect his flock with the same disease. He is destroying the sheep in his flock with even greater cruelty than wild beasts. These attack and wound the sheep that are scattered and away from the flock. But he is in the midst of the flock itself, and while he presents himself as their guardian and savior, he secretly brings error to those who trust him. It is possible to prepare against an attack from outside. But when the attack comes disguised as friendship, the victim is unready and easily harmed. The enemies attacking from inside are much more dangerous than those who attack from outside. (*Ep.* 50; PG 83:1414)

This resulted in an implacable enmity between Theodoret and Cyril that lasted until the death of the latter in 444. Cyril's successor, Dioscorus, not only held the same opinions, but was quite ready to take all sorts of actions in order to achieve the final condemnation of all Antiochenes. Through a series of maneuvers, he was named to preside over the council gathered at Ephesus in 449 that Leo the Great called the "robbers' synod" of Ephesus. There Theodoret was deposed, as were also Ibas of Edessa and all the other leaders of the Antiochene party. So matters stood until Theodore II, who supported Dioscorus, fell from his horse and died. Leo the Great urged the new ruler, Empress Pulcheria, to convoke a new council. This gathered in Chalcedon in 451 and undid what had been done two years earlier at Ephesus. Theodoret, now absolved of heresy, spent the rest of his life studying and writing, while enjoying the respect not only of the other Antiochenes, but also of many of the more moderate elements in the opposite party. He seems to have lived at least until 458, but the exact date of his death is unknown.

The writings of Theodoret are numerous. We have more than two hundred letters from him, while of his sermons all that we have are fragments quoted by others. Because of the christological controversies, his dogmatic writings have been much more studied than the rest. Even so, many of his dogmatic writings have been lost, because in the following century, in 553, the Second Council of Constantinople declared his teachings heretical, and after that time his writings no longer circulated widely. Most of those that have survived did so because they were erroneously attributed to another writer. The already-mentioned *Refutation of the Anathemas of Cyril* has been lost, but ironically it is possible to reconstruct it because in response Cyril quoted Theodoret extensively. This writing marks the entry of Theodoret into the christological controversy. He then wrote an extensive criticism of Cyril's theology, *Pentalogion*, of which only fragments are extant. As a further irony, two of Theodoret's theological works, *On the Holy Trinity* and *On the Incarnation of the Lord*, have survived because for a time they were attributed to Cyril! But today scholars agree that they are really the work of Theodoret. Similarly, several others of his works have survived by being attributed to others. Of these the most important is his *Exposition of the True Doctrine*. There is also a series of sixty-one *Questions and Answers for the Orthodox* that some believe is his.

Theodore's most important theological work is *The Beggar*, usually quoted under its Greek title, *Eranistes*. Theodore refers to the extreme Alexandrians as beggars who have collected little bits from other heretics here and there. The writing is presented as a long dialogue between a beggar (a Monophysite) and an orthodox believer. After three books devoted to this dialogue, the fourth is a systematic summary of the preceding. The core of the argument is the relationship between God's immutability and the humanity of Christ. As a typical Antiochene theologian, Theodoret wishes to make sure that the humanity of the Savior is not eclipsed by his divinity and therefore insists on the distinction between the two. Thus, in the final summary he says: "If Christ is both divine and human, as we are taught by Holy Scripture and the illustrious fathers have always preached, then he suffered as a man; but as God he remained impassible" (*Beggar* 4.2.13; PG 13:231).

Theodoret also wrote an important apologetic work, a series of *Speeches on Providence*, of which ten are extant. In these speeches or sermons, he compares Greek philosophy with Christian doctrine, seeking to show the superiority of the latter.

Although most often Theodoret is studied because of his participation in the christological debates, he was above all an exegete and an interpreter of

Scriptures. Probably the most influential of his works in this direction was his commentary on Genesis, which was followed by three others on Joshua, Judges, and Ruth—all of which have survived and often are called *Discussions on the Octateuch*. He also wrote similar works on the books of Kings and Chronicles, as well as on the Psalms, the Song of Solomon, as well as on various prophets. Among the books in the New Testament, he focused particularly on the epistles of Paul.

In these works, despite his Antiochene tradition, Theodore does not hesitate to make use of allegory when it seems appropriate. Thus, for instance, he interprets Psalm 23 by relating it with the work of Christ as well as with baptism and communion:

> This Psalm represents the joy of the nations whom he shepherds. It describes the mystical feast that their shepherd has prepared for them. . . . Those who eat of this saving meal proclaim: "The Lord is my shepherd, I shall not want. He makes me lie down in green pastures." After calling the one who provides all that is good a shepherd, it was also fitting to speak metaphorically about the food of the sheep. What is here called "pastures" is the sacred teaching of the divine words, which first instruct us with the word and then feed us with the mystical food.
>
> "He leads me beside still waters": this points to the water of the new birth, in which the baptized receives grace, is rid of the senility of sin, and becomes a youth rather than an old person. (*Comm. Psalms*, Ps. 23:1–2; PG 18:1025)

Having said all this, it is important to stress that Theodoret was also a historian. His *History of Heresies*, in five books, is a summary of all heresies, beginning with biblical times and leading up to Theodoret's own time. His *History of Monasticism* is actually a series of biographical data and anecdotes about thirty-one persons, three of them women, who led an ascetic life in Cyrus and the neighboring area.

There is no doubt that Theodoret's most important historical work is his *Church History*, which he wrote while he was in exile after the "robbers' synod" of Ephesus. In his prologue to this writing, while beautifully describing the task of a historian, he also declares himself a successor of Eusebius of Caesarea, intending to continue the work of that great historian:

> When artists paint on panels and on walls the events of ancient history, they alike delight the eye, and keep bright for many a year the memory of the past. Historians substitute books for panels, bright description for pigments, and thus render the memory of past events both stronger and more permanent, for the painter's art is ruined by time. For this reason I too shall attempt to record in writing events in

ecclesiastical history hitherto omitted, deeming it indeed not right to look on without an effort while oblivion robs noble deeds and useful stories of their due fame. For this cause too I have been frequently urged by friends to undertake this work. But when I compare my own powers with the magnitude of the undertaking, I shrink from attempting it. Trusting, however, in the bounty of the Giver of all good, I enter upon a task beyond my own strength.

Eusebius of Palestine has written a history of the Church from the time of the holy Apostles to the reign of Constantine, the prince beloved of God. I shall begin my history from the period at which his terminates. (*Ch. Hist.* 1, prologue; *NPNF*[2] 3:33)

But no historian is absolutely objective, for the narrative itself always has a purpose. Part of Theodoret's purpose becomes clear when we see that his history ends with words of praise for Theodore of Mopsuestia and Diodore of Tarsus:

When the divine Theodorus was ruling the church of Antioch, Theodorus, bishop of Mopsuestia, a doctor of the whole church and successful combatant against every heretical phalanx, ended this life. He had enjoyed the teaching of the great Diodorus, and was the friend and fellow-worker of the holy John, for they both together benefitted by the spiritual draughts given by Diodorus. Six-and-thirty years he had spent in his bishopric, fighting against the forces of Arius and Eunomius, struggling against the piratical band of Apollinarius, and finding the best pasture for God's sheep. (*Ch. Hist.* 5.39; *NPNF*[2] 3:159)

AN ONGOING TRADITION

The decisions of Chalcedon did not end the debate. On the contrary, just as the Alexandrian tradition continued in a number of churches that broke away from Greek Orthodoxy, something similar, although not as widespread, happened with the Antiochene tradition. Since many of its leaders at various points felt persecuted, or at least excluded, they crossed the border northeastward to settle in the city of Nisibis, where they established a school whose disciples soon spread throughout the Persian Empire. To this day there are still in the Middle East believers calling themselves "Assyrians" whose historical roots go back to the great Antiochene teachers.

31

Further Horizons

Most of the authors we have been studying up to this point wrote in Latin or in Greek, the two main languages of the Roman Empire. But by the time we are now studying, and somewhat earlier, the Christian faith has been making headway among other peoples and other languages.

As stated above, in the fourth century Ulfilas, or Wulfila—"little wolf"—served as a missionary among the Goths beyond the Danube, and as part of his labors he developed an alphabet for the language of the Goths, into which he then translated Scripture. However, since the Goths soon settled within the borders of the Roman Empire and became culturally assimilated, they did not produce an extensive literature in their ancestral language.

It was mostly toward the east and south, in Persia and Egypt, that Christianity began developing literature in other languages. In the East, particularly beyond the borders of the Roman Empire, the Syriac language was widespread. Since this was also the language of many Christians in Syria, the church there served as a bridge for an extensive missionary work that eventually would reach India and even China. Some of this literature has already been mentioned, such as the work of Aphrahat and of Ephraim the Syrian. But it was in the fifth century that the Syriac church gave rise to an extensive literature, so that by the end of the century that literature was entering its golden age. A contemporary of Augustine, Philoxenus of Mabbugh (Mabbug), produced a translation of the Bible as well as several biblical commentaries, but only fragments remain of his works, mostly from his commentary on Matthew.

Narses was born around 440 in a village near Mosul. For some time he lived and taught within the borders of the Byzantine Empire. But when Emperor Zeno ordered his school closed, he moved to Nisibis, which now became the center for the theological tradition whose enemies dubbed "Nestorian." He wrote commentaries on many books of the Old Testament, but most of these have been lost. On the basis of the extant fragments, it is possible to affirm that, as was to be expected given his Antiochene roots, he was primarily interested in the grammatical and literal sense of the biblical text, and from there would move to a typological interpretation that did not deny the historicity of the text itself. This may be seen, for instance, in his commentary regarding the sacrifice of Isaac, which Narses studies first of all to clarify the literal sense of each phrase and then to show how that history of Isaac pointed toward Jesus Christ. Narses also left a record of what took place at the Council of Ephesus in 431, which many historians believe to be more factual than what became the generally accepted story within the Orthodox Church and which raises serious questions about the behavior of Cyril. He also wrote a number of homilies and hymns, many of which are still extant and earned him the title of "Harp of the Spirit."

Possibly the most important early Christian writer in Syriac was Babai the Great, who lived late in the sixth century and early in the seventh and wrote some eighty books, including several biblical commentaries and lives of saints. His most important work is the *Book on the Union*, which is a defense of Antiochene Christology, for which Nestorius had been condemned. Quoting one of his hymns should suffice to show his adherence to Antiochene Christology, with its clear distinction between the humanity and divinity of Christ:

> One is Christ the Son of God, worshipped by all in two natures. In his Godhead begotten of the Father without beginning before all time: in his manhood born of Mary, in the fullness of time, in a united body. Neither his Godhead was of the nature of the mother, nor his manhood of the nature of the Father. The natures are preserved in their essences in one person of one sonship. *Hymn of Praise (Teshbokhta)*; http://assyrianpost.blogspot.com/2006/05/hymn-of-praise-teshbokhta.html)

Armenia, placed as it was between the two vast empires of Rome and Persia, had embraced Christianity when the king and his family were baptized in 314. Some hundred years later Mesrob, who first served as secretary to the king and later became a monk and a missionary, produced an alphabet that served as a foundation for the first literature in Armenian. He gathered a group of scholars who, with the support of the head of the church in Armenia, undertook the task of translating Christian literature from Greek and Syriac. This is why in earlier chapters we have repeatedly mentioned writings that have been lost in the original languages but are still extant in Armenian translations.

Gorium, a disciple of Mesrob, studied in Constantinople and after returning to Armenia translated the Bible as well as other classical Christian literature.

Encouraged by these translations, original Christian literature began to emerge. Gorium produced a *Life of Mesrob*. Eznik (or Yeznig) of Colb, who was part of the same circle of translators, wrote a work that modern scholars call *Refutation of the Sects*, for the extant manuscript has no title. It describes and then refutes the opinions of the pagans, of worshipers of the sun—a traditional practice in Persian lands—as well as of the Greek philosophers and of the Manicheans. Faustus (or Pavsdos) of Istanbul (thus named that because he had studied in Constantinople), after returning to Armenia wrote a history of his land and its religion. Akatangheos, a secretary to the king, wrote a *History of the Life and Deeds of Tirdat*, the Armenian king who brought Christianity to the land. Also among the sources for the history of Armenia, there is a *History of Vardan and the War of Armenia*, telling of the resistance of Armenian Christians to the Persian invasion and giving the reasons why the Armenians felt that their Christian brothers in Constantinople had forsaken them. But it was not until a later time, mostly in the eighth century, that Armenian Christian literature reached its golden age.

In Egypt, before the conversion of Constantine, Christianity had expanded among the Coptic population, the descendants of the original inhabitants before the Greek and Roman invasions. After the time of Constantine many Christians among this Coptic population resented the power and presence of Constantinople. Also, they clearly continued preferring their ancient tongue. Already in the fourth century there were Coptic translations of parts of Scripture. But the Coptic documents that have most interested scholars in recent times are the already-mentioned gnostic writings of Nag Hammadi. These are not originally Coptic documents but instead are translations from the Greek into Coptic that, thanks to the dry Egyptian climate, have survived while the originals have disappeared. The same may be said of a number of Manichean writings that exist only in Coptic, as well as of many of the apocryphal books both of the Old Testament and of the New: the *Apocalypse of Elijah*, the *Apocalypse of Moses*, the *Acts of Peter and Paul*, and many others. Possibly the most ancient Orthodox Christian document translated into Coptic that we now have is the Easter sermon of Melito of Sardis. This translation seems to have been made late in the second century or early in the third. Later, translations were made of several of the outstanding figures of the fourth and fifth centuries: Athanasius, Basil of Caesarea, Cyril of Alexandria, Gregory of Nazianzus, John Chrysostom, and others. The same is true of several acts of martyrs.

The earliest original Christian literature in Coptic arose in monastic communities, particularly in Pacomian communities, where acts of Coptic martyrs were written in imitation of those already existing in Greek.

After the Council of Chalcedon, when the Coptic Church broke communion with the church in Constantinople, several writings of Cyril of

Alexandria, the great defender of traditional Alexandrian theology, were translated into Coptic. Soon thereafter translations appeared of some of the works of Dioscorus, who had been condemned as a heretic by the Council of Chalcedon but was considered a saint by the Copts. In the sixth century, when Emperor Justinian was able to bring imperial power to bear on Egypt, such Coptic literature became an important instrument of resistance.

From Egypt, Christianity passed on to Ethiopia, where a translation of the Bible was an important factor in the development of the language of the land. Then a supposed translation of the works of Cyril of Alexandria appeared, although in fact only a few pieces in this fairly long collection were written by Cyril.

What has been summarized here in a few pages does not do justice to the growing body of Christian literature in languages other than Latin and Greek. Unfortunately, this literature has not been sufficiently studied, in part because there are not many scholars who are proficient in those languages. Thus there is still much material remaining to be studied and classified. Let it suffice to say that the collection Patrologia orientalis, whose publication began more than a century ago and thus far has surpassed fifty thick volumes, is still far from complete.

PART 6

Transition into a New Age

Introduction to Part 6

At this point we have summarized the narrative of early Christian literature up to the fifth century. Upon completing this history, we enter a period in which much of the intellectual and literary vitality of earlier centuries was lost, and therefore this may well be seen as the dusk of early Christian literature.

In the Greek-speaking East, christological controversies remained the focus of attention, becoming ever more subtle and bitter. Since those controversies were deeply rooted in the rivalries between Alexandria and Antioch as well as in a resurgence of ancient cultures and a resistance to Byzantine rule, the goal of unity was soon forgotten in favor of the path of schism. The defenders of Antiochene traditions who felt excluded by the Council of Ephesus and its aftermath took refuge in Persian lands, and from there they continued attacking their adversaries, employing mostly the Syriac language. That church, frequently forgotten by Western historians, was continually expanding eastward, to the point of reaching China in the seventh century. Those who took the opposite tack and were rather inexactly called Monophysites also withdrew from the Byzantine Orthodox Church and created independent churches partly on the basis of doctrinal differences, but also as a way of affirming their independence from Byzantine authorities, thus giving rise to bodies such as the Armenian Church, the Coptic Church, and the Church of Ethiopia. The seventh century brought with it the Muslim invasions. Soon both Antioch and Alexandria were under Arabic rule, and Constantinople could no longer claim effective authority over those churches. All those circumstances did little to promote original Christian literature, which was mostly limited to the refutation of opponents, usually repeating well-worn arguments and even expressions.

In the West the crisis had begun earlier, although it was not equally severe. The Germanic peoples who invaded Roman territories eventually took up most of the culture of the conquered, thus giving birth to what we now call Western civilization. But the process took centuries, and meanwhile wars and chaos were not conducive to the production of Christian literature at the level of its golden age of the fourth century. Muslim invasions also affected the area, soon occupying both North Africa, which until then had been a center of Christian theological and literary activity, and most of the Iberian Peninsula.

But after dusk there are stars in the sky. After the decline of early Christian literature, there were still important authors whose work shaped the literature of the following centuries, preserving and transmitting some of the culture and wisdom of antiquity. In this last section of the present history, we shall be looking at those authors, not in detail, but only to give a general idea of their relationship with the past and their significance for the following centuries. With that purpose, rather than discussing all the authors of this time of transition, we will focus on three influential figures in the West and three in the East.

32

The West

As we come to the closing of our narrative, a word must be said about the literature that served as a bridge between antiquity and the Middle Ages, eventually leading to a new order and new creativity as the chaos of repeated invasions subsided and medieval Western civilization was being shaped. There is no doubt that the Latin writer who most profoundly influenced the Middle Ages was Augustine of Hippo. But there are three others who deserve special attention as bridges between antiquity and the Middle Ages. These three are Benedict of Nursia, Gregory the Great, and Isidore of Seville.

BENEDICT AND HIS *RULE*

Of these three authors the least prolific was Benedict. His enormous impact is not due to vast writings, but rather to a single book commonly known as the *Rule of St. Benedict*, or simply as the *Holy Rule*, which shaped Western monasticism.

It is interesting to remark that this person of enormous importance for the history of Western Christianity was practically unknown during his lifetime. Since he devoted his life to the practice and ordering of monastic life, he did not participate in theological controversies, nor did he produce monumental writings. Furthermore, if it were not for Gregory the Great, who tells us of the life of Benedict in his *Dialogues*, we would know very little of that life.

Benedict was born around the year 480 and therefore lived in a chaotic time when Italy was repeatedly invaded by various Germanic tribes. He was not yet born in 476, when the Heruli, led by Odoacer, deposed the last Western Roman emperor. Political and social chaos were the background in which Benedict was

377

formed and in which he lived most of his life. In the midst of the disorder, there was a brief period of progress and reconstruction when the Ostrogoths, under the rule of Theodoric, sought to restore or recover the glories of Roman antiquity. It was during this time, from 492, when Benedict was twelve years old, to the death of Theodoric in 526, that Benedict was formed, made his first attempts at ascetic life, and created his first monastic communities.

Theodoric had just begun his work of restoration when Benedict, who was not yet twenty years old, went to study in Rome. Although the ancient city had lost much of its splendor, it was still the center of the Western world, and those who visited it spoke of its marvels. After some time there, Benedict decided to follow the monastic way of life. The process was long. First he undertook an extreme and solitary monasticism, leading to actions such as diving into thorn bushes in order to silence the desires of the flesh. As his fame grew, many saw him as a teacher of ascetic life. Eventually he was invited to leave his solitude in order to become the abbot of a nearby monastery. The result was a disaster. The monks considered him a tyrant and even attempted to poison him. Finally he decided to return to his solitude.

But once again he was followed by those who sought his teaching, and Benedict was finally convinced of the need to form some kind of monastic community. In this undertaking he was inspired by what he knew of the monastery that Pacomius had founded centuries earlier in Egypt. He tried to organize his disciples by creating twelve monasteries, each of them with twelve monks. But that also failed, partly due to the opposition of church authorities who looked upon it with suspicion.

It was then that, with a small group of his most faithful followers, Benedict settled in Monte Cassino. There he organized a compact community. They would all live under the same roof, following the same hours of prayer, eating together, and sleeping in a common dormitory. Above all, all property was to be held in common so that, while each individual monk would live in poverty, they would not live in misery.

In order to organize his community, Benedict composed his famous *Rule*, in seventy-three chapters. Although it is impossible to determine the exact date of this document, it seems to have been written in 529 or 530. Theodoric had died a few years earlier, and once again chaos threatened Italy, while Byzantine Emperor Justinian sought to reestablish imperial authority. In the midst of those conditions, the Benedictine monastery in Monte Cassino was an island of peace and order in a sea of violence and chaos. Soon, following its example, other monasteries emerged and were following the *Rule* of Benedict.

One of the reasons that made this document so important and successful was that it joined what Benedict had learned from his experience and his studies of Eastern monasticism with the best of Roman tradition, which underscored the value of the rule of law. On the basis of his earlier experiences, Benedict was convinced that the best monastic life is life in community. But he was also convinced that within that community there must be an established order to which all would be subject and that asceticism would be reasonably moderate. For this reason the *Rule* became a sort of constitution to which all, including the abbot, were subject, and which would regulate a moderate asceticism. This is expressed at the beginning of the *Rule*: "We are, therefore, about to found a school of the Lord's service, in which we hope to introduce nothing harsh or burdensome" (*Rule*, prologue; trans. B. Verheyen [reprint, Veritatis Splendor Publications, 2014], 23).

One of the pillars of Benedictine monasticism is stability. This means that a true monk does not go from one monastery to another according to his desires or convenience. Benedict did not believe that such wandering monks were true monks. At the beginning of his *Rule*, where he speaks of different sorts of monks, he comes to the last, which he considers despicable: "But the fourth class of monks is that called Landlopers, who keep going their whole life long from one province to another, staying three or four days at a time in different cells as guests. Always roving and never settled, they indulge their passions and the cravings of their appetite. . . . It is better to pass all these over in silence than to speak of their most wretched life" (*Rule* 1; Verheyen, 25).

Another of the pillars of the *Rule* is humility, which is to be joined with the obedience due to the abbot. In speaking of the office and characteristics of the abbot, he directs:

> Let him make no distinction of persons in the monastery. Let him not love one more than another, unless it be one whom he findeth more exemplary in good works and obedience. Let not a free-born be preferred to a freedman, unless there be some other reasonable cause. But if from a just reason the Abbot deemeth it proper to make such a distinction, he may do so in regard to the rank of anyone whomsoever; whether bond or free, we are all one in Christ. . . . Therefore, let him have equal charity for all, and impose a uniform discipline for all according to merit. (*Rule* 2; Verheyen, 27)

But the authority of the abbot is to be employed in accordance with the wisdom of the community:

> Whenever weighty matters are to be transacted in the monastery, let the Abbot call together the whole community, and make known the matter which is to be considered. Having heard the brethren's views, let him weigh the matter with himself and do what he thinketh best. It is for this reason, however, we said that all should be called for counsel, because the Lord often revealeth to the younger what is best. (*Rule* 3; Verheyen, 30)

While the abbot is to seek the counsel of the community on important matters, monastic community leads to obedience, for "the first rule of humility is obedience without delay" (*Rule* 5; Verheyen, 35).

Apparently the original text ended with chapter 7 and therefore was relatively brief. But then, as the community developed, Benedict wrote in more detail about the practices of common prayer that the monks are to share and about the organization of the monastery itself, including the distribution of responsibilities among the monks as well as their other activities.

Regarding prayer as a community, each day will have eight specific times for prayer. Referring to the psalmist as a prophet, and quoting Psalm 119, Benedict explains the reason for these hours:

> As the prophet saith: "Seven times a day I have given praise to Thee," this sacred sevenfold number will be fulfilled by us in this wise if we perform the duties of our service at the time of Lauds, Prime, Tierce, Sext, None, Vespers, and Compline; because it was of these day hours that he hath said: "Seven times a day I have given praise to Thee." For the same Prophet saith of the night watches: "At midnight I arose to confess Thee." (*Rule* 16; Verheyen, 53)

As a whole, these hours are the "Divine Office" or "work of God" (*opus Dei*). This work of God is the main task of the monastic community, which is to pray not only for itself, but also for all of humankind.

But monastic life is not to be limited to prayer and devotion. Benedict's understanding of monastic life is expressed in the words "pray and work" (*ora et labora*). On the basis of this principle, Benedict sets the schedule that monks are to follow:

> Idleness is the enemy of the soul; and therefore the brethren ought to be employed in manual labor at certain times, at others, in devout reading. Hence, we believe that the time for each will be properly ordered by the following arrangement; namely, that from Easter till the calends of October, they go out in the morning from the first till about the fourth hour, to do the necessary work, but that from the fourth till about the sixth hour they devote to reading. After the sixth hour, however, when they have risen from table, let them rest in their beds in complete silence; or if, perhaps, anyone desireth to read for himself, let him so read that he doth not disturb others. Let None be said somewhat earlier, about the middle of the eighth hour; and then let them work again at what is necessary until Vespers. (*Rule* 48; Verheyen, 83)

The *Rule* of Benedict made an enormous impact on the emerging Western civilization. Although there were many other monastic rules, eventually Benedict's became the most common, and most other Western monastic rules are derived from it. The movement expanded throughout Western Europe, and Benedictine monasteries left their imprint on the entirety of society. They were practically the only centers of study and learning. They served as places where manuscripts were copied and preserved, as shelters for sojourners, as pharmacies and centers of medical service for the ill, and as schools where parents took their children to be educated. In much of Europe, the population living near monasteries established its own schedule on the basis of the Benedictine hours of prayer and the bells announcing them. In remote areas, monasteries cleared lands, drained swamps, and established better agricultural practices.

Clearly, all of this did not happen during the lifetime of Benedict, for at the beginning the monasteries that followed his *Rule* were few, and Benedict himself was hardly known. It was much later in that sixth century, when Gregory the Great became pope, that the Benedictine movement took flight. Gregory himself had been a Benedictine monk, and now he employed his new office to promote Benedictine monasticism, which he used as an arm in his missionary interests and in his efforts to reorganize the life of the church. Two centuries after Gregory, Charlemagne, in his attempt to bring about political and religious uniformity within the lands that he governed, also promoted the expansion of the Benedictine *Rule*.

GREGORY THE GREAT

Even though Gregory did much to promote Benedictine monasticism, this was only one of the many reasons why he is called "the Great." He was born in Rome around 540, just a few years after Benedict wrote his *Rule*. His profoundly Christian family belonged to what little remained of ancient Roman aristocracy. He was a young man when he saw the great disasters that were taking place at Rome, first due to the early Germanic invasions, and then to wars between Goths and Byzantines, both invaders in Italy. Then came the invasions of the Lombards, more ferocious than the former. In his writings Gregory repeatedly refers to those harsh experiences, which continued throughout most of his life. Even before the Lombard invasion, he lamented:

> Wherever we look we see tears; everywhere we hear plaints. Cities are destroyed, settlements undone, fields deserted, and the land desolate. There is no one to tend the fields and hardly anyone in the cities. And what misery is left of the human race is still being felled and destroyed. And yet the wrath of heaven is endless, because even in the midst of that wrath evil actions are not abandoned. Some are taken

captive, some are maimed, and others killed. What pleasure is still left in this life, my brothers? . . .

We see the state of Rome, which at times seemed to be mistress of the world: repeatedly broken with unspeakable pain, with the desolation of its citizens, with the attacks of its enemies and its frequent ruin. (*Homilies on Ezekiel* 2.6.22; PL 76:1009–10)

After receiving as much education as was possible in those difficult times at Rome, and possibly led by the misery and chaos that he saw all around him as well as by his own ascetic tendencies, Gregory joined the monastery of St. Andrew, which followed the *Rule* of St. Benedict. But the peace of the monastery would not be his lot. He had been four years in St. Andrew when Pope Benedict called him to an active task in the organization of the church, and then Pope Pelagius II named him his ambassador before the court in Constantinople. He spent six years in that city, until he was allowed to return to Rome and to St. Andrew, where he became abbot. Shortly after the death of Pelagius, Gregory was elected bishop of Rome. Despite his efforts to reject that responsibility, he became pope in 590.

Gregory's work as a pope is the reason why he is known as Gregory the Great. When there was a threat of new invasions, it was Gregory who led negotiations to spare Rome. Since there was a severe shortage of wheat, Gregory organized a system to have it brought from Sicily. Under his leadership, aqueducts were rebuilt, lowlands that had been swamps were drained, and a system was established whereby the church would warehouse food to be distributed to the poor. In short, the ancient city was given new life.

But the actions of Gregory were not limited to the city of Rome and the surrounding area. In various ways, Gregory intervened in the lives of church and civil society not only in Italy, but also in Africa, Gaul, and even England, where he sent the Benedictine monk Augustine of Canterbury as a missionary. He repeatedly clashed with the imperial authorities in Constantinople, and his impact was felt even in distant Armenia.

What interests us here is Gregory's work as a writer. His earliest extant work, in thirty-five books, is his *Exposition on the Book of Job*, which he began writing when he was a legate in Constantinople and finished years later. There he applies the ancient distinction of three basic levels of meaning in the biblical text: literal, allegorical, and moral. Thus, after explaining the historical meaning of a certain passage, Gregory provides an allegorical interpretation of every detail in it, then finally applies it to the actual life of believers. It is on this third level that his interest lies. For this reason, this work is commonly known as his *Moralia*. The commentary is so detailed and extensive that the first five verses in the book of Job occupy fifty-six chapters of the first of Gregory's thirty-five books. At the same time, the moral applications that Gregory sees in the passages he studies make it clear that he is primarily addressing monastic communities. This commentary on Job, with its moral applications, became one of the most important sourcebooks for discussions of ethics during the early centuries of the Middle Ages.

His interest in the life of the church in Germanic lands led him not only to send missionaries such as Augustine, but also to interpret Augustine of Hippo and much of the earlier tradition in ways more amenable to this new flock. This may be one of the reasons for his simplification of the faith and his emphasis on morals and miracles.

His much shorter *Pastoral Rule* was even more influential. It was written in response to his friend John, bishop of Ravenna, who had chided Gregory for not having willingly accepted the bishopric of Rome. Gregory writes of the variety of pastoral tasks. The work is divided into four parts. The first two, that in general treat the responsibilities of a pastor and the character and attitudes necessary to be able to fulfill them, have eleven chapters each. The last of the four parts is a very brief chapter on the same subject. But the most extensive part of the work, the third part, with fourteen chapters, is a more detailed discussion of the manner in which a pastor is to deal with different situations and conditions.

At the very beginning of the work, Gregory expresses the need for anyone who is to practice pastoral ministry to follow a process of learning and formation:

> No one presumes to teach an art till he has first, with intent meditation, learnt it. What rashness is it, then, for the unskilful to assume pastoral authority, since the government of souls is the art of arts! For who can be ignorant that the sores of the thoughts of men are more occult than the sores of the bowels? And yet how often do men who have no knowledge whatever of spiritual precepts fearlessly profess themselves physicians of the heart, though those who are ignorant of the effect of drugs blush to appear as physicians of the flesh! (*Pastoral Rule* 1.1; *NPNF*² 12:1)

But studying is not enough, for it is also necessary to live according to the results of that study and to teach by example:

> There are some also who investigate spiritual precepts with cunning care, but what they penetrate with their understanding they trample on in their lives: all at once they teach the things which not by practice but by study they have learnt; and what in words they preach by their manners they impugn. Whence it comes to pass that when the shepherd walks through steep places, the flock follows to the precipice. (*Pastoral Rule* 1.2; *NPNF*² 12:2)

What made this book necessary reading for any medieval pastor who wished to be faithful to his calling was the third part, whose subject is how to deal with people in different conditions and attitudes. At the beginning of this section, Gregory lists the various subjects that he will be discussing. In that list the emphasis lies on the need to take into account the particular situation with which one deals. This is clearly shown by a quick look at the beginning of that list:

> Men and women.
> The poor and the rich.
> The joyful and the sad.
> Prelates and subordinates.
> Servants and masters.
> The wise of this world and the dull.
> The impudent and the bashful.
> The forward and the fainthearted.
> The impatient and the patient.
> The kindly disposed and the envious.
> The simple and the insincere.
> The whole and the sick.
> (*Pastoral Rule* 3.1; *NPNF*[2] 12:24)

The list continues to a total of thirty-six; but what is quoted suffices to show Gregory's emphasis on the need to deal with each person according to their nature and circumstances. The impact of this book in the Middle Ages was enormous. There were other books on pastoral duties, such as Ambrose's *On the Duties of the Clergy* and several similar works by Augustine. But this particular work by Gregory, partially because of its simplicity, became the most widely used.

There was another work of Gregory that enjoyed even wider circulation, his *Four Books of Dialogues*. This is presented as a series of conversations with a deacon by the name of Peter, who expresses doubts about some Italian saints and their miracles. Gregory tells him the life and miracles of these saints. It is a book full of surprising and marvelous events, many of them hard to believe and even laughable; but for that very reason it is a good source for understanding the beliefs of Gregory's time. Particularly important is the second of these four books, where Gregory deals with Benedict. This book, which frequently circulated as an independent piece in monastic circles, contributed enormously to the prestige of Benedict and to the diffusion of his *Rule*.

There are also two collections of sermons by Gregory. One of them consists of twenty-two sermons divided into two books, all on Ezekiel. Their method of interpretation is what we have already seen in his commentaries on Job. While he does explain the literal meaning of the text, he is mostly interested in what he calls the "mystical" or allegorical meaning of the text, as well as its practical application to life. The other collection of sermons, also in two books, includes forty sermons. The first twenty of these were written by him, but spoken before the congregation by someone else. Since his early youth, Gregory had suffered from a disease that he called a stomach ailment, which sometimes would not allow him to preach sermons he had prepared.

Gregory expresses his thought of the relationship between Scripture and its interpretation in preaching in the last of these homilies, on the parable of the rich man and Lazarus:

> Beloved brethren, when dealing with sacred Scripture one must first of all remain with historical truth, and then explore its meaning by understanding its allegory. The allegorical meaning can easily be understood if it is grounded on the historical truth. But, since sometimes allegory edifies faith, and the historical meaning edifies moral life, we who—thanks be to God—speak to you who are already believers, do not think that it is wrong to alter the order and, since you already have the true faith, say something on the allegorical meaning first and in a concise way, and hold back for the end of our exposition what you most need, the moral meaning of the history itself. We do this because it is usually easier to remember what one hears last. Let us then discuss briefly the allegorical meaning so that we may arrive sooner at the moral meaning. (*Homilies on the Gospels* 2.20.1; PL 76:1154)

Finally, Gregory's epistolary is extensive, including some 850 letters. This number is approximate because, as is often the case, although the collection includes a total of 859, scholars doubt the authenticity of some of them. Unfortunately, among those whose authenticity some doubt is a very interesting and oft-quoted correspondence between Gregory and Augustine of Canterbury. All the epistles of Gregory that have survived were written after he became pope, that is, beginning in 590. They seem to have been preserved because Gregory himself, as an able administrator, kept copies of them and circulated some of them among several readers. With few exceptions, they deal with the various administrative issues facing Gregory, and therefore they are an important source for historians trying to reconstruct the events and the life and organization of the church at that time.

Gregory was one of the important bridges through which the Middle Ages received the legacy of antiquity. It was through him that the Middle Ages read Augustine. Thus, while preserving the thought of the great bishop of Hippo, he also left his own stamp on that record so that medieval Augustinianism was probably as much shaped by Gregory as by Augustine himself.

ISIDORE OF SEVILLE

The third of the authors to be discussed in this chapter—again, not as a complete list but rather as examples of the bridge between antiquity and the Middle Ages—is Isidore of Seville. The date and place of Isidore's birth are not known. Most probably he was born in Seville or nearby around the year 560. He apparently was part of the Hispanic-Roman population that still subsisted amid the Germanic invasions and after those invasions provided the administrative and intellectual resources for the assimilation of the invaders into what remained of ancient Roman civilization. Isidore was very young when his parents died. He had at least three older siblings, Leander, Fulgentius, and Florentina. The first was bishop of Seville; the second, of Ecija; and the third was a virgin consecrated to monastic life. Apparently Isidore was much younger than the rest, for in an instruction on monastic life that Leander wrote to his sister, and commonly known as the *Rule of St. Leander*, he tells her:

> Do not forget our younger brother Isidore, whom our parents entrusted to his three surviving siblings when, happy and without having to worry for his childhood, they went with the Lord. And, since I love him as a son, and prefer his love to all temporal things, and rest upon his love, do love him ever more and pray for him ever more in view of the love our parents had for him. (*Rule of St. Leander* 31; PL 72:892)

Apparently Isidore went to live with his older brother Leander when he was orphaned. Leander took charge of his education and instructed him in matters of faith, with the result that when Leander died, Isidore succeeded him as bishop of Seville. This would have been shortly after the year 600 and therefore toward the end of the pontificate of Gregory the Great.

Isidore was a prolific author who was particularly interested in the use and meaning of words and in their relationship with ancient knowledge. Among his works are two that apparently Isidore conceived as separate but complementary writings. The first, *On the Difference of Words*, is apparently inspired by some works of the most famous students of grammar in classical Rome; it discusses a series of synonyms that are frequently employed as if they were interchangeable, but whose meaning is not exactly the same. The second, *On the Difference of Things*, is not about physical things, but rather about ideas and how they relate among themselves. Another apparently later work, *Synonyms*, is quite different from the other two, for rather than a discussion about how words and ideas are similar or different, it is a sort of penitential soliloquy in which Isidore uses chains of synonyms in order to say the same thing, although with different emphases. An oft-quoted example, appearing at the beginning of the work, is this: "Everybody hates me; nobody offers me love; all reject me; all despise me abominably; all fear me with horror; all reject me" (*Synonyms*, prologue; PL 83:829).

Isidore also wrote several works on biblical studies. Apparently the earliest of these was *Forewords*, which is mostly a series of short introductions to each of the books of the Bible, besides a general introduction to the entire canon. His marked interest in classifying and ordering everything may also be seen in *On the People in the Bible*, inspired by previous authors; its authorship is debated. It is a relatively popular introduction to the main characters in Scripture. The same concern for ordering ideas is to be found in his *Book of Numbers*, whose purpose is to explore the meaning of each number in the Bible. Thus, for instance, large sections are devoted to discussing the significance of the number 7 or of 5 and their multiples, quoting one passage after another using such numbers. The *Allegories* are another collection of studies of names in the Bible, now showing their allegorical meaning. *Questions* is mostly a series of allegorical commentaries on the Old Testament.

Isidore also sought to organize the historical knowledge of antiquity. His most complete work in this field is a *Chronicle* of the history of the world up to 615, when it was apparently written. Following the examples of Jerome and Gennadius, he also wrote *On Illustrious Men*. In order to reclaim the value of his Hispanic inheritance in the face of Byzantine claims, he wrote a *Praise of Spain*, followed by a history of the Goths, the Vandals, and the Suevi (Suebi). Along with these one may include *On Heretics* and *On the Origin of Ecclesiastical Offices*, which includes a history of Christian worship.

Isidore was also profoundly interested in the functioning of the world and in natural phenomena, with which he deals in the work *On the Universe*, written at the request of King Sisebutus. The purpose of this writing was both to explain natural phenomena and to reject the many superstitions surrounding them. Here he deals with subjects such as the winds, earthquakes, the movements of heavenly bodies, and eclipses. Frequently, after explaining the origin of any of these phenomena, he moves on to an allegorical discussion of their importance for faith and Christian life.

All of these works, and many others that have not been mentioned, seem to be but a series of exercises in preparation for Isidore's great work, the *Etymologies*. Although there is ample evidence that his other writings were read throughout the Middle Ages, there is no doubt that it was through the *Etymologies* that the Middle Ages had access to a goodly part of the knowledge of antiquity, particularly on matters having to do with the order of the universe.

The title of this work may be misleading, for it is not actually a series of etymologies, but rather an encyclopedia of all the knowledge of antiquity seeking to relate it with Latin and with the origin and meaning of words.

Thus, it is not mostly a sort of etymological dictionary explaining the origin of each word, although there is a long section dealing with such origins, but rather an encyclopedia in which, while discussing various phenomena and other realities, the origin of their name is explained.

A list of the titles of the twenty books composing this work suffices to show its encyclopedic nature:

1. *On Grammar*
2. *On Rhetoric and Dialectics*
3. *On Mathematics*
4. *On Medicine*
5. *On Laws and Times*
6. *On Books and Ecclesiastical Offices*
7. *On God, the Angels, and the Faithful*
8. *On the Church and Sects*
9. *On Languages, Peoples, Kingdoms, Militias, Cities, and Kinships*
10. *On Words*
11. *On Humans and Prodigious Beings*
12. *On Animals*
13. *On the Universe and Its Parts*
14. *On the Earth and Its Parts*
15. *On Buildings and Fields*
16. *On Stones and Metals*
17. *On Agriculture*
18. *On War and Games*
19. *On Ships, Buildings, and Dress*
20. *On Provisions and Domestic and Rustic Tools*

Each of these books includes an enormous variety of subjects. For instance, after twenty-three chapters on laws, book 5, *On Laws and Times*, includes forty-eight chapters on astronomy. Here he discusses the name of the science itself, the history of its main teachers and how it differs from astrology, in order to move then to the heavenly bodies, the movements of the sun, the moon, and the planets, and much more. These chapters express the best knowledge of the time. For example, in chapter 5.56, dealing with the movements of the moon, he says:

> The moon marks the length of its months according to when it loses and recovers its light. The course of the moon is oblique rather than straight, like the sun, so as to avoid being over the center of the earth and thus producing excessively frequent eclipses. Its orbit is close to that of the earth. When it is waxing, its horns look East; but they point West when it is waning. And this makes sense, for it is moving towards its dusk and will lose its light. (*Etymologies* 5.56)

These three authors, Benedict of Nursia, Gregory the Great, and Isidore of Seville, serve as illustrations of the three main means by which the Middle Ages received and adapted the legacy of earlier times. Benedict reminds us that monasteries were the center where the knowledge of antiquity was preserved and copied, including most of the writings discussed in this book. Gregory shows the essential role of the church in employing the writings of antiquity and in restoring a certain measure of order within which such writings could be preserved and studied. Finally, Isidore sets the path for a view of knowledge which consisted mostly in repeating and examining what others had said. It is for this reason that, upon reaching the time of these three great figures, we have come to the end of the period we have been studying and to the beginning of a new age.

33

The East

As in the West, also in the East the sixth century was a time of transition between antiquity and a new age. The changes were different from those that took place in the West, for the Byzantine Empire would continue existing for several centuries. While in the West the church was unifying and becoming more centralized under the leadership of figures such as Gregory the Great, in the East divisions became ever more frequent. The christological controversies, conjoined with a spirit of resistance against Byzantine authority, led to the birth of churches that still exist. And, while in the West the Germanic invaders eventually assimilated into the conquered culture and adopted its religion, in the East the Arab invaders kept their own religion and frequently imposed it on the lands they had taken. In many of those lands, ancient Christian churches now became a minority within a mostly Muslim population.

The first decades of the sixth century seemed to be a time of vitality and renewal within the Byzantine Empire. In 526 Justinian rose to the imperial throne and began a program of expansion and reorganization. Expansion led him to retake North Africa, until then ruled by the Vandals, and to intervene repeatedly in Italy and other Western regions. His program of centralization followed the policy of most other emperors of the time, seeking to unify a church that had been divided by christological controversies. But the expansion was ephemeral, for in the following century the Arab invaders conquered not only North Africa, but also much Byzantine territory in Asia. In those lands that were no longer part of the Byzantine Empire, new churches were formed that were independent of Constantinople and frequently opposed the Orthodox Church of the Byzantine Empire.

Even so, Justinian's reign is a landmark in the history of the Greek-speaking East. In 529, the same year when Benedict settled in Monte Cassino, Justinian closed down the ancient Academy of Athens. This was mostly a symbolic gesture, for that institution had declined greatly; but it is a sign that antiquity was passing, and a new age was opening. That very year Justinian also convoked a team of experts in jurisprudence and ordered that Roman law be codified and made more uniform. The resultant document, the *Corpus juris civilis*, is still an important source for this study of ancient Roman law. The fact that it was issued in Latin shows that Justinian, whose name was of Latin origin, still thought in terms of a unified empire that would continue the ancient glories of Rome. But the history of the document itself shows that times were changing. Although the *Corpus juris civilis* was intended to be a complete legal system, prohibiting the creation of new laws, Justinian himself had to issue new laws. These, known jointly as the *Novellas*, were incorporated into the *Corpus juris civilis*. It is interesting to know that, while the *Corpus* as a whole was written in Latin, Justinian's new laws were issued in Greek. Justinian felt free to dream about the restoration of the ancient Roman Empire, but reality was forcing him in a different direction.

In the preceding chapter, we dealt with Latin Christian literature during the sixth century; in the present chapter, instead of dealing with the vast number of Eastern writings during the same century, we shall refer to three authors who serve to illustrate the various dimensions of the bridge that was built between the literature and theology of earlier times and those of the Middle Ages. These three are Leontius of Byzantium, Dionysius the Areopagite, and John of Damascus.

LEONTIUS OF BYZANTIUM

As is often the case, it is impossible to determine the birth date of Leontius, which seems to have taken place in Constantinople near the year 475. We do know that in 519, when the christological controversies and imperial interventions in them were creating tensions between the Western and Eastern churches, Leontius went to Rome to promote a conciliatory attitude. The following year he settled in a monastery near Jerusalem, where he spent most of his life, although traveling repeatedly to Constantinople, where he died around the year 543.

Leontius was probably the most distinguished Byzantine philosopher of the sixth century. Although greatly influenced by Origen and his Platonist inclinations, his philosophy was mostly Aristotelian, particularly in his theory of knowledge, as may be seen in the following lines: "The simple perception of objects as a whole gives us the general and imprecise idea. But by means of thought we distinguish among various objects and thus come to a clear knowledge of them" (*Three Books against the Nestorians and Eutycheans* 1; PG 86:1296).

But in spite of his philosophical interests, much of the work of Leontius revolved around the christological controversies. Originally inclined toward the Antiochene Christology that is commonly called "divisive," eventually he became a defender of the decisions taken at the Council of Chalcedon. This may be seen in the title of one of his main works, *Three Books against the Nestorians and Eutycheans*. In this writing, as in all his work, his main interest is christological, for he is writing in an environment dominated by the controversies that had led to the Council of Chalcedon and still continued. Given the subtleties of the issues at stake, the style of Leontius is quite abstract and often difficult to follow. This may be seen in the following words, near the beginning of this work:

> [In the person of Christ] the properties of a substance are equally applied to the whole, and that which belongs the whole is also common to each of the two substances, for the whole is in each of them. For there would be no interchange of predicates [*communicatio idiomatum*] if the particular character of each of them did not remain the same, even within the union. That is the union of which we speak, which is more unitive than that which divides, but also richer than the one that confuses [the two natures], so that the two natures do not become one by virtue of the union. (*Ag. the Nestorians and Eutycheans* 1; PG 86:1304)

Apparently some time later, responding to the objections of the Monophysite theologian Severus of Antioch, Leontius published a *Solution of the Arguments of Severus* and *Thirty Chapters against Severus*. Many other works have been often attributed to him, but their authorship is doubtful.

The reason why the work of Leontius merits attention is that it exemplifies several of the characteristics of literature produced in the Christian East at that time. It is a literature almost completely dominated by the christological controversies and increasingly inclined to subtle distinctions. It is also a literature that drinks from the wells of both Plato and Aristotle. In all of this, the work of Leontius is an announcement and forerunner of most Byzantine theological literature during the Middle Ages.

DIONYSIUS THE AREOPAGITE

At approximately the same time when Leontius was producing his theological treatises and Justinian was codifying ancient Roman law, an unknown author wrote a series of works claiming to be the Dionysius that, according to the book of Acts, was converted in Athens after hearing Paul's speech at the Areopagus.

Today there is general agreement that these writings do not really come from that Dionysius, but rather from someone in the sixth century. But shortly after they were published, they gained wide circulation. Since they claim to come from a disciple of Paul, they were given an almost apostolic authority.

Nothing is known about this false Dionysius beyond what can be discovered from his five works. Scholars are in agreement that he seems to have written early in the sixth century and that he was profoundly imbued with the Platonic tradition. Little may be said beyond that. His five extant works are *The Celestial Hierarchy*, *The Ecclesiastical Hierarchy*, *On the Divine Names*, *Mystical Theology*, and a collection of ten epistles.

This Pseudo-Dionysius proposed a mysticism based on a hierarchical structure of the universe and inspired in the Neoplatonic conception of a single primordial being, from which all others are derived, thus creating a hierarchy that descends as each level is more distant from the original One. After pointing out that it is impossible to see God directly, Dionysius presents reality as a series of hierarchies through which the soul can ascend in order to reach God. Thus he says:

> He [God the Creator] modelled it on the hierarchies of heaven, and clothed these immaterial hierarchies in numerous material figures and forms so that, in a way appropriate to our nature, we might be uplifted from these most venerable images to interpretations and assimilations which are simple and inexpressible. For it is quite impossible that we humans should, in any immaterial way, rise up to imitate and to contemplate the heavenly hierarchies without the aid to those material means capable of guiding us as our nature requires. Hence, any thinking person realizes that the appearances of beauty are signs of an invisible loveliness. The beautiful odors which strike the senses are representations of a conceptual diffusion. Material lights are images of the outpouring of an immaterial gift of light. The thoroughness of sacred discipleship indicates the immense contemplative capacity of the mind. Order and rank here below are a sign of the harmonious ordering toward the divine realm. The reception of the most divine Eucharist is a symbol of participation in Jesus. And so it goes for all the gifts transcendently received by the beings of heaven, gifts which are granted to us in a symbolic mode. (*Celestial Hierarchy* 1.3; trans. Colm Luibheid, in *Pseudo-Dionysius: The Complete Works* [New York: Paulist Press, 1987], 146)

Here and in the rest of his writings, this false Dionysius draws a universal hierarchy in which, reflecting the Trinity, each element has three levels. In heaven, angelic beings are divided into three hierarchies, each of them with three levels. The first includes seraphim, cherubim, and thrones. The second, the dominions, virtues, and powers. The third, principalities, archangels, and angels. On earth, the church is divided into two hierarchies, each of them with three levels. First is the priestly hierarchy, which includes bishops, priests, and deacons. Then come the faithful, also divided into three, for first are the monastics, then the faithful who partake of Communion, and finally those who are not allowed to do so, among whom there are also three levels: the catechumens, the energumens—people for whom the church prays because they are possessed by demons—and the penitents.

On this basis Dionysius proposes a mystical ascent by means of the contemplation of each level of being in an ascending process. Also in this process are three stages or "ways": First, it is necessary for the soul to be rid of its impurity by the "purgative" way. Once purified, the soul may follow the "illuminative" way, in which it receives divine light. Finally, in an ecstasy, the soul is united to God, and this is the "unitive" way. While this mysticism is very similar to that of late Neoplatonism, it claims the name of Christian because in each of these stages the soul is guided by Christ, the Word of God.

By reason of the subapostolic authority that he was given, the impact of this false Dionysius was enormous. Shortly after being published, his works were translated into Syriac, then Armenian, and finally in the ninth century into Latin. As a result, in both Eastern and Western churches the sort of mysticism that Dionysius proposed became widespread.

This author is important for our history first because he left a profound imprint in all medieval theological literature, but also because he shows the degree to which Christian faith had been joined and even confused with classical philosophy, and finally because he is one more example of the manner in which the Middle Ages interpreted the early centuries of Christianity through the eyes of bridge figures.

JOHN OF DAMASCUS

John of Damascus, whom Eastern Christianity considers to be the last of the "Fathers" of the church, lived long after the other authors discussed in the present chapter. All the extant biographies of John are fairly late and not absolutely trustworthy, particularly in what they say about his youth. We do know that he was born late in the seventh century in Damascus, which a century earlier had been conquered by the Arabs. The Arabic name of his family was "Mansur," and apparently his grandfather, known as "Mansur ibn Sarjun," had been a civil servant who under Emperor Heraclius played an important role in the negotiations leading to the capitulation of Damascus, and then was a functionary at the court of the caliph.

We do know that early in the eighth century, probably in 706, John joined the monastery of Mar Saba (St. Sabas) near Jerusalem, where he spent most of his life. Some years later Emperor Leo III issued the first of a series of edicts against images, thus giving rise to the iconoclastic controversy. John was an active participant in the debate, as a defender of images, and for that reason the Second Council of Nicaea (787), frequently called the Seventh Ecumenical Council, declared him worthy of veneration jointly with the other "Fathers of the church."

The literary work of John of Damascus was extensive. Given his fame, a number of writings that were not his were also attributed to him. The most important of these is probably the *Dialogue between a Christian and a Saracen*, which is particularly interesting as a window into the relationships between Christians and Muslims in the caliphate of Damascus, but which was probably the work of an anonymous writer.

In the field of biblical studies, John has left only a commentary on the epistles of Paul, which is mostly a compilation of what others had said. Also, as was typical of theologians at that time, he wrote three works on Christology. Against the extremely divisive Christology that by then was known as "Nestorianism," he wrote two books *Against the Nestorians*. And against the opposite extreme, he wrote *Against the Jacobites* and *On the Two Wills and the Operations in Christ*. This latter work was directed against the new form that unitive Christology had taken at his time, commonly called "Monothelism." As guides to monastic life, he wrote *The Sacred Fasts*, *The Eight Spirits of Evil*, and *Virtues and Vices*. Of his homiletic labors only a dozen sermons are extant, the best-known one on Christmas. He also wrote numerous hymns that are still sung regularly in the Greek church and some of which are included in modern hymnals in other languages. In English, the most widely known is probably the one beginning "The day of resurrection! Earth, tell it out abroad; The Passover of gladness, The Passover of God" (*The Presbyterian Hymnal* [Louisville, KY: Westminster/John Knox Press, 1990], #118).

The significance of John of Damascus for the history of Christian theology and literature is due mostly to his three *Orations against Those Who Reject Sacred Images* and to his extensive work *Fountain of Knowledge*.

The essence of his argument in defense of images may be seen already in the first of the three *Orations*. There he says that the commandment against images that appears in the Decalogue was given partly to thwart the tendency of the Jewish people to idolatry, but also because at that time there was no adequate way of representing God. But this has changed radically after the incarnation of God in Jesus Christ:

In earlier times it was impossible to represent God, who has neither shape nor body. But now that God has been seen in the flesh
and relating with humanity, I do make an image of this God whom
I see. I do not adore matter, but rather the creator of matter who
for my sake became matter, who was ready to reside in matter, who
through matter has obtained my salvation. I cannot but honor this
matter that brought about my salvation. I do honor it, but not as if
it were God. . . . For this reason I also approach every other matter
with reverence, because God has filled it with his power and grace. It
was through matter that salvation came to me. (*Ag. Those Who Reject
Sacred Images* 1.16; PG 94:1245)

The other two speeches in this series reiterate that argument, although
sometimes with a different twist. In the second, John relates the honor and
veneration due to relics, such as the cross and the holy lance that tore the
body of Jesus, with the veneration due to images:

If I render honor and reverence to the cross, the lance, the thorns, or
the sponge with which those who killed my Lord mocked and killed
him, should I not also bow before images that believers have made
with the good purpose of glorifying and remembering the sufferings
of Christ? If I bow before an image of the cross, no matter of what
it is made, should I not also venerate the image of the crucified, who
saved me through the cross? (*Ag. Those Who Reject Sacred Images* 2.19;
PG 94:1305)

Finally, the third speech includes an interesting attempt to list or classify
various sorts of images and also asserts that the very first one to make an
image of God was God, who created humans after the divine image.

The great doctrinal work of John of Damascus, *Fountain of Knowledge*, was
preceded by others preparing it. Among them there is a treatise *On the Holy
Trinity*, another *On Right Doctrine*, and an *Exposition and Declaration of Faith*
that some say he professed at his ordination.

All of this, jointly with his writings on Christology and his defense of
images, is the background for the *Fountain of Knowledge*, which is undoubtedly
the most important of all the works of John of Damascus. Some have declared
that this is the first great theological summa, a forerunner of the great systematic works of the Middle Ages. In this work he deals with a vast variety
of earlier writers, whom he quotes abundantly in order to build his imposing
synthesis. The *Fountain of Knowledge* is composed of three parts. John himself
summarizes the purpose of each of them in the preface:

First, I shall expound the best contributions of great philosophers,
for any good to be found in them has been given to humanity by
God. . . . Then I shall expound in an orderly fashion the follies of

heretics, whom God hates, so that by knowing falsehood we may follow truth more closely. And then, with the help and grace of God, I shall expound the truth that destroys every falsehood and casts away error and has been embellished and adorned by the prophets as if placing it within the golden frame, and also by fishermen whom God set up as shepherds and teachers bearing the truth of God. (*Fountain of Knowledge*, preface; PG 94:524)

The sixty-eight chapters of the first part, frequently called *Dialectics*, deal with what John of Damascus considers preliminary matters to the study of theology, mostly—as he has announced—Greek philosophy. As the foundation for what he will be saying later regarding Jesus Christ, in this section he takes great care to define not only some of the traditional terms generally employed by philosophers, but also other terms that will be central in the final section. This includes words such as "nature," "form," "hypostasis," "person," "enhypostasis," and "anhypostasis."

The second part, *On Heresies*, includes not only what may properly be called sects or heresies within Christianity, but also other systems of thought that have impacted Christian doctrine. This includes, among many others, Judaism and Hellenism, as well as particular philosophical schools such as Pythagoreanism, Platonism, Stoicism, and Epicureanism. Then in more detail the discussion focuses on a long list of heresies, many of which are hardly known today, among which appear also the scribes, Pharisees, and Sadducees.

The third part of the *Fountain of Knowledge*, known as *An Exact Exposition of the Orthodox Faith*, or simply as *On Orthodox Faith*, is the most important portion of the entire work. It is here that we find the systematic theology or summa of theology that has gained John of Damascus wide recognition. In a way, it is an orderly and detailed review of the Nicene Creed, which seems to be its basic outline. Soon this third part of the *Fountain of Knowledge* began circulating apart from the rest of the work, to the point that it is frequently considered an independent writing. Although the author originally divided this section into a hundred chapters, in the Latin West it has circulated as divided into four books, perhaps in order to show its parallelism with the four books of *Sentences* of Peter Lombard. There was good reason for this, for to some extent the order of *On Orthodox Faith* is similar to the order that Peter Lombard would later follow. Thus the first book deals mostly with God as One and Triune, which is also the subject of Lombard's first book. Likewise, the second and third books are parallel in content to the second and third books of the *Sentences*. But this parallelism breaks down in the fourth book, where the Damascene focuses mostly on the theme of Christology, so widely debated during his time, in order finally to deal with the sacraments and with the life of faith.

As he approaches the end of this vast work, John of Damascus returns to the subject of images, which he always considered fundamental, and their relationship with the incarnation. In chapter 89—chapter 16 of book 4, according to the Western division of the work—one finds some of the most oft-quoted words of John of Damascus. It was words such as these that gained him his reputation as a champion of orthodoxy:

> But besides this who can make an imitation of the invisible, incorporeal, uncircumscribed, formless God? Therefore to give form to the Deity is the height of folly and impiety. . . . But after God in His bowels of pity became in truth man for our salvation, . . . He lived upon the earth and dwelt among men, worked miracles, suffered, was crucified, rose again and was taken back to Heaven, since all these things actually took place and were seen by men the Fathers gave their sanction to depicting these events on images as being acts of great heroism, in order that they should form a concise memorial of them. . . . We fall down and worship not the material but that which is imaged: just as we do not worship the material of which the Gospels are made, nor the material of the Cross, but that which these typify. (*Orthodox Faith* 4.16; *NPNF*[2] 9:88)

There is ample reason to consider John of Damascus the last of the "Fathers" of the church. He is a direct heir of the authors we have been studying in this volume, not only in their content, but also in their language and style. But his circumstances were very different. His context was no longer that of the Roman Empire, which had accepted and promoted Christianity since the times of Constantine. He lived under the rule of the caliphs of Damascus. Therefore, just as Benedict of Nursia, Gregory the Great, and Isidore of Seville had to find ways of living and transmitting the faith of their ancestors to a new world resulting from Germanic invasions, John of Damascus had to do likewise in a new world ruled by caliphs. Still, in contrast to the West, in the East a remainder of the ancient Roman Empire still subsisted, known now as the Byzantine Empire. John of Damascus did not live within the borders of that empire, but the faith that he professed and defended was that of Byzantium, even when other Christians around him were increasingly departing from Byzantine orthodoxy and becoming Nestorians or Monophysites.

Despite those differences, it is clear that both in the East and in the West a new age was dawning. It would be a time of new challenges, new achievements, new errors, and new failings. But it would be a new age that would still consider itself heir to the legacy we have been studying.

Epilogue

Thousands and thousands of years have passed since the day when that unknown ancestor of ours had the insight to place one stone atop another so that others might follow along the same path. Much later, less than two thousand years ago, others whom we can also call our ancestors—if not ancestors in the flesh, at least ancestors in the faith—began leaving a trail of their experiences and their faith in the vast literary production that through the centuries has shaped Christianity. Probably neither that remote ancestor nor those other more recent ancestors ever imagined that in this twenty-first century of the Christian era, the echoes of their work would still be heard. Yet, without that remote ancestor, civilization would never have developed, and without the more recent ones, the faith would not have reached our days. To all of them we are debtors; for all of them we must be grateful. Without the first, we would never have these electronic devices with which today we write and communicate. Without the others, we would not have the faith by which today we live.

What will the future say of us? Will it say at least that we preserved and sought to enrich such a legacy?

CPSIA information can be obtained
at www.ICGtesting.com
Printed in the USA
BVHW071250190720
583905BV00001B/52